COLLATERAL DAMAGE

COLLATERAL DAMAGE

Britain, America, and Europe
in the Age of Trump

Kim Darroch

PUBLICAFFAIRS

New York

PublicAffairs
Hachette Book Group
1290 Avenue of the Americas, New York, NY 10104
www.publicaffairsbooks.com
@Public_Affairs

Printed in the United States of America

First published in Great Britain in 2020 by William Collins, an imprint of HarperCollins*Publishers*

First US Edition: October 2020

Published by PublicAffairs, an imprint of Perseus Books, LLC, a subsidiary of Hachette Book Group, Inc. The PublicAffairs name and logo is a trademark of the Hachette Book Group.

The Hachette Speakers Bureau provides a wide range of authors for speaking events. To find out more, go to www.hachettespeakersbureau.com or call (866) 376-6591.

The publisher is not responsible for websites (or their content) that are not owned by the publisher.

Typeset in Minion Pro by Palimpsest Book Production Ltd, Falkirk, Stirlingshire

Library of Congress Control Number: 2020944287

ISBNs: 978-1-5417-5101-9 (hardcover), 978-1-5417-5102-6 (e-book)

LSC-C

10 9 8 7 6 5 4 3 2 1

To Vanessa, to whom I owe it all

Contents

1

Leaks and Tweets

*

'It's going to be a rough few days, Ambassador, but we'll get through this'

– the embassy media team, 5 July 2019

*

'WE'VE GOT a problem. There's been a leak.'
I looked at my chief of staff, poised in the doorway to my office. Normally a picture of unflappable calm and command, she looked anxious. The embassy media team were hovering just behind her.

It was Friday 5 July 2019, the day after US Independence Day: the embassy was half empty, with many staff away for a long weekend. And it was a typical summer's day in the Swamp: hot, humid, soupy. As usual, the air conditioning, perfect in the rest of the building, wasn't quite cutting it in my office; a consequence, I supposed, of inhabiting the largest space in the building. I was just seven days away from going on leave myself, to the refuge of our cottage in Cornwall and three weeks of messing around in sailing boats. My wife, Vanessa, would be returning to the UK that evening, to catch up with her 96-year-old mother. And I felt like I needed a break too, but not just to escape the heat. Being ambassador in Washington had always been a seven days a week, fifteen hours a day job. But even by these standards it had been a draining period: the President's

state visit to London, a succession of British ministers and parlia-
mentarians in town, a speech at the Aspen Ideas Festival, a visit to
Montana, and on the Washington circuit, a multiplicity of events
every night at which attendance was obligatory – all against the
background of the resignation of the British Prime Minister Theresa
May and the competition to succeed her.

The words 'there's been a leak' were ones I had heard regularly
during my time in Washington. They usually related to the porous
state of the plumbing and guttering in the outwardly majestic ambassadorial residence next door. Indeed, a bucket was permanently
stationed in the corner of the master bedroom, there to catch the
contents of Washington's occasional fierce cloudbursts. But it was
instantly clear to me that this was a different kind of leak. The media
team told me that the *Mail on Sunday* had tipped off one of the
Foreign Secretary's special advisers that they had a stash of communications from the Washington embassy to Whitehall. The newspaper
had sportingly provided a handful of screenshots of individual pages,
prompting a bizarre parlour game: how quickly could we identify
the full documents from the pages provided? We passed the test:
within an hour, we knew, with one exception, what they had.

The senior team assembled around my conference table. Copies
of the leaked texts were handed around. The *Mail on Sunday* were
telling our London colleagues that they had a lot of material, more
than twenty-five pages. The three documents we had identified were
cables (diptels – diplomatic telegrams, in Foreign Office jargon) from
the previous three weeks: on the state visit, on President Trump's
2020 campaign launch, and on US policy on Iran. These were sensitive but on a quick skim, I reckoned the blowback should be
manageable. But they came to considerably less than twenty-plus
pages: so what else did the *Mail* have?

The detective work continued. Bewilderingly, judging by the
screenshot, the remaining text was from 2017, two years earlier, and
was a letter, not a cable. Cables usually had a wide circulation, in
the hundreds: letters generally had more sensitive content and a
much smaller readership. So the letter format alone was worrying.
As was the fact of the long gap between this and the other docu-

ments, suggesting that someone had been curating my output for years, and selecting the most combustible material.

The minutes ticked past. My concerns mounted. While those around the table continued to chew over the leaks already identified, one of my private office team, at her desk immediately outside my office, scrolled through the document archive. I heard the photocopier whirring before she emerged with a sheaf of copies in her hand.

The remaining leak was a confidential letter from me to Mark Sedwill, cabinet secretary and national security adviser, dating back to mid-2017. This had been written as input for a top-level discussion of UK-US relations, some six months into the new US administration. My mood sank. This was really bad.

The National Security Council had been created by David Cameron and William Hague when the coalition government took office in 2010, in part as a reaction to claims that the previous government had decided to go to war in Iraq without proper consultation of senior cabinet ministers. As national security adviser from 2012 to 2015, I had organised its work. So when I wrote that letter in 2017, I had known what was required: a frank, unvarnished assessment of the Trump administration, seven months into office.

The letter had provided exactly that. Given its sensitivity, it had gone to a very small number of people in Whitehall. It had described the infighting inside the White House chronicled daily by the US media, drawing on dozens of sources inside the building. It had summarised the policy missteps, especially the executive orders banning travel from several Muslim countries, a measure quickly blocked in the US courts. It had highlighted the damaged relationships with NATO allies, in the wake of President Trump picking fights with many of them at a NATO summit, as well as hinting that he didn't agree with the cornerstone of the alliance, Article 5, which states that an attack on one is an attack on all. And it had assessed the growing cloud of scandal swirling around the administration, centred on accusations of collusion between the Trump campaign and agents of the Russian state. The letter had also, however, highlighted his killer instinct for the vulnerabilities of his opponents; his Teflon qualities; and his extraordinary empathy with his political base, who treated him less as a politician, more as a messiah. But I immediately doubted that these more positive comments would be given any prominence in the media.

I remembered that one of my predecessors, my close friend Nigel Sheinwald, had gone through a comparable experience when a less than totally flattering letter he had written about Barack Obama's qualities as a presidential candidate had leaked to a (different) newspaper. Nigel had survived. Obama's team had declined to respond to the leak. Was there any chance that the Trump White House might behave similarly? I had my doubts.

I returned briefly to the residence over lunchtime, for a meeting with a personal trainer with whom I was signing up: a specialist in dealing with chronic back pain. We agreed a schedule of appointments through to November, though I warned her – I hoped in jest – that I might be out on the street by Monday. She looked bemused.

The rest of the day was a rolling series of meetings. Sometimes stories take the government by surprise. But when there is some warning, the media machine swings into pre-emptive action. The aim is to produce a succinct, objective, calm, and factually correct text which presents government policy in the best possible light, and to which everyone sticks, whether sitting in No. 10, a Whitehall outpost, or an embassy thousands of miles away. And if, as is usually the case with stories involving the Foreign Office, another country is involved, the Holy Grail is a press line which the relevant foreign government has also agreed to use.

So my team talked to London and agreed some press lines. My media team telephoned the White House to warn them of the impending story. We had good relations with the White House press office, and they responded reassuringly, promising that they wouldn't react and would try to play the whole thing down. I then phoned the White House chief of staff, Mick Mulvaney, who was a good friend, to tip him off personally on what was about to unfold. Mick, too, was reassuring: 'This stuff happens to us every day.' But he added, ominously and, it turned out, presciently, that he couldn't predict how the President would react. The media team, drawing on their conversations with the White House, told me they thought it would be rough, 'but we'll get through it'.

On which note I took Vanessa to Dulles Airport to catch her flight to London. The generous Virgin team in Washington usually let us use their business lounge, even though we generally flew in economy. So we had a cheerful hour over cocktails, looking forward to swapping the Washington sweatbox for some honest Cornish rain. Not wanting to put her on edge, I mentioned casually that there might be a brief flurry in the Sunday papers about a leak from the Washington embassy: it would blow over . . .

Saturday was an agony of waiting for the British Sunday papers to hit the streets. The hours crawled past, each one more sluggish than its predecessor. Earlier in my career, I had been head of News Department and FCO spokesman. Every couple of months, I would accompany the then secretary of state, Robin Cook, to one of the Sunday morning political shows. I would need to brief him on the contents of the Sunday papers – which involved going to the news-stand outside Victoria Station at about 11 p.m. on Saturday to buy all the first editions. Nowadays, one would go online. But the image of the Victoria Station newsstand remained lodged in my mind. I whiled away the hours playing tennis, going for a swim, watching a Washington Nationals baseball game on TV. But I kept visualising the bundles of newsprint hitting the pavement – one of which would determine my future.

Around 5 p.m. Washington time, announced by a vibrating mobile phone, the first *Mail on Sunday* article landed in my email inbox. The first of several: it turned out that the newspaper had filled most of its first five pages with extracts from my reporting. And the reality – the screenshots of the pages – looked, well, terrible. As I had expected, on the front page at least, they had highlighted the criticisms – words like 'inept' and 'deeply dysfunctional', together with the comment that the administration, already mired in scandal, could be at the beginning of a downward spiral leading to disgrace. I had said that the President 'radiated insecurity'. Further in, the lead article had highlighted one particular sentence: 'We don't really believe this administration is going to become substantially more normal; less dysfunctional; less unpredictable; less faction riven; less diplomatically clumsy and inept.'

It wasn't all like that. At one point, underlining Trump's talent for eviscerating his opponents and his seeming indestructibility, I had likened him to that figure from Eighties cinema, the Terminator. The reference featured briefly in the inside pages. So did my judgement that, notwithstanding the administration's performance to date, there was a credible path for Trump to win a second term. But how many readers would reach the inside pages?

And there was a piece about me. Parts of it looked like a cut-and-paste reworking of a friendly *Financial Times* profile from a few months earlier. The piece observed in apparent wonder that I had been brought up in a council flat in Abingdon, Oxfordshire while attending Abingdon School, at that stage a direct grant establishment, now a fully fledged public school of some repute. I couldn't object to this: it was true (though my father, were he alive, would have pointed out that it was only for three to four years, while he saved to buy a house). Other parts were more questionable. The article asserted that I was a rabid Europhile, simply on the basis that I had twice worked in Brussels in the UK representation to the European Union, the second time as ambassador. But in mitigation, it asserted that at the same time I was deeply patriotic, on the grounds that the protective case for my mobile phone featured a Union Jack. Ye shall know them by their phone cases.

So overall, it was about as bad as it could be; a template for despondency rather than relief. Notwithstanding it being Saturday night, the story went immediately to the top of the UK media, leading all the bulletins. The embassy press secretary who had drawn the short straw of weekend press duty was besieged. So were her counterparts in Whitehall. The line was straightforward: 'We don't comment on leaks; ambassadors are paid to be candid and offer an honest unvarnished assessment of developments in their host countries.'

That Saturday night, the US media didn't really catch up. But we knew it was coming. And by Sunday morning, though it had broken too late for the US newspapers, it was leading most of the US news channels and spiralling across social media: top on both sides of the Pond. I got a mid-morning phone call from Vanessa, who sounded shocked. She said she had been woken by her mother at 7 a.m. with the words: 'You have to come and look at the television! Kim is all over the news.'

It is difficult to convey how the next few hours felt. There were moments when I was overwhelmed with dread at how the White House would react. I knew the President was spending the weekend at his New Jersey golf club. I could imagine him coming into the locker room after his round, there to meet some faceless adviser, who would pour poison into his ear about what the British ambassador had written, and then stand back and watch this notoriously thin-skinned individual erupt. There were minutes when I thought back on my years of public service and wondered what kind of a mark this would leave on my record. Was this to be how it ended? And there were more reflective moments when I thought to myself . . . that I had finally fallen off the tightrope. Particularly in the second half of my career, I had done some high-profile jobs – Foreign Office press spokesman, Europe adviser to the Prime Minister, ambassador to the European Union, national security adviser – in which I had carried out large-scale press briefings or appeared before parliamentary committees. The objective, at these moments, had been twofold: convey government policy accurately and persuasively; and avoid yourself becoming the story. There had been breaches – I had been named in a few articles. And during my time in Brussels, some Eurosceptic MPs and MEPs had attacked me publicly, apparently for just being in the job (I used to joke that I understood how the scientists, engineers and officials attacked during Stalin's Great Purge must have felt). But on the whole, and thanks to a large measure of luck, I had stayed on the tightrope and got away with it – until the 2019 weekend from hell.

In practical terms, it was another day of rolling meetings. The weekend notwithstanding, the embassy team gathered in the upstairs flat in the residence. We monitored the three main cable news channels, checking for nuances of difference in the coverage. I was fed regular updates from the FCO and No. 10 on how the story was playing in the UK. So there was intense activity all around me. But personally, I felt increasingly numb and detached. It was an out-of-body experience, in which I floated above the scene, disconnected from the mayhem unfolding below. Was this really all about me? Would I wake up in an hour and discover, like Bobby Ewing in *Dallas*, that it was all a dream? And everyone in the room knew that this was just the prologue: what counted was what the occupant of the White House would say.

The dread was justified. The President arrived back from New Jersey by helicopter, landing on the White House lawn late that Sunday afternoon. As was the tradition, a group from the White House press corps were waiting to fire questions at him. And inevitably, one of the first was about his reactions to the leaks of my report. The President said, 'The ambassador has not served the UK well, I can tell you that. We are not big fans of that man.'

My immediate thought was that, if this was it, it was survivable. Having escaped for a few hours in the late afternoon, the media and political teams returned that evening for a round-up of events and took the same view: it could have been worse. And Sunday night came and went without further comment from the White House. But I had always expected it to be a reckoning by Twitter; the President habitually saved his most personal attacks, and his most savage language, for his morning Twitter feed, his direct channel to his base.

And so it proved. On Monday morning, the President tweeted, 'I do not know the Ambassador, but he is not liked or well thought of within the US. We will no longer deal with him.' He then mysteriously digressed into an attack on the Prime Minister: 'What a mess she and her representatives have created. I told her how it should be done, but she decided to go another way. The good news for the wonderful United Kingdom is that they will soon have a new Prime Minister.'

As I read 'We will no longer deal with him', it flashed instantly through my mind that it was all over. But I didn't, at that moment, pursue the thought: with new information coming on stream at every moment, there was no space to think things through. No. 10

were saying that I continued to have the Prime Minister's full support. The Foreign Secretary, Jeremy Hunt, also issued a statement saying that he supported me, while adding that he didn't fully agree with my assessment. This qualification was something of a blow, but understandable: in my days as a press spokesman, I would have advised the Foreign Secretary to say exactly that for the sake of the relationship between the US and the UK. The British media were speculating on where former Foreign Secretary Boris Johnson MP stood on the issue, given that he was hot favourite to succeed Theresa May as Prime Minister.

And out of the blue, there was an emergency debate about me in the House of Commons. The chairman of the Foreign Affairs Committee, Tom Tugendhat MP, had put down an urgent question on the leaks of reporting from Washington. The minister of state at the Foreign and Commonwealth Office (FCO), Sir Alan Duncan (another close personal friend, I should declare), made a character- istically forthright statement in defence of me while also insisting on the importance of diplomats worldwide being able to report freely and frankly. The Hansard report of the subsequent debate, which I read a few hours after it took place, provided a reassuring picture of near complete support.

But what remained in my mind, of course, were the handful of dissenting views. There had been a furious intervention in the debate from Sir Bill Cash MP, who described my 'toxic attacks on the US President' as 'completely unjustified', adding that as chairman of the European Scrutiny Committee he was 'more than well aware of my prejudices'. (To give his remarks some context, I had appeared before his committee several times in my EU days, tasked with explaining and defending government EU policy: he has no more knowledge of my personal views or 'prejudices' on anything than he has of whether there is life elsewhere in the universe.) And for good measure, Dominic Raab MP, a former cabinet minister and one of the unsuccessful candidates for the Conservative leadership, said on *Newsnight* that I was wrong to have included 'personalised remarks' in my confidential reporting; while also perplexingly arguing that, by contrast, for Boris Johnson to say publicly, while mayor of London, that Donald Trump was 'stupefyingly ignorant' was completely fine.

The team also kept me updated on the war on social media: I was apparently well ahead on body count. One comment in particular caught my eye. Mia Farrow, icon of 1970s cinema and star of *Rosemary's Baby*, tweeted: 'The Ambassador is only saying what everybody knows. Trump continues to disgrace America, at home and abroad.' Actually, I didn't say anything remotely so forthright: but she was trying to help, and anyway, it would have been unwise to take issue with Satan's mother.

I was scheduled to have lunch that day with one of the senior Arab ambassadors. She was a longstanding friend and exceptionally well connected: knew everyone, was invited to everything. My plan had been to use the meeting to catch up on the latest on senior adviser Jared Kushner's long-awaited proposals for an Israel–Palestine peace settlement, and to find out when her country's leader would next be in Washington. In the event, we mostly talked about the leaks. She commiserated, and said that every ambassador was saying the same as me. But there was an air of finality about the discussion; I sensed that she didn't expect to see me again.

Liam Fox, the Secretary of State for International Trade, arrived in Washington that afternoon on a long-scheduled visit. I was due to accompany him on most of his calls the following day, including those to his counterpart, commerce secretary Wilbur Ross, to Ivanka Trump in the White House, and to a couple of Republican senators. I was also due to attend a dinner at the US Treasury that evening in honour of the ruler of Qatar: though the host was Steve Mnuchin, the Treasury Secretary, there were rumours that the President would attend. I quickly calculated that my participation (or not) in these events would demonstrate the scope and severity of the President's injunction against me.

I talked briefly to Liam Fox, who was as friendly, measured and supportive as I could have hoped. And then I stepped back onto the diplomatic treadmill, hosting a reception at the residence for the departing head of corporate affairs at the embassy. As I delivered some valedictory remarks – mostly, in the British tradition, jokes and unflattering stories about him from his colleagues – I was conscious of a slightly edgy atmosphere, and became aware that the guests from the administration were looking warily at me. Is he going to say something about the leaks? Is he going to get emotional? They should have known better: Brits don't emote, least of all in public. Afterwards, some of the embassy staff came with me to a well-known Mexican restaurant in Washington, Lauriol Plaza; nothing like a couple of margaritas to make the world look a better place.

Tuesday started ominously. I was told that Treasury Secretary Steve Mnuchin wanted to speak on the telephone. I had breakfast with Liam Fox and his team, and went into the embassy, in part to show them that I was still alive. I then heard that Wilbur Ross was no longer available to meet Liam – though strangely, he could take a telephone call from him at any stage during the day. The lie of the land could not have been clearer if someone had taped a 'get lost' message to a brick and thrown it through a window of the residence.

I phoned Mnuchin mid-morning. Sounding understandably uncomfortable, he said that it would be inappropriate for me to attend the Qatari dinner, given recent events. I said I was sorry to miss it, but I understood. I decided on the spot also to pull out of the meeting with Ivanka Trump; I could see myself being blocked at the White House security gates. Meanwhile, my congressional team were checking whether I would be welcome at Liam Fox's two meetings that afternoon with prominent Republicans, the North Carolina congressman George Holding and the long-serving senator from Iowa, Chuck Grassley. Quick answers came back from both: 'Of course!'

I took a couple of phone calls from colleagues in London: Mark Sedwill, cabinet secretary, and Simon McDonald, Foreign Office permanent secretary. Both insisted there was strong support in London, including in Parliament. Simon would ask how reporting on Brexit by the US Embassy would look if published. (I subsequently discovered from friends inside the US system that the US Embassy in London's reporting on the performance of the May government and its handling of the EU departure process made my comments on the Trump administration look like a prolonged round of applause.)

The meetings that afternoon in Congress went fine; indeed, better than fine. Congressman Holding joked that he was glad to see that I was still alive. Senator Grassley said pointedly: 'Ambassador, you are always welcome here.' Otherwise, both members of Congress knew Liam Fox well, and promised strong support for a future US–UK free trade deal.

On my return to the embassy, I took a phone call from Vernon Jordan. I had met Vernon within a few weeks of my arrival. He is near legendary in the US. A highly successful lawyer and a leading figure in the African-American community, he had in his early career been a prominent civil rights activist. When he first came to lunch with me, he told me the story of his game-breaking 1961 court victory, when he forced the University of Georgia to accept its first African-American students, and then personally escorted them onto the campus through a large crowd of angry protesters. Vernon told me how sorry he was about what was happening and that I was guilty only of telling the truth. From this heroic figure, that meant a lot.

The afterglow of Vernon's words survived through the next meeting: a drink with the visiting House of Commons arms export controls committee. They, understandably, wanted the inside story on the leaks and the US reaction, rather than an exposition on US arms control policy. They were warm, sympathetic and supportive. But the glow faded somewhat when I went back into the embassy, where I was ambushed by my political team. It was 10 p.m. in the UK; and the political event of the moment had been a televised debate between the two remaining candidates for the succession to Theresa May, Foreign Secretary Jeremy Hunt and his predecessor in the role, Boris Johnson. The team told me that Hunt had volunteered strong support for me – 'if I become Prime Minister, Darroch stays' – and had challenged his opponent to make the same commitment. Johnson had failed to do so. Instead, he had ducked and weaved and argued that this was not something that should be debated in public. And Johnson's apparent failure 'to back the British ambassador in Washington' had become the lead story out of the debate.

Someone thrust a mobile phone with the relevant clip from the debate between Hunt and Johnson into my hand. I watched but barely registered what I was seeing, distracted by the arrival of one of the media team brandishing a printout of the front pages of the UK newspapers. I was the lead story in at least two, *The Times* and the *Guardian*, though the latter headlined the President's attack on the PM rather than his comments about me. But the *Times* headline was chilling: 'I won't deal with British Ambassador, says Trump'. The sub-headline twisted the knife: 'President puts pressure on embattled envoy'. Even as I despaired at the words, however, I had to laugh at what lay immediately alongside them. *The Times* had chosen to place immediately next to their Trump story a large photograph of Snowball, a cockatoo with the most extraordinary golden plumage on its head. Snowball's presence on the front page was apparently the product of his talent for previously unseen cockatoo dance moves – rather than, say, any passing resemblance to the most famous coiffure on the planet. The British sense of humour really is matchless.

I then went back to the flat in the residence. A call came through from a longstanding contact who happened to be the political editor of a leading UK paper. I had been avoiding calls from journalists all day; this one I took. After asking how I was, he invited me to comment on the debate between Hunt and Johnson. I declined. He then paused before saying, 'I'm wondering whether you are going to fall on your sword.' I said instantly, 'Why should I?' But he had articulated exactly the question that was starting to bounce around in my head.

On the spur of the moment, I decided I needed to canvass views. I invited the team over for a casual supper, rustled up at zero notice by the brilliant residence staff. The mood was outwardly cheerful but brittle. I sensed it could be snapped with a single sentence. This was a collection of the best and the brightest from the most distinguished diplomatic service in the world, but they hadn't experienced anything quite like this before. By contrast, I had: though never with myself at the centre.

I said to them: 'Given what the President has said, do you think

I can now actually do the job of ambassador? Just theoretically, would British interests be better served if I wasn't around?' As I'd expected, this somewhat dampened the hitherto upbeat mood. Some of them made the argument that it would all calm down, especially if the incoming Prime Minister made it his business to smooth things over. I proffered the counter-argument that this was a President who held grudges; and that everyone in the administration to whom I spoke from then on would be holding the best stuff back. So while I could stagger on, I wouldn't be delivering the insights which they, and the wider government, had a right to expect from me.

We kicked the arguments around for a while without resolution, though inside, my own views were hardening. But I knew there was someone more important I had to consult before reaching a decision, even though, with the five-hour time difference, it was approaching 3 a.m. in the UK. I excused myself and went to phone Vanessa.

2

Off and Then On Again

*

'I think the PM has other plans for Washington'
                    – Jeremy Heywood, cabinet secretary

*

IT WAS July 2015. I was coming to the end of my four years as national security adviser. David Cameron had just won a surprise election victory. Change was in the Whitehall air. One of my outer office team telephoned me. 'Jeremy's office just rang. Can you pop down?' I guessed immediately that the summons from Jeremy Heywood, as cabinet secretary the most senior civil servant in the country, could be about a move; or possibly just an exit. There was no guarantee of another job after the national security post.

I was at Jeremy's door in thirty seconds. As I had anticipated, he got straight to the point: 'Have you thought about what you want to do next?' I had of course thought long and hard about precisely that question, and had reached a simple conclusion. It was arguably my time to move to the private sector; but there was one job which would keep me in the public service. 'I'd like to go to Washington,' I said. 'And the timing fits: Peter Westmacott will have done his four years at the end of this year.' Jeremy looked as if he had expected this, and came straight back with: 'I think the Prime Minister has other plans for Washington.'

I, in turn, wasn't surprised. If another civil servant had been ahead of me for the post, I would, after my time as national security adviser, have been disappointed. But I guessed there might be a political figure in the wings: Washington was a job which had often gone to political appointees. Indeed, as a junior press spokesman in the Foreign Office back in the 1970s, I'd had to defend then Prime Minister Jim Callaghan's appointment of his son-in-law, Peter Jay, to Washington. I could still remember the witty newspaper headline: 'The son-in-law also rises'.

Jeremy asked whether I would be interested in other roles. I said that I felt I had done enough time in Whitehall; and the job I had just completed had represented the summit of my ambitions, were Washington not an option. Jeremy asked what I would do. I said I would try my luck outside government. We left it at that.

As I retreated to my office, I was grateful to Jeremy for his frankness. He was one of the finest civil servants I had known; and he had been a friend, an ally and an invaluable source of advice throughout my time as national security adviser. His death of cancer in 2018, tragically young, remains a huge loss to the country. As for the possibility of a political appointee to Washington, I was philosophical. The Prime Minister had a perfect right to do so, given the pre-eminent importance of the relationship between the UK and the US. Anyway, the private sector would be interesting; if rumour was correct, less work for (much) more money.

I broke the news to Vanessa that evening. She was similarly philosophical, knowing that, in a diplomatic career, nothing was for sure until you got on the plane. She had learnt this early, through the protracted saga of my first posting, back in 1980. In practice, in those days, you went where you were sent. But in theory, you could express preferences. So we spent an evening choosing our top three preferences from the list of jobs available, and the three we wanted to avoid. It was with some trepidation, then, that I went home one evening and told her: 'I've got some good news and some bad news. The good news is: I've got a posting. The bad news is that it's Lagos, one of our bottom three!'

But that was just the start. One of the periodic Foreign Office economy drives led to the Lagos job being cut. So the FO's Plan B was that I should go to The Hague. I even took a couple of Dutch lessons, from which I remember the phrase *Der tafellaken is helder wit*: 'the tablecloth is bright white'. It didn't seem to me the most useful observation, but perhaps I hadn't attended enough diplomatic dinners. In any case, my efforts at Dutch were wasted when the FO decided to keep the incumbent on in post for another year. So I waited another few weeks, to be told I was going to Tokyo at a month's notice. As it turned out, Tokyo was a fabulous posting, where we made friendships that have lasted to this day. And from that episode on, we knew that the unexpected was to be expected. We grew to treasure the unpredictability of diplomatic life.

Two days passed. For the first time in my life, I started to read about my pension arrangements – but found the details utterly baffling. And then, out of nowhere, a second summons to Jeremy's office arrived.

Jeremy came straight to the point. He told me that the Prime Minister thought I had done a good job as national security adviser, and was inclined to find a way to meet my Washington ambitions. But it would only be for two, perhaps two and a half years, rather than the usual three to four. How would I feel about that?

I said immediately that I would be fine with it. A small part of me was thinking that by mid-2018 I would have done four decades in the diplomatic service and might want a change of scene. But a bigger part of me was calculating that if a week was a long time in politics, two years was an eternity: a lot could happen in that time.

A few days later, I picked up a plausible rumour about what the plan might have been. The story was that David Cameron was not going to fight the 2020 election. He was instead intending to stand down in the second half of 2018, to leave his successor a clear run in office, eighteen months before the election. And Ed Llewellyn, the Prime Minister's chief of staff, would be sent to Washington when David resigned. Ed was a good friend whom I had known for close to twenty years, an accomplished and well-liked linchpin in No. 10, and a natural diplomat. So I wouldn't have begrudged him the job for a second. In the end, however, the great roulette wheel of life took another spin, as I had guessed it might: within a year of my conversation with Jeremy, Cameron would resign and Ed would go to Paris rather than Washington. There are worse second prizes.

Washington is, in the eyes of most in the British diplomatic service, the most coveted post on the planet. So over the inevitable long celebratory dinner at our local, The Glasshouse in Kew, Vanessa and I talked about the circuitous route which was taking us to 3100 Massachusetts Avenue; and about quite how big a part luck had played in the journey. *Sliding Doors*, starring Gwyneth Paltrow – in the days when she did more films, less lifestyle – is a minor but entertaining British romcom from 1998, built around the intriguing idea of two parallel stories. In one, our Gwyneth is running for a train on the London Underground, gets distracted by a lost earring, and just misses it: the doors slide shut with her stranded on the platform. In the other, she makes it onto the train. The two stories then play out. In one scenario, life works out well; in the other, badly. It thus illustrates an eternal truth: that in everyone's life, there are chance moments, or seemingly small decisions, which can in prac-tice change your life irrevocably.

So what journey brought me to this point? The Darrochs are a Scottish clan, concentrated mostly on the island of Jura, off Scotland's west coast: beautiful if you like bleak and windswept, famous for Jura whisky, the Corryvreckan whirlpool, just off the island's northern tip, and the fact that George Orwell wrote *1984* in a farm-house on the island whilst dying from tuberculosis (in a letter to his agent, he complained of 'a quite unendurable winter'). But Scottish ancestry notwithstanding, I was born in South Stanley, County Durham, where my grandparents on my mother's side lived – my grandfather was a miner. My brother, Neil, followed some twenty-two months later. I lived until the age of six in Nairobi, Kenya, where my father taught at the local expatriate school. My parents then split up and my brother and I returned to England with my father: apart from a brief visit she paid to the UK a few months later, I never saw my mother again. And as a typically inhibited, or perhaps repressed, Englishman I have never tried to track her down. I'm told she left my father after meeting someone else in Kenya – this was, after all, the Happy Valley era. Hence she stayed there and my father returned to England with my brother and me. I'm also told that somewhere, I have two half-sisters. But life has moved on.

I sometimes wonder what would have happened if, as might have been more usual, my brother and I had stayed with her rather than accompanying my father – the first of those life-determining sliding doors moments. I suppose I might still have gone to university. But I can't believe I would thence have joined the Foreign Office. And to focus on the important stuff, if nothing else I would have been known as Nigel rather than Kim; the former was my mother's choice, the latter my father's – a lifelong Rudyard Kipling fan. And I would thereby have escaped four years in Tokyo where, until they met me, most Japanese assumed I was Korean, as in Kim Dae Ryung; and three years in Washington where, until they met me, most Americans assumed I was a woman.

On arrival back in England, my father initially got a teaching job at a school in Midhurst, Sussex, leaving my brother and me with my grandmother, who was headteacher at the village primary school in the hamlet of Farnborough in Berkshire: he would drive up to see us at weekends. Farnborough's only claim to fame is that it is, at 720 feet above sea level, the highest village in . . . well, Berkshire. Perhaps that's why the headteacher's cottage was so cold.

It was a gentle but isolated existence, in a community dominated by farming. There was a village squire, living in what looked to me like a stately home at the top end of the village. But it was also clear, even to a child of my age, that there was a good deal of rural poverty around. And the village school was genuinely tiny; around forty pupils, of all ages from five to eleven. There were some primitive touches, such as outside lavatories, and school meals delivered daily by van, in metal containers the size and shape of milk churns. The meals were, I suspect, already overcooked by several hours before being deposited in the containers, and the subsequent van journey encouraged the process of deterioration to continue. There are things which to this day I cannot eat, among them custard and gravy, so traumatic did I find some of the contents of those churns.

There was another side to this modest village school. My grandmother was formidable: a force of nature. She had been an army teacher during the Second World War, and had been evacuated out of several locations in North Africa. The British Army had actually missed a trick; had they promoted her to field marshal, the enemy would have fled. As it was, she imposed strict discipline and an iron rule on the school, I daresay on the whole village. My brother and I always felt that she was harder on us than anyone else; no doubt she was anxious to head off accusations of favouritism.

But whatever, it worked. I did well enough academically to be entered for the scholarship exams for Abingdon School, about thirty miles away. There was a Darroch history with the school; two of my uncles had gone there, though not my father. Abingdon was at that stage a direct grant establishment (it's now fully independent), which meant that while most pupils there were fee-paying, the local authority funded a small number of scholarship kids – of whom I turned out to be one, when I lucked through the exams. I was one of the last of the direct grant generation; the Labour government abolished the scheme in 1975, thus denying bright children from less well off backgrounds the chance to go to great schools. No doubt those responsible for the decision could justify it; but to me, to this day, it looks like an act of tribal political vandalism.

Abingdon was a mixed experience. It was a wonderful school, which has since become famous as the alma mater of Radiohead (coincidentally, I'm sure, a new music school was built in the school grounds while I was there). But I was a difficult and disruptive teenager, setting school records for the number of detentions and beatings in a single term and constantly on the edge of expulsion. A psychologist would no doubt attribute this to a broken home and an absent mother. But for me, it was much more about an instinctive and, it turned out, lifelong resistance to authority; to this day, if I am ever 'ordered' to do anything, as opposed to being politely asked, my inclination is to do the opposite.

I was also painfully conscious at school of being different from everyone else – in terms of where I'd come from and where I lived. When I won a scholarship, my grandmother retired from the village school, and we moved at short notice to Abingdon – with my father at that stage still visiting at weekends. As was straightforward in those days, we were assigned a first-floor flat in a council estate about fifteen minutes' walk from the school; the British equivalent of US public housing. Abingdon School had a distinctive school uniform, and as I walked out of the estate every morning, instantly identifiable as the only Abingdonian on the estate, I imagined every curtain twitching and ambushes being hatched. The reality, though, was quite different. There were no attacks, and my brother and I ended up playing impromptu games of football with the local youths most evenings. And when my father got a job in the area, remarried and bought a house, I missed the estate.

I just about survived at Abingdon. I was one of only a handful to be given no responsibility whatever: I was made neither a school nor a house prefect. I played tennis for the school, and some rugby (though I never reached the glamour of the first XV, for which I would have traded a lot, especially since my younger brother, though at a different school, was a star rugby player). But I got some good O levels; and then, despite picking the wrong subjects for A level – Biology, Chemistry and Physics when I should have done English and History – got good enough grades to head north, to Durham University, to study Zoology. I never even considered Oxbridge.

Durham was in some ways a re-run of Abingdon. The university had a collegiate system, and I had chosen, pretty much at random, Hatfield College. I discovered when I arrived that Hatfield, while modest in its academic record, was comfortably the strongest college at sport; one of its students, Pete Warfield, actually played rugby for England while at the college. I wholeheartedly embraced the spirit of the establishment, barely attending a lecture in my first year, with the result that I failed all my first-year exams, and was threatened with expulsion unless I resat and passed them all in August. To the visible surprise of my tutors, I managed to replace three fails with three passes. In the second year, I failed to complete my dissertation (on the concentration of certain ions in the body fluids of Chilopoda and Diplopoda) by the deadline of the end of the summer term (the truth was, I had failed even to start it); so I lost another summer to catching up and scraping through. On the other side of the ledger,

I played rugby for the college and fives and squash for the university. And most important, I met Vanessa, who became my girlfriend. One of my opening gambits was to take her on a hunting expedition for specimens for my dissertation – centipedes and millipedes. With romantic dates like that, no wonder she later agreed to marry me.

My university career ended, predictably enough, with a lower second class honours degree in Zoology. Strong-armed by Vanessa into doing some work, I actually came quite close to getting an upper second; but the faculty debated long and hard and decided, I was told on a split vote, that my failure to deliver a dissertation on time should disqualify me. I had, meanwhile, been offered a place to do a masters at Imperial College in Applied Entomology. But with only a lower second, there was no government grant forthcoming. So I had to go and find a job.

I stayed up in the North-East for that post-university summer. I got a summer job a few miles away from Durham in Spennymoor, at a factory making fluorescent strip lights. My role was in the paint plant. The job was simple enough. The metal carcasses for the lights were placed on hooks on a raised conveyor belt. They disappeared into the paint machine, then reappeared a while later, gleaming white and hot to the touch, the paint having been blow-dried en route. My job was to unhook them from the conveyor belt and stack them neatly on a pallet. They would then be picked up by a forklift truck and transported to their place of union with the lighting tubes. There was a problem, however; try as I did, I couldn't lift the carcasses off their hooks quickly enough – with the result that some of them were making a second circuit through the paint plant, acquiring an unwanted second coat. This initially caused hilarity amongst the permanent workforce – 'you've been to university but you can't do this' – then eventually exasperation. But in those far-off kinder days, I wasn't fired as I deserved: instead I got a welcome transfer to driving the forklift trucks, notwithstanding my never having done this before. Health and safety wasn't such a downer in those days.

Meanwhile, in the heat of that 1975 summer – at the time, it was the hottest August on record – I also started to look for a more permanent job. My co-workers at the factory were worried about me. They could see that I wasn't up to manual labour. And they were bemused when I told them of my degree in Zoology. As one of them put it to me: 'How many zoos are there in the country? And there's already that Johnny Morris on the TV.' Encouraged by this show of confidence, I fixed an appointment with the university careers advisory office. My interviewer asked me what I wanted to do. I confessed that I had no idea, but mentioned the Foreign Office. Vanessa's father had suggested this to her previous boyfriend who was studying Classics at Oxford. The ex had dismissed the idea, but she found a readier audience in me. Diplomacy, after all, sounded just the ticket for someone who had read Ian Fleming's entire literary output by the time I was fifteen.

The careers adviser, however, was less persuadable. She looked quizzically at me, observed that leaping from zoology to diplomacy was a bit of a stretch, and added that it was in any case almost impossible to get through the entrance exams. She suggested instead that I think about a career in business, and try applying to some of the big British multinationals with graduate schemes. I took away a sheaf of application forms; but also a growing determination to try for the Foreign Office, primarily to spite another authority figure.

There were two entry levels to the Foreign Office: the 'fast stream' and the 'executive'. Knowing no better, I applied for both – as well as throwing in a handful of applications for companies, chosen on a more or less random basis. The FO process kicked off well before anything else stirred in the employment jungle. Within a few weeks, I found myself in a large hall somewhere in Oxford, working through a day of exams – a strange mix of IQ-style tests and an essay about how you would respond to some sort of existential national crisis, a plague, invasion by zombies, that sort of thing. Mysteriously, I passed – and got invited to two days of further tests and exercises. These were intriguing, including an interview with a psychologist, more essays, more IQ tests, a general knowledge exam, and a session where groups were created and everyone took turns in chairing a meeting.

Having somehow survived this – especially the interview with the psychologist – I was invited to the third stage, the final selection board. And here I came seriously unstuck. Having drifted into the interview with no thought or preparation, I was stumped on basic questions like, why did I want to join the Foreign Office? Saying that I enjoyed travel didn't hack it. The rejection letter popped through the letterbox a few days later.

I had in parallel been pursuing the process for Foreign Office entry at executive level – or 'the slow stream' as I subsequently discovered it was dismissively called within the system. It was much simpler: a half day of exams and then a final interview. And some of the companies to which I had applied had offered me interviews. About a week before the first of these, with ICI, then the largest industrial conglomerate in the UK, the Foreign Office accepted me. Vanessa and I pondered for at least a couple of hours that evening how I should respond – and we agreed I should give it a go. There was nothing to lose: if I didn't like it, in those golden days there were many more career options available for even the most average of university graduates. And after all, the Foreign Office had been the first to offer me a job.

I moved to London and joined the Foreign Office in September 1976. I found a basement flat on Mount Ephraim Road, a few hundred yards from Streatham Hill Station. It was basically a bedroom about the size of a large bed, with a small bathroom and an even smaller kitchen. But its overriding feature was damp – mould on the walls and the carpets, cracks and holes in the plasterwork, peeling paper on the ceiling. I thought it was great and still feel nostalgic about it. As for life in government, Labour were in power. Jim Callaghan was Prime Minister and Anthony Crosland was Foreign Secretary (though he died in office with a cerebral haemorrhage). I rapidly discovered what being in the 'slow stream' meant. My entry group were given a single day's induction, which concentrated on where the lavatories were and how a file of papers should be put together. We heard that the fast streamers had a welcome to the service lasting a week, during which they were told many times how wonderful they were to have triumphed against such intense competition. Their week reportedly concluded with a glass of sherry with the permanent under secretary. All of us, whether fast or slow, were then dispatched to departments to learn our trade. But there was a hierarchy here too. The fast streamers were sent to the elite political departments, with names like Near East and North Africa Department and Latin America Department: NENAD and LAD for short. I was sent to Protocol Department – Protocol Department for short – to labour on the diplomatic privileges and immunities of the foreign diplomatic community in London, mostly cheap cars, cheap booze and unpaid parking tickets.

I found this more incentivising than discouraging. Even in the unglamorous surroundings of Protocol Department, I was enjoying the proximity to power, and the buzz from working next door to Downing Street – not to mention the events to which I got invited because, although protocol didn't involve high policy, it did involve lots of parties. I remember being given a lift to one of them by one of the Queen's ladies-in-waiting. As we approached the gates of some appropriately grand building, she said to me: 'Young man, could you please get my tiara out of the glove compartment?'

Nevertheless, fifteen months later, as soon as I was allowed, I retook the fast stream exams. This time I passed. Possibly, after a year in the institution, I could better answer the question 'Why do you want a career in the diplomatic service?' Vanessa and I celebrated with the luxury of the day: a bottle of supermarket cider. And my course was set.

And thereafter I was, in essence, extraordinarily lucky. There were many 'sliding doors' moments when my career could have taken a different course. I remember three in particular. The first came towards the end of my first posting in Tokyo. There didn't seem to be any interesting jobs coming up back in London – until Prime Minister Margaret Thatcher unexpectedly decided she wanted to build the Channel Tunnel. I became the UK secretary of the Anglo-French Channel Fixed Link Treaty Working Group ('Channel Fixed Link' because it was thought at the time that it might be a bridge rather than a tunnel). And that led to my organising the ceremony to mark the signing of the Channel Tunnel treaty. I chose, and sold to No. 10, Canterbury Cathedral Chapter House for the ceremony; and the dean of the cathedral's house for Thatcher's lunch with François Mitterrand.

When, some ten years later, my son arrived for his first day at King's Canterbury, the wonderful school in the grounds of the cathedral to which both my children went, I was able to show him the plaque commemorating the event. I'm not sure he was impressed! But No. 10 were happy; and it launched me, in terms of making the senior levels of the Foreign Office aware of my existence.

The second moment came in the mid-1990s, when I was deputy head of European Union Department. It was time for me to bid for an overseas posting. I was vaguely attracted to the job of deputy ambassador in Prague; a beautiful city, an interesting country, and fascinating politics, a few years after the fall of the Berlin Wall. So I bid. A few weeks later, my boss, the head of the European Directorate, called me in and said he was about to go to the postings board. Did I really want to go to Prague? For some reason – perhaps the cold grey drizzle that day, which struck me as all too central European – I said, 'Not really. I've changed my mind.' He told me a few hours later that I would have got it, had he not intervened to kill it.

Had I not, on the spur of the moment, said no, I would have missed out on one of the most exciting jobs of my career. Six months later, by which time I would have been in Prague, I was asked at short notice to become head of Eastern Adriatic Department, which was then dealing with the war in Bosnia. It was the biggest foreign policy issue of the moment, and it catapulted me to a different level in terms of profile in the FO, No. 10 and Whitehall. It also sent me, within a few weeks, on a military plane into Sarajevo, a city terrorised by Bosnian Serb snipers who manned the surrounding hillsides, shooting at any residents within range. Perhaps out of boredom, they also shot at our plane as it came in to land, prompting the cancellation of our flight out that evening. I thus spent the night in besieged, war-torn Sarajevo, which at the time was suffering from frequent electricity and water cuts. It also led to one of the more memorable meals of my career, in one of the few functioning restaurants – 'Sarajevo schnitzel', an unidentified piece of meat deep-fried in breadcrumbs. Judging by its corrugated appearance, whatever it was had been run over by a tank.

And the third sliding doors moment came in 2004, when I was director general for Europe. Stephen Wall was the Prime Minister's Europe adviser – the most important European policy job anywhere in the system. This is Stephen's story rather than mine, but because of policy differences with Tony Blair, especially in relation to the euro, he unexpectedly and suddenly resigned. A few months previously, I had run for, but failed to get, the post of political director in the Foreign Office. Suddenly, I was the only credible candidate on the scene for Europe adviser to the Prime Minister – a job that was actually a grade higher than political director, elevating me to the ranks of permanent secretaries. I spent three years in No. 10 advising Tony Blair on Europe policy – which led directly to my appointment as ambassador to the European Union in 2007. This in turn led to my becoming national security adviser to David Cameron in 2012; which in turn led to Washington. I owe a lot to Stephen Wall . . . or as Bob Dylan put it: 'Blame it on that simple twist of fate'.

3

Discovering 'Real America'

*

'*I like Donald Trump; he says what I'm thinking*'
– an Uber driver in Jackson, Mississippi, November 2015

*

'DONALD TRUMP is making quite an impact, and leading in the opinion polls. But he won't win the nomination.'

It was late 2015. The words were spoken by one of America's leading political pundits, to general agreement around the table. Thanks to the hospitality of the then British ambassador, Peter Westmacott, and his wife Susie, Vanessa and I were staying at the British residence in Washington DC for a couple of days before embarking on an American road trip; a personal journey around 'real America' before I took up my posting in late January 2016. And I was attending one of the regular 'pundits' breakfasts' which generations of British ambassadors in Washington have hosted.

A US road trip, exploring the freedom and romance of the endless highway, had been a longstanding ambition of mine, ever since being hooked by the classic American 'road movies' of the late 1960s and early 70s: *Easy Rider, Vanishing Point, Two Lane Blacktop*, and my all-time favourite film, *Five Easy Pieces*. And with three months' 'preparation' for my posting to Washington, it seemed like the perfect time. Like most Britons of my generation, I had visited New York and Boston, and San Francisco and Los Angeles on the West Coast.

But the rest of the country was uncharted, imagined through watching too many American films. It being November, we had to go south to avoid the cold, snow and ice. So we planned a drive from Nashville, where our son Simon was teaching at Vanderbilt University, down to New Orleans through the heart of the Deep South. We were then going to fly to Las Vegas for a two-day introduction to that symbol of American excess; after that we would drive across to Utah to see something of the American south-west, and in particular to experience the wonders of Zion and Bryce National Parks. As for where we finished, our oldest friends, Nigel and Lou Graham, whom we had known since our university days, had volunteered to join us for the trip: they offered their apartment in Long Boat Key, a short drive and long bridge across from Sarasota in Florida, as the perfect oasis for the final week.

It wasn't just about reliving the Seventies. I would be arriving in Washington at the start of election year. Who is running America matters to everyone. Every government has a reason to want to influence the White House on one issue or another. And the central figures in a future White House tend to be drawn from the leading figures in the campaign team. So tracking the election, and building relationships with the top advisers, would be an overriding priority. And I wanted to get a head start by understanding how the candidates were seen in other parts of America.

But before flying down to Nashville, there were two more events in Washington. We attended a dinner in the residence at which the guest of honour was Frank Luntz. This was the first of many encounters with Frank, who became a good friend. He is a big, colourful personality; to see Frank interrogate a focus group is to see an artist at work. He describes himself as a political and communications consultant, pollster and pundit. He is a lifelong, but mainstream, Republican: a familiar face on US TV politics shows. Most of all, he is a great Anglophile from his days at Trinity College, Oxford, where he advised our current Prime Minister, Boris Johnson, on his bid for the presidency of the Oxford Union. Successive British ambassadors have benefited from his knowledge and judgement and his generous nature. Frank duly presented to the assembly his latest polling figures, and concluded that, while the Republican race was still open, Hillary Clinton was likely to win the Democratic nomination and eventually the White House. To be fair to Frank, every pollster was saying the same. And every pundit was transfixed by the Democrats' Blue Wall: the theory that the Democrats were 'guaranteed' 240 electoral college votes from states which were 'certain' to vote Democrat, and only needed another 30 or so to reach the 272 required to win the presidency.

We concluded with a day exploring Washington. On the way to look at the White House, we drove past the Watergate building. As someone who, while a university student, had followed every twist of the Watergate saga, it felt like touching history. But the highlight was a trip to the top of the Washington Monument – all 555 feet of it. We were accompanied and guided by an engagingly enthusiastic park ranger. I confess that we took the lift up, saving the spiral staircase for the downward journey. But so knowledgeable was our guide that we probably climbed half of it anyway, so frequently on the descent did we double back to see things we had missed. His potted history of the monument included the information that its construction had been halted for more than a decade in the mid-1800s, because its backers had run out of money; a reminder that, in America, the land of private enterprise, it is for the most part wealthy philanthropists that build the monuments, not the state. The ranger pointed to the visible manifestation of this temporary bankruptcy: halfway up, the stone changes colour slightly because when construction restarted, the stone from the original quarry had been exhausted. Once you know this, it leaps out at you to a degree which the monument's original backers must have found vexing. But the view from the top remains timeless. Dusk was falling as we gazed out across Washington; as the lights came on across the city, we looked down the Mall, glimpsed the White House, and thrilled at the adventure to come.

Nashville was utterly different. We stayed with our son, Simon, who, having done his doctorate at Yale, had been made assistant professor of geology at Vanderbilt University, right in the heart of the city. Knowing Nashville only by reputation, I imagined a bar on every corner, each with a resident country and western singer. This wasn't actually far from the truth, except it wasn't only country and western. Nigel and Lou joined up with us at this point; and on that first night, Simon took us to the epitome of a dive: an old-fashioned Nashville music venue called The Basement, a sweaty, shabby and stained cellar with a tiny ramshackle bar in one corner, selling beer and some of the worst wines on the planet. There was no stage, with the performers standing a few feet from the audience. A succession of bands performed, some with recording contracts, some just hopeful wannabes; but all were exceptional musicians. The show opened with brief singer-songwriter acoustic sets, but swiftly moved on to loud, hard rock music and blues. We loved it.

It being after midnight, we took an Uber back to Simon's apartment. The driver was female – married, young children, earning some extra money. I asked her how she saw US politics. She said she 'kinda liked Donald Trump'; she remembered him from *The Apprentice* and thought he must be a smart businessman. I expressed surprise: wasn't she hoping to see the first woman President? She said emphatically: 'I'm not with Hillary Clinton. I just don't trust her.' I asked why. The response carried an edge of genuine dislike. 'She just says what she thinks you want to hear. She doesn't really care about people like me.'

Back in the apartment, I reflected on what I'd heard, and how perceptions confounded reality. Hillary Clinton had been raised in a classically middle-class family, her father the owner of a small drapery business and lifelong Republican, her mother a Democrat. And her presidential campaign was about 'inclusive capitalism': keeping jobs in America, sharing profits with the workers, equal pay for women, more affordable healthcare. Donald Trump was the billionaire son of a New York property developer, who had been loaned $400 million by his father to start his business career, had his own jet, and ran expensive hotels, casinos and golf clubs. Yet Trump was seen as the authentic one, who cared about America's blue-collar classes, and Clinton as the fake. There was clearly something very wrong about how Clinton was marketing herself or very right about how Trump was selling himself.

Back on the music trail, we also went to a much larger, but similarly raw, Nashville venue called Cannery Ballroom, there to see a nationally renowned Southern rock band, with a multiple-album recording history, called The Drive-By Truckers. I had grown up with the rock music of the American South – The Allman Brothers Band, Little Feat, Lynyrd Skynyrd – so I knew what to expect; and they were terrific. Their best tracks remain on my playlist to this day. Add to these musical experiences some great restaurants and a wonderfully cool cocktail bar called The Patterson House, and we could have stayed in Nashville for weeks.

But we didn't. Instead, we set off for New Orleans. There were limits to our embrace of the 1960s counterculture; we hired a large SUV rather than a couple of Harley-Davidsons. We loaded up with emergency rations of that wonderful American invention, trail mix, from Trader Joe's and hit the road.

It is a little over 500 miles from Nashville to New Orleans; a day's drive for an American, three for those of us lacking the frontier gene. On a map, it is due south, then about an inch to the left, so there were several route options. We decided to drive down the length of Mississippi, mostly using the Natchez Trace Parkway, a famous road built in the 1930s; it follows the route of the Natchez Trace, a historic forest trail created and used by Native Americans from prehistoric times, then colonised by early European explorers and settlers. During the War of 1812, the US army used the Trace to supply General Jackson's forces in New Orleans. This led directly, I suppose, to Jackson's decisive and fabled victory against the invading British forces in the Battle of New Orleans on 8 January 1815, his ascension to national hero status, and ultimately to his election as President in 1829. The 'simple twist of fate' here is that the battle should never have happened: the two governments had already signed a peace deal, the Treaty of Ghent, on 24 December 1814. But news travelled slowly in those days, with the British forces in the area not learning of the treaty until a month later. I could not but wonder whether Jackson would have made it to the White House if WhatsApp had been invented at the time.

Notwithstanding the Trace's crucial role in the defeat of our countrymen two hundred years earlier – perhaps we had deserved it for burning down the White House and the Capitol in the same war – we joined it a few miles outside Nashville. It was extraordinarily beautiful; a two-lane blacktop through a fairytale, sun-dappled forest that stretched to the horizon. And with scarcely a building visible on the entire route, the view to each side was the one the early explorers would have seen – when the Trace was known as the Devil's Backbone, because if the diseases didn't get you, the high-waymen and bandits would. We rapidly discovered, however, one drawback to this journey through a woodland wilderness. In the days when the Trace was the main route southwards, there were trading posts along it where travellers could get provisions, eat and sleep. These were all long gone. Around lunchtime, we googled the nearest diner: I think it was called Maisie's Family Cafe. But when we arrived at it, a couple of miles off the Parkway, it was a scene from a post-apocalypse movie; a wrecked shell of a building, broken windows and a kicked-down door. Even worse, it wasn't even serving food: so, trail mix for lunch.

After another hundred miles of glorious greenery, we turned off the Trace and took the short detour to Jackson, the capital of, and largest city in, the state of Mississippi. And yes, it is named after the victor of New Orleans and scourge of the British: more humble pie. We stayed at the Old Capitol Inn, a pleasingly quirky independent establishment just across the road from the Mississippi State Capitol. And on their recommendation, we set off by Uber for 'the best Mexican restaurant in Jackson'.

Still intrigued by what I had heard in Nashville, I asked this Uber driver whether he was following the early days of the election race. 'I'm interested,' he said. I asked him who he liked. He replied, in an echo of his female Nashville counterpart: 'I like Donald Trump, he says what I'm thinking.' I asked about the rest of the field. He shrugged dismissively. 'They've all been bought up by big business; they're working for them, not us. But Trump is different. He's self-financing.' 'Could Trump actually win?' I asked. 'Maybe,' he replied, 'a lot of people agree with what he's saying.'

The Mexican restaurant was indeed good. Among its specialities was guacamole freshly made at the table. One of the waiters pitched up with some avocados and proceeded to perform his party trick. Hearing our accents, he said, 'Are you Australian?' We told him we were visiting from England. 'Why on earth have you come to Jackson?' he said, looking genuinely amazed. We explained that we were driving from Nashville to New Orleans. 'Well, I'd get out of this place as soon as possible if I were you,' was his parting comment.

The guacamole was excellent.

Actually, we didn't get out of Jackson quickly. We stayed a day, seeing the sights of the city. The highlight was a guided tour of the Capitol building. The Mississippi legislature wasn't sitting and there were few visitors, so we had the building, and the tour guide, almost to ourselves. Built in 1903, it was ancient by American standards and a formally designated 'Historic Place'. Intriguingly, in a typically American back story, it had been financed by the proceeds of a successful law suit for unpaid taxes won by the state of Mississippi against the Illinois Central Railroad; and it was built on the site of the old state penitentiary, which presumably helped to focus the minds of successive generations of Mississippi politicians.

The guide took us into the debating chambers and invited us to sit in the Speaker's chair. As we wandered the corridors, I found myself gazing at the group photographs of generations of Mississippi state senators; on a less than comprehensive survey, it looked as if the first African-American senator had appeared in the mid-1980s. I also noticed an unexpected feature in the top left-hand corner of the state flag, and I asked the tour guide why Mississippi was still showcasing the Confederate flag in that way. He looked hugely embarrassed and said: 'I really can't discuss that.' Surprised at this, I asked how people like him felt about the Civil War. He paused, looked at me intently, and said: 'You have to realise, the Civil War was mostly fought here in the South. It was our homes that were burnt down, our crops that were pillaged, our economy and our way of life that was destroyed. That's how we feel.'

Outside, in the autumn sunshine, we walked through the gardens surrounding the Capitol – and found more echoes of the Civil War. Right in front of the building stood a large monument, created as late as 1917, to 'The Women of the Confederacy – mothers, sisters, wives and daughters'. A little further from the building was a statue of a Confederate soldier. I found myself recalibrating. I had expected our trip through the Deep South to resonate with echoes of the civil rights clashes of the Sixties; to remind me of places like Selma and Montgomery and Birmingham, Alabama, and of grainy black-and-white TV footage of protests and burnings and beatings. Instead, there were reminders and relics everywhere of another, wider and more savage conflict that had taken place a century earlier, the wounds of which seemed as deep and as open as if it had happened yesterday.

That evening, we again went to a downtown restaurant, this time by regular taxi rather than Uber. The vehicle was a huge SUV, but we found it more cramped than expected for the four of us; the driver had reclined his seat back to a near horizontal position, primarily to provide adequate space for his large stomach, which was more a beer barrel than a six-pack. The pile of empty fast food cartons in the passenger footwell provided a clue as to the cause of his condition. As with his predecessor, I invited his views on the election process. 'Not interested,' came the reply.

When we set off the next morning, heading for New Orleans via Natchez, I put Lucinda Williams's *Car Wheels on a Gravel Road* on the car CD player. Williams was born in Louisiana and her music is soaked in the Deep South. The album is a raw, heartfelt travelogue of the land we were travelling through: of Jackson, Vicksburg and Baton Rouge, of dusty back roads, cotton fields and dilapidated shacks. My travelling companions were insufficiently appreciative of the brilliance of the music first time round, so I made them listen to it all over again.

And so to Natchez – for lunch and a wander around a city that, prior to the Civil War, had boasted more millionaires than any other city in America. It enjoys a spectacular setting on a high bluff overlooking the Mississippi River. We started at the visitor centre, where the main attraction was a short film on its history. Founded by French colonists in 1716, it was fought over for several years by the French and the Natchez tribe of Native Americans, traded to Spain in the Treaty of Paris of 1763, and sold again a few years later to, yes, the British. We then ceded it to the US after the American Revolutionary War. The combination of the cotton boom and Mississippi River trade made it, for a few decades, exceptionally wealthy. The film painted a picture of an era of extraordinarily gracious living; of wealth and privilege, society balls and horse racing, and the most beautiful antebellum mansions in all America. But it explained little of Natchez's decline and depopulation, beyond the damage done to the cotton industry by the boll weevil infestation that struck the Deep South in the late 1800s.

As we left the centre, we concluded that there must have been more to the Natchez story. It was a warm still afternoon, so we bought some food and sat on the heights of the bluff, in the open air, overlooking the river. The Mississippi stretched out before us, as wide as a lake, mud-brown and sluggish. The far side was so thickly wooded that scarcely any buildings were visible; we realised that we were gazing upon a landscape that hadn't much changed over the last two hundred years. And we trawled the internet for a more complete history of Natchez.

As we had expected, there was a darker side to the story. Natchez had also prospered thanks to slavery. The cotton plantations had thrived on slave labour, while Natchez itself had hosted the Forks of the Road Market, one of the largest slave markets in the whole of the South. The city was lucky enough to survive the Civil War largely undamaged; indeed, in 1863, Ulysses S. Grant set up temporary headquarters in one of Natchez's finer antebellum mansions. And Natchez continued to prosper for some decades after the war. But then the boll weevil landed, and destroyed the cotton crops, and the railroads replaced the steamboat traffic, bypassing the river cities and drawing away their commerce.

Throughout, Natchez remained a centre of Confederate defiance, troubled race relations, Ku Klux Klan activity, and opposition to civil rights progress. African-American activists were targeted and churches burned down. In the mid-Sixties, E. L. McDaniel, the Grand Dragon of the Ku Klux Klans of America, had his office on Natchez's Main Street.

As we mused on this alternative history, a minibus drew up behind us, and a dozen men emerged and started hoeing a large municipal flowerbed. I watched them for several minutes before I realised what I was seeing. They were prisoners. Dressed in identical overalls, they were the modern equivalent of a chain gang, though without the leg irons. It was a moment straight from the movies; *Sullivan's Travels*, or perhaps *Oh Brother, Where Art Thou?*. I didn't, however, dare to take a photograph; who knew what crimes they had committed?

On that note, we hit the highway for the final leg to New Orleans; the last stretch of Mississippi, then into Louisiana and *True Detective* territory. We arrived early evening, checked into another quirky hotel, this time in the French Quarter, and headed out to dinner with the honorary consul for the United Kingdom, James (Jimmy) J. Coleman Jr, CBE. Jimmy was from an old New Orleans family. A Princeton graduate and Oxford University postgraduate, he was a successful and wealthy lawyer and property developer, a friend of the British royal family, a philanthropist – and, at forty-four years, the longest serving British honorary consul anywhere on the planet. He was also exceptional company. (Sadly, Jimmy died in March 2019 after a fall in his parents' mansion, and New Orleans thereby lost one of its great characters.)

The first evening, Jimmy took us to Antoine's Restaurant, a New Orleans institution since 1840, where we sampled the eclectic fusion that is French-Creole cuisine while soaking up Jimmy's lifetime experience of his city. We quizzed him in particular for his take on the US elections. He said that he looked at them as a businessman. In his view, Obama had been 'anti-business', always imposing new, profit-sapping regulations. So he would be voting Republican, along with most of his businessmen friends. 'Including if Trump is the Republican nominee?' I asked. Jimmy shrugged: 'I don't like him and hope he isn't, but yes, he's a businessman too, and he will know what needs to be done.' This was my first experience of the other component of the growing Trump coalition; over the coming months I was to hear the same from the American business community up and down the country.

I also asked Jimmy about his experience, as a New Orleans resident, of Hurricane Katrina. He said that his own property had been virtually untouched. The same went for his immediate uptown neighbourhood. He also reminded me that there had been a 24-hour gap between the storm striking and the levees failing. So when he had walked around the city in the storm's immediate aftermath, there hadn't been that much damage. Then the flood waters came. And some parts, like New Orleans East, had never really recovered.

Intrigued by his account, we visited a semi-permanent Katrina exhibition in central New Orleans the next morning. After absorbing it, especially the TV film clips, I talked to one of the curators. He told me that the oldest, wealthiest families in New Orleans had built houses on the best, usually the highest, land. So although 80 per cent of the city had flooded, some of the New Orleans 'aristocracy' had escaped, while the poorest parts of the city, largely home to African-American communities, had been hardest hit. And afterwards, it had taken several years to get back to normal. In his view, both in the hours immediately after the storm and in the long-term clean-up, the authorities, both state and federal, had screwed up badly; and the weakest had suffered most.

Of course we did the usual things in New Orleans: the French Quarter, the French Market, Jackson Square (we couldn't escape the humiliator of the British Army), the Mississippi towpath. That afternoon we walked around the picturesque streets of the Garden District (where I was disappointed not to run into film stars Sandra Bullock and John Goodman, or Trent Reznor of Nine Inch Nails, all supposedly residents of that neighbourhood). And I insisted on visiting the cemetery where part of *Easy Rider* was filmed. Devotees of the film will remember that in these scenes, having watched the Mardi Gras procession, Wyatt and Billy pick up two girls, go to the cemetery, take acid, and make inappropriate use of the marble chambers in which the dead are entombed in New Orleans (the water table being so high in the city that if coffins were buried in the ground, they would simply float away). As with the Harley-Davidsons, this was another part of the script we lacked the nerve to recreate.

Then on to Sin City, the gambling capital of the world. We really didn't get Las Vegas. I've been there since, for work reasons, and I still don't get it. We landed there from New Orleans at dusk; from the air, awash with neon, it looked like an exotic glittering piece of jewellery carelessly discarded on the desert floor. But that was the best of it: close up, it was bleak, tawdry, grasping and plain weird. It is, for example, almost impossible to walk outside for any distance on a pavement in Vegas; you can only walk through the shopping malls. Indeed, the entire metropolis appears explicitly designed to separate visitors from their money as quickly as possible. And there are few more dispiriting experiences than wandering through the vast gambling floor of a hotel on the Vegas Strip: endless lines of slot machines, acres of blackjack and roulette tables, an air conditioning system in which air freshener fights a losing battle with the fog of nicotine, and hosts of dead-eyed punters losing their money.

I recognise that this may be a minority view; Vanessa fell into conversation in the hotel lift with a lady of mature years who told her that she visited Vegas three times a year, and always counted the days until her next trip. We had a good evening watching Cirque Du Soleil at the next-door hotel, and enjoyed one quintessential Vegas experience. According to TripAdvisor, the best Italian restaurant in the neighbourhood was in a nearby shopping mall. We duly went there for dinner, to find ourselves in a reimagined shopping street in Italy. The restaurant was located in one corner of someone's idea of a piazza. We sat and ate some perfectly decent pasta, while above us, the artificial sky darkened and started glinting with fake stars.

We set off the next morning in another rented SUV for the 150-mile sprint eastwards to Springdale, Utah, just across the border with Nevada. Springdale is on the edge of Zion National Park and about ninety minutes from Bryce National Park; and it is Mormon country, having originally been established by a community of Mormon farmers in 1862. It is tiny: according to the last census, its population is 529. But it is also spectacular, surrounded by towering cliffs of red Navajo sandstone. The same red sandstone makes the fifteen-mile Zion Canyon, which we saw the next day, a truly exceptional experience, which we thought couldn't be matched. But then, the day after, we saw Bryce. Its pink, red and amber phantom-like sandstone rock formations are simply otherworldly, transported from a galaxy far away.

We also had a run-in with Utah's draconian alcohol licensing laws. It happened to be Thanksgiving. To get into the spirit of this uniquely American holiday, we tried to buy some wine for the evening. This was a problem. It turned out that state laws prohibited supermarkets from selling wine, which could only be purchased from state-run 'liquor stores', and the one in Springdale had closed hours earlier. So we ate at a neighbourhood diner at the deeply un-European time of 6 p.m. (their last sitting), and as we paid the bill, we asked whether we could buy some wine to take back to our hotel. The waiter looked deeply troubled and disappeared to consult his boss.

He returned and launched into a negotiation. Where were we going to drink the wine? Our hotel room, we said. This seemed okay. Were we content to carry the wine in a brown bag, and not take it out of the bag while walking down the road? We promised that we could make it the 800 yards back to our hotel without needing alcohol on the way. This also seemed okay. And then came the clincher. They couldn't open the bottles for us; so if we didn't have a corkscrew, we would be in trouble. We said this was fine. We didn't have a corkscrew, but we knew that we could rely on the time-honoured technique, employed by generations of students, of pushing the cork down into the bottle. Honour and local law satisfied, we were allowed our two bottles. And as we discussed on the walk back, we really didn't mind the interrogation or the local rules; better this than the spectacle of helpless drunks lying on the pavement (as seen in some British town centres on a Friday night). And our wives were thrilled to be asked to produce ID proving they were over twenty-one.

In the event, the wine accompanied our viewing of an American football game, the New England Patriots at the Denver Broncos, so we unwittingly participated in what I now know is an American Thanksgiving tradition. Or at least Nigel and I watched it. As I recall, it was snowing in Denver, and the Broncos won with a dramatic overtime play, a 48-yard touchdown by C. J. Anderson.

We returned to Las Vegas the following day, but went straight to the airport for our flight to Orlando. By that evening, we were on the freeway to Longboat Key, via Sarasota. This final leg was about rest and recreation as much as further exploration: sun, sea, tennis. Nigel and Lou's apartment overlooked a long, virtually empty, white sand beach with pelicans wheeling past the windows and dolphins 'team-fishing' offshore. We knew and liked Sarasota from previous trips. It has some great waterside restaurants, an old-fashioned cinema showing indie films, and a pleasingly laid-back vibe.

Sarasota also has a feature of some fame, or perhaps notoriety. There is a famous photograph, taken by Alfred Eisenstaedt in Times Square on VJ Day, 15 August 1945, of a sailor kissing a nurse. In 2005, the sixtieth anniversary, a man called Seward Johnson created a 25-foot-high statue of the couple, which he called 'Unconditional Surrender', and was given permission to place it prominently, but temporarily, on the Sarasota waterfront. In 2007, it was loaned to the Port of San Diego, travelling there on a flatbed truck, which must have been quite a sight on the freeway. It was returned to Sarasota in 2012, in the teeth of some opposition: the then chair-woman of the Public Arts Committee said of it, 'it doesn't even qualify as kitsch'. Nevertheless, it has remained, even surviving a car driving into it in 2012; it is now permanently owned by the city, having been bought and donated by a Second World War veteran. It has, however, suffered a more recent mishap. The sailor in the iconic photograph, George Mendonsa, died on 18 February 2019. The next evening, someone sprayed a #MeToo logo on the statue; 1945's romantic moment had become 2019's sexual assault.

Our time in Sarasota wasn't all play. Florida, with its twenty-nine electoral college votes, is the most important swing state in America, so there was value in sniffing the state's political air. And Sarasota is a leading refuge for Midwesterner 'snowbirds', fleeing the bleak northern winters by driving straight down I-75 to Florida's west coast. The Midwest is where US elections tend to be decided.

So what was in the air? Judging by what I heard, hopes were building around the local boy, Florida senator Marco Rubio (reminding me that he'd also been tipped by some of the Washington pundits at that breakfast at the residence several weeks earlier). But Donald Trump seemed to be everyone's second choice from the field.

These were mostly rich retirees, but Trump's rhetoric seemed to be connecting with them as much as with the blue-collar classes. The overwhelmingly dominant theme, however, was deep dissatisfaction with President Obama. The apartment block was equipped with gym, swimming pool and tennis courts. I visited the gym most mornings, to hear the other residents complaining about taxes and regulations and government waste. One morning, two of them had an entirely serious conversation about whether Obama was actually a communist. Another morning, the discussion focused on the President's attendance, a few months previously, at the funeral of Reverend Clementa Pinckney, a South Carolina state senator killed in a mass shooting at an African-American community church in Charleston. This was the service where Obama memorably broke into 'Amazing Grace' during his eulogy. My fellow gym enthusiasts didn't think Obama would have attended the funeral had the victims been white. Given the hopelessly small size of my survey, I hesitated to draw judgements. But with the benefit of hindsight, the signals were already there that Florida wasn't going to vote for Obama's Secretary of State.

I usually can't sleep on aeroplanes. So as we flew back to London, I had plenty of time to think about the messages I had heard during the trip. I had been to the borderline South (Tennessee); the Deep South (Alabama, Mississippi, Louisiana); the West (Nevada and Utah); and Florida. I had scarcely heard a positive word anywhere about Obama, or Hillary Clinton. By contrast, I had heard a lot of approving comments about Donald Trump, and almost nothing about the other Republican candidates. In short, it had been the polar opposite of Washington, where Obama was spoken of with respect and Trump with contempt or derision. America seemed to be two different countries.

But it was the Deep South which left the deepest imprint on me, as it does on so many travellers. An American might say 'Well, of course; everyone knows what's been left behind.' But I simply hadn't understood the legacy of the Civil War: the memories, the hurt, the bitterness, the defiance and the rewritten history, all contributing to an abiding sense of resentment and separateness, and a distrust of the Northern elites in their Washington and New York fortresses. With a little research, I uncovered what was known as the Lost Cause of The Confederacy: a revisionist ideology which held that the Confederates had been fighting, not to retain slavery, but for their homes, the rights of their states, and the Southern way of life. It reached its peak in the years of the First World War, at the same time that the statue of 'The Women of the Confederacy' was being erected in front of the Mississippi State Capitol. And I realised that there were echoes of the Lost Cause in many of the moments of the trip: the tour guide's heartfelt exposition of Southern victimhood in the Capitol; or the nostalgic, sepia-tinged, account of the history of Natchez presented in its visitor centre. Oscar Wilde, one of my favourite writers, visited America in 1882 for a 'talking tour', in which he appeared in 150 cities. He wrote five years later, in 'The Canterville Ghost', of 'the beautiful, passionate, ruined South, the land of magnolias and music, of roses and romance . . . living on the memory of crushing defeat'.

4

Snowzilla

*

*'I could stand in the middle of Fifth Avenue and shoot somebody
and I wouldn't lose any voters'*
                                        – Donald Trump, 23 January 2016

*

WE ARRIVED in Washington DC at the start of my posting
on the afternoon of Wednesday 20 January; a clear, sunny
but cold day, with the temperature hovering around minus 8°C. We
spent the evening having supper with some of the senior members
of the embassy. The next day was unpacking, meeting the residence
team, hearing about the building's state of disrepair, and walking
around the compound. And on Friday morning, I went into the
embassy building for the first time as ambassador, to be met by the
worried faces of the deputy head of mission and the head of corporate affairs. A monster blizzard was heading towards the north-eastern
seaboard, with Washington right in its path. One meteorologist
described it somewhat inarticulately as 'kind of a top-ten snowstorm'.
The *Washington Post* dubbed it 'Snowzilla'.

The advice from the team was clear and insistent: I should close
the embassy at lunchtime to allow staff time to get home before the
roads became dangerous. I looked out of the window at the clear
blue sky and wondered about the optics of my first decision as
ambassador being to close down the embassy. But the same advice

was coming in from every direction, with the 24-hour news channels already approaching maximum hysteria: 'Everyone should get home!' And I heard that Amanda Downes, the residence social secretary of twenty-eight years' standing, had taken Vanessa shopping at the local Whole Foods to 'provision up' and head off the risk of starvation over the ensuing few days.

So I signed off an email to all staff telling them all to abandon ship and head for the lifeboats. They complied. Meanwhile, the sun continued shining.

But not for long: the sky gradually turned from blue to grey and snow started to fall that Friday afternoon. It was, at first, a few flakes floating prettily to earth, like Hollywood's concept of Christmas. But through the evening, it increased steadily in ferocity. As we went to bed, we were conscious of a raging blizzard outside. We woke to the extraordinary sight of four feet of snow, lying in drifts against every door in the residence. And the snow was still coming down. Every feature in the residence garden had been obliterated by a thick white blanket. Massachusetts Avenue, in normal times a four-lane artery into the heart of Washington, was silent and unrecognisable; a snow-mobile, or a skier, might have made some progress down it, but nothing with wheels.

This was genuinely once-in-a-generation, one of those episodes of Big Weather that characterise the United States. There were tragic consequences; among the more than 100 million people affected by it, there were 55 deaths, including three in Washington. The cost of this officially designated 'Category 5 Extreme Event' was estimated at $3 billion.

Inevitably, the snowstorm also generated some knockabout politics. At the time, the Republican presidential primaries were in full swing. Chris Christie, Governor of New Jersey (who later became a good friend), was campaigning in New Hampshire, flew back briefly to his state to assess the damage, which by then was more about the risk of flooding from melting snow, but returned almost immediately to the campaign trail. A storm of criticism erupted around his swift exit. A frustrated Christie said to a reporter: 'I don't know what you expect me to do, go down there with a mop?' A New Jersey resident instantly crowd-funded the purchase of 1,000 mops for the governor.

Two of our best friends from my time in Brussels as British ambassador to the European Union were already in Washington when we arrived. David O'Sullivan, the EU ambassador to the US, and his wife Agnes lived about a mile down Massachusetts Avenue from us. We invited them round for supper on Saturday evening, though we wondered whether they would be able to make it through the snowdrifts. They could: they pitched up in full winter gear, wearing ski suits and snowshoes. And they reciprocated, inviting us back on Sunday evening. We lacked the ski gear, but dressed in what was available and set off down a silent and still impassable Massachusetts Avenue. Though the road was still covered in feet of snow, the emergency services had created a narrow pathway, allowing us to walk to the side street where the O'Sullivans lived. We turned off the main road to be greeted by a hill of snow twelve feet high. It took us twenty minutes to climb it and then slide down the other side; ice axes and crampons would have helped. We heard subsequently from David and Agnes that the first house on the street was an outpost of the Russian Embassy. The Russians had hired some private excavators and cleared the snow from the road in front of their building – by pushing it all back down the street. They had thereby opened their way to the main road while creating an impassable obstacle for the rest of the street. I surmised that it wasn't one of those neighbourhoods where new arrivals were greeted by neighbours bearing meat loaves or pumpkin pies.

We reopened the embassy the following Tuesday, though perhaps a third of the staff were still stranded down impassable roads. I eventually delivered the traditional arrival address to the whole embassy on Thursday, which was followed by an equally traditional drinks party. Life gradually returned to normal, apart from the lingering grey, grubby piles of snow that littered the landscape, melting reluctantly in the frigid air. I started on a round of introductory calls, beginning with the State Department. And within a few days, I found myself presenting my credentials to President Obama at the White House.

'Letters of credence', as credentials are more properly known, date back to the fourteenth century. In those days, when an ambassador pitched up at the court of a neighbouring king, there were risks attached. If the relationship had somehow soured during the journey, which would perhaps have lasted months, the ambassador might find himself taken hostage, imprisoned, or even dismembered. The modern generation is fortunate that such practices have largely died out. Ambassadors are now processed by conveyor belt. Most heads of state, at least in the world's major economies, get through the business of receiving credentials as rapidly as decently possible, by seeing new ambassadors in job lots: no lengthy discussions over refreshments about the state of bilateral relations. So in Washington, a group of the newly arrived is assembled once every few months. Each of them gets sixty seconds, a handshake and a photograph with the President.

I had never actually experienced a credentials ceremony before. There was no such procedure for ambassadors to the European Union, as the EU was not a country, despite the superstate dreams of the Brussels idealists. Unsure what exactly I was meant to be doing, I was completely unprepared for the photograph and so was captured in a robotic pose, looking somewhat uncomfortable. The result was Andy Warhol's fifteen minutes of fame, with much accompanying ribaldry on social media.

I avoided the Twitterstorm by immersing myself in a succession of meetings to learn about the embassy. Washington, as the capital of the most powerful country in the world and our strongest ally, was rightly regarded as having the most important bilateral British diplomatic mission. It had more than 450 staff, divided into 22 teams, and oversaw a network twice that size, with consulates (which nowadays are more about trade than lost passports) in Atlanta, Boston, Chicago, Houston, Los Angeles, Miami, New York and San Francisco, and pure trade offices in Denver, Minneapolis, Raleigh, San Diego and Seattle. The embassy connected to every department of government in the UK, and got involved in pretty much every conceivable aspect of the UK–US relationship. Around half of the embassy staff were Americans ('locally engaged', in the Foreign Office jargon), including the entire congressional liaison team and two-thirds of my private office; coming from all parts of the country, they brought invaluable knowledge and understanding. The biggest single section was the 150-strong defence team. Their tasks included looking after the welfare of the several hundred British servicemen and women embedded in the US armed forces, overseeing the dozens of joint US and UK equipment and technology projects, and managing the day-to-day interactions necessitated by our forces' joint operations in Afghanistan and Iraq. And I quickly discovered that, somewhere in the embassy, there was someone covering each and every conceivable interaction between the UK and the US, from British nationals on death row to future trade deals and everything in between.

I started to think about how I should spend my time, given that there were three or four options for every hour of life as British ambassador to the US. First, it was election year. We needed to get alongside the leading campaigns, build relationships with the main advisers, and provide London with a constant flow of insights and analysis; crucially, material that they weren't reading in media reports. Second, supporting British business had to be one of the highest priorities. National wealth is created by the private sector, not by government; and 19 per cent of total British exports go to the US, by a long way our largest bilateral market. So I told the commercial team that I would see any senior visiting British businessman who was coming through Washington, and that I would host at the residence any export promotion events they wanted to put my way. Third, I resolved to spend two afternoons a week in Congress, seeing senators and congressmen; more time with them than some of my predecessors had spent, but I reckoned it would be repaid, sooner or later.

I also recognised that I had to get out of Washington and around the country, as I had learnt on my road trip. DC wasn't America, there were eight consulates to visit, and I was personally intrigued to visit Silicon Valley and the headquarters of the internet giants. Beyond this, I knew that each week was bound to be filled with the normal business of bilateral diplomacy: a steady stream of senior ministers and officials visiting from London, and the daily task of understanding, assessing, reporting and, most important of all, building the relationships which would enable me to intervene on any aspect of US federal and state activity that had implications for British interests.

That was the day job. There were also the evenings. Washington comes alive at night. And the British ambassador is in the fortunate, if demanding, position of being invited to pretty much everything. I got into the habit of spending an hour a week with Amanda Downes and the private office team, deciding which of the dozens of invitations I received each week should be accepted – and often, how many different events could be crammed into one night. There was a real art to this, and I was seriously lucky in having Amanda at the table. In particular, she warned us against accepting all but a handful of a Washington speciality, the 'charity gala dinner'. The best of these could be spectacular. The worst were a deadly combination of endless speeches preceding a meal of shoe-leather steak, followed by more speeches stretching into the late hours. Throughout my diplomatic career, I had reckoned that if I didn't get at least a couple of insights worth reporting back to London from each and every evening event, then I had been wasting my time. Thanks in part to Amanda's judicious advice about which invitations to accept, and in part to Washington being the most political, and gossipy, of cities, the problem became, not collecting worthwhile insights, but finding the time to report all of them, so rich an environment was the Washington social circuit.

And then there was the residence. Designed by Sir Edwin Lutyens, considered the greatest British architect of his age, and completed in 1928, this was a building designed for parties – whether an intimate dinner for a dozen in the smaller of the two dining rooms, a reception for 350 in the ballroom (under a portrait of the Queen by Andy Warhol), or a garden party for 600 to celebrate a royal wedding. Adding together breakfasts, lunches, receptions and dinners, Vanessa and I found ourselves hosting some 800 events a year there; and thanks to a brilliant head chef and his team, as well as an accomplished front-of-house operation, it ran like a well-oiled machine.

The biggest of these 800 events was the annual embassy open day. There was a Washington tradition that all the embassies opened their doors to the public over a couple of Saturdays in May. For us, this had become, over the years, a Cecil B. de Mille style spectacular. Jaguar, Bentley and Rolls-Royce displayed their latest models. There were stalls showcasing British food and drink. The residence was decked out for a black-tie dinner. The Washington Shakespeare Company performed extracts of his plays on the terrace. The rose garden looked at its most glamorous. Local TV news film crews roamed the compound. On a sunny day, around 10,000 people would come through the gates, producing a queue half a mile up Massachusetts Avenue.

The first year, I lingered for a while near the Jaguars, eventually sitting in one for the benefit of a TV crew. I noticed among the thousands of visitors a young man, studying me with intent. As I clambered out of the car, he approached me and asked for a photograph with me. I readily agreed. He then said, 'I really love your show. When's the next season?' I asked who he thought I was. He said, 'Aren't you Jeremy Clarkson?' I explained that I was someone far less important than the presenter of *Top Gear*, namely the ambassador. Did he still want a photograph? Looking mildly embarrassed, he said, 'Yeah, okay then,' did the selfie thing, and vanished. One of the embassy staff overheard: by Monday, several thousand people knew the story.

The Foreign Office also required us to make the residence generate income by hiring it out commercially. So we found ourselves hosting everything from company boards to gala dinners. The one disadvantage to this otherwise lucrative practice was that a short speech by the ambassador came as part of the package. So I found myself speaking about an extraordinary range of subjects to a highly varied range of audiences. Night after night, I gave silent thanks to a succession of creative speechwriters. And most nights, as the guests filed out, dazzled by the grandeur of their surroundings, I wondered what they would think if they knew that, thanks to decades of under-investment, the fabric of the building was in a parlous state. There were leaks whenever it rained, floods whenever a pipe failed, misbehaving fire alarms, periodic power cuts, and unreliable lifts. Late one evening, Vanessa was trapped in a lift for fifty minutes. Dodgy lifts are a feature of British residences worldwide; there was a similarly troublesome example in the Brussels residence, though my jamming it by stuffing a redundant Christmas tree in it one January may not have helped.

We started to settle into a pattern of life. Vanessa had also started work as a teacher at the British International School of Washington. (She had worked throughout every posting of my career, finding it kept her grounded and gave her a life outside mine.) So we rose at 6 a.m., Vanessa to get ready for her 7.30 start, while I caught up on the US news and the emails from London. Vanessa had a short walk through the woods and I did the thirty-second commute to the embassy at about 8 a.m., unless there was a working breakfast, and spent most days on a combination of meetings, video conferences and calls. Vanessa got back to the residence at about 5 p.m., giving her an hour's turnaround before the evening event. I generally went straight from work. If it was one event, we might be home by 8 p.m.; if two or three, 10 p.m. or later. In short, it amounted to an extraordinarily interesting and rewarding life; but also to an unending and sometimes exhausting succession of fifteen-hour days.

Within a couple of months of our arrival, the residence acquired two additional occupants. Vanessa took on two rescued Washington street cats, which she named Monty and Pico (both names inherited from former occupants of the family cat position). The rescue charity carefully vetted the residence and gardens for their suitability for homeless cats before releasing them to us. They became well-known figures around the compound, and indeed in the New Zealand Embassy next door and the Naval Observatory across the road – the latter the official residence of Vice President Mike Pence and his wife Karen. The cats even took to following Vanessa on her walk through the woods to school. Sadly, Pico was killed on Massachusetts Avenue a couple of years later. Monty, however, thrived, and stayed on after our departure, in the care of the residence manager. He developed into an exceptionally effective – that is, lethal – hunter. We came home one evening to discover he had dragged a rabbit through the cat flap into the kitchen, there to dismember it – leaving entrails on the carpet and splashes of blood halfway up the walls.

Mrs Pence famously kept rabbits; and I pondered briefly, but dismissed, the notion that Monty's victim was one of hers. As I swabbed the blood from the kitchen walls, however, it did occur to me that it was a fitting metaphor for the political times in Washington.

At the weekends, we started to get to know the city. To a Londoner, it feels compact; in the car, in some directions, one can be out of it in twenty minutes. Perhaps appropriately, as the capital city of the melting pot that is America, it is a mash-up of architectural styles, from the neoclassicism of the Capitol, the White House and Union Station through the Norman style of the Smithsonian, the gothic revivalism of the National Cathedral, all the way to the African influences in the extraordinary new Museum of African American History on the Mall (designed, as it happens, by a brilliant British architect, David Adjaye). It is also a strikingly low-rise city, thanks to the Height of Buildings Act of 1910. This restricts buildings in business areas to 110 feet in height, and those in residential areas to a mere 90 feet. But most of all, we enjoyed walking around the quiet, leafy nineteenth-century streets of old Georgetown, some fifteen minutes' walk from the residence. Or at least, we usually did: there is one month when those streets should be avoided. The streets are full of ginkgo trees. But they planted females, not males; and for a month in autumn, the pavements are covered in seeds from the trees – which smell, precisely and disconcertingly, of vomit.

Those first weeks passed in a blur of social gatherings – save three events which remain in the memory. The first was a Washington institution called the Alfalfa Club. Though it is called a club, it meets but once each year, on the last Saturday in January, for a black-tie dinner at the Capitol Hilton. Its membership is a combination of corporate America and Washington politics. Its proceedings are, in sharp contrast to the more famous White House Correspondents' Dinner, entirely private. But they are similar in the sense that the entertainment comprises a series of theoretically humorous and disrespectful speeches. The club's name is a tribute to the alfalfa plant, which has an exceptionally wide-reaching root system, designed to capture all available moisture; a plant, in other words, that is willing 'to do anything for a drink'. It was founded in 1913, by four Southerners, to celebrate the birthday of the Confederate general Robert E. Lee. It didn't admit African Americans until 1974, and women until 1994. The serving President would always be invited. Sportingly, President Obama attended twice, in 2009 and 2012. In his 2009 speech to the dinner, Obama noted that 'if General Lee were here with us tonight, at this dinner in his honour, he would be 202 years old. And very confused.'

So I pitched up for my first Alfalfa, to be greeted by a sea of faces including many of the most famous corporate figures in America; from the giants of Wall Street to the stars of Silicon Valley. I was one of about a dozen ambassadors in attendance, and we were treated mysteriously well. At a certain point in the pre-dinner drinks, we were selected out and ushered into a 'VIP area', from which Wall Street and Silicon Valley were excluded; only ambassadors and senior American politicians were allowed entry. Hence mysterious; anywhere to which I am allowed access while, say, Jeff Bezos and Warren Buffett are excluded has to be strange. As I walked in to this exclusive gathering, I could scarcely believe my eyes: among the twenty or so people there were two former Presidents, George H. W. Bush (in a wheelchair) and George W. Bush; several senior White House figures including presidential adviser Valerie Jarrett; and a sprinkling of cabinet secretaries, including Secretary of State John Kerry. I gleefully made the rounds, picked up what gossip I could, and sent an email to London on Monday morning, beginning 'I talked to both George Bushes, John Kerry and Valerie Jarrett on Saturday night . . .'

A week or so later, there was the National Prayer Breakfast, traditionally held on the first Thursday in February. By comparison with Alfalfa, this was a newcomer, having been founded by President Eisenhower in 1953 with the encouragement of the Reverend Billy Graham. But it is the bigger event, with more than 2,000 guests packed into the Washington Hilton's largest room, several hundred more in an overflow room, a handful of visiting heads of state, and live coverage on national TV. It also always gets a keynote speech from the President.

I had no idea what to expect when I walked into the vast auditorium in the hotel basement. But in fact, it was exactly what it said on the tin: a range of national figures, mostly politicians, but also Church leaders, leading a series of prayers. Obama gave a brilliant, deeply personal speech, in part about his relationship with his daughters. It reminded me that, at his best, Obama had few equals as a public speaker. The unexpected highlight, however, was the performance of the two unannounced 'mystery speakers'. These turned out to be Mark Burnett, a TV producer, and Roma Downey, an actress.

Had I been in America longer, I might have known that these were national figures. Downey played the angel (yes, really) in a long-running TV show, *Touched by an Angel*; and Burnett was a giant of TV production, having invented two hugely successful TV shows, *Survivor* and *The Apprentice*, in the latter casting as the CEO figure an aspiring TV star called Donald Trump. They gave a confident and professional performance, and I was struck in particular at hearing a British accent from the podium. Mark Burnett had been born in London and had served in the Parachute Regiment, including during the Falklands War, before emigrating to the United States in 1982. I emailed him later that day to congratulate him on his performance and to say how nice it had been to see a Brit as the star speaker at such a quintessentially American event.

Then, a month after my arrival at the embassy, I had my first taste of American election campaigns. The first two events on the Republican calendar, the Iowa caucus and the New Hampshire primary, had been and gone, with Donald Trump winning both, in continuing defiance of the Washington pundits. The next primary was South Carolina. Vanessa and I flew down to the state capital, Columbus, on the day of the vote. We had lunch with the local Republican Party representatives. They insisted we eat catfish, which was apparently caught by being wrestled by hand out of muddy riverbanks. They were outstanding (the Republicans, that is – the catfish was okay): friendly, frank, full of insights. We then talked that afternoon to some of the journalists covering the primary. Everyone thought Trump would nail a hat-trick of successes, but there was uncertainty over the margin of victory and the order of the runners-up. And no one, especially not the local Republicans, seemed happy. They didn't like the tone of the Trump campaign, and they didn't see him as a proper Republican.

The tradition is that every campaign, whether winning or losing, holds a party (sort of; warm beer in plastic cups) as the results come in. The Trump campaigners were holed up somewhere else in South Carolina, a fair distance from Columbus. So Vanessa and I and the embassy political team went to the Marco Rubio event. Rubio was a young, charismatic, good-looking senator from Florida, with a striking back story. His father had fled Cuba in the 1950s and worked as a bartender, initially in Nevada, then in Miami. A lot of knowledgeable people thought Rubio had a real chance of winning the Republican nomination.

In the event, he never came close to challenging Trump. His candidacy was effectively destroyed by Chris Christie. At the televised debate preceding the New Hampshire vote, Christie, a gifted exponent of bare-knuckle politics, metaphorically beat Rubio up, accusing him of spouting vacuous, pre-programmed, robotic soundbites. A flustered Rubio was prompted into responding with some words best described as, well, vacuous, pre-programmed, robotic soundbites. When I heard this, I felt a stab of sympathy for Rubio, given my own trial by Twitter a few weeks earlier; we robots had to stick together. That said, Rubio actually ran second in South Carolina, prompting an upbeat mood at the event I attended. Rubio spent a few minutes with me and the team, and then delivered a speech to the assembled crowd that would have been spot on had he actually won the primary rather than come second. But it was a false dawn; a few weeks later, after being ridiculed by Christie, losing his home state of Florida to Trump, and having run out of money, Rubio pulled out.

The big news, however, from South Carolina, apart from Trump's third victory, concerned another candidate. Jeb Bush, George W. Bush's younger brother, had been a successful governor of Florida from 1999 to 2007. As George W. Bush's presidency began to fall apart under the pressures of failure in Iraq, senior Republicans could be heard increasingly to say 'we got the wrong Bush'. So when Jeb announced his candidacy for President in June 2015, money poured in (some $100 million). He immediately became front runner. But that was as good as it got. Of his campaign, it was said 'he never walked without stumbling'. Once under the national spotlight, he emerged as a clunky, uninspiring public speaker and a diffident, nervous performer in debate. In particular, he couldn't cope with Donald Trump, looking like a deer in the headlights whenever Trump attacked him. Trump dubbed him 'low energy Jeb'; Bush never got close to an effective response. Some debaters have an instinct to go for the jugular; Jeb's habitual response was to deliver the harmless glancing blow.

So by the time the Bush campaign reached South Carolina, it was the land of the last chance saloon. I was due to call on both Bush and on the senator for South Carolina, Lindsay Graham, that afternoon. Both cancelled at short notice. I was told that they were in conference, with Graham providing some campaign advice and analysis. If this was true, then Graham's advice must have been sharp-edged; Bush withdrew from the presidential race the next day.

A few weeks later, I went down to see Jeb Bush in his Florida office. He gave me a lot of his time, spoke freely and frankly, and came across as a transparently decent human being and a serious policy thinker. But he also looked and sounded like he had been hit by a truck. He fretted about letting down his team by being such a weak candidate. He worried about the Republicans becoming the anti-immigration party on the back of Trump's success. He said he had spent decades building support for the Republican Party in the Latino community, only to see Trump destroy it in a few months. But most of all, he seemed shattered by the experience of the campaign: his precipitous fall from front runner to roadkill in the space of a few months. And the anger was still there. As I left, he said, 'Trump may win the nomination. But you can be sure of this. He will not win the presidency.'

Back in Washington from the South Carolina primary, and just over a month into my posting, I wrote to London with my first considered assessment of the presidential race. On the Democratic contest, I predicted that Hillary Clinton was likely to win, but noted that she was facing much tougher opposition than anyone had expected from Senator Bernie Sanders of Vermont. Sanders, who described himself as a democratic socialist, and who looked to me disconcertingly like Doc Brown from the *Back to the Future* films, had virtually dead-heated with Clinton in Iowa, and had then convincingly won New Hampshire; but had been blown out of the water in South Carolina, where the African-American community voted overwhelmingly for Clinton.

As for the Republicans, I wrote that Trump had been underestimated throughout his presidential run; that 'the likeliest outcome' was that he would win the Republican nomination; that Clinton was damaged goods with serious likeability and trust issues; and that it was therefore conceivable that Trump would go on to win the presidency. For the record, this judgement was made on 25 February 2016.

5

The Brexit Vote

*

'I think it's a very great thing that has happened . . . basically, they took back their country'
        – presidential candidate Donald Trump, 24 June 2016

*

"WHAT YOU need to do now is develop a career anchor."
        These words of advice came from a friend in the human resources department of the Foreign Office. His point was well judged. After twelve years in the office, I had been a junior press spokesman; I had spent four years in Japan, but not as a language specialist; I had done two years running the Channel Tunnel treaty negotiations; and I was in the middle of three years as senior private secretary to the minister of state dealing with the Middle East. Meanwhile, my colleagues had been learning 'hard' languages like Chinese and Arabic, and developing career specialisations. Having early in my career achieved a historically low score in the hard language aptitude test, none of this was for me; I had instead been following an enjoyable but utterly random path.

I pondered these words and, a few weeks later, talked to him again. I said that I wanted to become a specialist in the European Community – the EC, as it was known around the system. He was taken aback. This was a career path that tended to involve future postings in Brussels; pleasant enough but no one's idea of a glamorous city. And it had the reputation around the corridors of being a sixty-hour-a-week grind, mostly spent in airless conference rooms negotiating the widgets directive. So there wasn't much of a queue at the door for this particular career path. But I told him that I liked the idea of negotiating for a living; and that I thought the European Community was 'the future', in that it would come to play an increasingly large role in British politics and governance. As we talked it over, he started to agree.

When I finished as private secretary a few months later, there wasn't anything available in Brussels. So I was asked to go to Rome as first secretary (EC and Economic). This involved a course on economics of, well, all of four and a half days – leading my colleagues to dub me 'the Economic Miracle' when I subsequently opined on the subject. It also involved a month in Florence learning Italian, and then three years of living in an extraordinary apartment in the sixteenth-century English College, the Venerabile Collegio Inglese for trainee Catholic priests, in the Centro Storico, the ancient heart of Rome: hardship piled upon hardship. The college had a picturesque history; and our showcase high-ceilinged apartment was where, back in the 1700s, the most famous British visitors, including in 1635 Thomas Hobbes, the English political philosopher, would stay before making the short walk to the Vatican. Just as our days in Rome were drawing to an end, we learnt that the apartment was rumoured to be haunted. It was as well that Vanessa hadn't discovered this earlier. As for me, looking back, I rather warm to the idea that the ghosts of illustrious guests of the past are still roaming those corridors. If Hobbes is amongst them, he must be gratified that his concept of the absolute leader, wielding supreme and unchecked power over his subjects, has such notable modern-day adherents.

After a joyous three years of *la dolce vita*, I returned to London as deputy head of the European Union Department. I subsequently took time out from what was now known, post-Maastricht Treaty, as the EU, the European Union, to lead the department dealing with the break-up of Yugoslavia and the Bosnia war; and then a couple of years as the Foreign Secretary's press spokesman. But after that, it was back to the EU for more than a decade: director of the Foreign

Office European departments: then Prime Minister Tony Blair's Europe adviser: and then over four years as British ambassador to the European Union.

The Foreign Office is somewhat lazily characterised in parts of the British media as a den of crazed Europhiles, eager to sell out their country if it contributes to the next stage of the construction of the European superstate. The reality is that there are both enthusiasts and sceptics inside the machine – both remainers and leavers, in these more tribal days – though it would be a fair guess that remainers are the majority. I personally was, and am, neither a sceptic nor a super-enthusiast. I took the pragmatic view that, overall, it served British interests to be part of the European project.

I felt this in particular because I had grown up during an era of seemingly relentless British decline, culminating in the three-day week of 1974 and then the uncollected rubbish and the unburied bodies of the 1978–79 Winter of Discontent. In comparison with these convulsions, Europe had seemed to be flourishing. I thought that the single market, essentially a British idea, was one of the greatest projects of the twentieth century. I felt equally strongly about the EU offering membership to central and Eastern European states, a project to which I felt I had contributed by chairing the EU Enlargement Working Group during the British EU presidency of 1998 (the 'presidency' of the European Union rotates among the member states, each getting six months). But I also recognised what a strange, 'un-British' construction was the European Commission. I despaired at times about the lowest common denominator outcomes of internal EU negotiations. And I thought that the British Treasury had a point in its critique of the euro: that it wouldn't work without a single fiscal and budgetary policy across the single currency zone, and large-scale financial transfers from the richer regions to the poorer. I was also conscious, however, that, for our European partners, the European project was about much more than trade and economics. Only a generation or two earlier, they had lived through two world wars, with millions killed and their cities destroyed. Indeed, the entire history of Europe had been one of wars between neighbours. So their attachment to the ideals and ambitions of building Europe was rooted in history. It was emotional as well as intellectual, and was fundamentally about peace and security, and an end to war in Europe forever.

Whatever my mixed feelings about the characteristics and policies of the European Union, I thought from the outset, privately, that the Cameron proposition of holding a referendum on membership of the European Union was seriously risky. I could see a lot wrong with the EU. I could sense the mounting unhappiness within the Conservative Party. No one could miss the rise of UKIP. All of us British officials working in Brussels would, on occasion, become incensed at the seemingly magisterial powers of unelected Commission officials, especially when their proposals were wrong-headed, as with the catastrophically misguided Working Time Directive of the 1990s. A decade later, the Eurozone became a low growth disaster area after the 2008 financial crisis. And members of the euro responded to that crisis as if they were a privileged inner court within the EU, entitled to take decisions without recourse to the views of the rest. But overall, it was still, surely, in our interests to work for reform from within? And what if we lost?

David Cameron has written about his thought processes before making his famous announcement on an EU referendum at Bloomberg's London headquarters in January 2013. He relates that he concluded that the best way of keeping the UK within the EU was to renegotiate the terms of our membership, get a better deal, then put the question to the British people and win the argument, settling the Europe issue for party and country for a generation. I worked for Cameron for almost four years. I thought he was a seri-ously talented politician, streets ahead of his contemporaries as a leader; that he made a lot of good, often brave, decisions; and that he was a thoroughly decent human being. But I have never accepted the argument that the referendum was unavoidable and unstoppable – that it was somehow written in the stars. The fact was that we had negotiated for ourselves a privileged form of EU membership, full of British exceptionalism: Mrs Thatcher's rebate, our unique perma-nent exclusion from the euro, and our partial exclusion from those bits of Schengen, 'Europe without Frontiers', that we didn't like. In short, we had managed to get ourselves effectively the best of both worlds; the advantages of membership, absent the obligations we didn't like, and with a special discount on costs. But then, as a civil servant, I have never had to run for election and navigate the tides of public opinion.

Whatever my personal feelings on the issue, I arrived in Washington with the referendum only six months away, with the renegotiation of our EU membership in full swing, and with a US administration frankly puzzled about why the British government had decided, from choice not necessity, to take such a huge risk. On my round of introductory calls, I would be asked repeatedly, 'Can you just explain again why you are doing this?' I would use the approved lines, which centred on the supposedly unstoppable public pressure for a vote, given how much the European project had changed from the one they had supported in the 1975 referendum. I could tell from their body language that none of the Obama team bought this; and I could readily imagine the US Embassy in London reporting that the referendum promise had been about heading off the UKIP threat in the 2015 election, and that Europe never featured in polls listing the top ten concerns of the British electorate. The more assertive of my contacts would then say, 'We really need you inside the EU, so we trust you will win this.' I tried to reassure them: winning was the plan.

The concerns of the Obama team were real. But in telling us how important we were to them, there was an element of flattery. I vividly recall an informal drink with a friend from the Obama team, who revealed that on a lot of European business, their first call was to Berlin: Merkel was seen as the one calling the shots, while we were perceived to be somewhat marginalised. The areas where we ranked ahead of the Germans were wider international affairs, especially defence and security. But even here, our reputation had been tarnished by the British Parliament's vote, in August 2013, against UK involvement in proposed air strikes against President Assad's forces in Syria, following his use of chemical weapons against his own people. That said, they were ready to help. And there was an opportunity coming with a presidential visit to London in April 2016.

This was to be Obama's last trip to London as President. The Obamas got on famously with the royal family, so the programme involved a private lunch with the Queen and the Duke of Edinburgh, and a private dinner with the Duke and Duchess of Cambridge (where the photos of the US President meeting two-year-old Prince George made front pages everywhere). With Cameron, there was an afternoon meeting and a big press conference in one of the Foreign Office's grand conference rooms. I worked with Susan Rice, Obama's national security adviser, and Jeff Zients, his economic adviser, on the agenda for the talks. Jeff asked me whether the Prime Minister would want the President to say anything at the press conference about the referendum. I said I thought it was likely that he would; that in any case, the President was bound to be asked about it at the press conference; but that the precise words would have to be for discussion between the two of them.

In the event, unsurprisingly, the referendum was the first, and dominant, subject of the discussion. Obama had already written a piece for the *Daily Telegraph* saying that, while the decision was a matter for British voters, the EU magnified British influence across the world. Cameron set out how the Remain campaign were doing, conveying simultaneously that it was close, but that he was confident of winning. The discussion turned to the arguments of the Leave campaign, in particular their claim that the single market could be replaced by a multiplicity of free trade deals around the world, including with the United States. Obama said that, given the much bigger markets with which deals could be done, he couldn't see a free trade deal between the US and the UK being a priority. George Osborne suggested he say something to that effect during the press conference.

At the end of the meeting, we duly walked across to the Foreign Office, and into a Locarno Room packed with journalists. When the moment came, Obama said: 'I think it's fair to say that maybe, some point down the line, there might be a UK–US trade agreement; but it's not going to happen any time soon, because our focus is in negotiating with a big bloc, the European Union, to get a trade agreement done, and the UK is going to be in the back of the queue.

Not because we don't have a special relationship, but because, given the heavy lift on any trade agreement, we need to be having access to a big market with a lot of countries rather than trying to do piecemeal trade agreements, which is hugely inefficient.'

As the Obama convoy left the Foreign Office, the heavens opened, leaving us in the UK team wondering whether it was an ill omen. The President's words on a trade deal immediately captured the news cycle, leading all the TV news bulletins and most front pages the following morning. The Leave campaign reacted angrily. Dominic Raab, then justice minister, said that he didn't believe Obama's comments would reflect future US trade policy, and that 'what you had here was a lame duck American President doing an old British friend a political favour'. Boris Johnson, at the time in his last days as mayor of London, called Obama 'hypocritical'. Nigel Farage said he was the most anti-British American President ever. Some in the British media, noting that Obama had said 'back of the queue' rather than the more American 'back of the line', speculated that the Prime Minister had given him a script. I was there: he didn't. The choice of words was Obama's own.

Over the ensuing months, I would be asked many times by members of Obama's team whether the President's intervention had been counter-productive. Some of the instant opinion polls after the visit suggested that more people in the UK had been offended than had supported his words; other polls suggested it was fifty-fifty. Personally, I thought 'back of the queue' was a little harsh and sharp-edged; a softer formulation would have been better. But I also think that it made no difference one way or the other. People weren't interested in 'technicalities' like trade deals; they were voting to punish the Establishment.

The Obama visit stirred up a new wave of US interest in the referendum. Both Hillary Clinton and Donald Trump were asked about it. Clinton sided with Obama: her senior policy adviser, Jake Sullivan, told the *Observer* that she 'valued a strong United Kingdom in a strong European Union'. Trump took the opposite view. He said to Fox News, 'I know Great Britain very well. I have a lot of investments there. I would say that they're better off without the EU. But

I want them to make their own decision.' All of this was as expected. Whitehall took it entirely calmly. They took it less serenely, however, when we picked up rumours that Trump would be visiting the UK at around the time of the actual vote, on 23 June. We were asked to check with the Trump camp. It turned out that he was indeed visiting, for personal and business reasons; he would be presiding over a ceremony to mark the relaunch of one of his two Scottish golf courses, Trump Turnberry, after a £200 million redevelopment. But, we learnt, he would be flying overnight and not arriving until the morning of 24 June, after the polls had closed. So no campaigning; the Foreign Office calmed down. Until, that is, they realised the next question coming down the track: should the Prime Minister offer him a meeting?

There was form between Donald Trump and David Cameron. Back at the beginning of the year, in the context of Trump's campaign-trail rhetoric attacking Muslims, Cameron had said, when challenged at Prime Minister's Questions, that Trump's words were 'stupid, divisive and wrong'. He had also said, however, after Trump had nailed down his party's nomination, that 'anyone who makes it through the primary process deserves respect'. And somewhat uncharacteristically, Trump hadn't really retaliated to Cameron's criticism of his comments on Muslims. As for the possible meeting, the thoroughly sensible line that emerged from No. 10 was that the Prime Minister would in principle of course be ready to see Donald Trump, as was the tradition with visiting US presidential candidates. We in the embassy were, however, asked to talk privately to the Trump team to warn them that, if they asked for a call on 24 June, the Prime Minister might be rather busy. Prescient words, as it turned out, though not for the reasons we might have hoped.

I had fallen into the habit of checking in with the Prime Minister's chief of staff, Ed Llewellyn, every few weeks through the campaign, ostensibly so I could have some inside knowledge when talking to the White House, but also just because I wanted to know how things were. Ed was entirely consistent throughout: he always sounded extremely worried. He told me that the private polls from the Northern and Midlands towns were 'terrible'. He was deeply critical of the leader of the opposition, Jeremy Corbyn, for his failure to do any serious campaigning in the Labour Party heartlands. He said to me, once or twice, 'We can lose this, you know.'

So perhaps I should have been better prepared when a group of us from the embassy assembled at my deputy's house on the evening of 23 June to watch the results come in. Instructions had, incidentally, gone out from the centre to the entire diplomatic network that there should be no public 'watch parties', so there were no outside guests. But the final opinion polls, or at least those that I saw, suggested that Remain had recovered a narrow lead. And I was guessing that all of the warnings about the implications of leaving for the economy, for jobs and for incomes, would prey on people's minds as they went into the privacy of the polling booth. A British friend had emailed me a sort of ready reckoner for the results, a constituency-by-constituency table showing what the figures should be if the final opinion polls were right.

At about 7 p.m. Washington time the results started to flow. It was the Sunderland result that rocked me back. I knew the town from my time at Durham University; I used to go and watch the Sunderland football team play at Roker Park, long since demolished to make way for the optimistically named Stadium of Light. In those days, Sunderland had been the epitome of post-industrial decline. Once known as 'the largest shipbuilding town in the world', with more than four hundred shipyards, by the Seventies it was better known for its appallingly high unemployment rate. Standing in the upper reaches of the football stadium, I could look out over rows and rows of terraced houses towards abandoned shipyards, and beyond to a grey, bleak North Sea. Sunderland's luck had turned, however: it was revitalised through being chosen, in 1984, as the location for the first Nissan car plant in Europe. The plant is still thriving, now making a best-selling electric car. Most of its output goes to Europe.

Sunderland was nevertheless expected to vote Leave, but by a majority of about 6 per cent. The returning officer, on live TV, announced a result that sounded instantly way out of line with that estimate. A quick calculation showed a Leave vote of 61 per cent, as against Remain at 39 per cent. A longstanding British friend of mine happened to be one of the country's top pollsters, a regular on BBC election nights. I texted him to ask what I should make of Sunderland. He texted back almost immediately to say that he thought it was an outlier, and that later results would be more in line with the pre-vote opinion polls.

They weren't. The Newcastle result was another killer. And throughout Northern and Midland cities, Leave was winning by huge margins, approaching 70–30 in some cases. I knew that London and the South-East were expected to vote heavily for Remain. But I started to question whether it would be enough. Then my pollster friend texted again to say that he was 'now much less confident about the accuracy of the polling data and the final result'.

We didn't stay much longer at the gathering. I thought I could see the lie of the land. But I also thought that it would be hours before the result was certain. At 4 a.m., however, I woke and knew I had to catch up on the news. I went through to the study, where my phone was charging. I pressed the Home button. The screen flashed: 'David Cameron announces his resignation as Prime Minister'.

Further sleep being impossible, I was early in the embassy that morning. There must have been colleagues who had voted Leave, as they had every right to do. But no one was skipping down the corridors. People looked shocked. The atmosphere was funereal. One or two were in tears. I did a quick all-staff meeting, at which I set out what I thought would happen next, including that David Cameron would stay on as caretaker Prime Minister until a successor had been chosen through that convoluted two-stage Conservative Party process. And I emphasised that, however individuals felt about the outcome, whether jubilation or despair, the face we should present to the outside world was one of calm acceptance of the result and confidence about the future: this had been democracy in action. Fortunately, it was a Friday, with the weekend beckoning. By the following Monday, the mood had lightened a bit.

As for the world outside the embassy gates, a rare thing was happening; the UK was leading the US news. There were dozens of requests for me to do interviews; the instruction from London to every one of us around the network, however, was that we should decline all bids, at least for the moment, and let the Prime Minister's words from Downing Street speak for themselves.

David Cameron phoned President Obama later that day. As he himself has recorded, he told Obama that he'd had a strategy to keep the UK in the EU, that he'd executed it, that it hadn't worked and that he was sorry. I didn't listen to the call, but the subsequent record showed that Obama had replied in classily empathetic terms. Within a day or two, however, I was hearing from friendly White House journalists that the private reaction inside the building was much harsher, with the President asking his staff, 'How could Cameron even ask the question without being sure of the answer he would get?' Or as one of the White House team put it to me: 'we think you guys are screwed'.

A different line was, however, emerging on home soil. Donald Trump had landed in Scotland and had arrived at Turnberry, to be met by a small crowd of onlookers and a large crowd of journalists and cameras. An hour after Cameron had announced his resignation, Trump was doing an impromptu press conference in front of the Turnberry clubhouse. He said: 'I think it's a great thing that happened, an amazing vote, very historic. Basically, they took their country back.' On David Cameron, he said, 'He's a good man, but he didn't get the mood of his country right.' Asked why Leave had won, he replied: 'People are angry. They are angry over borders, they are angry over people coming into the country and taking over and nobody even noticing. They are angry about many, many things.' On the European Union, he said that break-up 'looks like it's on its way'. He observed that lots of Germans, some of whom were 'members of Mar-a-Lago' – the Trump-owned Florida resort – had told him they were leaving Germany 'because of the tremendous influx of people'. And asked about the implications of the vote for the British economy, he said, 'When the pound goes down, more people are coming to Turnberry, frankly.'

In short, it was vintage Trump: outspoken, opinionated, dismissive of contrary views, occasionally unattached to the facts, but also newsworthy and crystal clear; no one could wonder afterwards where exactly he stood on the issues. And approve of the underlying thought or not, there was undoubtedly truth in his assertion that immigration had been a central issue in the referendum outcome. There was, however, one notable false step. Trump tweeted on arriving in Scotland: 'Place is going wild over the vote. They took their country back, just like we will take America back!' Almost right: Scotland voted by 62 per cent to 38 per cent to remain in the EU.

6

The Rise and Rise of Donald Trump

*

'Nobody knows the system better than me, which is why I alone can fix it'
— presidential candidate Donald Trump's speech to the Republican Convention in Cleveland, Ohio, 21 July 2016

*

MID-MAY, AND I was hosting a small lunch in the Residence for a combination of visitors from London and some senior Republican Party figures. None of the latter were Trump supporters: some would later sign the 'Never Trump' letter. Their biggest concern was around foreign policy: Trump seemed to be a Putin admirer; he saved much of his harshest criticism for America's allies and partners; and he didn't believe in free trade. In short, they didn't think he was really a Republican. I asked whether these could be tactical positions, adopted for the campaign, to be discarded if elected? To my surprise, one of the Brits dissented vigorously, arguing that Trump had always held these views. And he directed me to a YouTube clip as proof.

I tracked down the clip that evening. It was from a BBC TV chat show, hosted by the British equivalent of Johnny Carson, one Terry Wogan. The guests comprised of Donald Trump, his first wife, Ivana, and Dame Edna Everage (the Australian comedian, Barry Humphries, in drag). Trump was there to promote his book

Art of the Deal. Dame Edna was there to lampoon the other guests, at one point saying to Trump: 'The book is wonderful. It's very entertaining. It's got lovely photographs of you two adorable young people. I love the one of you standing there caressing your skyscraper.'

Mid-interview, Wogan asked Trump whether there was truth in the rumours that he has political ambitions. Trump said: 'Well, I hate to see what's happening to the United States. It's a great country. But the United States is being taken advantage of by Japan and so many other countries. I mean it's really a shame. I see what's happening in terms of our leadership. I mean they are being outplayed and outsmarted by every country. It's just one of those things.'

The year was 1988. Twenty-seven years later, America 'being taken advantage of' would be a central element of the Trump campaign. He would rage about America's 'terrible' trade deals, suggesting that they had caused millions of jobs to be exported overseas. He would also target illegal immigrants, especially Mexicans. And of war hero and elder statesman John McCain, he would say: 'He's a war hero because he got captured? I like people that weren't captured.'

And it worked. As my Republican guests acknowledged, Trump was already the 'presumptive nominee', with the withdrawal of the two last remaining competitors, Senator Ted Cruz and Governor of Ohio, John Kasich. On 26 May, Trump would nail down his nomination by securing his 1,238th delegate, and thus a definitive majority of the votes available, leaving the cream of the Republican Party scattered in his wake. Or as one of my guests put it: 'What the . . . happened there?'

Having told London, back in February, that Trump would be the nominee, I had spent the intervening months, while reality caught up with prediction, trying to understand the secret of his appeal. I concluded that it was a combination of elements, some unique to the candidate, some reflecting the mood of America. But it started with Trump's reality TV career. Notwithstanding its global success, not everyone, especially in the business community, was a fan of *The Apprentice*. But there is no doubt that the CEO, played by Lord (Alan) Sugar in the British version and Trump in the original American version, is a covetable role: a mythical, god-like figure Who Is Never Wrong. Trump fronted *The Apprentice* for a decade, right up until his run for the presidency. So in those early overstocked primary debates, with sixteen candidates on the stage, Trump would have been, for many TV viewers, the only recognisable face.

Then they liked what they heard. Trump was box office. He didn't duck and weave; he didn't hedge, or try to bridge both sides of an argument; he didn't obey the rules of political correctness. He said what he thought, in strikingly clear and simple terms (one analyst assessed, in a much-quoted article, that Trump's language would have been understandable to a fourth or fifth grader, 9–11 years old, while the other candidates were speaking at ninth grade level, 14–15 years old). And then there were his speeches. Measured by normal standards, they were shapeless, rambling and policy free; Trump would just stand at the podium and talk. But they were addictive, even at times electrifying. There was no knowing what he would say next.

It wasn't, however, just about tone and unpredictability. Trump's messages were resonating to a degree very few had anticipated. America in 2016 seemed in an uncertain mood, anxious about its future and its place in the world. There were still wounds and resentments from the 2008 financial crisis; ordinary people had lost their jobs, but no bankers had gone to jail, and within a year or two, the Wall Street bonuses were as unreal as ever. People were worried about globalisation and the flight of well-paid factory jobs overseas. They hated being told that they had to learn how to code because robots would take over all the blue-collar jobs. They resented the flow of illegal migrants across America's borders. They couldn't understand why successive US governments had got bogged down in 'un-winnable' wars in Afghanistan and Iraq. They despised the culture of political correctness, which they perceived as being told what to think by the East and West Coast elites. Most of all, they saw themselves as ignored and abandoned by a self-serving Washington.

Donald Trump seemed to be addressing all these concerns. He presented himself as a self-made, successful businessman who could restore economic growth and create jobs. He was a climate change denier. He raged against international trade deals, claiming that they cost American jobs. He asked why American lives were being lost in the 'sand, blood and death of the Middle East' and promised to bring the boys home. As he was self-financing his campaign, he could claim to be an outsider, not beholden to corporate America, and not part of the Washington conspiracy. And in the eyes of many Republican voters, he was the only politician to 'get it' on illegal immigration. It was an intoxicating mix. In essence he promised a return to better, more secure times, when the factories and the coal mines were working, and when America won its wars. His slogan 'Make America Great Again' was really an appeal to sepia-tinged nostalgia: a promise to turn back the clock.

Although it would all go sour later, in these early days of the campaign Trump also used the media brilliantly. He might not have known much about foreign policy (actually, any form of policy); but the art of manipulation he did know. He had reputedly learnt his trade, as a New York man-about-town, in the bare-knuckle world of the New York tabloids. One story from that time was that he had once placed a quote on the front page of the *New York Post*, supposedly by the woman who became his second wife, Marla Maples, that he had given her 'the best sex I've ever had'. And once campaigning, while other candidates would control their media appearances rigidly, he would appear anywhere, anytime: perfect for the 24-hour news channels trying to fill time and space. One of the leading morning news shows, MSNBC's *Morning Joe*, would phone him what felt like daily for his latest thoughts. The news channels also loved his 'what's-he-going-to-say-next' speeches; so much so that they preferred to show an empty podium, with Trump about to perform, to any other of the candidates actually speaking.

I tracked Trump's march to the nomination from Washington, and sent my political team to schlep around the primary circuit. I used the time to exploit one of the privileges of being British ambassador in America's capital: the opportunity to learn from some of the great figures of recent American history, and in particular to get their take on the election race. I focused particularly on Republicans: what did they make of this unconventional likely Republican nominee? I called on Donald Rumsfeld, a controversial figure during his time as Secretary for Defense in the George W. Bush administration. He could not have been more gracious or more entertaining. Having myself borrowed many times Rumsfeld's famous delineation of the world into known knowns, known unknowns and unknown unknowns, I asked him where it came from. He explained instantly that he himself had borrowed it from a senior NASA scientist with whom he had worked back in the 1990s on the Commission to Assess the Ballistic Missile Threat to the US. As for Donald Trump, he seemed relaxed about the prospect of him being the nominee. I asked him whether he wasn't worried about what this said about the national mood: had America ever felt more divided, or more angry? He said, gently: 'When I was a young congressman in Washington in 1968, I woke up one morning to find the city on fire. This is nothing compared to those days.' Intrigued, when I returned to the office I reminded myself of the 1968 events. After the assassination of Martin Luther King on 4 April that year, Washington was hit by six days of riots, damage to hundreds of buildings, and more than a thousand fires.

It wasn't just Rumsfeld. I also consulted Colin Powell, chairman of the joint chiefs of staff during George H. Bush's presidency, then Secretary of State during George W. Bush's first term. Over lunch, we reminisced about the Blair/Bush days and about Colin's exceptionally close relationship with the then British Foreign Secretary, Jack Straw. I asked for his take on the Republican race: it turned out he wasn't an admirer of candidate Trump (as he has since made clear publicly). And I called on the grand old man of the Republican Party, Senator John McCain, who recalled his many encounters with British politicians, back to Mrs Thatcher. He had a long-running feud with Trump, so it was no surprise to hear him express the hope that someone else, indeed almost anyone else, would get the Republican nomination. But I also sensed with McCain, as with Powell before him, an edginess. They hoped Trump wouldn't be the nominee, but they were already sensing that he might be, and calculating the decisions that they would then face.

A few weeks later, I heard more of the same when I had a drink with Michael Bloomberg, zillionaire and Republican mayor of New York from 2002 to 2013 (though he would briefly run for the presidency in 2020 as a Democrat). He spoke judiciously but left me with the indelible impression that he was finding it impossible to stomach the rise of Donald Trump, a minor figure amongst the New York elite compared to himself. (New Yorkers would say that Bloomberg had given away more money than Donald Trump had ever made.)

And in a typically DC moment, I turned up at a *Washington Post* event at the George Town Club, sat down at a random table to eat, and introduced myself to the others at the table, to hear one of them say, 'Hi, I'm Bob Woodward.' When you unexpectedly meet such a celebrated figure, it is hard to sound cool. I recall saying something completely banal about how closely I had followed Watergate, and how much I admired what he had done then and since. He forgave me this, and invited me to lunch. We kept in touch over the next three years. He would write, in the form of *Fear*, the best, most authoritative book about the first phase of the Trump presidency. And when I resigned two years later, he sent me a personal note so precious I feel like framing it. That said . . . he doesn't really look like Robert Redford.

Alongside this stroll through the pages of history, the political team and I were trying to build up our contacts with the Trump campaign. These took some tracking down, as Trump had assembled a collection of fringe figures and unknowns – largely because the big names had either hung back or gone with Jeb Bush or Marco Rubio or Ted Cruz. Indeed, a counter movement of 'Never

Trumpers' was already developing. Significant figures from previous Republican administrations were signing up to letters asserting that they would never work for a Trump presidency. But we made some progress, starting with Wilbur Ross. I first met Ross when he attended one of our regular commentators' roundtables to discuss the election race. He had been out in the media supporting Trump, notwithstanding his past as a registered Democrat. It was hard to find anyone in Washington who would 'speak for Donald'. So Ross found himself an isolated voice in the discussion. He didn't seem to mind, and I was so intrigued that I invited him to a one-to-one lunch.

In preparation, I briefly scanned his life and times. He was a fascinating figure: a Wall Street multi-millionaire known as 'The King of Bankruptcy', the nickname reflecting a career in which, first for Rothschild & Co. investment bank and then for himself, he had acquired and restructured failed companies in industries such as steel, coal and textiles. This had earned him his critics; to this day there are financial journalists trying to chase him down with stories of corners being cut or disclosure rules being ignored. Yet I could not but be intrigued by someone who seemed repeatedly to have invested in disaster and come away ahead.

When we started to talk, I asked about his relationship with Trump. The connection turned out to be a bankruptcy. In the 1980s, Trump had gambled massively on casinos on the Atlantic City board-walk. He ultimately acquired three, finally spending almost a billion dollars on what was at the time, with a typically Trumpian flourish, claimed to be the largest casino in the world, the Taj Mahal – all financed by junk bonds at 14 per cent interest. By 1991, he was haemorrhaging money and filed for bankruptcy. Ross was asked to represent the bondholders. Plan A was involuntary bankruptcy and the ousting of Trump. After negotiating with him, Ross persuaded the investors to keep Trump on – albeit with only a 50 per cent stake in the business, and after being required to sell his yacht, the unim-aginatively named *Trump Princess*. I asked Ross why he had saved Trump. He told me that there had been two reasons. First, he had been impressed by how Trump had handled the negotiations. He could have come across as a broken man, but he had been calm, organised and on top of all the detail. And second, Ross had noticed Trump's star appeal – the way people had crowded around his car and mobbed him in his casinos. So a condition of the bailout had been that Trump should personally be present in the casinos as much as possible.

I stayed in touch with Ross throughout the election season. I asked him at one point whether he would take a job in a Trump administration. People usually hedge when you ask them that sort of question: Ross said straightforwardly that he would. He duly became commerce secretary – in which capacity he several times went out of his way to help us. The Atlantic City casinos, however, fared less well; they went bankrupt again and have all closed. News reports suggest that the Taj Mahal has found a role as a home for feral cats.

We didn't stop at Wilbur Ross. My deputy developed a good relationship with Corey Lewandowski, Trump's campaign manager. This was useful until, on 20 June, Trump fired him. Meanwhile, I got to know Jeff Sessions, a senior Trump adviser, a long-time senator for Alabama, and as courtly a Southern gentleman as you could meet. He was one of the first senior Republicans to come out for Trump, and hence, we reckoned, a likely pick for a Trump cabinet. We were right: he became attorney general, though he later fell out with the President and also got fired. And in common with a number of embassies in Washington, we became aware of a young man called George Papadopoulos, who was putting himself around town as a leading foreign policy adviser in the Trump team. Having spent a year at University College, London doing his masters, he was quite the Anglophile, and though I never met him, my team got to know him quite well. But although he was indeed a member of the campaign foreign policy advisory panel, he never really convinced: in that memorable Texan phrase, he was all hat, no cattle. So when he asked us to set up a number of meetings with British ministers before a visit to London, we instead put him in front of the desk officer in the Americas Department. As the history books will relate, Papadopoulos got up to a number of other things in London which ultimately landed him in prison. Maybe we should have filled his diary for him.

My political team also came across a British element to the Trump campaign. It was a small company called Cambridge Analytica. They described themselves as a political consulting firm specialising in data analysis, digital campaigning and strategic communications. They already had something of a track record in American politics, having been engaged on several campaigns in the 2014 midterm elections. In the 2016 presidential elections, they were initially carrying out data analysis for Ted Cruz's campaign. But they ended their association with Cruz after the 20 February South Carolina primary – according to the Cruz camp, because they really weren't delivering anything of value; according to some in the media, because their founder, the reclusive American billionaire Robert Mercer, switched from Cruz to Trump.

The Cambridge Analytica team were based in New York, alongside the Trump campaign, rather than in Washington. So our contacts were more on the telephone than in person. At the time, it was never entirely clear what precisely they did; they certainly weren't the only pollsters inside the campaign (indeed, the story was that this particular candidate was so obsessed with polling data that if presented with figures suggesting he was doing badly, he would demand new data be found from a different source that told a better story). But the CEO, Alexander Nix, would come through Washington from time to time, have a coffee with one of the political team, and provide some snippets on campaign dynamics – who was up, who was down, who counted and who didn't. They were useful, though second-order, insights.

That a British company, albeit American-owned, had managed to break into the extraordinarily competitive world of US political consultancy was quite a story; that they had been hired by the likely winners of the Republican race made them hot property. So there was growing media interest in Cambridge Analytica's life history. Initially, in the British media, the tone was celebratory – a bunch of Brits outsmarting the American companies and grabbing the best job in town. I wondered idly whether they would be up for one of those prestigious business awards at the end of the year. But as is now exceedingly well documented, it all turned bad – though not until a year or so later. It was revealed that the company had used an unauthorised intermediary to acquire the personal data of 87 million Facebook users. They had then used this data for profiling and targeted campaign messages; they were eventually banned from using the Facebook platform for any future messaging or advertising. *Channel 4 News* produced a seriously damaging piece of investigative journalism on the company, from which it never recovered. Cambridge Analytica would file for insolvency on 1 May 2018 and would ultimately close down.

The enduring known unknown is, did they make a difference? Cambridge Analytica's calling card was 'micro-targeting of voters'. The technical term for it was 'psychographics' – which, it has to be said, conjures up instantly an image of mad-eyed scientists conducting brainwashing experiments. In layman's language, it amounted to analysing data to predict the behaviour, interests and opinions held by specific groups of people and then serving them the messages to which they were most likely to respond: hence the value of data from 87 million Facebook users.

It is of course impossible to know for sure whether many, or any, of the almost 63 million people who voted for Donald Trump in 2016 were influenced by messages on social media. The Trump campaign itself downplayed the company's contribution, describing it as modest and suggesting that it was claiming credit for work done by others. A cynic might observe that, once the company got into trouble, they would say that, wouldn't they. But more persuasively, the view amongst political scientists was and is one of deep scepticism about the effectiveness of micro-targeting. One prominent figure in the field, Eitan Hersh of Tufts University, said 'Every claim about psychographics made by or about Cambridge Analytica is bullshit.' And personally, I was with the sceptics. The claims of the digital crowd reminded me of a different era and the ludicrously inflated claims made in 1979 about the role in Margaret Thatcher's victory of the Saatchi 'Labour Isn't Working' posters. I think that voters were rather more influenced by the spectacle of James

Callaghan's government being plainly out of ideas and staggering from confidence vote to confidence vote. Success tends to have many fathers, while failure is an orphan; and none shout louder than political consultancies associated with the former, or run for cover faster if attached to the latter.

We weren't, of course, only building relationships with the Republicans. There was a Democratic campaign too. It was clear Hillary Clinton was going to be the nominee, though it was equally clear that there were serious doubts about her among Democratic Party insiders, and a manifest lack of love for her among large swathes of the American public. But the die was cast early; the party thought Bernie Sanders too far to the left to be electable, and Joe Biden wasn't running. And the Democratic establishment circled the wagons around her.

We knew most of this entourage. Many had worked in the Obama administration. Some dated back to Bill Clinton's two terms. Generations of British ambassadors and politicians had connected with them. Yet building links with the 2016 campaign was an unexpectedly frustrating experience. The Clintons were notorious for running two parallel sets of advisers. There was the official team: the chief of staff, the campaign manager, the pollster, the policy advisers. And then there was the circle of longstanding Clinton friends and confidants, with whom every shred of advice from the official team had to be checked and tested. So it was a divided and, one sensed, unhappy team, and far less accessible than anticipated. It was weirdly easier to talk to senior members of the Trump team.

From what I heard and saw, journalists were finding themselves similarly excluded. Trump was everywhere on the news channels; Clinton's team built a wall around her. There were exceptions: Jake Sullivan, a friend from the Obama days and Clinton's lead foreign policy adviser, stayed in close touch. Democratic Party royalty like Tom Donilon, one of Obama's national security advisers, did the same. There were lots of well-connected Democrats around Washington who were happy to critique the Clinton campaign from a distance (though they would have expected jobs had she won). And the middle rankers in the campaign team were happy to escape for an evening to share their insights. But the senior figures – the inner campaign team – might as well have been working from Mars.

As we tracked the two campaigns, and kept London informed through our reporting, we also tried to bring out an unusual, perhaps unique, feature of this particular race. It was Democrat against Republican. But it was also Establishment against Insurgent. Trump was sometimes described, with good reason, as engaging in a hostile takeover of the Republican Party. He was at odds with some sacred tenets of the Republican faith, such as support for open markets and free trade. And he had assembled around him a team of outliers and unknowns: Steve Bannon, Corey Lewandowski, Paul Manafort, Kellyanne Conway, Peter Navarro, Steve Mnuchin, Jeff Sessions, Michael Flynn. Some of this was by choice, but much was by necessity; the Republican mainstream was by and large refusing to work for him. It made for a wild ride, presenting a profound contrast between the style, tone and approach of the two campaigns, and the starkest of choices for the American people.

Meanwhile, I was putting a tricky question back to London. All of my predecessors, during US election campaigns, would have sought meetings with the two protagonists as they went head to head. But with one of these two candidates, there was the possibility, even the likelihood, that tweets or comments might be made after the meeting, perhaps in exaggerated terms – which might in turn cause problems with the other campaign team, or unwelcome stories in the media. So I reckoned I needed cover from London before making a move. I wrote to the Foreign Office setting out the argu-ments for and against; leaning towards doing it, but leaving the final call to them. And then I waited. And waited. I checked and was told that the issue was stuck somewhere in the senior levels of the system. Which is where it stayed.

Though this was frustrating, I didn't really blame London, or agitate for a response. They were in the middle of a horribly close and intense referendum campaign. I guessed they were in a deeply risk-averse mood and really didn't need this question. What they had done, in not replying, amounted to a soft no. I let it rest.

In amongst all this, the UK was acquiring a new Prime Minister. Theresa May was always the favourite to succeed David Cameron and was handed the role on 13 July by acclamation when her run-off opponent, Andrea Leadsom, pulled out in the wake of some tactless comments about the advantages of her being a mother, in contrast to the childless May. And May immediately appointed a new Foreign Secretary, former mayor of London and prominent Leave advocate Boris Johnson.

I met Boris Johnson in my days as Foreign Office press spokesman. He was at that time the Brussels correspondent of the *Daily Telegraph*, already a well-known figure for his almost single-handed creation of the 'Euromyth': the supposed ambitions of the Brussels bureaucrats to ban prawn cocktail-flavoured crisps, or to harmonise condoms in a one-size-fits-all regulation. He in effect created a new genre of journalism, prompting other editors to demand similar stories from their journalists – and in the view of many, in both politics and the media, played a significant role in poisoning British public attitudes towards the European Union. Chris Patten, the former British EU Commissioner and Conservative Party elder statesman, said of Boris at the time, in an unwitting anticipation of a favourite line of a future American President, that he was 'one of the greatest exponents of fake journalism'. Johnson himself once said: 'I was sort of chucking these rocks over the garden wall and I listened to this amazing crash from the greenhouse next door over in England as everything I wrote from Brussels was having this amazing explosive effect on the Tory party.' All that said, as a participant at briefing sessions, he was straightforward: with me, at least, he asked well-informed questions, listened to the answers, and unlike some of his colleagues, never became querulous if he wasn't getting the story he wanted: his critics would no doubt say, recalling his firing from *The Times* for inventing quotes, that that was because he then just made it up.

Johnson's appointment as Foreign Secretary prompted a lot of surprise. And he was instantly a marked man on the Continent, where, from what I was hearing from around the network, his early encounters with his European counterparts didn't go well. The reaction to him in Washington was different; there he was welcomed and admired. He visited several times in his two years as Foreign Secretary (before resigning in protest at Theresa May's handling of Brexit in July 2018). So I saw a lot of him, and the Americans simply liked him. They found him charismatic; they admired his erudition; they laughed at his jokes. One of his visits coincided with an annual reception I gave for the Shakespeare Theatre Company of Washington. Johnson agreed to speak, and then delivered, to a dazzled audience, a speech made up almost entirely of quotations from Shakespeare's plays. On another occasion I was with him in Boston, where he was seeing US Secretary of State John Kerry, whose home town it was. That evening, we took him briefly to a reception with the local British-American Chamber of Commerce, where he enlivened his impromptu speech by waving a British teabag, lifted from his hotel room, in front of his audience: proof, he asserted, that Boston Tea Party notwithstanding, the British were still big in that town. As we later walked from the reception to a local crab restaurant, we heard, from the opposite pavement, in an unmistakably British accent, the cry: 'Hey, Boris, you fucker!' We all tensed: was the Foreign Secretary about to be assaulted? The answer was, on the contrary, that this group of Brits just wanted a selfie with him. Their opening gambit was, we explained to our bemused American secret service detail, a traditional British greeting of amity, employed once the evening was several drinks old. And Johnson of course did the selfie; several more votes notched up.

On a more conventional note, Johnson also delivered the Bentley. Jaguar have a deal with the Foreign Office to provide flag cars for ambassadorial vehicles in most of our biggest posts. The United States is Bentley's biggest market; and when time was up for the Jaguar in which I was being transported around town, Bentley launched an audacious bid to undercut them for the replacement. It was the deal of the decade. They offered a car that would normally have cost at least three times as much as the Jaguar for a broadly equivalent price, threw in free servicing for its lifespan, and added the bonus that the embassy could keep whatever money we could get for it when it was sold on. I put this back to the Foreign Office for a decision. There were understandable worries that the car would be too showy and would be a bad story in the media. But both Alan Duncan, the minister of state, and the foreign secretary prioritised value for money for the taxpayer, as represented by the Bentley offer. So that's what we got. When Johnson next visited Washington, he relived his time as motoring correspondent for *GQ* magazine, 'testing' it by driving it around the embassy compound at a healthy pace.

Johnson seemed fascinated by Donald Trump. When mayor of London, he had once said that a good reason for avoiding New York was the risk of rounding a corner and coming face-to-face with Trump. In most respects they were about as different as two people could be – in their attitude to issues like immigration, and especially in their relationship with the written word: Johnson a prolific writer, Trump famously averse to reading. But they shared a single-minded ruthlessness and political ambition. By the time Johnson became Foreign Secretary, Trump had secured the Republican nomination and was preparing for the Republican Convention and the run-off with Hillary Clinton. I think Johnson, while no supporter of most of the policies Trump was promoting, was intrigued by his success, and in particular by Trump's use of language: the limited vocabulary, the simplicity of the messaging, the disdain for political correctness, the sometimes incendiary imagery, and the at best intermittent relationship with facts and the truth.

Back to American politics. Presidential nominating conventions date back to the early nineteenth century. Both the major parties hold them, with the formal purpose of selecting their nominees for the presidential election. For much of US history, conventions were murky, heated, even corrupt events at which factions quarrelled and backroom deals were done, sometimes producing unexpected results. Indeed, the term 'dark horse' first migrated from the horse racing track, where it was used to describe a horse unknown to the gambling community, into politics at the Democratic Party's 1844 convention, where the almost unknown James K. Polk emerged as the nominee after delegates had split irretrievably over the front runners. Polk may have been unknown, but he went on to win the election and become the eleventh president. And the 1924 Democratic Convention needed to go through 103 successive votes to decide on a candidate, John W. Davis, who, unlike Polk, lost.

But these proceedings in smoke-filled rooms became increasingly unacceptable to the rank and file of both parties, culminating in the historically disastrous Democratic Convention in Chicago in 1968. The United States was deeply divided over the Vietnam war. Senator Eugene McCarthy of Minnesota ran against the war and energised tens of thousands of supporters. Vice President Hubert Humphrey didn't compete in a single primary, but controlled enough delegates to secure the Democratic nomination. Angry McCarthy supporters joined forces with anti-war demonstrators and confronted the Chicago police outside the convention hall. Riots broke out, and the convention was conducted against a backdrop of tear gas grenades. The Democrats rightly concluded that this couldn't be allowed to happen again. They adopted, on the recommendation of a commission headed by South Dakota senator George McGovern, a comprehensive primary system in which candidates would be allotted convention delegates based on their performance in the primaries. These delegates were then compelled to vote for 'their' candidates. The Republicans adopted a similar system in 1972.

Thanks to these changes, the conventions lost most of their drama. It was still theoretically possible that no candidate would arrive at the convention with an overall majority of delegates, necessitating a 'brokered convention' in which delegates could eventually be released from their commitments to vote in specified ways. But in practice, conventions morphed into coronations for the chosen candidates, with a succession of speakers lauding them on prime-time TV in front of, they hoped, tens of millions of viewers.

Whatever the lack of drama, I looked forward to my first and only experience of these unique events. The parties choose the locations carefully, in swing states, hoping to win extra votes by bringing thousands of delegates to key cities, filling the hotels and restaurants and boosting the local economies. The Republicans went first, from 18 to 21 July, in Cleveland, Ohio, in the heart of the Midwest. Hotel prices tend to quadruple during a convention, so my parsimonious political team reserved an Airbnb months in advance. Some British MEPs were attending, so we made a point of inviting them round for tea, to show how we were saving taxpayers money. The house was actually fine; and by chance, it was right next to the open-air venue of the biggest music event of the week – a concert by Lynyrd Skynyrd. Though ticketless, I was able to hear 'Sweet Home Alabama' and 'Free Bird' with crystal clarity from the balcony of the house.

As for the main event, it was irredeemably strange. We were able to get onto the convention floor, in among all the banners. A succession of senior Republicans, tiny figures on a distant stage, were making speeches, but no one seemed to be paying attention. The speeches, in any case, tended towards repetition, with every peroration acclaiming 'the next President of the United States – Donald J. Trump!' All, that is, except Ted Cruz, who managed to get through his fifteen minutes without endorsing, or even mentioning, Trump. Cruz left the stage at a rare clip, to a few scattered boos. Otherwise, the crowd became energised only when Hillary Clinton's name was mentioned, at which point the whole hall broke into a chant of 'Lock her up!' This was commonplace at Trump speeches, as I had seen on television. But now was the first time I had experienced it in the flesh. I looked around me at the clenched fists and angry faces: it felt like genuine mass hatred.

The main event at conventions is, of course, the speech by the nominee: the showcase moment on prime-time TV. Trump's speech, late on Thursday night, was dark and grim – and really, really long, finishing around midnight Eastern time. It contained a savage attack on Hillary Clinton – someone who 'had committed terrible, terrible crimes' – and it painted a picture of an America that was impoverished and crime-ridden, threatened by terrorism and with its soldiers 'dying on distant battlefields'. For neutrals, listening to it in the hall while chants of 'USA, USA!' rang out, it was an uncomfortable and unsettling experience. Sharp-eared journalists, egged on by Trump's team, highlighted its similarities to Richard Nixon's address to the 1968 Republican Convention, delivered at a time when America was genuinely torn apart over Vietnam. In short, it felt excessive and unbalanced; belonging to a different universe from Reagan's 'Morning in America'. Cormac McCarthy's post-apocalypse masterpiece, *The Road*, with its marauding tribes of cannibals roaming a destroyed America, depicted a happier place.

There were two shafts of light in the darkness. The first was a meeting with Chris Christie. I had long wanted to meet the man who had for a while been the Great Hope, the Republican Party's President-in-waiting. But he was damaged by a troubled second term in New Jersey, and his presidential bid never really left the launch pad. As an old friend of Trump, he declared for him when pulling out of the race. He then did a warm-up for a Trump speech in Florida, and remained on the stage, in camera shot, looking somewhat uncomfortable, while Trump did his piece. As one commentator gleefully noted, Christie looked like he was being held hostage. Social media went wild: 'Free Chris Christie!'

I didn't mention this when I saw him. Instead, we talked about his campaign run, his takedown of Marco Rubio and his friendship with Donald Trump. He was generous with his time, smart, insightful and exceptionally funny, not least because he is a gifted mimic. An hour went by in a flash. I saw him several times over the next two years; no meeting in my diary was ever more fun.

And then there was the party of the week. John Kasich, Governor of Ohio, should have been the host of a convention in his home state. But his personal relations with Trump were poor; and as a moderate Republican, I think he couldn't bring himself to stand on the convention stage and endorse his rival. So he stayed away. Instead, he hosted a party at Cleveland's main tourist attraction, the Rock & Roll Hall of Fame. I went an hour early, toured the exhibits, talked to Kasich and attended the party. It was great, though inevitably it was impossible to agree with all of the names on the Hall of Fame inductees list: what were Aerosmith doing there?

While I was away at the convention, the embassy had a Harvey Weinstein moment. A senior embassy colleague received, out of the blue, a phone call. The voice at the other end announced that it was Harvey Weinstein, that he and a group of colleagues were about to set off by private jet from South Africa to London, and that one of their number lacked the necessary visa in his passport, but would want to accompany the rest of them to dinner in London. Could the embassy sort this out and ensure that visa requirements were waived?

The Home Office were consulted. They said, firmly, 'No': there were strict criteria for visa waivers and this individual didn't qualify. The decision was immediately passed back to Weinstein. He exploded. Did we not realise who he was? Didn't we know he had been a personal friend of successive British Prime Ministers? Did we not care that he had invested tens of millions in the British film industry? My colleague wearily promised to check again, further up the ladder. He did so. The answer was an even more emphatic no. He called Weinstein back to pass on the bad news. Weinstein told him that this would be a career-destroying call, that Weinstein would personally follow up with his friends in London, and that, after Washington, his next job would be the North Pole. My colleague found this disturbing: would Weinstein really go after him? When I got back, he asked me what I thought. I told him not to worry. I think that was a good call.

The Democratic Convention, a week later, was in Philadelphia. We again opted for an Airbnb, this time literally on the wrong side of the railway tracks. The house in which we stayed was modest but clean, but the vacant lot next door was a wilderness of broken bottles and used syringes. I took photographs to offer as evidence of my five-star lifestyle the next time the House of Commons Public Accounts Committee came to Washington. The convention itself was a much more controlled and choreographed affair; much less chanting, much more optimism. It also had better speakers: both Obamas (and Michelle was exceptional), Joe Biden, Bill Clinton. Michael Bloomberg, who ran New York as a Republican, took the stage and tore into Trump: 'As a New Yorker, I know a con when I see one.' And unlike the Republican version, it ran to time; the star speakers hit the prime-time TV slots. Even Hillary Clinton, no one's idea of a sparkling public speaker, did well. The Democrats left feeling good about themselves, and confident about their prospects.

I got by with very little sleep; we all did. Outside the main hall, conventions are an endless rolling party. These are not drinking parties, since the beer tends towards the thin and weak, and the wine towards the undrinkable. Instead, they are festivals of gossip, intrigue and speculation. A keen observer of American politics can learn more in a night than in an average month. Looking back on the two conventions now, however, my overriding question is: what did they matter? Republican choreography was a shambles; Democratic organisation was immaculate. The Republicans portrayed America as a savage, feral place, beset by failure; the Democrats, by contrast, did their 'hopey-changey stuff' and were full of optimism. Michelle Obama provided the soundbite of the moment: 'When they go low, we go high.' And yet, a few months later, notwithstanding Philadelphia having hosted the Democratic Convention, Hillary Clinton couldn't even win Pennsylvania.

7

Fear and Loathing in Washington

*

'The Fox News exit poll numbers had Hillary Clinton winning Wisconsin, Pennsylvania, states that Trump eventually won . . . and it wasn't even close: it looked like she was going to win big'
— Frank Luntz, pollster and TV pundit

*

'Fifty percent of people won't vote, and fifty percent don't read newspapers. I hope it's the same fifty percent'
— Gore Vidal

*

'BUT WHAT about the first Nixon–Kennedy debate in 1960?' The political team and I, at the end of a longish day in the office, and with the debates between Trump and Clinton on the near horizon, were swapping presidential debate stories. It is a rich field, if you like your history quirky and anecdotal.

Debates are a relatively recent feature of US elections, at least in the modern format. Back in 1858, Abraham Lincoln and Senator Stephen Douglas held no fewer than seven face-to-face debates, two years before confronting each other in the 1860 election. The format involved hour-long speeches each, followed by ninety-minute rebuttals; perhaps not the perfect model for the future television age. For the following hundred years, occasional challenges were thrown down, but always rejected; for example, Wendell Willkie challenged Franklin D. Roosevelt in 1940 but Roosevelt refused. Debates started to become regular features of primary campaigns, however, and proved popular, so the pressure grew for them to be part of the presidential election too. The dam finally broke with the Kennedy–Nixon debates of 1960. And although the face-to-face debate format then disappeared again for sixteen years, since the 1976 revival they have become fixtures, and the highlights of election season, consistently drawing audiences in the range of 60 to 80 million.

As for the highlights of previous debates, most of which I saw at the time when replayed on the BBC, there was the famous debate between Gerald Ford and Jimmy Carter in 1976. No one remembers the first round, on domestic policy, which Ford was thought to have won. But many recall Ford's gaffe in the second debate: 'There is no Soviet domination of Eastern Europe and there never will be under a Ford administration.' The cartoonists and humorists particularly enjoyed the morning after, some of them borrowing from Martin Luther King: 'Free at last, free at last!' Ford, who had been building momentum, stalled; and Carter won a narrow victory.

Then there was Reagan–Mondale in 1984. Ronald Reagan had performed poorly in the first debate, especially with a muddled closing statement loaded with half-digested statistics, leading observers to question whether age was taking its toll. But in the second debate, he struck back with a no doubt carefully rehearsed zinger that both amused the nation and seemed instantly to kill Walter Mondale's comeback: 'I will not make age an issue of this campaign. I am not going to exploit, for political purposes, my opponent's youth and inexperience.' We also reminded ourselves of the only vice-presidential debate ever to make big headlines: 1988, and Lloyd Bentsen to Dan Quayle, 'You're no Jack Kennedy.' Quayle still became Vice President, but Bentsen will live forever on that one line. And finally, a personal favourite. In the 1992 debate between George H. W. Bush and Bill Clinton, the camera caught Bush checking his watch some fifteen minutes from the end, as if he had a train to catch.

And what was the story around Nixon–Kennedy? It was about the importance, not of what you said, but how you looked. Those listening on radio to that encounter, the first presidential debate of the modern era, thought Nixon had won, because he sounded more knowledgeable, experienced and authoritative. Those watching on television, however, noticed his five o'clock shadow, the sweat gathering on his upper lip and his unhealthy pallor, and preferred the youthful and Hollywood-handsome Kennedy. There were three more debates between Kennedy and Nixon; one draw, two clear Nixon wins. But no one remembers these, and that first debate is forever cited as proof of the supposedly superficial and capricious nature of the TV audience – when all it really signifies is that appearances matter.

There were to be three debates between Hillary Clinton and Donald Trump. In the run-up, they were generating an exceptional degree of excitement and speculation. This in part reflected a sharp change in media attitudes towards one candidate. Donald Trump might have been good copy. Ratings might have gone up when he was on screen. But in a tight two-horse race, most of the nationally available outlets, both TV and newsprint – Fox News excepted – seemed to have concluded that this man was not fit to be President. They turned on him, highlighting his lack of policy answers to the problems of the moment, his ignorance of foreign policy, his fondness for conspiracy theories and his dog-whistle pronouncements on immigration and race. And there was a palpable sense of anticipation that the famously policy-wonky Clinton would expose these deficiencies in a one-to-one debate.

Trump of course started to fight back. At his campaign rallies, he would consign the press to an enclosure and then condemn the 'fake media' from the podium, prompting many in the audience to shout abuse at them, if not worse. In short, he started to run a media campaign against the media – revelling in the copious attention he was securing while disparaging both individual journalists and the media as a whole every time he stood behind a podium. And it was working. His attacks on the press became guaranteed applause lines during his speeches. More significantly, they took the public discourse away from policy issues – weak ground for Trump – into a debate about whether or not the media were biased. They also arguably neutralised the numerous negative stories about Trump's past uncovered by investigative journalists during the campaign – about the Trump Organisation bilking a succession of small-time contractors, about Trump's tax issues, about the Trump Foundation's illegal activities. If his supporters, or indeed neutrals, bought the campaign rhetoric about the fake news media trying to bring him down, that gave them licence to discount these stories.

The first debate, at Hofstra University in New York on 26 September, I watched on television. In doing so, I was among the largest TV audience for a presidential debate in US history, at 84 million, not counting those watching online. It was a comprehensive, even overwhelming, victory for Clinton, with the opinion polls unanimous. The CNN poll of TV viewers had her winning by 62–27; NBC by 52–21; ABC by 53–18. Clinton seemed immaculately prepared, Trump the opposite. And Trump found himself constantly defending things he was accused of saying or doing in the past: 'stiffing' contractors on building projects, claiming that Obama hadn't been born in the US, and a history of sexist comments. In particular, Trump seemed completely thrown by Clinton's accusation, in her closing remarks, that when he had owned the Miss Universe contest, he had dubbed the 1997 winner, Alicia Machado, 'Miss Piggy' (because after winning, she had put on weight) and 'Miss Housekeeping' (because of her Latina heritage). In the moment, Trump reacted angrily: 'Where did you get that from?' But the following morning, he was on Fox News confirming it; Machado had indeed been 'the worst winner ever', becoming 'an eating machine' and 'gaining forty-two pounds'. Machado herself was also quickly out on the networks, blaming Trump for a personal history of eating disorders, and suggesting, to absolutely no one's surprise, that she was leaning Democrat in her election vote.

As part of our analysis of the event for a Whitehall that couldn't get enough on the US election, we canvassed some of Washington's leading political pundits. The view was unanimous and amounted to 'this was just what we predicted'. The debate, they thought, had illustrated that, as anticipated, Trump was uninformed, a policy lightweight, and had a lot of indefensible stuff in his back story. I noticed, however, that his weak performance didn't make much of a dent in his poll ratings, or in the enthusiasm of the crowds he was attracting. Had his base not been watching? Or had they seen something to which the rest of us were blind?

The second debate, at Washington University in Midwestern St Louis, was on 9 October, a couple of weeks on from the New York event. And we, I think alone in the Washington diplomatic community, had tickets. Amanda Downes, through a friendship she had built up over her years in the embassy, had managed to secure Vanessa and me places in the auditorium for both this and the third debate in Las Vegas. Having watched the TV coverage of every presidential debate since 1976, I was fascinated to see one in person.

Then, two days before the two candidates took the stage, another monster from the Trump undergrowth broke cover: the 'Access Hollywood' story. *Access Hollywood* was an NBC show. The *Washington Post* acquired, presumably from a source at NBC, a video clip of Donald Trump and one of the show's hosts, Billy Bush, having a pre-show discussion about women. Trump was filmed saying of Bush's co-host, Nancy O'Dell, 'I moved on her very heavily . . . but I couldn't get there . . . Now I see her, she's got the big phony tits and everything . . . she totally changed her look.' He said of the actress Arianna Zucker, with whom he was appearing, 'I better use some Tic Tacs, in case I start kissing her.' And he added, seemingly discussing his seduction technique, 'When you're a star, they let you do it . . . you can do anything . . . grab them by the pussy . . . you can do anything.'

The story immediately dominated the media. It became the most viewed piece in the history of the *Post*'s website. The journalist who nailed the scoop, David Fahrenthold, would go on to win the Pulitzer Prize for it. And instantly, the air became full of the sound of Republicans running for cover. A number of senators, governors and members of Congress, including John McCain, rescinded their endorsements of his candidacy. Arnold Schwarzenegger, who had found time to serve as Governor of California between *Terminator* films, announced that, for the first time since he became an American citizen, he would not be voting Republican. Some in the party called for Trump to withdraw, to be replaced by running mate Mike Pence, former Governor of Indiana.

Trump himself responded within hours of the videotape becoming public. But it would be fair to say that his initial statement somewhat undershot the target. He put out a statement on his campaign website saying: 'This was locker room banter. Bill Clinton has said far worse to me on the golf course. I apologise if anyone was offended.' Presumably advised by his campaign team that this had made things worse, he then released a lengthier statement by video the following morning, in which he said 'I was wrong and I apologise', and promised 'to be a better man'. But he also alleged that Bill Clinton had abused women, and that Hillary Clinton had bullied the victims to stay quiet.

As for reactions from the non-political world, Billy Bush apologised for his contribution to the conversation with Trump, saying he was embarrassed and ashamed. It didn't save him; on 17 October he resigned from NBC. The media were understandably intrigued by his famous family. He was related to two Presidents, nephew of the elder President Bush and cousin of the younger one. *The Economist* magazine observed, 'Who would have thought that Mr Bush, an NBC presenter, could end up playing a more influential role in this election than his cousin Jeb, who many expected to win it?' Meanwhile, a number of prominent athletes said that they had never heard, and would not have tolerated, this kind of talk in locker rooms – spawning the hashtag #NotInMyLockerRoom. And Tic Tac, presumably concerned that their product might become pegged as the appropriate preparation for sexual misconduct, issued a statement on Twitter that 'Tic Tac respects all women and finds the recent statements and behaviour completely unacceptable.' They somehow resisted the obvious second sentence: 'So suck on that.'

To those of us following the story in the embassy, it was hard to see how Donald Trump could recover from this. Indeed, judging by the Saturday and Sunday morning US newspapers, the emerging consensus amongst political commentators was that the story would terminate his candidacy, and not just because Arnold Schwarzenegger had dumped him. There were also intriguing stories about divisions within the Trump camp. Running mate Mike Pence had just about stayed on board, releasing a statement that he had been 'offended by the words and actions described by Donald Trump . . . could not condone or defend them . . . but still supported him because he had expressed remorse and apologised to the American people'. Melania Trump took a similar line: 'the words my husband used are unacceptable and offensive to me'; but she hoped 'people will accept his apology, as I have'. Less convincingly, she asserted that 'this does not represent the man that I know'. But it also emerged that Chris Christie, who had become a close adviser, had said that Trump's comments were 'completely indefensible' and that this had opened up a serious rift between him and Trump. Steve Bannon, at that stage campaign director, would say later that members of the campaign team became defined by how they reacted to *Access Hollywood*; Christie had failed the test, hadn't shown up for the flight to St Louis, and as a result, had trashed his prospects of a cabinet post.

The rest of us, however, did set off for St Louis. As the debate hour approached, it became clear that Trump had decided that offence was the best form of defence. His team, and his surrogates on the news channels, were pushing out a lot of material on the Clintons. The media were then summoned to an impromptu press conference an hour or so before the debate, to be met by the presidential candidate and three women who claimed to have been victims of sexual misconduct by Bill Clinton. The plan apparently was that they would confront him in the debate chamber, an idea the organisers quickly vetoed. But the strategy was clear.

The debate was another comprehensive win for Hillary Clinton – if measured by the strength and coherence of the arguments and policies advanced by the two candidates. But from the outset, when there was no handshake, the tone was exceptionally nasty. When Clinton raised *Access Hollywood*, Trump said, of Bill Clinton, 'There's never been anybody in the history of politics that's been so abusive to women; mine are words and his are actions.' He also, in effect, threatened to put Hillary in jail were he elected. But for those of us in the audience, denied the TV close-ups but able to see the whole stage, perhaps the most striking feature of the debate itself revolved not around words, but around actions. This was a town hall format, with questions from members of the audience sitting at the wings of the stage. When questions were addressed to Clinton, she would approach the individual concerned to establish eye contact. And Trump would follow her, and stand immediately behind her, looming over her shoulder. After the debate, some in the media suggested this amounted to stalking. Personally, I was irresistibly reminded of pantomime villains; I was half tempted to shout 'He's behind you!'

At the end of the debate, while the audience was queuing for the exit, there was a moment, while the cameras were still running, when the families of the two candidates gathered around the protagonists, in two sharply separated groups: social distancing before its time. I was transfixed by the picture this created. The Clinton group, on the left of the stage, looked, well, normal verging on homely, and a touch elderly. The Trump group, by contrast, looked otherworldly. To the forefront were Melania Trump, Ivanka, and the two daughters-in-law, wives of Don Jr and Eric Trump. They appeared, up above us on the stage, improbably glamorous: impossibly tall in their stiletto heels, pencil-thin in their tailored designer dresses, identikit shoulder-length blond hair; aliens from Planet Perfect. I wondered what sort of impression they were making on the TV audience. 'They have nothing in common with us'? Or 'I want to be like them'?

Afterwards, I found my way into the 'Spin Room'. This is where advocates for both candidates gather with the media to persuade them that their man, or woman, won. Or at least, that is the theory. I had imagined something relatively disciplined and organised: perhaps a couple of huddles of journalists with the respective campaign spin doctors. Instead, I came across a scene from Bedlam. In the centre of a cavernous space, there was a circular area, surrounded by a sturdy fence along which the journalists and cameras were lined up. Inside this stockade were the women who were accusing Bill Clinton of sexual misconduct, moving from camera to camera, telling their stories. Other figures, presumably those needing less protection from the media mob, were scattered around the rest of the space, each one identified by a banner displaying a name. Rudy Giuliani was in one corner; John Podesta, the Clinton campaign chairman, in another; and there were dozens more. I listened to Giuliani for a few minutes. Trump had, at one point in the debate, alleged widespread election fraud. Giuliani was saying to a group of journalists something like: 'Of course it happens. You all know this. They say that in Philadelphia, all the Democrats vote three times, with a bus provided between the polling stations.'

Spin Room stunts notwithstanding, the opinion polls again concluded that Clinton had come out ahead, though by a smaller margin than in the first round; NBC, for example, had her ahead by 44 per cent to 34 per cent, with 21 per cent undecided. I didn't disagree with the polls. But I thought that in those few days running up to the debate another important factor had become evident: that Trump possessed extraordinary levels of resilience. Almost the entire Republican establishment had disassociated itself from him after the videotape story broke. Reince Priebus, chairman of the Republican National Committee, had reportedly told Trump that he should either resign his candidacy or go down to the worst defeat in recent US political history. The US mainstream media were also telling him that he was finished. He ignored them all. Not just that, but he went on the attack. Whatever I thought of his policy prescriptions, such as they were, or his rounding up of the Clinton accusers, a part of me had to marvel at his resolve, when others might have crumbled. This seemed to me to make him an exceptionally dangerous opponent for Hillary Clinton. He wasn't going to give up or go away; he would keep climbing back up from the canvas.

A week later, we were in Las Vegas for the final debate at the University of Nevada. By then, election day was little more than three weeks away. On the afternoon before the debate, I had managed, to my surprise, to arrange a meeting with a major financial backer of Donald Trump. Sheldon Adelson, one of the richest men in America and the founder of the Venetian hotel complex in Las Vegas, arguably the gaudiest hotel on the entire Strip. He also had casino interests in Macau and Singapore. Of Ukrainian Jewish ancestry, he had been brought up in modest circumstances in a blue-collar district of Boston, where his father drove a taxi and his mother ran a knitting shop. But he started his business career at the age of twelve and was a millionaire by the time he was thirty. He had been a Democrat until 2012, when he announced his switch to the Republican Party via an op-ed in the *Wall Street Journal*. In the 2012 election campaign, he was reported to have donated $92 million to losing campaigns; first Newt Gingrich, then Mitt Romney. In 2016, he interviewed a range of candidates including Jeb Bush, Chris Christie and John Kasich before deciding on Trump; and then, according to the media, donated $25 million to his campaign (though some reports put the figure at over $80 million).

I made my way to The Venetian. It is extraordinary; its recreation of Venice landmarks extends to a purpose-built artificial waterway on which gondolas circulate (motorised, of course: this is still America). Adelson was waiting for me in his appropriately vast office. One entire wall, seemingly the length of a tennis court, was covered by framed magazine covers featuring the face of . . . Sheldon Adelson. On a quick study, they all seemed to be different; it appeared he really had been on that many front covers. We talked about why he was supporting Donald Trump. He said that his approach was to back the candidate who was the strongest friend of the state of Israel, adding that, in his mind, this equated to strong support of his close friend, Bibi Netanyahu. He had spoken to a selection of the Republicans running in the primaries, but had held off a decision until late in the game – and had then gone with Trump. He didn't endorse everything Trump said, but thought America needed a proper businessman as President. And Trump was tough; the rest had seemed weak by comparison.

I asked about his own business career. He laughed and said he had been the third richest in the United States. But he'd had 'a bad few years' and was now only sixteenth. I commiserated. I noticed in the corner of his office a collection of model jets hanging from the ceiling and asked why they were there. He said they represented his personal fleet of twenty-odd jets. I wondered why he needed so many. He explained that his family used them and each would go simultaneously to a different part of America; so they needed a jet each.

I left after an hour or so, parting on friendly terms; he said, 'Come back and see me whenever.' And I would see him from time to time over the next two years, when he came through Washington. In particular, he would be guest of honour at a reception I held in the residence to mark the one-hundredth anniversary of the Balfour Declaration, the 1917 statement by the British government announcing support for 'the establishment of a national home for the Jewish people' in Palestine. His views about Israeli policies on the Palestinians were some distance from the position of the government I served. But there was something extraordinary about the son of a taxi driver becoming the twenty-fourth richest person on the planet. And he would go on to have a major influence on the Trump administration's policies on Israel, in particular the move of the US Embassy from Tel Aviv to Jerusalem.

While I was hearing about the consequences and burdens of extreme wealth, Vanessa and Amanda Downes were exploring the neighbourhood, and they came upon some sights that perfectly captured the Vegas vibe. The Trump International Hotel on the Strip was one of the few that refused to negotiate contracts with unions. So the Culinary Workers Union, for obvious reasons a big deal in Las Vegas, had organised, to coincide with the debate, a demonstration outside his hotel. This comprised half a dozen taco trucks, tricked up to look like, yes, a wall. The accompanying workers chanted 'Dump Trump' for the TV cameras. Meanwhile, to add to the noise levels, a vintage, open-topped, bright pink Cadillac was cruising the Strip towing a platform displaying a giant-sized effigy of Donald Trump, wearing only underpants. I don't think it was the official advert for that evening's debate, and there was no sign of a Hillary Clinton equivalent. To this day, footage of it can be found on YouTube, accompanied by the tune of 'Hail to the Chief', but with some deeply inappropriate alternative lyrics.

The debate that evening was, like its predecessors, a clear win for Clinton. The tone was marginally less vicious than in St Louis a week earlier, though this was relative: Trump still called Clinton 'a nasty woman', while she said he was 'the most dangerous person to run for President in the modern history of America'. But it was memorable mostly for Trump's response to a question from the moderator, Chris Wallace of Fox News, about whether he would accept the result, were he to lose. His reply: 'I will tell you at the time. I will keep you in suspense.' The media went into meltdown, suggesting that he was casting doubt on American democracy. To a degree, he was; but to me, it was partly about his determination never to back down, and partly about reminding his supporters of his claims that the election might be rigged against him and, by association, all of them too. He was stoking up the suspicion, and the anger.

Having flogged across to the West Coast, Vanessa and I lingered through the weekend, using the opportunity to see another bit of America. We stayed overnight with some friends in Los Angeles. We drove to Death Valley, where we stayed in a modest hotel in the appropriately named Furnace Creek, which holds the record for the highest recorded air temperature ever: 134°F, in July 1913. It was somewhat cooler during our stay. We went for dinner, however, at the historic Inn at Death Valley, perched on a nearby hill. This was built in the 1920s, by the Pacific Coast Borax Company, in an effort at diversification; sales of borax, which they mined in Death Valley, were slowing, and they needed a showcase hotel to create some custom for their Death Valley Railroad. For a while, the cream of Hollywood came. But by the time we got there, it was Stephen King's Overlook Hotel recreated in the desert. Almost empty, there seemed to be ghosts in every corner. The barman, the image of the apparition in *The Shining*, served margaritas so powerful that it was difficult to stand upright after drinking one; true 'Death Valley specials'. To this day, I wonder what on earth he put in them.

The absolute highlight of the mini-break, however, was 'Desert Trip' at Palm Springs. This was the rock concert of the decade: a three-day festival featuring, on successive evenings, Bob Dylan and the Rolling Stones, Neil Young and Paul McCartney, and, the night we were going, Roger Waters from Pink Floyd and The Who. The media had dubbed the event 'Oldchella', though at fifty-seven, the average age of the audience was significantly lower than that of those on stage. It may have been the best concert I ever attended; it was certainly up there. It was a perfect, warm desert night, with the sun setting behind the surrounding mountains. And to hear The Who's 'Baba O'Riley' or Pink Floyd's *Dark Side of the Moon* floating up into the night sky was genuinely magical.

Back on the campaign trail, the polls were sending a bleak message to the Trump team. In the week after the third debate, every national poll had him trailing Clinton, by margins varying from two points to twelve. On my return to Washington, I talked to a senior Clinton adviser; he sounded supremely confident, and talked about the possibility, if their lead continued to stretch, of taking some of the flakier Republican states like Arizona. And then, on 28 October, less than two weeks before election day, FBI director James Comey made an announcement which many – notably Hillary Clinton – argue 'forever changed history'.

I met James Comey a couple of times: first, when as national security adviser, I accompanied David Cameron on a visit to FBI headquarters; and then when, in my early months as ambassador, I made an introductory call on him. He was likeable, affable, and exuded competence and professionalism. He spoke with genuine warmth about the Bureau's relationship with, and admiration for, the UK security service. But for me, he conveyed above all a palpable air of unbending moral rectitude; he really was the FBI agent from central casting. Add to that, at six foot eight, he towered four inches above me.

The FBI had opened an investigation into Hillary Clinton's use of a private email server while she was Secretary of State as long ago as July 2015. Comey himself had announced in July 2016 that the FBI had concluded, and had recommended to the Department of Justice, that no criminal charges be filed against her; she and her senior aides had been 'extremely careless' but 'no reasonable prosecutor would bring such a case to court'. FBI agents were however pursuing a separate investigation into the activities of a former congressman, Anthony Weiner, who happened to be married to Huma Abedin, Hillary Clinton's closest aide and adviser. And they discovered emails between Abedin and Clinton on Weiner's computer. At this point, Comey made two decisions of critical importance. He reopened the email investigation, on the basis that new evidence had emerged. And he decided to write a letter to Congress to inform them of the reopening. On the former decision, he probably had no choice. But the latter was instantly challenged by colleagues in the Department of Justice, who warned Comey that he could be violating FBI procedures, in particular a policy of not commenting on investigations close to an election. Comey nevertheless went ahead, having decided that not releasing the information would make him guilty of misleading Congress and the public.

The media went into another meltdown. The reopening of the investigation went instantly to the top of the news cycle and seemed to stay there for days. And the race immediately tightened up. Both YouGov and CBS, in polling conducted between 28 October and 1 November, had the gap down to three points; a Fox News poll conducted two days later had it at one point. Moreover, the news seemed to re-energise Trump, who added extra stops to his last week of campaigning; meanwhile the Clinton team appeared seriously rattled. As the storm blew through, I telephoned a senior figure in the Clinton campaign. He raged about the unfairness of Comey's announcement, claimed that it had destroyed the momentum that they had been building, but also argued that the polls had now stabilised and they were still ahead. Then on 6 November, only two days before polling day, Comey announced that the investigation into the extra emails had been completed, and the conclusion reached that there should be no further action.

Historians will argue for decades about the impact of Comey's announcement. Clinton herself would come to blame Comey directly for her loss, saying a few days after the election that 'our analysis is that Comey's letter to Congress raised doubts that were groundless and baseless, but stopped our momentum'. Nate Silver, the pollster who had made his name by predicting the 2012 election exactly right, would write months later that the Comey letter might have shifted the race by three or four percentage points towards Trump, swinging Michigan, Wisconsin, Pennsylvania and Florida his way, enough to change the outcome of the electoral college. Moreover, he would question whether the media carried the biggest responsibility by giving Comey's intervention disproportionate coverage. On the other hand, David Axelrod, the Democratic guru behind Obama's election victories, would argue that the Comey announcement was only one of several factors underlying the outcome: 'Comey didn't tell her not to campaign in Wisconsin after the Democratic Convention; Comey didn't say don't put any resources into Michigan until it's too late.' And a post-election deep dive by the specialists into the polling data in the swing states would suggest that, in these constituencies, Clinton's slide had started before the Comey announcement; perhaps by as much as between three and six points in the week preceding 28 October, thanks to 'Republican voters coming home'. In short, as the *New York Times* would later conclude: 'we shall never know'.

As election day dawned in Washington, however, the media and pundit classes were united; Clinton was going to win. The polls might have narrowed, but every national poll still had Clinton ahead. And this was also the outcome that Washington wanted; it is a strongly Democratic town. In the embassy, we had sent a cable to London the day before, in which we had led with the consensus amongst the experts that America was about to have its first woman President. But fortunately, as it turned out, we had noted that there was still a path to victory for Trump, given the unpopularity of his opponent (these were the two most unpopular candidates since polling began) and the reality that, because of the electoral college system, American elections were actually decided by the voters in about six states.

It was a day of hanging around, trying to work normally, but in reality waiting for the polling stations to close and the TV stations to launch their election coverage. In the late afternoon, my political team touched base with the pollsters in the two campaigns (Cambridge Analytica in the case of Trump). The Clinton camp were convinced they had won; the Trump team were sure they had lost – as many of them would tell us in the succeeding weeks. We also talked to our friend Frank Luntz, whose own polling predicted a comfortable Clinton win.

Election night for Vanessa and me started with supper with Elizabeth Drew at her home in Georgetown, along with, among others, a Supreme Court judge. Elizabeth was one of the leading journalists of the Watergate era, and the author, at last count, of fourteen books about American politics. She agreed with the Washington consensus: Clinton would win, the question was by how much. And it was mostly too early for evidence to emerge to the contrary, except that, in US elections, much of the vote counting is done by machine and running totals shown on the news channels. So instead of a series of announcements of final results by otherwise obscure returning officers, as is the case in the UK, it is possible to watch the votes mounting up, state by state. The TV stations then use these figures to predict the eventual result, and when they are confident about the outcome, they 'call' the state for one or other candidate. The striking feature of this election night, to the disquiet of our dinner companions, was how many states were being designated 'too close to call'; not just the swing states like Ohio, Florida and Pennsylvania, but also states like Virginia, Georgia, Michigan and Nevada, normally guaranteed for one candidate or the other.

As the mood at the Drew residence grew more anxious, we moved on to the *Washington Post* party. By the time we arrived, it was anything but happy hour. The atmosphere was palpably tense, the noise level a low murmur. People were gathered around the TV screens, mostly watching silently as the running totals mounted, state by state. Some looked stricken, others just worried. As I checked the totals myself, I could see that Clinton was behind the count in all the swing states. I said to Vanessa: 'I think I'm experiencing another Brexit moment.'

We didn't stay long; I had a cable to London to write. I thought it was essential that some reporting from Washington should have arrived on the desks of ministers and senior officials by 8 a.m. the following morning; otherwise, people would be wondering what on earth the embassy had been doing on this once-every-four-years night. This meant pressing the send button by 2 a.m. Washington time. So at about 10 p.m., I joined the political team in the embassy and we started discussing what to write.

Shortly after I arrived, at about 10.20 p.m., the news channels called Ohio for Trump. This was a huge moment; Ohio was the quintessential swing state, having voted for the eventual winner in every US election since 1964. Virginia, the home state of Tim Kaine, Clinton's running mate, then went Democrat. So the outcome still looked to be balanced on a knife edge. And all eyes turned to Florida. There was a particular focus on Broward County, full of Democratic voters, who needed to turn out in force if Clinton were to make up enough ground to take the state. They didn't, and she didn't. At around 11 p.m., the news channels called Florida for Trump. North Carolina, which some optimistic Democrats thought Clinton might take, followed for him a few minutes later.

Three things were clear by then. First, it was already a bad night for the Democrats: it looked as if both the Senate and the House of Representatives were going Republican. Second, the outcome of the presidential election was going to hinge on four states: Nevada, Wisconsin, Michigan and Pennsylvania. And third, it would be touch and go whether the result would be clear by our 2 a.m. deadline. At around 12.20 a.m., Nevada was called for Clinton. But while she was never far behind in the other three states – at moments she was within a few thousand votes – she was always in arrears, and the clock was ticking. In terms of my cable, my options were to hedge, saying it was looking like a Trump victory but that the outcome was uncertain at the time of writing; or to take a punt and call it for Trump. I chose the latter.

At the last moment, I wanted to add some colour to the otherwise purely factual text. The Foreign Office of my early career had been wedded to classical allusions in its reporting. My tastes were more lowbrow: fewer Romans, more Rolling Stones. I used to read Hunter S. Thompson's pieces, and on a last-minute whim I tried to capture the mood of the *Washington Post* party earlier that evening by adding that 'fear and loathing' were stalking the Washington corridors. Not my best idea: the words would feature prominently when the cable would be leaked to the *Sunday Times* a few weeks later. But it seemed harmless enough at that late hour. I pressed send at about 1.55 a.m.

The news channels called the election for Trump about twenty minutes later. I decided to stay up for his victory speech (Clinton delivered her concession speech the following morning). At 3 a.m., Donald Trump took the stage at the Hilton Hotel in New York. He delivered a short and uncharacteristically magnanimous speech, praising his opponent, thanking his campaign team, calling for America 'to heal the wounds of division', and promising 'to be President for all Americans'. As he left the stage, he was accompanied by The Rolling Stones' 'You Can't Always Get What You Want', as he had been at the Republican Convention back in July. The Stones have an extraordinarily rich back catalogue, and this is one of their best. They hated the Trump campaign using it, and had issued a statement asking them to stop, to no avail. As the song rolled out, I could not but wonder: surely this should have been Hillary Clinton's song?

8

Loose in Trump Tower

*

'*That pink marble maelstrom . . .*'
– Ada Louise Huxtable, architecture critic,
on the Trump Tower atrium

*

'*We are just temporary occupants of this office. That makes us guardians of those democratic institutions and traditions – like rule of law, separation of powers, equal protection and the civil liberties – that our forebears fought and bled for. Regardless of the push and pull of daily politics, it's up to us to leave those instruments of our democracy at least as strong as we found them*'
– President Barack Obama, as he left office, in a letter
to incoming President-elect Donald Trump

*

THE DISTRICT of Columbia had voted 92.8 per cent for Hillary Clinton. So on that post-election dawn, the faces of the early-morning commuters were as grey as the skies above the city. Colleagues arriving at the embassy told me that there were people in tears on the metro. There were shocked faces among the large contingent of Americans working in the building. And the post-mortem on the news channels was already underway – with pollsters struggling to explain how they had got it so wrong.

We in the embassy, however, had different concerns. Though we knew several figures in the Trump team, there were two we did not: Jared Kushner, the President's son-in-law, and Steve Bannon, the 'CEO' of the Trump campaign. In this, we weren't alone; so far as I could discover, none of my colleagues in the Washington diplomatic community had been able to connect with either man. We wanted to be the first. Also, I needed these connections to calm London down; I was hearing of a Whitehall meltdown at the news that this unknown and controversial figure, rather than the reassuring and familiar Hillary Clinton, was heading for the White House.

And there was an even more immediate task. The British Prime Minister always telephoned the US election winner on the morning after the victory. It was presentationally important, and symbolic, that this should be among the very first phone calls that the President-elect took. We had been preparing for this for several days. My friend Chris Christie had been charged with leading the transition team, and he in turn had put us in touch with the individual tasked with assembling the 'early phone calls' list. We had booked our place; we were promised, should Trump win, one of the first three calls, alongside the Canadian and Mexican leaders. We phoned our contact before 8 a.m.; he told us that the victors were 'sleeping off' their late night, and that they would be back in touch with us around midday.

Time passed. We chased our contact a couple of times; there was no answer. We started to wonder whether something had gone wrong. And then, around mid-afternoon, the news channels started reporting that Trump had taken a couple of telephone calls, from the Egyptian and Turkish presidents. This sounded completely bizarre; not that the two individuals were insignificant, but it was hard to imagine any circumstances in which they would have been top of the list. We checked with other contacts in the Trump entourage and heard that earlier that morning, Chris Christie had been fired, and that Trump's inner circle had taken a deliberate decision to ignore all of the preparations made by the transition team. So there would be no carefully choreographed succession of congratulatory phone calls; it was every man for himself.

It was the moment for Plan B, and for some scrambling. We thought the President-elect was holed up in Trump Tower in New York. We needed the telephone number of someone in the room with him, or at least in the room next door. It clearly wasn't Chris Christie. So between us, I and the political team telephoned pretty much every Republican we knew. They all promised to help. But we struck gold with Tommy Hicks, a Texan who had been a prominent fundraiser for Trump, but was more importantly a close friend of the Trump children. He'd been to the residence a couple of times; he'd said 'Call if you need help'; and he'd delivered – by giving us the telephone number of Rhona Graff, senior vice president of the Trump Organisation, and executive assistant to Trump himself.

I phoned Rhona. She could not have been friendlier. I said that I was the British ambassador, phoning on behalf of my Prime Minister, who wanted to congratulate the President-elect. She said 'Great. He's right next to me. Shall I pass the phone over?' I explained that I needed to get the Prime Minister on the line first. She said 'Call me whenever.' So I telephoned No. 10, to discover that the Prime Minister had gone to bed (with the five-hour time difference it was after 10 p.m.). I asked whether they wanted to wake her; they argued that a phone call the following morning would be fine. So I went back to Rhona and booked the call for around 8 a.m. Eastern time the next morning.

With the wisdom of hindsight, it was a mistake not to ask that the Prime Minister be disturbed; not a mistake that changed the trajectory of history, or indeed the course of anything, but one that created an unnecessary story, and put the Washington embassy under serious pressure for the next few weeks. If I had pressed for the call to take place that evening, I think I could have enlisted the No. 10 media team in my support, because they would have seen what was coming. James Kirkup, at that time political editor of the *Daily Telegraph*, and a smart journalist whom I knew from my time as press spokesman, wrote prominently the next day that because the British Prime Minister's was only the ninth of the phone calls taken by Trump, it showed how little the UK mattered, how empty the 'special relationship' had become, and how little influence the UK had with the Trump team. In reality, it didn't signify anything of the sort. The real story was that all the carefully laid plans and arrangements had literally been thrown in the bin, and that this wasn't going to be an administration that operated by the usual rules and procedures. But I didn't blame Kirkup; the story was a gift.

As it happened, the phone call went fine. I listened in. Trump talked about his Scottish mother, his golf courses in Scotland, and said the UK was a special place for him. She talked about the UK–US alliance, and about the prospects for increased trade as the UK left the EU. He invited her to visit him in the US 'as soon as possible'.

We also carried out something of a post-mortem. The Australians had got their call just before us. I asked the Australian ambassador how they had beaten us to the punch. He said that they had realised at around the same time as we did that all the pre-cooking had been thrown away. They too had wondered how to get through to Trump Tower. And then one of them had remembered that Trump had played golf several times with the top Australian golfer, Greg Norman. They had contacted Norman, who had indeed been able to supply Trump's mobile number. I had to congratulate him on some brilliant lateral thinking, while concluding privately that we should have gone straight to Nick Faldo or Rory McIlroy.

Lessons in lateral thinking aside, it became clear over the next forty-eight hours that the Kirkup story had rattled Whitehall, and No. 10 in particular; and that questions were being asked about whether the Washington embassy was up to the challenges ahead. No one from London said this to me directly. But I had friends in the system telling me that something of a blame game was underway, and that we were among the targets. Moreover, we were starting to get a flurry of requests for background on Trump, analysis of his policy proposals (such as they were), and guesses about his likely cabinet picks, who might of course, unlike in the UK system, come from anywhere: the business community, the armed forces, Congress, the medical world, even the media. And I could imagine what lay behind this sudden surge of interest: ministers across Whitehall asking officials 'what do we know about him?'

The mood in Whitehall deteriorated further on 12 November when, from nowhere, the 'photo of the year' appeared. One of the curiosities of the US election campaign had been a cameo appearance and supportive speech at a Trump campaign rally in Mississippi by Nigel Farage, anti-EU campaigner and 'architect of Brexit'. The story was that Trump and Farage had been introduced by the Governor of Mississippi, Phil Bryant, and had hit it off, leading to a sponta- neous suggestion from Trump that Farage speak at the rally. There were a handful of further such appearances on the campaign trail, and judging by their on-camera interactions, there was real chemistry there. Nevertheless, the photo released on Farage's Twitter account on 12 November, of him and the President-elect laughing together while standing in front of glittering golden elevator doors in the upper reaches of Trump Tower, took the world by surprise, and by storm. Wherever one stood on the political spectrum, the symbolism was unavoidable: the two victors over their respective establishments, celebrating together, wreathed in gold. It felt like a vision of the future: 'O brave new world, that has such people in't'.

Meanwhile, I was pursuing Trump's inner circle. We got hold of Steve Bannon's email address through a friendly member of the Trump campaign team. Jared Kushner was a bigger challenge, but a senior British businessman who knew him well offered to act as a go-between. So I fired off introductory emails to both, offering to come up to New York to meet them. It took a while, but both even- tually responded in reasonably friendly terms, though neither would offer immediate meetings, arguing that they were swamped with planning for government. This rang true. Given that the entire tran- sition team had been sacked and its work junked, they were in effect starting from scratch.

Then it was back to London for a few days, on the Sunday over- night Virgin flight. Twice a year, a small group of us – including my colleagues from Beijing, Moscow, Berlin and Paris, plus a sprinkling of smaller posts – returned for an informal day of discussions with the senior leadership of the FCO. I always added on a couple of days, so I could make some calls around the rest of Whitehall and plug in to the zeitgeist. Given Whitehall's angst about this 'unknown' US President, I knew I also needed to offer reassurance.

I stayed in my usual haunt, a modest tourist hotel a few streets behind Victoria Street, within walking distance of Whitehall. On Monday night, my first night there, I put my mobile phone on recharge and quickly fell asleep, having barely slept on the overnight flight the previous day. I was half conscious of the phone buzzing and vibrating constantly through the night, but never sufficiently disturbed actually to get up and check it. But at about 5.30 a.m., I could resist no longer; I unhooked it from the charging cable and gazed blearily at the screen. It was full of 'Breaking News'. Trump had tweeted some hours previously that 'Many people would like to see Nigel Farage represent Great Britain as their Ambassador to the United States. He would do a great job!'

This would have been a challenge to process at any stage in the day. At five thirty in the morning, my first thought was to wonder how big a story it would be. I made some coffee and switched on the BBC, waiting for the 6 a.m. news that would start *BBC Breakfast*. I got the answer soon enough; it was the lead story. And there was already a comment from Farage, who said he was flattered, and that it had been 'a bolt from the blue'; yeah, right, I thought. Farage was also reported as saying that he did not see himself as a typical diplomatic figure, 'but this is not the normal course of events'. On those two points, at least, I had to agree.

The 6 a.m. bulletin featured no government reaction. I knew from my stint as FCO press spokesman that the media would have been pressing for some official comment, and I pondered for a moment whether I should ring the Downing Street switchboard and get hold of the duty press officer. But I concluded that it would sound too needy and pathetic to phone and say, 'Er, Kim Darroch here, just ringing to ask – what are you going to say about me!' I should trust the system. As it happened this was a good call. When the 6.30 news bulletin came round, the presenter added, 'And we've just had a statement from No. 10, who say there is no vacancy in Washington.'

At 8 a.m. I was due to speak at a briefing circle breakfast at the

Reform Club on Pall Mall. This was a smallish gathering, twenty or so; a mixture of senior figures from the private and public sectors. I had talked to the group a couple of times before, as ambassador to the EU and as national security adviser. My mind was still whirling from Trump's tweet, and on the twenty-minute walk to the venue, I wondered how I would be received during the half-hour of 'mingling' before the breakfast started and I delivered my presentation (which was inevitably billed as being about how Trump had won and how he'd perform as President). The answer was that my audience behaved exactly as you would expect from a group of Brits. No one mentioned the tweet. Everyone looked at me as if I was suffering from a grave, probably fatal illness. And everyone talked about the weather. So monstrous and overwhelming was the elephant in the room that when I stood up to speak, I opened by saying how nice it was to see them all there at what might well be my farewell appearance. The line got a laugh; Brits like their humour black.

The story rumbled on for a few days, drifting to the inside pages. Some commentators asked whether the President-elect understood that his job would be to nominate US ambassadors serving outside America, not foreign ambassadors coming to the US. Others questioned whether Nigel Farage realised that ambassadors had to represent the views of the government of the day, not their own. But there was a significant minority, especially but not exclusively on social media, saying that it might be a good idea to appoint a personal friend of Donald Trump as British ambassador. And Farage himself was out on the airwaves a fair amount, slamming the government for its instant rejection of the idea, and attacking me personally as a fanatical Europhile. He also said, in an interview on Russia Today – an interesting choice of outlet – that I had once come to his office in Brussels and 'it was one of the most unpleasant conversations' he'd ever had.

This last point puzzled me somewhat. Part of the job of British ambassador to the EU was to meet all the British MEPs. We held an annual reception at the residence in Brussels for them, to which I think Farage sometimes came. Once every six months, a lunch was held for the ambassadors of the twenty-seven member states, the president of the European Parliament and the leaders of the various parliamentary groups, of which Farage was one. He wasn't popular with the other, more mainstream group leaders (in the sense that they wouldn't talk to him), so the organisers invariably sat me next to him. We would talk amiably enough, provided we stayed away from government policy on Europe. The only occasion which remotely fitted the description of this 'unpleasantness' was when London had asked me to go and see him. The European Parliament had (wrongly in our view) been given the power to change legislation agreed by the member states in the Council of Ministers. The parliamentary committees had the key role in deciding what changes to propose. On some committees, the only British representative was a UKIP MEP. So London asked me to find out whether UKIP was prepared to work with the government in these committees to achieve the best possible texts in terms of British objectives; in short, would UKIP MEPs work to a British government brief in these instances? I got the answer from Nigel Farage that I had expected: 'no', expressed in reasonably clear, even abrupt, terms. But that was it. As unpleasant meetings go, it didn't rank in the top ten of those I'd had, or would have, in my career. So was this really the encounter he had found so upsetting? If it was, apologies now for my apparent offensiveness.

Back in Washington, the story had made quite a splash too. The mainstream US media wondered why Trump thought it conceivable that the British Prime Minister would send the leader of an opposing political party as her ambassador to Washington. But in the US system, most senior ambassadors are political appointees, and resign after an election. A lot of Americans accordingly assumed that, with Theresa May's arrival as PM (albeit not through a general election), British ambassadors would change too. So on my return to Washington from London, I was asked for weeks afterwards when I was leaving, and whether Farage would be replacing me. Vanessa had just started teaching at Washington's British school; the anxious parents of children in her class would come up to her and say 'Is it true? We're so sorry you're going.' And throughout my time in Washington, but especially as the end of my tour approached, people would ask whether Farage was going to succeed me. It was, in short, a story which stuck around.

During my week in London, the embassy political team had been approached by the Trump camp with a clear and significant message: that they wanted, as soon as possible, to begin their conversation with the British government at senior political level. This was not straightforward. The convention was that foreign governments shouldn't seek formal meetings with the incoming administration, and especially the President-elect, before inauguration, the logic being that there could only be one US government at a time. The Japanese had broken the convention instantly; on the back of a friendly phone call with Trump, Prime Minister Abe had journeyed to New York for a very public meeting with Trump in Trump Tower. The Obama White House had been furious and had rapidly warned others, including us, against following the Japanese. Even before this explosion, however, I hadn't thought that a meeting between May and Trump was the right answer. I wanted instead to set up an entirely private discussion, with no publicity, between the Foreign Secretary, Boris Johnson, and senior Trump advisers. This partly reflected the Trump team's wishes – Johnson was one of the few British politicians with a public profile in the US and the one they most wanted to meet – and partly my own view that he would carry out this first encounter well. Johnson was getting mixed reviews in the role of Foreign Secretary, particularly in Europe, but he had gone down well on a visit to Washington earlier in the year. He 'spoke American'. And his leadership of the Leave campaign in the referendum, while making him a marked man in Brussels, had made him a hero in Trump Tower.

I rapidly discovered, however, that No. 10 took a different view. I never found out whether the Prime Minister personally had been consulted, or if it was just the view of her notoriously controlling twin chiefs of staff, Nick Timothy and Fiona Hill. But the message that came back to my recommendation that I be allowed to set up a visit to New York by Boris Johnson to see the Trump team was initially a flat 'no': no one was to see any senior member of Trump's staff until the Prime Minister herself had met him. This seemed to me a mistake, and damaging to British interests; but although I enlisted the support of senior officials in the Foreign Office and Cabinet Office – and indeed the Foreign Secretary himself – I couldn't get the ruling overturned. Meanwhile, our Trump contacts were becoming frustrated: 'Where are you?' 'Why don't you want to talk to us?'

After a couple of weeks of head-banging, I happened upon a different idea – why not try to have Timothy and Hill themselves come to the US for these first contacts, in the hope that they would then agree to a follow-on visit from Boris Johnson? I tried this on No. 10. For a couple of weeks, there was silence; and then, miraculously (or so it felt), the dam broke. Timothy and Hill agreed to a visit at short notice, two weeks before Christmas. They didn't want to be spotted entering Trump Tower. And their priority was a meeting with their future counterpart, Reince Priebus, already Trump's pick as his chief of staff, who was based mostly in Washington, working out of Republican National Committee headquarters near the Capitol. So it was a day in DC, on Friday 16 December. The centrepiece was a teatime meeting with Priebus. But we also fixed an off-the-record session with political commentators, a couple of meetings with senior backroom figures in the Republican Party, and a call on Newt Gingrich, Trump's friend and adviser, and former Speaker of the House of Representatives.

In the event, the visit wasn't a success. Nick Timothy arrived carrying some variety of flu virus, as a result of which he was in subdued form throughout, while Fiona Hill was monosyllabic by her normal high-energy standards, giving every appearance of wishing she wasn't there. I initially sensed their discomfort at the breakfast with political commentators, where they seemed uninterested in the picture of American politics that the guests were presenting. And they then seemed utterly nonplussed by the force of nature that was Newt Gingrich. I used to love taking visitors to see Newt. He had his idiosyncrasies; for example he would begin meetings by handing visitors a reading list of his latest articles. But he was unfailingly courteous, interesting, insightful and indiscreet. Even if one disagreed with much of what he was saying, he was guaranteed good value. But I found myself carrying most of the conversation, with Timothy and Hill largely silent.

And then to the centrepiece, the meeting with Reince Priebus. This was the most disappointing of all. Priebus, whom I already knew a little, was palpably looking to build a relationship with his future UK counterparts. I think he imagined a future in which they would be speaking on the phone every week. But there was no chemistry, no spark in the room. At one point, Priebus asked, 'What does the May government stand for?' There was a heavy silence for what felt like minutes before Timothy said, 'It's about making the economy work for the many, not the few.' The meeting broke up soon afterwards.

That said, the visit served its purpose. The veto on senior ministerial contacts with the Trump team wasn't exactly lifted; but it sort of crumbled, in that No. 10 moved towards setting conditions for Johnson to visit, rather than vetoing the idea in principle. The first and most important condition, however, was that no meeting would be held with Trump.

All of which gave me a pretext to intensify my efforts to see Steve Bannon and Jared Kushner. And eventually, both of them agreed to see me, in Trump Tower. I went up to New York on the Acela train on a cold and snowy 4 January. Trump Tower is a grandiose 58-storey building in midtown Manhattan, right on the face of Fifth Avenue. It contains a hotel, shops, condominiums, the Trump Organisation's HQ and Trump's private apartment; and in those weeks before the show moved to the White House, it was perhaps the most important piece of political real estate on the planet. On the street outside, there were barriers everywhere, and a seething crowd of onlookers. It took twenty minutes to get through the various security checks, whereupon I found myself in the entrance hall, looking at the famous golden escalator down which Trump had descended in July 2015 to launch his campaign. The lobby was staked out by dozens of cameras and journalists, flanking the entrance to the lifts, filming and accosting any recognisable faces amongst those entering and leaving. I told myself that no one would recognise me, that I was just another faceless suit. I was right.

Arriving at Trump HQ, some twenty floors up, I was met, taken along a corridor cluttered with cardboard boxes of Trump campaign material, and ushered into an anonymous meeting room. Jared Kushner arrived a few minutes later.

The media had been full of Kushner's importance as a close and – being family, untouchable – adviser to the President, with a portfolio that focused on Israel/Palestine but gave him a free hand to roam pretty much everywhere. So it was something of a setback when it turned out to be, at least for the first half – no, make that three-quarters – a seriously testy encounter. As one of its last acts of diplomacy, the Obama administration had discreetly encouraged a United Nations Security Council resolution stating that Israeli settlement activity was a 'flagrant violation of international law' and had 'no legal validity'. The resolution had passed on 23 December, with fourteen votes, including that of the UK, in favour and none against. The fifteenth vote, that of the United States, had been an abstention; an unprecedented step in US diplomacy after decades of vetoing any UN resolution criticising Israel. Trump had, before the vote, publicly called on Security Council members not to support the resolution; another largely unprecedented move, given the tradition that incoming administrations should not try to 'co-govern' during the transition. Kushner started into the issue immediately and radiated genuine anger. He said that the President-elect was deeply disappointed at how we had voted, and suggested that this was exactly the kind of core issue on which Trump would judge the worth of friends and allies. I tried to explain that opposition to Israeli settlement policy was a long-established UK position and that it would have been inconceivable for the British representative to have taken any other stance. But there was no meeting of minds; although I was able to confirm Kushner's agreement to see Boris Johnson a few days later.

I was then scheduled to see Steve Bannon. I texted him to ask if he was ready. He texted back to say that, notwithstanding our appointment, he was at that moment in Washington. We exchanged a few more texts to rearrange a meeting there in forty-eight hours' time. And then I took stock. There had been meagre returns for my three-hour journey from Washington: one difficult meeting, where I hadn't exactly struck up a warm relationship with a key figure for the future, and one no-show. So I thought about how I could prolong my stay in Trump Tower. A few days earlier, I had been told that Trump's personal lawyer, Michael Cohen, was an important figure in the inner circle, and I had been given a mobile number for him. Thinking I had nothing to lose, I texted the number, introducing myself as the British ambassador, saying I was in the building, and asking whether I could introduce myself. To my surprise, a text pinged back almost instantly, giving me floor and office numbers and saying 'come on up'.

By that stage, the meeting with Kushner over and no escort reappearing, I was on my own. I made my way back to the lifts and ascended as Cohen had instructed. I emerged into a sizeable lobby area, with Cohen's office, door closed, a few strides away. But my eye was caught by another office on the corner of the building, with open double doors; it was clearly huge, with a panoramic view of the Manhattan skyline. I edged towards it, and glimpsed a famous profile; the President-elect was in the room, standing with his back to the doors, talking on his mobile phone. I hung around for what felt like about ten minutes but was probably much less, thinking that when the phone call ended, I could knock on the door, go in and introduce myself. The problem was that the call wasn't ending. Indeed, judging by the volume of Trump's voice, it was becoming difficult and contentious. So, reluctantly, I backed away and knocked on Cohen's door.

A voice from within told me to enter. It was a tiny office, lined with shelves, each copiously stacked with folders and unruly piles of papers. Apart from Cohen, seated behind his desk, which was also overflowing with paper, there were two others in the room, both with the appearance of office juniors. He introduced them, then asked them to leave, and we had a friendly thirty-minute one-to-one conversation. I noticed that his windowsill was full of photos of someone playing baseball, and asked about them; it turned out that his son was a baseball prodigy, with the prospect of a professional career. We talked about the campaign and I asked whether he would be moving to Washington. He said that nothing was definite, but it was likely; he hoped for a job in the White House. Noticing a tennis racquet in the corner, I asked if he played. When he said that he did, I invited him to a game on the residence court; we almost, but not quite, fixed a date there and then. We concluded by exchanging further contact details and agreeing to stay in touch. When leaving, as a final favour, I asked whether he would introduce me to the President-elect on my way out. He readily agreed, but we found the tennis-court-sized office empty. Trump had gone to a meeting elsewhere in the building.

As has been well documented, it wouldn't subsequently go well for Michael Cohen. He wouldn't be offered a job in Washington. And the Mueller investigation into Russian interference in the 2016 election would finish him. All of those folders and piles of paper in his office would end up in the hands of the FBI. He would be fired by Trump in May 2018 and would plead guilty in August that year to eight criminal counts, including tax fraud, bank fraud, and violating campaign finance laws. He would appear before Congressional committees at which he would try, ultimately unsuccessfully, to implicate Trump in some of his crimes. Ben Stiller would play him in *Saturday Night Live* sketches. He would be sentenced to, and serve time in, a federal prison. And he and I would never get to play tennis.

A day or two after the visit to Trump Tower, an interesting letter arrived from the Republican National Committee. Signed by senior Republican politicians, it invited the Prime Minister to speak at the Republican 'Retreat' in Philadelphia on 26 January, a few days after the inauguration. This looked to me instantly like an attractive option. The retreat would pull together pretty much the entire Republican representation in both the House and the Senate; and the Republicans controlled both houses. The Prime Minister would probably be the only foreign leader invited to address the assembly. In short, it was a fantastic platform. And as I thought about it, it occurred to me, in a sort of 'road to Damascus moment', that it could also be a way of short-circuiting the usual tortuous procedures for organising a prime ministerial meeting with the President. Donald Trump, by then in his first week in the presidency, would certainly be addressing the retreat. So what about a meeting between May and Trump in the margins? Even better, could the Prime Minister go on from Philadelphia to Washington and meet the President the next day in the White House?

As it happened, I was seeing Steve Bannon the next day for our rescheduled meeting. He had invited me for a coffee at his house in Washington, a location known to the media as Breitbart Towers because Breitbart News, the right-wing news and opinion website, was supposedly run from its basement. Bannon was a controversial figure, way to the right of the Republican mainstream and he had contacts, of which he made no secret, with some of the more dubious European political parties, amongst them the National Front in France and Alternative for Deutschland in Germany. But he was also likely to be a central figure in the Trump White House, having just been announced as chief strategist. He was clearly wildly busy and overstretched, as evidenced by his postponing our encounter from early to late morning; but when I got through the door, he was friendly and direct. Not wanting to waste his time, I mentioned that we might get Boris Johnson to New York within the next couple of weeks, and that he would want to meet Bannon. This having met with a positive response, I then pitched my idea of the Prime Minister accepting the invitation to the Republican Retreat and meeting President Trump while in the neighbourhood.

I added, however, that it would be even better if, rather than having a meeting in Philadelphia, she came up to Washington and saw the President in the White House. I highlighted the symbolism of the Prime Minister being the first international leader through the door after inauguration. Bannon said instantly, 'That's a great idea. I like it.' I asked whether he was speaking on behalf of the Trump team. Could we take this as a green light and start planning? 'Absolutely,' he said. 'Let's do this.'

This left but one more connection to be delivered before inauguration: Boris Johnson's visit. No. 10 were still reluctant to sign off on the principle of the visit; they wanted a cast-iron guarantee that there was no possibility of an encounter with the President-elect. In reality, it was impossible to give an absolute guarantee of this; Trump was simply too unpredictable. But in the end, I concluded that I had to take the risk. And so I told No. 10, not entirely accurately, that there was definitely no chance of a meeting because Trump would be away in his Florida resort of Mar-a-Lago on the only dates when the Foreign Secretary could cross the Atlantic (I had been told that Trump's departure for Florida was likely, but not certain). This assurance was enough: the Foreign Secretary was confirmed for Sunday and Monday, 15–16 January. He would fly into New York overnight, arriving on Sunday morning; would meet Bannon and Kushner in Trump Tower; would come down to DC on Sunday evening; and would make some Congressional calls on Monday.

I nearly didn't make it to the New York meeting. I was on the Sunday morning Acela train when it broke down at the Baltimore Airport stop, about thirty miles out from Washington. My driver, Brian Gale, drove to the station, picked me up, and continued on to New York. We missed our rendezvous at JFK Airport, but connected with the Foreign Secretary and his party at the consul general's apartment in midtown Manhattan. And after a short briefing session and a sandwich lunch, we set off on the short trip to Trump Tower. We had arranged to come in through the back 'tradesman's' entrance to avoid the media stakeout in the lobby. So we arrived, unseen, in the same anonymous and windowless meeting room where I had met Kushner.

It was a long meeting, close to three hours. The Foreign Secretary was accompanied by Mark Lyall Grant, my successor as national security adviser and No. 10's representative at the meeting. Unexpectedly, there were three on the other side of the table. Bannon and Kushner were there, as anticipated, but so was someone I'd not previously met: Stephen Miller, who was introduced to us as Trump's speechwriter. Miller would become one of the leading, and most durable, survivors in the Trump White House, and arguably, after Bannon's departure in August 2017, the most controversial, given his hard-line views on immigration and his evident influence on the President. On this first meeting, however, he was a silent onlooker.

The meeting kicked off with Kushner complaining to the Foreign Secretary, as he had to me, about our support for the UN Security Council resolution on Israeli settlement policy. The Foreign Secretary explained British policy. Kushner explained why the President felt so strongly. There was some back and forth. I watched Steve Bannon during the exchange. He could not have looked more indifferent. And as soon as he could, he changed the subject. He was much more interested in Brexit; he spoke at length about what he believed was an inexorable tide of populism sweeping Europe, fuelled by a flood of economic migrants from North Africa and the Near East, which had in turn been accelerated by chronic instability in those regions. It was a compelling picture, though one in which Bannon explicitly saw the rise of right-wing populist parties as the solution, not a worrying symptom of the problems.

Iran was the other main subject. Trump had said, dozens of times, on the campaign trail that the Iran nuclear deal concluded by his predecessor was the 'worst deal ever' and one from which he would withdraw once in power. Kushner, in particular, channelled this line. Johnson pushed back firmly, pulling Mark Lyall Grant into the conversation to talk about the detail of the deal, and indeed quote chunks of it. They didn't really attempt to contest Mark's arguments, or to engage on the technical substance; but nor did they look persuaded.

There was plenty of warmth as the meeting broke up. The Foreign Secretary threw his weight behind the possible prime ministerial visit straight after inauguration; Bannon said he was working on it. Mobile numbers and email addresses were exchanged (notably between Johnson and Bannon). And we slipped out again unseen, my mind working overtime as we traversed the service corridors at the back of the building. As I'd anticipated, Johnson had handled the meeting deftly; he'd pushed back where necessary, while building relationships for the future. He did equally well that evening at the residence. I had invited a selection of senior Republican Party figures there to meet him. He circulated, sprinkled a touch of stardust, and finished up with a funny speech, full of arcane references and florid language. They loved it. And he similarly charmed the Republican leadership on the Hill the next day. I particularly enjoyed his opening sentence to a startled Paul Ryan, Speaker of the House of Representatives: 'Paul, you're obviously great. Why on earth didn't you run for the presidency?'

9

American Carnage

*

'And so, my fellow Americans, ask not what your country can do for you – ask what you can do for your country. My fellow citizens of the world: ask not what America will do for you, but what together we can do for the freedom of man'
   – John F. Kennedy's inauguration speech,
   20 January 1961

*

'. . . Mothers and children trapped in poverty in our inner cities; rusted out factories scattered like tombstones across the landscape of our nation . . .'
   – President Donald Trump's inauguration speech,
   20 January 2017

*

AFTER THE rigours of the transition, inauguration week was a ball; actually, several of them.

It wasn't always thus: the first inauguration, that of George Washington, on 30 April 1789, took place at Federal Hall in New York, and amounted to little more than a simple swearing-in ceremony. The next two, in 1793 and 1797, were likewise simple affairs, held in Congress Hall, Philadelphia, before the event moved to the recently completed city of Washington in 1801. The only absolute requirement – because it is in Article 2 of the Constitution – is the recitation of the presidential oath of office, typically delivered to the Chief Justice of the Supreme Court. Over the decades, the date of the inauguration has shifted around, only becoming established on 20 January in the Twentieth Amendment to the US Constitution, passed in 1933; as has the venue, with the event being held in a variety of locations around the city, including the chambers of both the Senate and the House of Representatives in the Capitol building, as well as the White House itself. But the modern pattern was established by Ronald Reagan, with his actor's eye for setting and spectacle, when he held his first inauguration, in 1981, in front of the west face of the Capitol, looking down on the National Mall, the Washington Monument and the Lincoln Memorial. Since then the inauguration has grown into a day-long series of events, with parades and, yes, lots of balls, though the centrepiece has become the inauguration address, delivered by the incoming President straight after the swearing-in. And though generations have tried, no one, not even Obama, has ever matched the soaring, timeless rhetoric of John F. Kennedy's 1961 speech.

With the balls mostly held on the evening of the ceremony, and since the inauguration fell on a Friday, the preceding week was devoted to parties. We hosted a reception for about four hundred at the residence, to which a pleasing number of Trump's entourage came, including Rudy Giuliani, Newt Gingrich, Kellyanne Conway, deputy chief of staff Katie Walsh, former campaign CEO Corey Lewandowski, Reince Priebus, press spokesman Sean Spicer, party life-and-soul Chris Christie, and Rick Gates, who would, months later, become a central figure in the Mueller investigation. Not even I could claim, however, that this was the standout event of the week. That honour fell to the Chairman's Global Dinner, an innovation introduced by the 2017 presidential inaugural committee.

These committees are a recurrent feature of presidential inaugurations. In shorthand, they are a collection of the incoming President's wealthiest friends, who donate large sums of money to ensure that their boy gets a great sendoff and the biggest balls ever. The big donors often reappear a few months later as nominees to some of the glitzier ambassadorial posts around the world. The Trump inaugural committee was worth a quick study. Chaired by Tom Barack, a West Coast billionaire and long-time friend of Trump, its members included Steve Wynn, the casino magnate, Sheldon Adelson, and Woody Johnson, heir to the Johnson & Johnson empire, owner of the perennially useless New York Jets American football team and soon to reappear as nominee for ambassador to the Court of St James. The committee raised an extraordinary sum, an unprecedented $107 million, twice the amount of any of its predecessors. Around half of this went to four 'event-planning companies', a couple of which were run by friends of the Trumps. Some $1.5 million was spent at the Trump Hotel in downtown Washington. But a substantial sum, some tens of millions, seems never to have been spent. Moreover, there were persistent rumours of illegal donations, through front companies, from shadowy Russian and Middle Eastern individuals. Investigations by federal prosecutors in Brooklyn and New York continue.

But all this strife lay in the future. The Chairman's Global Dinner was billed as an event where the Washington diplomatic community could meet senior figures in the incoming administration. There was no promise that either Trump or Vice President Pence would be there, but the buzz was that they might be. So we ambassadors turned up in force, in an endless parade of gas-guzzling limos queuing at the Andrew Mellon Auditorium, one of the more expensive Washington venues. So lengthy was the line, Vanessa and I abandoned the car and walked the last quarter-mile.

It was quite a gathering. There were indeed some senior figures from the incoming administration in attendance. I had a long talk over dinner with Michael Flynn, who had been appointed national security adviser. I told him that had been my job before Washington. He seemed, well, unimpressed. 'Hey, I'd like to hear about your experiences,' was exactly what he didn't say. A number of Trump's biggest financial backers were there too. I saw Steve Wynn across the room, looking wealthy and at home. And I talked briefly to Sheldon Adelson. Gazing around the crowd, I calculated that there would have been hundreds of billions of dollars in that one, admittedly large, room.

But it still lacked the main man; until the curtains on the stage parted and Mike Pence walked on. We diplomats wondered whether that was it and Pence was the main attraction – until it turned out that his role was that of warm-up man for Donald Trump. A role he performed competently enough, if his act was a little over the top for the neutrals in the audience. But I had to admire the theatre with which the evening was unfolding. And within a few minutes, Trump took the stage. His speech was solid boilerplate, but it didn't matter. I and, I would guess, all of my fellow ambassadors were much more focused on the central question: when he finished, would he disappear off to another event, cocooned in his security detail, or would he come down off the stage and mingle?

Trump walked to the side of the stage. At this point, he could either exit stage left, or he could take the steps down to where the crowds were. He tantalised us for a few minutes, remaining on the stage while talking to a small group who had been bold enough to climb up onto the stage with the President-elect. I guessed they were the event's backers; paying for it all presumably gave you the right to go anywhere. But then, to an audible tremble of anticipation around the room, he descended.

It was important not to look too desperate. So I waited fifteen minutes before casually inserting myself into his personal space. I introduced myself as the British ambassador. For one crazy second, I almost blurted out 'And what's more, my first name is Nigel'; fortunately, I didn't. He paused for a second, prompting me to wonder if he was about to say 'Why are you still here? Didn't you see my tweet?' Instead, of course, he said, 'Good to meet you. How is Brexit going?' I told him that it was all on track, words that I was to use constantly over the next two years; this was probably the only occasion, early in the game as it was, when they were broadly true. I then told him that the Prime Minister was likely to come over to the US for the Republican Retreat the weekend after inauguration, and that she would like to come up to the White House the next day to see him. This actually wasn't quite true: No. 10 were still vacillating over the idea. But what is life without risk? He said, 'That would be great.' Job done.

The following morning, I sent a short email back to the No. 10 team and the FCO, reporting that I'd talked to Trump the previous evening and that he'd be keen to see the Prime Minister in the White House the day after the Philadelphia retreat. This was perhaps a bit more specific and definitive than justified by the conversation, but anything to get No. 10 over the line. And within a day or two we received a short administrative note saying a recce team would be arriving early the following week. We were on. And a day later, I noticed that someone, somewhere in Whitehall, had told the British media that I'd met Trump. It was portrayed as if he and I had done a lightning *tour d'horizon* of the world's trouble spots before deciding where we'd invade first, rather than holding a three-minute conversation about visits in an increasingly sweaty room. But no matter, it had registered: more than one Nigel had met Trump.

Back at the dinner, I spent the rest of the evening watching the future President as closely as I could without looking like I was stalking him. I noticed two things. First, he was genuinely skilful at schmoozing his donors. He worked the room. He didn't get stuck with anyone. He appeared to remember names. He affected genuine interest in what people were saying to him. And he had, at least when surrounded by supporters, real charisma and stardust. I could see instantly how he'd been able to electrify the huge crowds which had attended his campaign rallies. (By contrast, it had been said of Hillary Clinton that her crowds had pitched up for the rock stars who opened her rallies, like Bruce Springsteen, but had drifted away by the time she actually stood up to speak.) And second, he gave every appearance of actually enjoying the experience. He liked 'feeling the love'. It energised him. No wonder he had been such an indefatigable campaigner. And no wonder that, once he was in office, his White House staff would continue to schedule regular campaign-style rallies around the country; he actually needed that regular injection of adulation.

When he sat down to dinner, I noticed that he spent the next forty minutes in deep conversation with the new Secretary of State, Rex Tillerson. The body language was fascinating; it looked like a getting-to-know-you session, not a piece of deep policy planning. When I checked up the next day, I saw why. The story was that Tillerson had been hired on the basis of one thirty-minute conversation and the fact that he'd been a businessman, not a career politician. So they barely knew one another: Trump the Disrupter.

Inauguration Day dawned cold, grey and drizzly. This being one of the great events of state, ambassadors and spouses were invited en masse. This was good of the State Department, and guaranteed great seats; the alternative would have been to join the thousands on the Mall. But there was a downside: to get through all of the security checks that any vague proximity to the President involved, we all had to turn up hours in advance and hang around at the State Department building, located at quaintly named Foggy Bottom district of Washington (oh, what fun the State Department's critics had enjoyed with that name over the years). So we joined our colleagues for a couple of hours of terrible coffee and slightly better pastries.

Days later – or so it felt – as we boarded the buses to take us to the Capitol, each of us was handed a small plastic bag containing a lapel badge for security identification, a programme for the day, a bottle of water, a blanket, and a plastic poncho complete with hood. And then we sat in a traffic jam, most streets in central Washington being closed for, well, security. As I grew increasingly bored, I examined my poncho, and noticed that while its packaging said it was a 'deluxe' version, one of my European colleagues, sitting across the aisle from me, had a different model that seemed somewhat more 'economy'. I mischievously pointed this out to him, suggesting that it was possibly a slight against his nation. To my horror, he immediately agreed and set off for the front of the bus, to complain to the unfortunate protocol official sitting next to the driver. She shrugged her shoulders helplessly; they were clean out of deluxe ponchos. He sulked for the rest of the journey (possibly the rest of the day); a grave case of poncho envy. I felt a touch guilty for what had been intended as a harmless joke.

When we arrived at the Capitol, we were separated into two groups. The ambassadors were given ringside seats in the temporary grandstand behind the stage from which the President would take his oath and deliver his address; spouses were sent off to a seating area below the stage, from there to look up at these historic events. In other words, we ambassadors were thought worthy of forming part of the backdrop to the ceremony; spouses were not. But from where I sat, right at the top of the stand, next to my irreverent friend the Australian ambassador, I could see all the way from the stage down the Mall to the Washington Monument. I could see that there was a huge crowd of spectators, filling perhaps half of the stretch back to the Monument. If I had anticipated the controversy that would break the next day, I might have started counting.

As mere background figures, we were ushered into our seats early, while the rest of the grandstand was largely empty. We whiled away the time until the ceremony started identifying the illuminati taking their seats. It was a Who's Who parade of American politics: former Presidents, Supreme Court judges, senior figures from Congress, and as the hour approached, members of the President's family, President Obama and the First Lady, and then The Man himself. It's not, in fact, a given for the outgoing President to attend. In 1800, John Adams ducked the inauguration of Thomas Jefferson. In 1829, John Quincy Adams could not bear to witness the accession of Andrew Jackson. In 1869, Andrew Johnson was so enraged by his loss to Ulysses S. Grant that he held a cabinet meeting while Grant was being inaugurated. Woodrow Wilson did not go to Warren Harding's 1921 inauguration; and Richard Nixon had skipped town when Gerald Ford was inaugurated in 1974. I wonder about the chances of a sixth no-show if events unfold in a certain way in 2020.

In truth, the first part of the ceremony passed in a flash. There were prayers from three religious figures. There was a hymn from the Missouri State University choir. There were short speeches from two senior senators, Republican Roy Blunt, also of Missouri, and Democrat minority leader Chuck Schumer. Vice President Mike Pence was sworn in by Supreme Court Justice Clarence Thomas, and the President was sworn in by Supreme Court Chief Justice John Roberts. Had that been it, it would have been underwhelming. But the address was still to come.

The President would say publicly, later that day, that it had rained through the early part of the ceremony, but had miraculously stopped when he stood up to speak. My recollection is the exact opposite. At least where I was sitting, perhaps thirty yards from the presidential podium, it started raining at precisely the moment President Trump started speaking. Indeed, his first few sentences were wiped out in my section of the grandstand by the rustle of 150 diplomats donning plastic ponchos. I stole a look at my European colleague; his budget model seemed to be functioning well enough, though his disgruntled look remained. In any case, we all quickly became gripped by the words we were hearing. Within a minute, the President said:

> Today's ceremony, however, has very special meaning. Because today we are not merely transferring power from one administration to another. We are transferring power from Washington DC and giving it back to you, the American people. For too long a small group in our nation's capital has reaped the rewards of government while the people have borne the cost. Washington flourished, but the people did not share in its wealth. Politicians prospered, but the jobs left and the factories closed. The establishment protected itself, but not the citizens of our country. Their victories have not been your victories. Their triumphs have not been your triumphs. And while they celebrated in our nation's capital there was little to celebrate for struggling families all across our land. That all changes, starting right here and right now.

This critique of the American establishment had been a mainstay of Trump's stump speech. The difference here was that the 'small group' he was accusing of selfishness, enrichment and corruption was sitting right behind him, ashen-faced and fuming.

There was more. A few minutes further in, he said:

Americans want great schools for their children, safe neighbourhoods for their families, and good jobs for themselves. But for too many of our citizens, a different reality exists: mothers and children trapped in poverty in our inner cities; rusted-out factories scattered like tombstones across the landscape of our nation; an education system, flush with cash, but which leaves our young and beautiful students deprived of knowledge; and the crime and gangs and drugs that have stolen too many lives and robbed our country of so much unrealised potential. This American carnage stops right here and right now.

These dystopian images transported me instantly to some of my favourite American films. The reference to crime and gangs and drugs took me back to Walter Hill's Seventies classic about New York gang life, *The Warriors*, itself inspired by the Ancient Greek classic, Xenophon's *Anabasis*. But the rusted-out factories and American carnage? They were zombie movies reincarnated.

But I needed to pay attention – because by that stage, only half of the audience had been insulted. We representatives of foreign governments were next. The President continued:

For many decades we have enriched foreign industry at the expense of American industry . . . spent trillions of dollars overseas while America's infrastructure has fallen into disrepair and decay. We've made other countries rich while the wealth, strength and confidence of our country has disappeared over the horizon. But that is the past. And now we are looking only to the future. From this day forward a new vision will govern our land . . . from this moment on it's going to be America First. We must protect our borders from the ravages of other countries making our products, stealing our companies and destroying our jobs. Protection will lead to great prosperity and strength. We will follow two simple rules: buy American and hire American.

We exchanged glances in the diplomatic seats: so this was how it was going to be. And I thought to myself that the President had completed the job; with these comments on America's allies and trading partners, he had offended everyone. Meanwhile, back at the podium, there was, after the carnage, a slightly incongruous passage of Reagan-style lyricism:

> And whether a child is born in the urban sprawl of Detroit or the windswept plains of Nebraska, they all look up at the same night sky, they fill their hearts with the same dreams, and they are infused with the breath of life by the same Almighty Creator. So to all Americans, in every city near and far, small and large, from mountain to mountain and from ocean to ocean, hear these words: you will never be ignored again. Your voices, your hopes, and your dreams will define our American destiny . . . together we will make America great again.

As the address ended, I studied the faces of the former Presidents in the audience. They seemed nonplussed. Obama, unsmiling, shook hands with Trump. Michelle Obama looked furious. And George W. Bush leaned across and said a few words to Obama. I was too far away to have any chance of lip reading. But the TV channels brought in close-ups and experts. Bush had apparently said: 'That was some weird shit.'

As we diplomats trudged back through the rain to our buses, we discussed what we had heard. We guessed, and the media subsequently confirmed, that the speech had been written by Stephen Miller, but inspired by Steve Bannon, with his vision of a populist uprising sweeping the Western world. But all of us had been shocked by the primordially angry tone, combined with an almost complete lack of hard policy content. The mainstream media took the same view. MSNBC anchor and former Republican congressman Joe Scarborough called it 'less an inaugural address, more a primal scream aimed at Washington'. The *Washington Post* managed to find George Bush, and asked him what he thought. His reply: 'Good to see you,' as he ran out of the door.

Back at the buses, we were reunited with our spouses. Vanessa had buddied up with the EU ambassador's wife and the Irish ambassador's partner. The latter, a wonderfully witty New York lawyer, had noticed on arrival that the seats they had been allocated were still wet from overnight rain and gallantly dismembered his newspaper, placing some pages on each seat. When Vanessa stood to leave, she realised she had spent the preceding two hours sitting on a full-page photograph of Donald Trump's face.

10

Theresa May Meets Donald Trump

*

'Great days lie ahead for our two peoples and our two countries'
– President Donald Trump to Theresa May, 27 January 2017

*

'Thank you for inviting me so soon after your inauguration . . .
the invitation is an indication of the strength and importance of
the special relationship that exists between our two countries; a
relationship based on the bonds of history, of family, kinship and
common interest'
– Prime Minister Theresa May to Donald Trump,
27 January 2017

*

THE WEEKEND after inauguration should have been about preparations for the Prime Minister's visit to Philadelphia and Washington the following Thursday and Friday. The No. 10 reconnaissance team were arriving on Monday. A critically understaffed White House were making it up as they went along, hampered by unfamiliarity with, really, everything about the White House: the media were writing sneering stories about meetings conducted in semi-darkness because no one could find the light switches. But first, we had the glorious diversion of 'Crowdgate'.

Most media coverage of the inauguration had focused on the dark and ominous content of the President's address. Understandably so: it was a long way from Ronald Reagan's 1985 inauguration vision of America: 'hopeful, big-hearted, idealistic, daring, decent and fair'. So when the White House press spokesman, Sean Spicer, summoned the media to an unscheduled press briefing in the White House late Saturday afternoon, his words were awaited with some eagerness. He approached the rostrum, in front of the massed TV cameras, and began talking angrily about crowd size. Looking extremely uncomfortable, he accused the media of misrepresenting the size of the inauguration crowd in order to 'minimise the enormous support' the President had enjoyed for his big moment. He asserted that Trump had attracted 'the largest audience ever to witness an inauguration, period', and added that 'these attempts to lessen the enthusiasm for the inauguration are shameful and wrong'. Tirade over, he then fled the stage without taking questions.

Two things were immediately clear to me and, I would guess, to most of those watching. First, everything about Sean Spicer screamed 'Get me out of here.' All that was missing was the guy behind him with a gun pressed to his neck. Second, it instantly killed the theory that, once in office, Trump would mellow down, become 'presidential', and back away from his unceasing war with the mainstream media.

The media, of course, went into hyperdrive. Within minutes, they were comparing and contrasting overhead photographs of the Trump crowd and that for Obama's first inauguration. It was, frankly, no contest. The Obama crowd stretched perhaps three times as far down the Mall. Then the Washington Metro released figures for the numbers travelling on the metro system on the morning before the event. The Trump figure was 193,000; the Obama figure had been 513,000. In short, every piece of evidence pointed towards Obama attracting an audience about three times bigger than Trump's.

As a former press spokesman myself, I had some sympathy for Sean Spicer. I pictured him being summoned into the Oval Office by the President – on, moreover, his first full day at work – and being told that his continued employment depended on his willingness to defy reality from the White House podium. I liked to think that I would have walked rather than done it, but that's easy to say from a distance. Sadly for him, but inevitably, his reputation as spokesman never recovered from this first-day horror-fest. There would, over the next few months, be endless stories in the media that Trump was considering firing him, until he sensibly beat his boss to the punch by resigning after about six months in the job.

I got to know Sean quite well during his period in office, and we stayed in touch afterwards. He was a New Englander, brought up in a small town in Rhode Island, and a committed, though mainstream, Republican. He was also a naval reserve officer, in which he took some pride: he always came to our annual Trafalgar Night dinner at the residence. But we bonded, in particular, over a shared passion for dinghy sailing, though he had reached greater heights than me in the sport, being at one stage on the fringes of the US Olympic team. At least with me, he never really wanted to talk about the crowd size episode. But he did tell me some terrible stories about going shopping in Washington with his young children and finding passers-by hurling profane abuse at him. Of his time in the White House, he seemed happiest about choosing his own moment to leave, rather than, like so many of that first generation, being forced out. Thereafter, he would become a regular presence on the late-night chat shows, smiling amiably while the hosts made jokes about him; and in 2019, he ventured into the celebrity twilight zone that is the American version of *Strictly Come Dancing*. And then, irony of ironies given his contentious relationship with the media, he crossed the floor, launching in March 2020 his own political talk show for Newsmax TV.

There was one more twist to Crowdgate. The newspapers weren't sure whether outrage or ridicule was the right response: so they did both, at great length, in the Sunday papers. The administration's response to the onslaught was to put campaign strategist and White House counsellor Kellyanne Conway on the Sunday politics shows.

On NBC's *Meet the Press*, she was pressed by the host, Chuck Todd, on why Sean Spicer would 'utter a provable falsehood' during his very first appearance as White House press spokesman. Her reply was one for the ages: 'Sean Spicer gave alternative facts.'

We also got to know Kellyanne Conway well during our time in Washington. She was a great Anglophile, her fondness dating, she said, from her term at Oxford University. In contrast to many of her White House colleagues, she appeared regularly on the social circuit. When not on camera, she had friendly, joshing relationships with many journalists. She helped us whenever she could in terms of getting messages through to the President, especially about what not to say. She came often to the residence, where she charmed everyone, including our children. But when playing defence for Trump, she was ferocious. I think she would argue, regarding the phrase 'alternative facts', that all she had been trying to say was that there was no definitive figure for the size of the inauguration crowd, so it was legitimate for the White House to have a different estimate from the media one. But the media melted down all over again. 'Alternative facts' became one of the phrases of the age. Memes and tweets multiplied. Among the more memorable: 'Next time I stand on the scale to check my weight, I will only accept alternative facts' and 'I tried putting alternative facts on my tax forms and now I'm serving fifteen to life.'

Meanwhile, Winston Churchill was occupying my attention. It was a convoluted story. There had long been a bust of Churchill in the White House, just outside the President's private quarters. George W. Bush had been such an admirer, however, that he had wanted a second bust, this one actually in the Oval Office. So the British government had lent the White House a bust for the purpose. Obama, on assuming office, had thought, not unreasonably, that one was enough and had replaced the one in the Oval Office with a bust of Martin Luther King. The unwanted bust was returned to the British government; in fact, to the residence, where it had pride of place in the library. So far, so unremarkable, except that the Republicans, on hearing of Obama's decision, had constructed a political attack around it, claiming it as evidence that Obama didn't rate Churchill.

News of the supposed slight quickly crossed the Atlantic, where Boris Johnson, at the time leading the EU Leave campaign, suggested in an article in the *Sun* that Obama had 'an ancestral dislike of the British Empire' – words that would be thrown back at him by the US media during his first visit to the US as Foreign Secretary. So, with the issue never far from the headlines, it was inevitable that, egged on by senior Republicans, Trump would declare that once in office he would restore the Churchill bust to the Oval Office. And then, equally inevitably, the timetable accelerated: it had to be there by the time of Theresa May's visit.

The bust had actually been restored to its position by the afternoon of the inauguration. In the following weeks, I was sometimes asked how I had managed to get it back into the White House so quickly. My answer always left the listener nonplussed. It was that, once the White House gave clearance – which given the President's view, came quickly – the bust had been carried from the residence, put in the boot of an embassy Land Rover, suitably secured against movement in transit, and driven there: no police escort, no accompanying ambassador, half an hour's work, no fuss, no hassle.

There was one more twist. On the afternoon of inauguration day, after the swearing-in and address, a pool of White House journalists were invited into the Oval Office to see the President signing his first executive orders. They all flagged the newly restored bust. But one of them, Zeke Miller of *Time* magazine, thought – and tweeted – that Martin Luther King had been removed. He hadn't; it is quite a big space and the King bust was now simply in a different part of the room, with, by chance, a secret service agent standing in front of it. The White House leapt on the error, with the President himself saying in a speech the next day, 'This is how dishonest the media is . . . the retraction was like, where?' In fact, Miller had tweeted a retraction and an apology within an hour or so of the original error. But this was the shape, and tone, of things to come. Meanwhile, the two twentieth-century icons shared the space, and still do, gazing out across the most powerful few square feet of carpet in the world.

A small group of us left for Philadelphia on the Wednesday after inauguration, there to meet the Prime Minister before her speech to the Republican Retreat the next day. She arrived in good shape. I had a look at the draft speech, which I think was largely the work of Nick Timothy. It was a clever piece of writing. Deliberately designed to appeal to, and align the British government with, the traditional internationalism of the Republican Party, it meanwhile reminded the audience that, whenever the US had intervened overseas, challenging tyranny and striving to make the world a better place, the UK had generally been alongside them. So it touched on the UK–US alliance that had endured through the First and Second World Wars and the Cold War. It highlighted the path running from the Magna Carta to the American Constitution. It explained that Brexit would not mean the UK was going to withdraw from the world. It emphasised the importance of the post-war multilateral institutions which the UK and US had constructed together, especially NATO and the UN. And it called for an ambitious UK–US free trade deal once departure from the EU had been completed. The point, of course, was that these were assertions with which most Republicans could not possibly disagree; but except for the free trade deal, they had absolutely not been part of Trump's manifesto for his presidency.

In the event, when delivered to the massed ranks of Republican senators and congressmen, the speech was a triumph. It was interrupted by standing ovations so often that it must have lasted double the time that the words alone would have required. I wonder if the Prime Minister had ever experienced a more enthusiastic reaction to a speech. Afterwards, a long queue of Republican politicians formed to shake her hand and get a photograph with her for their campaign literature. One senior Republican said to me: 'That was way better than the speech we got from the President this morning.'

The selfie queue satisfied, we returned to Washington for a private supper at the residence and preparations for the White House the next day. We were alerted on arrival to a misspelt White House press release announcing a meeting the following day between the President and 'Teresa May'; the stage name of a glamour model and star of adult films. The Prime Minister (Theresa with an 'h') was entirely relaxed, reminding us that she had been filmed alongside her near-namesake on a daytime TV sofa. The accompanying British press made the obvious joke that the President might be keen to meet the 'h-less' Teresa too.

The big day started with the traditional prime ministerial visit to Arlington Cemetery to lay a wreath at the Tomb of the Unknown Soldier. It was clear, still, but above all cold, with the temperature hovering around 4°C. The US military carry off these ceremonies brilliantly – almost as well as the Brits. So the approach to Arlington was lined with a guard of honour, and the wreath-laying itself, although over in a few minutes, was conducted with the appropriate mix of solemnity and pageantry. Then we went on to the White House.

As we approached, I noticed that the President was waiting at the main doors to the building, and he stepped out to greet the Prime Minister as she got out of the car. This looked to me a break with previous practice; when I had visited the White House with David Cameron, I didn't think Obama had met him at the entrance. So as not to spoil the camera shot, I waited in the car until the Prime Minister and President had gone inside; then I followed them, but slipped away into a side room. The idea was for them to have some one-to-one bonding time before the formal talks began. I hung around there for about fifteen minutes, until a member of White House protocol materialised from the atmosphere (or so it seemed) and ushered me towards the Oval Office.

As I entered, the President and Prime Minister were standing on the other side of the room, next to the Churchill bust. As I advanced towards them, the President pointed at me and said. 'Good job.' I must have looked puzzled, because he repeated himself: 'Good job.' Then he turned to the Prime Minister and said: 'Your guy did a great job on Fox News talking about this meeting. He's from central casting.' I glanced at the Prime Minister. Sadly but understandably, she looked amused rather than impressed. And much as I would like to think that I'd done a brilliant interview – and Trump did watch the cable news channels a lot – I wonder to this day whether the President's comments weren't in some way intended to compensate for his tweet two months earlier recommending that Nigel Farage take my post.

The two delegations came in for the formal plenary session. The UK side included Fiona Hill, Nick Timothy, and Mark Lyall Grant, the national security adviser. I was fascinated to see who made the cut on the US side. The answer was, pretty much everyone. Priebus, Bannon, Kushner and Spicer were all there, along with General Flynn, the US national security adviser (who would last another two weeks in the job before being fired for lying to the FBI and the Vice President about his contacts with the Russian ambassador to the US, Sergey Kislyak). And as we sat down, I noticed something unusual about the US team: none of them was carrying a notebook. Over the length of my diplomatic career, I'd never seen that: it was second nature that someone, and usually several of the officials present, would take notes of the meeting, for transmission around the system, and to record what had been agreed. Instead, everyone on the US side seemed to be a special or senior adviser, no one a mere notetaker. Perhaps, to be charitable, the proceedings were being relayed into an adjoining room, packed with transcribers.

This wasn't the only quirk. As the talks unfolded, it became clear that the President didn't intend to work methodically through an agenda. He wanted a conversation, the more free-flowing and anecdote-rich the better. Within the first few minutes, he had touched on North Korea and the behaviour of its leader, Kim Jong-Un; the Middle East and the deadlock between the Israelis and Palestinians; his congratulatory telephone call from Pakistani Prime Minister Nawaz Sharif; and the unacceptability of protectionist Chinese trade practices, behind which Beijing had run up a $500 billion trade surplus with the US. Trump then did his campaign pitch about the Iran nuclear deal being the worst in history; the Prime Minister disagreed.

As I listened to the discussion unfold, I thought how strange the world of government must look to the other side of the table. Scarcely any of them had served even a day in any form of public administration before. In real estate, if you spent money, you got something: a piece of land or a building. In government, it was somewhat cloudier; you usually couldn't see what you were buying. Moreover, Trump's comments on the US defence budget and over-seas aid – 'what are we getting for our money' – mirrored discussions around the UK National Security Council table in my days as national security adviser. For Ohio class submarines, read our two giant aircraft carriers; for Trump's comments on US aid, read our endless, circling British debates about whether to reduce our overseas aid budget and spend the money on the National Health Service.

I also noted that Trump was completely dominant and was being treated with extraordinary deference by his team. None of them spoke unless specifically invited, and the invitations did not flow freely. The only individuals called upon were General Flynn and Steve Bannon, each being invited briefly to contribute some factual background information. Otherwise, silence – and a tension you could almost touch.

Halfway through our allotted time, we moved on to lunch. At this point, the President changed gear, and spent most of the rest of the discussion asking the Prime Minister about the state of Europe. From the tone and direction of his questioning, three things became clear. First, he had a real grudge against the European Union. He told an anecdote about the greens on his Doonbeg golf course on the west coast of Ireland being damaged because he'd been prevented by EU regulations from building a sea wall. (When I later recounted this to my Irish colleague, he said that it had been nothing to do with the EU; it had been a combination of local opposition and domestic legislation.) Second, he was convinced that Brexit had been delivered by the same forces that had swept him to power; that it would be a success; and that other member states would follow the UK out of the European Union. He asked the Prime Minister, 'Who will be next?'

Third, he was really bothered about Germany. He argued that Merkel had made a historic error in allowing a million refugees into Germany in 2015; that she had, as a result, forfeited her role of leadership in Europe; and that Germany was shamelessly free-riding on US defence expenditure. This last point provided an opening for the Prime Minister to make a pitch for NATO, notwithstanding its under-resourcing by European states. Trump listened politely and said he agreed. This was important, given that he had publicly described NATO as obsolete. The Prime Minister asked whether she could highlight his agreement at the press conference. Trump said that was fine.

The Prime Minister finished the meeting by inviting the President to pay a state visit to the UK. This surprised me. I had been asked a few days earlier whether I thought such a thing would be a good idea. I'd said that I thought it unnecessary and premature; we would look a bit desperate and, having secured the first White House visit, we could afford to wait and see how the Trump presidency panned out. I had also pointed out that state visits usually took place during Presidents' second term. London had, however, taken a different view. I allowed myself a brief surge of irritation before my usual conclusion when overridden: advisers advise, ministers decide, suck it up and move on.

The press conference went about as well as we could have hoped. On NATO, May said: 'On defence and security cooperation, we're united in our recognition of NATO as the bulwark of our collective defence and today we've reaffirmed our unshakeable commitment to this alliance.' For good measure, she added: 'Mr President, I think you've confirmed that you're 100 per cent behind NATO.' Trump nodded in visible endorsement. She also mentioned the state visit invitation, at which the British media started scribbling. What we hadn't seen, however, was that when the two of them had walked together along a colonnade linking the meeting room to the press room, they had, just for a few seconds, been holding hands. And brief though the moment was, the media hadn't missed it: there had been a mass of cameras tracking their progress. If one had ever wondered why photographers wasted so many hours of their time filming prosaic events like leaders walking from car to door, or from one room to another, here was the answer: the chance of capturing moments such as this.

When we arrived back at the residence, the Prime Minister's media team instantly asked her – why the handholding? She looked at them witheringly and said: 'He grasped my hand. What was I supposed to do?' More generally, she conveyed the sense that this had been a meeting like no other, while declining to set out any personal impressions: I guess she was worried about leaks. So, after a residence tea, it was off to the airport. The Prime Minister was flying straight to Ankara to see Recep Tayyip Erdoğan, the Turkish President. So she had a rather different encounter awaiting her; or perhaps not.

As the team and I discussed the visit over a drink that evening, we were exultant at having got in first: there wasn't an embassy in Washington that wouldn't have coveted the first meeting with the new President. And it effectively killed the narrative that had been attached to the Prime Minister, that she had been only ninth in line with a post-election congratulatory phone call. The first editions of the British newspapers emerged a few hours after May and party had departed for Ankara. Inevitably, the handholding photo was on most of the front pages. But the Prime Minister's success in gaining the President's endorsement of NATO was given prominent coverage, and was in itself enough to ensure the visit was rated a success. The state visit invitation, however, was less well received. Lord Ricketts, former permanent secretary at the Foreign Office, summed up the emerging consensus when he said: 'It would have been far wiser to wait to see what sort of President he would turn out to be before advising The Queen to invite him.'

Others did the maths. Neither George W. Bush nor Barack Obama had made a state visit until the third year of their presidency; having been invited on his eighth day in office, Trump could in theory have made his within six months.

The story might have run and run had it not been completely eclipsed by an extraordinary White House announcement late that Friday afternoon. A few hours after the Prime Minister's departure, the world was told that the President had signed Executive Order 13769. With immediate effect, this suspended the US Refugee Admissions Program for 120 days and temporarily barred from entry into the US all those holding passports from seven Muslim-majority countries: Iran, Iraq, Libya, Somalia, Sudan, Syria and Yemen. It was immediately dubbed 'the Muslim ban'. Initially imposed for ninety days, it also applied to Green Card holders – permanent legal US residents. Trump justified the action by arguing that it was necessary on security grounds, to give government agencies time to develop a strict vetting system and ensure that visas were not issued to individuals who posed a national security threat. 'To be clear, this is not a Muslim ban, as the media are falsely reporting. This is not about religion. It is about keeping our country safe. There are over forty Muslim-majority countries worldwide that are not affected.'

The order was the work of Steve Bannon and Stephen Miller, aided by a couple of government lawyers they had informally co-opted. The text, it appeared, had been nowhere near the experts in the State Department or the Department of Homeland Security. And it caused instant chaos. Dozens of individuals from the seven countries were already in the air or had just landed when the ban was announced. They were either detained at the airport or deported – including Green Card holders who were returning to their families and their careers. Overall, hundreds of thousands of people were actually, or potentially, affected.

Neither was the disruption confined to US airports. Heathrow was a major transit point from the Middle East to the US, so Heathrow-based carriers had to take instant decisions to stop passport holders from the seven countries boarding their flights to the US. The same issue cropped up at major international airports across the globe. And this being America, hundreds of lawyers instantly descended on US airport arrival areas, offering to represent those in detention or about to be deported. We in the embassy were immediately asked to intervene with the administration to ask if the ban could be lifted until we, and the airlines, could organise ourselves. We started with Homeland Security, which was in a state of total confusion, not having known that the order was coming. So we talked direct to the White House. They wanted to help – but it was the early hours of Saturday morning and they had no idea how to end the chaos they had just unleashed.

The confusion continued through the weekend and into the following week. Then on 3 February a Seattle federal judge suspended the order nationwide, on the back of a challenge from the attorney general of Washington state. The grounds for suspension were that the executive order violated a clause in the US Constitution that prohibited the favouring of one religion over another. The administration appealed. The suspension was reaffirmed two days later by the Ninth Circuit Court of Appeals in San Francisco. The administration tried again. The same court confirmed its earlier judgment, notwithstanding arguments from the Department of Justice.

Executive Order 13769 never came back into force, though many of its provisions would survive in a reworked version, Executive Order 13780, which emerged a couple of months later. This too would be challenged and temporarily suspended, but was ultimately saved by the Supreme Court in a landmark judgment in June 2017. Immigration policy, however, would become the biggest legal and political battleground of the Trump presidency.

For us in the embassy, meanwhile, this short-lived 'Muslim ban' held another message. Hours after it concluded, a successful prime ministerial visit had been eclipsed by an extraordinary – and amateurish – act of political disruption. It had seemingly come from nowhere, and had taken most of the administration, all of the US media, and the rest of the world, allies and enemies alike, by surprise. It had been the first dip in the Trump rollercoaster ride, and we guessed that many more would follow. Or, as poet Robert Browning put it, 'Never glad confident morning again.'

11

'No Collusion, No Obstruction'

*

'This is the single greatest witch hunt of a politician in American history!'
> – President Donald Trump on Twitter, 18 May 2017

*

IT WAS the best of times in Washington: the afternoon of 9 May 2017, the dogwood trees in bloom across the city, blue skies, the sun shining, but not yet the heavy, swampy heat of the DC summer. London, satisfied that relations between the UK and the US were in good shape in the wake of Theresa May's visit three months earlier, and preoccupied with the Brexit process, were letting us get on with our work – of which there was plenty. I was in my office, dealing with a succession of visitors and meetings. I wandered into the outer office, glanced at the TV screen, which was permanently tuned to one of the 24-hour news channels, and saw an astonishing news headline flash up on the screen: 'BREAKING NEWS. Trump fires FBI Director James Comey'.

The office of FBI director had existed since 1908. Over those ninety-nine years, only two directors had ever been fired. The first, in 1993, was William Sessions, fired by President Clinton on the recommendation of the attorney general, Janet Reno, because of 'a loss of confidence in his leadership of the organisation': code for allegations of serious impropriety, such as the use of an FBI plane for personal journeys. And the second was James Comey, the man many Democrats blamed for Hillary Clinton's election loss. So why had the President soured on the man who had by some accounts turned the tide of the 2016 election?

Within two days the President provided the answer, overriding the staffers who were claiming that the firing reflected a loss of confidence among the FBI rank and file in Comey's leadership. In an interview with NBC anchor Lester Holt on 11 May, Trump explicitly linked his action to the FBI's Russia investigation.

The Russia investigation is a complicated story, which eventually ran for over three years, with lots of twists and turns, blind alleys and dead ends, and an arguably ambiguous and incomplete ending: even in summary, it is something of a trudge. As compensation, however, it features a colourful cast of characters: schemers, crooks, charlatans, imposters and fantasists. It begins some eighteen months earlier, and has, improbably, a former British intelligence officer at its centre. Christopher Steele was a leading UK government expert on Russia. He left the foreign service in mid-career to set up his own private sector company, Orbis Business Intelligence. In May 2016, knowing that Donald Trump was about to win the Republican nomination, the Democrat National Committee, using Seattle-based law firm Perkins Coie as intermediary, hired a commercial research and strategic intelligence company, Fusion GPS, to conduct some opposition research on Trump. It is common practice in US politics for those running for public office – or at least those who can afford it – to commission research on their opponents; and Fusion GPS were in pole position for the contract because they had carried out some research on Trump for one of his opponents in the Republican primaries. Fusion GPS in turn hired Christopher Steele to conduct some of the research, in part because Steele and the head of GPS knew each other well, and in part because Fusion GPS wanted to focus on Trump's supposed links with Russia, long the subject of gossip and rumour.

In late June 2016, Steele submitted a report to Fusion GPS which alleged that the Kremlin had 'cultivated' and 'compromised' Trump, and was moreover feeding Trump and his team damaging intelligence about Hillary Clinton and her campaign. Steele also had a long-standing relationship with the FBI, dating from his days as an intelligence officer. Believing that his information on Trump had national security implications, he briefed his FBI contact on his findings. And he kept in touch throughout with an old friend in the Department of Justice, Bruce Ohr.

As it happened, the FBI were already looking at whether Russia was interfering in the election process, and were trying to assess the truth of allegations that some of the Trump campaign team were working with Russians. They were focused in particular on two individuals: Carter Page and George Papadopoulos. Page was an unpaid volunteer in the Trump campaign from January 2016, and had been interviewed by the FBI about his contacts with Russia as early as March that year. Papadopoulos had joined the campaign, as a 'foreign policy adviser', only at the beginning of March; but in the following weeks he travelled to Italy, where he met an individual who claimed to be in touch with senior Russians. Shortly after this encounter Papadopoulos emailed other members of the campaign team about the possibility of a meeting between Trump and Putin.

Meanwhile, as Steele was concluding and submitting his first report, stories started to circulate around Washington that Russian hackers had infiltrated the Democratic National Committee's internal communications network and grabbed tens of thousands of emails. The reports were true: within a few weeks, on 22 July, the stolen emails were uploaded onto WikiLeaks. As this was three days before the Democratic Convention, it looked like deliberate political sabotage. And it might have worked. The emails suggested a conspiracy between Hillary Clinton's campaign and senior committee officials to marginalise her opponent, Bernie Sanders. It could have wrecked the convention, had an inspired unity speech by Michelle Obama not won the day. Shortly afterwards, on 31 July, the FBI opened a formal investigation into Russian interference in the election, with a particular focus on links between Trump associates and Russian officials. In a nice touch for Rolling Stones fans, they called it the Crossfire Hurricane investigation.

There were several more reports from Steele in the run-up to the election, each containing new allegations of collusion between members of the Trump campaign and Russians, with the objective of damaging Clinton's chances. One of these suggested that Michael Cohen, the Trump Organisation lawyer I would later meet in Trump Tower, had met Kremlin officials in Prague that summer – an allegation which Cohen would strenuously deny, and which no one could ever stand up. Another report alleged that Page had met senior Russian officials during a trip to Moscow in July and had floated a 'deal' with them: the lifting of US sanctions on Russia in exchange for Russian favours. Collectively these reports made up what would come to be called the 'Steele dossier'. The FBI would say later that their investigation would have proceeded anyway, but the dossier 'aided it'.

There were also more Clinton campaign email dumps on WikiLeaks. And in September, Steele and Fusion GPS agreed that Steele should share his findings with the Washington press. He also briefed State Department officials. By the end of September, it was the talk of the Washington social circuit.

And then the questions started – to me, and to the embassy political team. The first to ask me was a senior State Department official; the next time it was an anchor on one of the news channels. 'Do you know someone called Christopher Steele?' My answer was a straightforward and truthful 'No'. But I knew why people were asking. We in the embassy would have had to have been living underground not to have picked the story up. We pointed out to all who raised the subject that Steele had left UK government service some years previously: 'nothing to do with us, guv'. If our contacts privately thought that no one ever really left Steele's line of work, they were too polite to say so to our faces. So we watched and waited.

The Washington media were, in the event, strikingly cautious in their handling of the story. From what we were hearing, a lot of them had the full dossier, but understandably, none was sufficiently confident in the credibility of the material to risk the lawsuits. So the election came and went. Steele continued producing his reports. Then, on 6 January, during the transition, senior FBI officials visited the President-elect in Trump Tower to brief him on Russian efforts to meddle in the US elections and alert him to the contents of the Steele dossier – emphasising that, while the US intelligence community was emphatically certain about the former, the latter was unverified. News of the meeting leaked, and provided the opening for CNN, a couple of days later, to break the dossier story. CNN didn't publish the dossier itself; but on the back of their story, Buzzfeed did, on 9 January – all thirty-five pages of it.

At this point, the narrative moved abruptly to the newly appointed national security adviser, General Michael Flynn. The media had been circling around Flynn for a while. He'd had a distinguished military career, including a central role in dismantling insurgent networks in Iraq and Afghanistan, and on the back of this had been made director of the Defence Intelligence Agency in July 2012. But he was effectively fired in April 2014: I was told by a senior member of the Obama team that he had been difficult to work with, and had seemed excessively hostile to Islam. Flynn, for his part, would say later that he had repeatedly warned the Obama administration about the rise of Islamic terrorism, but had concluded that they 'did not want to hear the truth'. Whichever, he went into the private consultancy world for a while; some work for a couple of Russian companies led to an invitation to a dinner in Moscow at which he sat next to Putin. Notwithstanding having been a registered Democrat, he then talked to a number of the Republican campaigns before joining the Trump campaign in February 2016.

Flynn rapidly became a central figure in the Trump team. His military background gave the campaign some much-needed national security credibility. He adopted the warm-up role at Trump rallies, stirring the crowd up, and in particular leading it in the Clinton-targeting chants of 'Lock her up'; and he used his Twitter account to encourage a (completely baseless) conspiracy theory linking senior Democrats to a child sex and human trafficking ring. Meanwhile, he was maintaining his channels to senior Russians. It subsequently emerged that there had been more than a dozen contacts in the course of the campaign. And he was also talking to Turkish government officials about US policy on Fethullah Gülen, a prominent Turkish dissident and Islamic cleric residing in Pennsylvania on a Green Card: the Turkish government wanted Gülen extradited. Whatever these offline activities, Flynn was everyone's prediction for national security adviser, should Trump win, and he was duly offered and accepted the post shortly after the election victory (though not before Obama had warned Trump personally and specifically against appointing him).

The national security adviser is one of the central figures in any US administration. So everyone in the Washington diplomatic community wanted to talk to him. I already knew Flynn and set up a meeting between him and his UK counterpart. Others had tracked him down too. My Russian colleague, Sergey Kislyak, had developed a relationship with him, and managed to snare him for more than one telephone conversation on 29 December – the day the Obama administration announced retaliatory sanctions and the expulsion of thirty-five Russian diplomats in response to Russian interference in the elections. Flynn would later admit in court that they had discussed the new sanctions, and that he had urged Kislyak to ensure that the Russian government didn't escalate the situation. Unfortunately, he had at the time told his administration colleagues, including Vice President Mike Pence, the opposite. So when the fact of the phone calls between Flynn and Kislyak leaked, Pence went on national TV, on 15 January, and said Flynn and Kislyak 'did not discuss anything having to do with United States' decision to expel diplomats or impose censure against Russia'. To his later cost, Flynn maintained this fiction when the FBI interviewed him on 24 January. But the net was closing. On 13 February, Flynn resigned as national security adviser, after twenty-four days in the post; it was the shortest tenure in history.

The Kislyak curse struck again a few weeks later. Jeff Sessions of Alabama was the first senior Republican senator to come out for Trump, became a foreign policy adviser to the campaign, and looked a certainty for a cabinet job. With the election won, he was nominated for attorney general – a post many had expected to go to Chris Christie. In his Senate confirmation hearing on 10 January, he was asked whether, during the campaign, he had 'communicated with the Russian government'. Sessions said: 'I did not have communications with the Russians.' On 1 March, the *Washington Post* reported that he had in fact met Sergey Kislyak twice. Sessions later qualified his initial denial: he had 'never met with any Russians to discuss issues of the campaign'. His spokeswoman clarified further – the senator had met Kislyak 'in his capacity as a member of the Senate Armed Services Committee', not in his role supporting the Trump campaign.

It didn't wash. As rumours continued to swirl, Sessions announced on 2 March that he was recusing himself from the FBI probe into Russian interference and all other campaign-related investigations – thus leaving decisions on these to the deputy attorney general, Rod Rosenstein. Trump never forgave him.

Two weeks later, we were in the line of fire. As he usually did when there were bad stories around – in other words, almost every day – the President went on the offensive. At the beginning of March, he claimed that President Obama had put Trump Tower under surveillance during the 2016 election campaign. The Senate Intelligence Committee, chaired by a Republican, Senator Richard Burr of North Carolina, looked into the allegation and concluded: 'Based on the information available to us, we see no indication that Trump Tower was the subject of surveillance by any element of the United States government either before or after Election Day 2016.' Sean Spicer inevitably came under sharp and sustained attack on the issue at his press briefing the next day. In some desperation, I suspect, he repeated a story from Fox News: 'Three intelligence sources have informed Fox News that President Obama went outside the chain of command. He didn't use the National Security Agency, he didn't use the CIA, he didn't use the FBI and he didn't use the Department of Justice: he used GCHQ.' (GCHQ are the British equivalent of the US National Security Agency, with whom they work closely; they gather security information by intercepting communications.) Against all precedent – the UK security agencies almost invariably refuse either to confirm or deny press stories – GCHQ issued an immediate and magisterial rebuttal: 'these claims are totally untrue and quite frankly absurd'. The story thereafter died within twenty-four hours. But it served to remind us in the embassy that there was a daily risk that conspiracy theories might erupt.

Thereafter, the *Washington Post*, the *New York Times* and the TV networks put whole teams of journalists into the search for new angles and insights. There were several strands, with Page, Papadopoulos, Flynn and Sessions all appearing to have been talking to Russians. And there was an enticing possible link to Julian Assange, founder of WikiLeaks, who at that stage was holed up in the Ecuadorian Embassy in London. So the stories kept coming, usually on the front page, day after day; until they were fired into the stratosphere, thanks to the booster rocket of the Comey firing.

Comey would later claim that Trump had been contemplating firing him for months – since, in fact, a private dinner between the two of them shortly after the inauguration. By Comey's account, Trump had used the one-to-one meeting to demand his total loyalty, or else; in short, a bid for a 'patronage relationship', which Comey had resisted. Comey would subsequently comment that 'This only added to the strangeness of the experience: the President of the United States had invited me to dinner and my job security was on the menu.' Thereafter, the President would periodically vent to his staff about his perception of Comey's inadequacies – which someone would then brief out to the *Washington Post* or *New York Times*.

Nevertheless, the timing of Comey's dismissal seemed to take the administration machinery by surprise, and the announcement was comically mishandled. Someone was dispatched to FBI head-quarters to pre-warn Comey personally, but he was actually giving a speech in Los Angeles. The announcement went ahead anyway – with Comey learning about it from a TV screen. To compound the chaos, it was originally presented as a response to Comey's handling of the Clinton email issue, and the claim that, more generally, he had lost the support of the rank and file of the FBI. But within a few days, the President had linked it to the FBI's Russia investigation: 'When I decided to fire Comey, I said to myself – you know, this Russia thing with Trump and Russia is a made-up story.'

Some commentators likened the President's decision to Richard Nixon's infamous 'Saturday Night Massacre', when he fired Special Prosecutor Archibald Cox, who had been investigating Watergate. Others described it as an abuse of power. A *New York Times* editorial called the President's explanation 'impossible to take at face value' and stated that Trump had 'decisively crippled FBI's ability to carry out an investigation of him and his associates'. Most Republican politicians either supported the President or ran for the hills: all but one or two, notably Bob Corker of Tennessee, chair of the Senate Foreign Relations Committee, distanced themselves, while John McCain called for an investigation by a special congressional committee. As for me, I always thought that the firing was primarily about Comey's unwillingness to promise absolute loyalty; his refusal to 'kiss the ring'. Trump was never one for constitutional niceties.

The Democrats, for their part, intensified their calls for the appointment of a special prosecutor to continue the investigation into Russian interference during the election. The White House disagreed; the President tweeted that those calling for a special prosecutor were 'phoney hypocrites'. But the pressure was intensifying daily. There seemed to be no possibility of the story dying, and ultimately, this was a Department of Justice decision, not one for the White House. And on 17 May, Deputy Attorney General Rod Rosenstein appointed former FBI director Robert Mueller as special counsel to oversee the Russia investigation.

The appointment of Robert Mueller as special counsel marked the end of the first act of the Russia drama. We had followed it closely from the embassy, and had reported regularly to London. The story had a big global profile, so tended to be the first question on the lips of visitors, so we had to be able to talk knowledgeably about it. And though none of us in the embassy really believed this was the new Watergate, neither could we ignore it, just in case it was. In wider Washington, however, our scepticism wasn't shared: in a classic case of the wish being father of the thought, much of the town seemed to believe it would actually bring the President down.

Mueller's appointment received a great press. The papers seemed dazzled by him, as the embodiment of an FBI man. He had attended Princeton. He was a war hero, having joined the Marines and served in active combat in Vietnam. He had been awarded both a Purple Heart and a Bronze Star, the latter for rescuing a wounded fellow Marine under enemy fire. He subsequently studied law at the University of Virginia, served in private law practices, then rose steadily up the ranks in government service, eventually becoming, in 1990, US assistant attorney general for the criminal division – in which role he oversaw the prosecution of Mafia boss John Gotti. In 1998, he became US attorney for the Northern District of California. And in July 2001, George W. Bush made him director of the FBI. In searching for the man behind the exceptional curriculum vitae, journalists alighted upon his reputation for absolute integrity, his un-showy taste in clothes (invariably dark grey suits, white shirts and boring ties), and his modest taste in accessories, as demonstrated by his $35 Casio watch. What they should perhaps have made more of was his record for caution, and for playing by the rules: Garrett Graff, in his book *Inside Robert Mueller's FBI and the War on Global Terror*, described Mueller as 'probably America's straightest arrow, very by-the-book, very professional'. Note the 'by-the-book' observation. But at that stage Washington was in love with Mueller; he was going to get his man, because that was what he did.

For us in the embassy, however, there was an unexpected bonus in Mueller's appointment. In a town which lived on leaks, he ran the tightest ship imaginable. The Mueller team just didn't leak. They released information when it suited them. Otherwise they were a locked black box. So while the story didn't disappear, it became more manageable. There was no longer a new twist each day. This was just as well: Mueller eventually submitted his report, under the catchy title *Report on the Investigation into Russian Interference in the 2016 Presidential Election*, on 22 March 2019, no less than 674 days after his appointment: Washington could have died waiting.

As some compensation, however, the juiciest story of the whole saga appeared from nowhere in July 2017. On 8 July, the *New York Times* reported that, about a year earlier, in June 2016, there had been a meeting in Trump Tower between the President's eldest son, Donald Trump Jr, son-in-law Jared Kushner, the soon-to-be Trump campaign chairman Paul Manafort, and a Russian lawyer with links to the Kremlin, Natalia Velnitskaya. It had indeed taken place: Trump Jr issued a statement the same day calling it a short introductory meeting about Americans adopting Russian children. This explanation unravelled almost instantly. Within three days, the *New York Times* had somehow acquired the entire email chain leading up to the meeting, which told a somewhat different, and completely bizarre story – and one, moreover, with another British connection.

In a crowded field, Rob Goldstone was perhaps the most colourful character to emerge from this whole narrative. Of British nationality, born near Manchester, he had left school at sixteen, had become a trainee sports reporter on the *Jewish Gazette*, moved into tabloid journalism, and then linked up with the music business after covering Michael Jackson's 1987 concert tour of Australia. He thereafter founded Oui 2 Entertainment, a publicity, marketing and events planning company, and having somehow developed links in post-Soviet Russia, started managing an Azerbaijani pop star, Emin Agalarov. Meanwhile, in 1996, the Trump Organisation bought the Miss Universe Pageant and ran the annual beauty contest until 2015. In 2013, they took the event to Moscow – and hired Goldstone and his company to help with its organisation, in part because Agalarov's billionaire father, Aras Agalarov, had agreed to host – and presumably help finance – the event. Hence the link between Goldstone and Trump was established.

The email chain, courtesy of the *New York Times*, revealed that, on 7 June 2016, Goldstone had emailed Donald Trump Jr to ask that he see Velnitskaya (whom he described as 'a Russian government attorney'). Goldstone added that he was acting on behalf of Agalarov, who wanted to help the Trump campaign by passing them some official documents and information which would damage Clinton. Trump Jr replied, somewhat unwisely, 'If it's what you say, I love it, especially later in the summer.' The meeting duly took place on 9 June in Trump Tower. As well as Velnitskaya, Goldstone attended, as did a former Russian intelligence officer named Rinat Akhmetshin.

This meeting has become the stuff of legend. Trump Jr described it as 'political opposition research' but also 'such a nothing . . . a wasted 20 minutes', on the grounds that Velnitskaya had provided nothing of value. One of the Russian participants alleged later that Velnitskaya had handed over a document, not about Hillary Clinton, but about 'violations of Russian law by a Democrat donor'. And Goldstone would say that the idea he was part of some Russian plot 'was the most ridiculous thing I've ever heard'. Personally, I rather bought into Goldstone's description: it was hard to imagine this particular group contributing anything of value. There were, however, plenty of voices in the media and among Democrats in Congress who saw the meeting as the smoking gun – the proof of attempted collusion between the Trump campaign and Russia. Democrat senator Mark Warner said: 'This is the first time that the public has seen clear evidence of senior members of the Trump campaign meeting Russians to try to obtain information that might hurt the campaign of Hillary Clinton.' The stories, and Congressional investigations, ran and ran, not least because of the shifting narratives emerging from those directly involved. And inevitably, within a few weeks, the Trump Tower dossier joined the growing pile of papers on Robert Mueller's desk.

Mueller got to work. The next eighteen months saw a succession of arrests and indictments. Fridays were the teaser. In August 2017, Mueller set up – 'empaneled' – a grand jury in Washington to work with his investigation. (Though the UK shares the common law system with the United States, we no longer use grand juries. But in the US system, a grand jury is empowered to subpoena documents, require witnesses to testify under oath, and issue indictments for criminal charges if probable cause is found.) Though its meetings were never announced, the belief around Washington was that Mueller's grand jury always and only met on Fridays. So, on most Fridays for the next eighteen months, there were expectations around town that another indictment was about to be announced. Those expectations were usually wrong. But not always: Mueller indicted thirty-four people – seven Americans, including five members of the Trump campaign, twenty-six Russians and one Dutch national – and three Russian organisations.

The first of these was Papadopoulos. He was arrested in late July 2017, and in October pleaded guilty to lying to the FBI about his contacts with Russian agents. Then on Monday 30 October, Paul Manafort and his long-time business associate and deputy campaign manager, Rick Gates, surrendered themselves to the FBI. The previous Friday, the grand jury had approved charges against them including conspiracy against the United States, money laundering, and working as unregistered foreign agents for Ukrainian clients. This was a huge story; after all, as campaign chairman, albeit for only a few months, Manafort must have talked frequently to Trump. The problem lay, however, in the small print: Manafort and Gates had been indicted for actions unrelated to the Trump campaign. Trump, for his part, said Manafort was 'only with the campaign for a very short period of time: I haven't spoken to him in a long time'.

Michael Flynn was next, pleading guilty on 1 December to lying to the FBI about his contacts with Russians. Thereafter, however, there was a pause, at least in terms of indictments of Americans: for the next seven months, it was all Russians. These were worth reporting, but nothing like as exciting as the indictment of well-known figures from the Washington social circuit. On 16 February 2018 Mueller indicted thirteen Russian nationals and three Russian companies for using social media to spread fake news, promote discord in the United States and engage in 'information warfare'; in short, for trying to affect the outcome of the US election. On 8 June, he indicted Manafort associate Konstantin Kilimnik. And on 13 July 2018 he indicted twelve Russian intelligence officers for hacking Democrat internal emails and then releasing them online.

Alongside all of this, there was a rich crop of Manafort stories. The more detail that emerged, the more colourful – and crooked – he appeared. Lots of people around Washington knew him and regaled me with their stories; they would conclude by shaking their heads and say 'we knew he'd gone to the dark side'. His accomplice, Gates, quickly did a deal with the prosecutors, giving evidence against Manafort in exchange for a reduced sentence himself. And the charges against Manafort mounted up. In the end, there were five counts of tax fraud, two counts of bank fraud, one count of failing to disclose a hidden foreign bank account and two counts of conspiracy. He was eventually found guilty on eight counts, including the conspiracy accusations, and sentenced to seven years in jail. He was initially sent to the Federal Correction Institution in Loretto, Pennsylvania, and is due for release in December 2024, potentially the end of Donald Trump's second term.

The stories about how Paul Manafort spent his money made even better copy. The federal prosecutors laid out his spending habits in court. He had seven houses, spread through New York and Virginia; and several cars, including three Land Rovers (nice that he bought British). He spent a scarcely believable $1 million on oriental rugs from a shop in Alexandria, a suburb of Washington bordering the Potomac. Where did he put them all? And then there were the clothes. He spent more than $1 million over five years on suits, jackets and shirts. On reading this, I found myself studying photographs of Manafort on his endless progress in and out of courtrooms. I really couldn't see anything special; the same creases and bulges as any other grey suit, usually matched with a tie that was just a touch too gaudy. And best of all, he owned a $15,000 ostrich-skin jacket. This was much photographed. It was a black bomber jacket with a white satin lining. Judging by the widely reproduced photographs, it looked worth all of $150.

Meanwhile, there was increasing speculation about whether the next Americans indicted might include a member of the Trump family, as a result of the Trump Tower meeting. Not for the first time, the speculation was wrong: the next domino to topple was Michael Cohen, the Trump Organisation lawyer and 'fixer' I had met in January 2017. He had been under investigation for months, for payments of hush money during the election campaign to women who claimed to have had affairs with Trump (this would have been, under America's complex campaign financing laws, an illegal use of campaign funds). The FBI raided his offices in April 2018, taking away some 700 paper files and close to 300,000 electronic files: on reading this I was reminded of the shelves full of papers I had seen in his office when I'd visited him. Cohen surrendered himself to the FBI on 21 August. He immediately pleaded guilty to five counts of tax evasion, one count of making false statements to a financial institution, one count of causing an unlawful corporate contribution, and one count of making an excessive campaign contribution for the purpose of influencing the election.

Cohen subsequently spent dozens of hours with the Mueller team; and he cooperated with New York State investigators in a separate case involving the Trump Foundation, a supposedly charitable body which turned out mostly to be giving money to itself. In December, he was sentenced to three years in prison. At around the same time, he also pleaded guilty to lying to the Senate and House Intelligence Committees about the 'Moscow Project', a proposition that concerned the building of a Trump-branded hotel in Moscow on which he had been leading for the Trump Organisation. Cohen had told the committees that the negotiations had ended in January 2016, when they had actually broken down in June 2016.

Roger Stone came next. A legendary figure with a chequered past, he had a long association with Republican politics, having worked on the campaigns of Richard Nixon, Ronald Reagan and Bob Dole. He had been a lobbyist, co-founding a Washington-based firm in 1980 with none other than Paul Manafort; the firm became notorious for representing Third World dictators like Mobuto Sese Seko of the

Congo and Ferdinand Marcos of the Philippines, leading them to be dubbed 'The Torturers' Lobby'. He was a champion purveyor of conspiracy theories, some of which he turned into books. For example, he published in 2013 a book alleging that Lyndon B. Johnson was behind a conspiracy to assassinate Kennedy; in 2014 a book alleging that John Dean, White House counsel during the Nixon presidency, had orchestrated the Watergate break-in to cover up his involvement in a prostitution ring; and in 2015 a book depicting Bill Clinton as a serial rapist and Hillary Clinton as an enabler. According to the writer and journalist Jeffrey Toobin, Stone described his political philosophy as 'admit nothing, deny everything, launch counter-attack'. A newspaper profile of Stone called him 'the boastful Black Prince of Republican sleaze'. And if all of this wasn't enough . . . he was a long-term friend of Donald Trump, and claimed to have planted in Trump's mind, as long ago as 1998, the thought that he could be President.

With all of this behind him, it is probably fair to assume that there was not a damp eye in the house when, on 25 January 2019, Stone was arrested at his home in Fort Lauderdale, Florida. The Mueller team had been investigating him for months, in particular with regard to allegations by associates of Stone that he had been collaborating with Julian Assange over the timing of the WikiLeaks dumps of Clinton campaign emails. Stone was charged with witness tampering, obstructing an official proceeding, and five counts of making false statements. He was convicted on all seven accounts on 15 November 2019. At the time of writing he awaits sentencing.

Exciting though it was to witness the settling of so many scores, Washington was still waiting for the indictment of a family member. And on 22 March, Mueller's 448-page report was handed to the Department of Justice and went straight to the attorney general, William Barr. Two days later, on 24 March, Barr wrote to Congress with his 'principal conclusions' from the report.

I vividly recall watching the live TV coverage, alongside the embassy political team, as Barr's letter was made public. There had essentially been two charges against the President: that his campaign had coordinated or conspired with the Russian government in its interference with the 2016 election; and that he had obstructed justice. On the collusion charge, the report concluded that, while the campaign had expected it would benefit electorally from information stolen and released through Russian efforts, the evidence of conspiracy didn't stack up. To quote in full the key paragraph:

The Russian contacts consisted of business connections, offers of assistance to the campaign, invitations for candidate Trump and Putin to meet in person, invitations for campaign officials and representatives of the Russian government to meet, and policy positions seeking improved US-Russian relations. While the investigation identified numerous links between individuals with ties to the Russian government and individuals associated with the Trump campaign, the evidence was not sufficient to support criminal charges. The investigation did not establish that members of the Trump campaign conspired or coordinated with the Russian government in its election interference activities.

As for obstruction of justice, the decisive words were:

Unlike cases in which a subject engages in obstruction of justice to cover up a crime, the evidence we obtained did not establish that the President was involved in an underlying crime related to Russian election interference.

Barr helped the obstruction issue over the line by asserting in his letter to Congress that he and the deputy attorney general had concluded that the evidence developed during the special counsel's investigation 'is not sufficient to establish that the President committed an obstruction of justice offence'.

We switched between TV channels as they each assessed the letter in real time. With the exception of Fox News, the disappointment was visible on every journalist's face. Their expressions said 'We've waited twenty-two months for this?' It was like the denouement of an Agatha Christie murder mystery in which, as Poirot assembles the suspects to reveal whodunnit, the victim walks in, miraculously revived: 'There was no murder!' And it turned into perhaps the best day of the Trump presidency. He hit the airwaves, and his Twitter feed, to claim total exoneration (not a word which appears in the report, but the victor gets to write the script).

A redacted version of the full report was issued on 18 April, whereupon it turned out that Barr had been highly selective in his summary. In particular, he had skimmed over a pointed passage which said:

> If we had confidence after a thorough investigation of the facts that the President clearly did not commit obstruction of justice, we would so state. Based on the facts and the applicable legal standards, however, we are unable to reach that judgement. The evidence we obtained about the President's actions and intent presents difficult issues that prevent us from conclusively determining that no criminal conduct occurred.

The Democrats, and some commentators, tried to make something of this; and some heavyweight legal analysts claimed that the Barr letter was a deliberate misrepresentation of the report. Mueller himself, according to the *New York Times*, wrote immediately to Barr, expressing his and his team's concerns that the attorney general had inadequately portrayed their conclusions. And the issue, and its handling, rumbled on for a few weeks. But really, it was all over; or at least that's what the opinion polls started to suggest about views around the country. It seemed as if the majority of Americans wanted to believe that Mueller had settled the issue; that he had delivered a clear verdict. Arguments that it was neither black nor white, but actually an ominous shade of grey, didn't interest them.

Back in the embassy, once we had done the immediate reporting, we reviewed how we had handled the story over the previous two and a half years. We had never predicted that it would bring Trump down; on the contrary, we had consistently foreshadowed the opposite. Even if it had reached the stage of impeachment proceedings, the Republican majority in the Senate would surely have saved him. But we had spent a lot of time tracking each development, each twist and turn: with hindsight, perhaps too much time. I recalled that, when I had visited Atlanta, Georgia, some eighteen months earlier, I had spent two hours over breakfast at the consul general's house with a group of locals involved in politics: party activists, journalists, political campaign consultants. Over that two hours, not a single one of them, neither Democrat nor Republican, had raised the Russia story, though it was on the front page of the *New York Times* and *Washington Post* every day. When, as the session was drawing to a close, I remarked on this, one of the guests said: 'That's just Washington stuff. There's always something like that going on. No one down here is interested.' Had we been trapped in a Washington echo chamber, while the rest of America got on with life?

As we kicked the question around, we concluded that we couldn't have risked ignoring the story. What if Mueller had concluded differently? He had clearly been deeply conflicted, especially over the obstruction issue. But in common with the entire US mainstream press and TV, and the rest of the Washington crowd, we had been drawn in, surfing along with them on a wave of bizarre revelations and Technicolor characters, coupled with the ever-present question: who will be next, and might it be someone you had dinner with last week? Also, there was a clue in the indictments. The Americans were being prosecuted for past crimes, for bank or tax fraud, for campaign finance violation, or for lying to the FBI. It was the attempted cover-up that did for some of them. No smoking gun was ever found, nor any incriminating message from the man himself. As he was fond of saying, 'I'm not an email person.'

All that said, there was some extraordinary stuff going on. The Mueller investigation found there were over a hundred contacts between Trump campaign advisers and individuals affiliated with the Russian government, before and after the election. The *New York Times* put the figure at 140. That is, by any measure, a lot of meetings and telephone calls; and it begs the question 'why?' What were they talking about, and to what end? Moreover, certain of the encounters were exceptionally reckless. For example, my Russian colleague Sergey Kislyak, thanks to his contacts with Flynn and Sessions, was at the centre of some of the stories. It shouldn't have been like that. Kislyak and I used to have lunch once a quarter, alternating between his residence and mine. They were interesting discussions. He was experienced, clever, and amusingly cynical. But I would always be accompanied by a senior member of the embassy, who would take copious notes which would be turned immediately into a report back to London. I noticed Kislyak was always accompanied too; I would have been offended if that hadn't been the case! Yet a group of the dodgiest Russians imaginable had been invited into Trump Tower, to meet members of the family, on the back of an email from a self-styled music publicist who was promising dirt on Hillary Clinton. In their shoes I think I might have put Mr Goldstone in touch with a junior member of the campaign team – perhaps the volunteer who answered the telephones – and suggested they meet at the local Starbucks. In short, at the very least, the Trump campaign were guilty of extraordinary naivety. Whether there was any more to it is one for the investigative reporters of the future.

Two more thoughts emerged from our discussion. The first was that we had underestimated the impact of the President's endless denunciations of the Mueller investigation. He called it 'a witch-hunt'. He would vent about it almost daily on Twitter, and in every encounter with the press. At the time, it just seemed like wallpaper – a line repeated so often that no one noticed it any more. With hindsight, it was highly effective, at least with his base. When I travelled outside Washington, especially in the South and the Midwest, I was struck by how many people believed the whole Russia investigation was a Washington conspiracy against a President whom the elite had never accepted. Had impeachment been pursued, it would have split America in half.

And finally, we realised that all of us – in the embassy, but arguably also in the wider Washington milieu – had missed the big point. We had been so distracted by allegations of collusion between the Trump campaign and Russia that we had risked missing the enormity of what the Russians had actually done. The Internet Research Agency, based in St Petersburg, and known to internet cognoscenti as a troll farm, had created thousands of social media accounts that purported to belong to Americans supporting radical political groups. They had planned or promoted events supporting Trump or opposing Clinton. They had reached millions of social media users in the run-up to the elections. Fabricated articles and disinformation had been spread from Russian government-controlled internet sites and promoted across these platforms. Computer hackers affiliated with Russian military intelligence had broken into the Democratic National Committee's email systems and released what they had found on WikiLeaks during the election campaign. The Mueller investigation concluded that Russian interference had been 'sweeping and systematic' and had 'violated US criminal law'.

Why did the Russians interfere? Absent some political explosion in Moscow and a turning out of the archives, we are unlikely ever to know the truth. There will always be speculation about Trump's dealings with Russia. But for me, the likeliest theory is that in part they really didn't want Hillary Clinton as President: anyone but her. They knew her well from her time as Secretary of State and hadn't liked what they had seen. And in part, it was because they could. Putin's formative years had been in the KGB. He knew what they could do, and believed in using their skills and capabilities. Once a KGB man, always a KGB man.

We will also never know how decisive an impact this Russian activity had on the election outcome. Hillary Clinton has occasionally said that she lost the election because of Russian interference. Donald Trump says the opposite. It was an extraordinarily close race, determined by 70,000 votes across three states. But were people influenced by what they read on social media: who can say? What is unarguable, however, is that this was a ruthless and shocking attempt to interfere with a democratic process. If systematically repeated in future elections around the world, it might discredit democracy for a generation. So it was an exceptionally serious act of disruption. And those of us living in democratic countries do not yet know how to respond. Whether we should be turning to collective expulsions and sanctions, or should try to kill the problem at source with a technical solution, denying this sort of material an internet platform through some clever algorithm, we need to find an answer soon.

12

The Conduct of the Presidency

*

'We are drifting dangerously close to an imperial presidency that exists above and outside the rules we thought were designed to prevent such an occurrence'
— New York Times, 12 May 2019

*

MY FIRST encounter with Jared Kushner, up in Trump Tower during the transition, was not a success. The second went better. He and Ivanka Trump came to a small dinner at the residence. Kushner had by then been in the White House for a few months. We talked about his extraordinarily wide portfolio; he could basically intervene on anything. We had a more constructive conversation about the Middle East. And he said something that stayed with me: 'We're businessmen and we're going to do things differently.'

Few truer words have ever been spoken. No one in recent history – maybe ever – has run the US presidency like Donald Trump. From the every-man-for-himself White House, through the war with the media, via his revolving-door cabinet, to his highly personalised diplomacy, and most of all his casually intermittent relationship with facts, he has done it his way. Before the Trump experience, most of us with a career in public service behind us would have said that it was impossible to run a government in such a manner; that it would fall apart and the men in grey suits would move in and engineer a more conventional leader. But as Donald Trump enters the final year of his first term, few observers would rule out his getting re-elected. So what's the story here?

It has to start with the unprecedented inexperience of both the President and his team. They had mounted a successful hostile takeover of the Republican Party. But none of the senior figures had ever served a day in government. Some of them had at least done time in politics: Stephen Miller had been a staffer for Senator Sessions; Kellyanne Conway had run her own political consultancy. But most of the main figures were from the private sector: Steve Bannon, Gary Cohn and Steve Mnuchin from Goldman Sachs; Jared Kushner and the President himself from real estate. Moreover, far from worrying about this lack of familiarity with public administration, they exulted in it, and they were highly suspicious of advice from career officials on how things should be done.

They didn't just not know *how* to get things done. They didn't really know *who* to hire either. Any new President has to fill roughly 4,000 politically appointed positions, of which around 1,200 require Senate approval. The Republicans had last been in charge of the White House under George W. Bush, from 2000 to 2008. So there should have been a pool of experienced and talented individuals with relatively recent experience of government available to the new administration. The problem was that, in reaction to some of the inflammatory and divisive rhetoric of the Trump campaign, many had signed 'Never Trump' letters saying they would not serve under Trump. Chris Christie, moreover, while leading the transition team, had put together a comprehensive list of possible senior appointees; but that had been binned when Christie was fired immediately after the election. And to complicate the task further, the Trump team, from the top downwards, didn't know many people – and yet set great store by loyalty. So those comparatively few Republicans who had declared early for Trump, when no one thought he could win, were first in line for cabinet jobs. As for the rest, the Trump team were either combing through the rightward fringes of the Republican Party, going outside politics completely, or leaving jobs empty. And with each unknown that they put forward for a senior post, they were running the risk of not getting Senate approval.

The result was that a lot of jobs remained unfilled. And many of the early appointments that *were* made didn't work out. National Security Adviser Michael Flynn was fired after three weeks. By the end of September 2017, eight and a half months in, Katie Walsh had resigned as White House deputy chief of staff; K. T. McFarland as deputy national security adviser; Michael Dubke as White House director of communications; and Sean Spicer had resigned as White House press secretary. Reince Priebus had been fired as White House chief of staff, Steve Bannon as White House senior strategist, Sebastian Gorka as deputy assistant to the President. And Tom Price had resigned as health and human services secretary in the wake of a string of stories about ethics violations.

Then there was the Anthony Scaramucci episode. Scaramucci was another larger-than-life figure from the Technicolor world of Donald Trump. An Italian-American, he started his banking career with Goldman Sachs, then founded his own investment firm Sky Bridge Capital. He also dabbled in politics, fundraising for Barack Obama in 2008, but falling out with the Democrats over what he saw as excessive regulation of Wall Street. Having joined the Republicans, he was national finance co-chair for Mitt Romney's 2012 presidential campaign. And in the 2016 race, he started by endorsing Wisconsin Governor Scott Walker, then backed Jeb Bush – while, on the Fox Business TV network, calling Trump a 'hack politician whose rhetoric is anti-American and very, very, divisive'. Nevertheless, he eventually signed on to Trump's campaign by joining the Trump finance committee. His reward, initially, was nomination as assistant to the President and director of the White House Office of Public Liaison and Intergovernmental Affairs. The nomination, however, somehow got blocked in the system, and by March someone else had been appointed. Scaramucci would tell me later that because of a longstanding feud, Reince Priebus had vetoed it; Priebus would always deny this. And in June Scaramucci was given the consolation prize of chief strategy officer for the US Export-Import Bank.

Meanwhile, Scaramucci started appearing regularly on the news channels, defending Donald Trump's performance as President. The media was already established as a prime route into senior office: many of the replacements for the first round of senior casualties had been recruited from the Fox News bench of pundits. Scaramucci was actually rather good at it, living up to his name (*scaramuccia*, in Italian, means 'little skirmisher'). And there was unquestionably a need for better surrogates for the President. Some of those speaking for him sounded unhinged. Others looked weird, like the customers at the bar on planet Tatooine, at the edge of the galaxy in *Star Wars*. Yet others seemed to be in a permanent towering rage. Scaramucci looked the part: he never lost his temper; he was coherent, measured, and came across as a member of the human race. So it was no surprise, to me at least, when on 21 July 2017 he was appointed to the post, by that stage vacant for four months, of White House communications director. The unexpected twist was in the small print; Scaramucci would report directly to the President, not to Chief of Staff Priebus. Sean Spicer resigned the same day; the *New York Times* reported that he – and Priebus – had vehemently objected to Scaramucci's appointment. Within a day or two, a photograph appeared in the national press showing Priebus and Scaramucci staring at each other in the Oval Office. This was, even in grainy newsprint, an image that shouted Mutually Assured Loathing. If body language could kill, both would have been corpses.

It couldn't last – and it didn't. On 26 July, Scaramucci spoke to Ryan Lizza of the *New Yorker* about his White House colleagues. He said of Priebus that he was a leaker; and more colourfully, that he was a 'f***ing paranoid schizophrenic'. He then said, in comparing himself to Steve Bannon, that 'I'm not trying to suck my own c***; I'm not trying to build my own brand off the f***ing strength of the President.' Throughout, he failed to say that the conversation was 'off-the-record', arguably a rather basic mistake for a communications director. As it happened, Priebus was doomed anyway, with Trump telling him he wanted a new chief of staff: Priebus resigned on 28 July. Trump then appointed General John Kelly, formerly secretary for homeland security, as his new chief of staff; and three days later, on 31 July, Kelly fired Scaramucci. This meant Scaramucci had served six days (though appointed on 21 July, he hadn't actually started until 25 July). It made Michael Flynn's twenty-four days seem like a lifetime.

I later got to know Anthony Scaramucci. I had lunch with him. He came to a couple of receptions at the residence. He was good value: smart, outspoken, knowledgeable, entertaining, scabrous. Time passed quickly in his company. And in 2019, he performed a remarkable pirouette. On 3 July, he tweeted that Trump would win forty-plus states in 2020. By the middle of August, he had become, as he continues to be, one of the President's most vocal public critics – prompted, he says, by Trump's attacks on Democratic women of colour and a misplayed Trump visit to meet the victims of a mass shooting in El Paso, Texas.

Back in the White House, the revolving door continued to spin. By the end of the year, two more had gone: Dina Powell from her post as deputy national security adviser and Omarosa Manigault (whose main claim to fame was her appearance on Trump's *The Apprentice* TV show – which she didn't even win) from her mysterious job as director of communications in the White House Office of Public Liaison.

More followed in 2018. Rob Porter, White House staff secretary, left in February, in the wake of accusations of domestic abuse from two ex-wives. David Sorensen, one of the White House speechwriting team, left two days later, also following domestic abuse stories. Later that month, the comparatively long-serving Hope Hicks, who had succeeded Anthony Scaramucci as communications director, resigned. On 6 March, Gary Cohn resigned as White House chief economic adviser. And then, on 13 March, the big one: Secretary of State Rex Tillerson was fired. According to a leak, Tillerson had, in an internal meeting a few months earlier, called the President 'a f***ing moron'. Whether he actually said this or not, Tillerson afterwards conspicuously failed to deny it, instead simply refusing to comment. So his days had been numbered for a while. But firing your Secretary of State is still something.

And the door continued to revolve. General H. R. McMaster, Flynn's successor as national security adviser, a highly decorated

Afghanistan veteran, a close contact, an excellent official and a good friend of the UK, resigned later in March 2018, to be replaced by ultra-hawk John Bolton. David Shulkin, secretary for veteran affairs, was fired six days later, in the wake of accusations of ethics breaches. (One of these offences seemed to be that he and his wife had paid an official visit to London, staying on afterwards at government expense in order to attend the Wimbledon tennis tournament; when I heard this I guiltily recalled telling Shulkin a few months earlier how wonderful an event Wimbledon was!) Joe Hagin resigned as White House deputy chief of staff in June. Scott Pruitt, administrator of the Environmental Protection Agency, resigned in July, having been accused of a series of ethics scandals. Marc Short, White House director of legislative affairs, also stepped down in July. Don McGahn resigned as White House counsel in August, Nikki Haley as UN ambassador in October. Jeff Sessions was fired as attorney general in November, and deputy national security adviser Mira Ricardel was fired the same month. John Kelly stepped down as chief of staff in December and Ryan Zinke resigned as secretary of the interior five days later, also for ethics violations. And then, just before Christmas, another big-name casualty: defense secretary and war hero Jim Mattis resigned in protest at the President's decision to withdraw US forces from Syria (though the President claimed Mattis was about to be fired anyway). Bill Shine, the Fox News executive, and the fourth to sit in the director of communications chair, left in March 2019. Kirstjen Neilsen resigned as Homeland Security secretary in April. Sarah Huckerbee Sanders stepped down as White House press spokesperson in June. And Patrick Shanahan resigned as acting Secretary of Defense later that month.

This turnover was without precedent in recent political history. Both Ronald Reagan and Bill Clinton got through a lot of staff in their first terms, but neither spilt anything like this volume of blood. And the appearance of chaotic infighting was exacerbated by the way many of these departures were signalled in advance. Stories would appear in the media saying that the President was dissatisfied with a particular cabinet secretary's performance, or that he was consulting friends (often outside the White House) about whether he should replace someone. And once these stories appeared, though it could take months, the individual concerned was always doomed. A lot of the apparently self-generated resignations were actually of individuals who saw the writing on the wall.

The net result of all these hirings and firings was that, after just two and a half years in office, Trump was on his third national security adviser; his third chief of staff; his fifth director of communications; his third White House press spokesperson; and his fourth secretary for Homeland Security – to highlight just some of the changes. Moreover, some posts were occupied for prolonged periods by 'acting' officials – even roles as senior as defense secretary, Homeland Security secretary and attorney general. All of this must have played havoc with the business of government; no sooner would a department have briefed a new secretary than he or she was on the way out of the door. For us in the embassy, it made one of the pillars of the bilateral relationship really difficult to manage. We wanted every British cabinet minister to be on good personal terms with his or her US counterpart. Most members of the cabinet would come through at least once a year – the Chancellor, the Foreign Secretary and the Defence Secretary rather more often. But we were increasingly asking ourselves whether we should advise a busy minister to cross the Atlantic if we believed their counterpart was about to be fired. I remember writing to one private office to say, 'We would, of course, welcome the Secretary of State coming to Washington: but we are hearing that the President is unhappy about the performance of the current Homeland Security secretary and is looking for a replacement; so you might want to wait.' And of course, we knew that, once we had made the call and dispatched that advice, it was more or less guaranteed that the individual at risk would manage to cling on for a few more months.

The revolving door was, however, just one of the several unusual features of the new administration. There was so much more, starting with the lack of structure and teamwork inside the White House – a situation otherwise known as 'the White House wars'. The President himself had run his business with an exceptionally flat management structure: everyone answered to him. If the usual bureaucracy was a pyramid, with the CEO at the top, then the Trump Organisation was a spider's web, with Trump himself at the centre, no real deputy, and all the senior figures reporting direct to him. He wanted to run the White House in the same way. Moreover, everyone was a senior adviser or a chief strategist, but almost no one had a clear, specified portfolio. So it sometimes seemed to us outsiders that everyone was doing everything (or perhaps nothing). Moreover, I was told that, as with Theresa May's meeting with the President, all the senior figures were going to every meeting on every subject – because Priebus was allowing unrestricted access to the President, and no one wanted to risk not being there when a decision was actually taken. There was also a daily contest to be the last person to see Trump at the end of the working day – because there was then a good chance of being invited up to supper in the private apartment and getting the President's ear for a couple of hours. Whatever else, it can't have helped their work–life balance.

And then there was the war between the globalists and the nationalists. When I had accompanied Foreign Secretary Boris Johnson to Trump Tower, I had noticed a certain tension between Jared Kushner and Steve Bannon; not in terms of their actually quarrelling in front of us, but in the way Bannon had looked so dismissive of everything Kushner was saying. Within a few weeks in the White House, this tension had turned into open warfare. And it was no surprise: Kushner was at the time essentially a New York Democrat; Bannon saw himself as a standard bearer for the 'alternative right' movement and the beating heart of the 'new populism' which he believed would sweep across Western democracies. So they must have disagreed about pretty much everything. Kushner, however, had a crucial advantage – he was family and couldn't be fired. Not so Bannon. The White House essentially divided between the two camps, and they waged battle on just about every policy issue.

And simply everything leaked. The *Washington Post* and the *New York Times* would write about the White House wars every day, usually claiming between a dozen and twenty separate sources. They sometimes had more material than they could process, with their White House sources queuing and climbing over each other to make sure their version of events was included in the next day's story. The sources would also get personal, briefing against each other, or claiming that the President was about to act against someone on the other side of the argument. One of the top White House journalists told me that, so bountiful were the backstabbing briefings, he had needed to set up a queuing system on his phone: 'If you want to brief against Priebus, press one; against Bannon press two; against Kushner, press three.' I think he was speaking only partly in jest.

It couldn't last; and it didn't. I remember in particular my last meeting with Steve Bannon. I saw him in his cramped White House office in the middle of June, just a few days after Theresa May had lost her majority in the UK general election. He was scathing about her tactics: 'You work with what you've got, and never believe the opinion polls.' His office walls were covered in large whiteboards, on each of which he had written Trump campaign promises, annotated with progress reports. To change the subject from the Prime Minister's problems, I asked him how it was going. He claimed that Trump was delivering like no President in US history. He talked about how, in Trump's wake, a populist wave would vanquish the mainstream parties in Europe, with Le Pen's Front National and Alternative for Germany leading the way. And I asked him how he was faring in his war with the globalists; he said, 'I can look after myself in a knife fight – can they?' Two months later, in August, he was gone. Someone in the White House briefed anonymously that the last straw for the President had been Bannon's photograph adorning the cover of an edition of *Time* magazine under the headline 'The Great Manipulator'.

To add another layer of complexity to the picture, while individuals in the White House were providing their chosen journalists with the juiciest, most colourful copy imaginable about their internal battles, the White House as an institution, led by the President and abetted by his press team, was engaged in total war with the mainstream media. In my time in diplomacy, all the Prime Ministers for whom I have worked, and all the US Presidents I have observed, have had an edgy relationship with the media. It is, in a way, inevitable; each needs the other but neither believes it is being treated fairly. The media think they are constantly misled, fed spin and sometimes deliberate untruths; the politicians think that facts and narrative are twisted, and context avoided, in order to produce critical coverage. Tony Blair, for whom I worked for three years as Europe adviser, had as benign an attitude to the press as any leader I have come across. But in one of his final speeches as Prime Minister, he accused the media of 'hunting as a pack', of being 'like a feral beast just tearing people and reputations to bits' and of having 'a seriously adverse impact on the way public life is conducted'.

No one I ever came across, however, had quite the sense of burning injustice that seemed to live inside Donald Trump. The relationship with the media had already deteriorated in the second half of his campaign. But once he was in office, it became still more toxic. He raged daily by tweet against the media: sometimes individual journalists, sometimes entire organisations. He had two particular feuds: with Jeff Bezos of Amazon, owner of the *Washington Post*; and with the *New York Times*, his hometown newspaper, because in his eyes it was the closest thing America had to a national newspaper and they never treated him as a local boy made good. But everyone was a potential target – even Fox News if they headlined unfavourable polls or gave airtime to the Democratic primaries. He also, over the first two years of his presidency, stripped away the structures through which successive Presidents had communicated with the press. The daily news briefing, traditionally conducted five days a week by the White House press spokesperson, took place only intermittently and then dwindled to almost nothing. And rather than formal press conferences, the President preferred an impromptu gathering on the White House lawn; a free-for-all where penned-in journalists shouted questions at him and he chose the ones he wanted to answer. As for one-to-one interviews, he abandoned the practice of spreading himself equally between the three main TV networks and spoke almost exclusively to Fox News, sometimes phoning them unbidden in the middle of their morning show.

All of this made the job of White House press spokesperson, one of the most high-profile in any US administration, a nightmare. After Sean Spicer walked away, Sarah Huckabee Sanders, the daughter of former Governor of Arkansas Mike Huckabee, took over, and was initially given good reviews by the White House press corps. She was also a good friend to the embassy, going out of her way to help us whenever she could. And it became clear when she and her husband came to dinner that they were transparently decent people. But her relationship with the media became tetchy and combative and, eventually, embittered, on both sides. As a former spokesman myself, I could see how those daily televised press confer- ences from the White House podium, those jousting matches between Sanders and the media, were becoming unworkable: so many of the questions that were being posed were impossible to answer truthfully without damaging the President. Sarah eventually walked away in June 2019. I was surprised she lasted so long.

One of the substitutes for the daily briefing was the President's Twitter feed. There is no doubt that, for Trump, it was and is an exceptionally effective way of communicating with his base: direct, immediate and unfiltered. But it wasn't the only purpose for which Trump employed Twitter. He also used it as an assault weapon against his critics. And it seemed to become a sort of pressure valve – a route through which he could rage and vent against the injustices to which, in his eyes, he was subjected daily. We rapidly came to learn that there were two modes of Trump tweeting. During White House working hours, when his staffers were around him, he tended to tweet about what he and the administration were doing – announcements in the pipeline, decisions taken, hirings and firings. But tweets late at night, or in the early hours of the morning, when he was by himself, were pure, raw Trump, and could be about anything, including what he was at that moment watching on TV. It was, moreover, possible to gauge his mood – just how angry he was – from the quantity and tone of his tweets through the long watches of the night. When he was really wound up, it was a torrent.

The tweets could be funny – sometimes intentionally, sometimes not. Among so much material it is hard to pick out a handful. But when, in 2018, there was a spate of stories questioning his mental health, he tweeted that, 'Actually, throughout my life, my two greatest assets have been mental stability and being, like, really

really smart . . . I went from VERY successful business man to top TV star to President of the United States (on my first try). I think that would qualify as not smart, but genius . . . and a very stable genius at that.' At the low point of his clash with Kim Jong-Un, he tweeted: 'North Korean leader Kim Jong Un just stated that the nuclear button is on his desk at all times. Will someone from his depleted and food starved regime please inform him that I too have a nuclear button, but it is a much bigger and more powerful one than his, and my button works!' And in the course of a long feud with the Republican senator for Tennessee, Bob Corker, Trump tweeted that Corker had 'helped President Obama give us the bad Iran deal, couldn't get elected dogcatcher in Tennessee, and is now fighting tax cuts'. Corker responded, 'Same untruths from an utterly untruthful President . . . #AlertTheDayCareStaff.' And the vice president of the National Animal Care and Control Association, one Robert Leinberger Jr, complained that President Trump's pejorative use of 'dogcatcher' was divisive and derogatory: 'it's not a proper representation of what we do . . . it's a profession now and people have to go through training . . .'.

In amongst all this mayhem, however, the President didn't completely ignore the traditional media. A couple of Fox News presenters became close to Trump – almost attaining the status of unofficial advisers. Both did the evening shows, which were less about news, more about comment. Both had something of the Howard Stern shock jock about them. One was New York-based Sean Hannity. The other, Tucker Carlson, lived near Washington, so we invited him along to lunch at the residence. He didn't deny that he talked regularly to the President. And in private, in contrast to his public reputation, he was measured, thoughtful and insightful.

There were also some journalists who flourished despite working for publications Trump appeared to hate. Three in particular stood out. Robert Costa of the *Washington Post* had covered the Trump campaign and, at least while I was in DC, acquired stories on the internal dynamics in the White House that no one else was getting – not least because the President would sometimes phone him direct. The brilliant Maggie Haberman of the *New York Times* had come from the hard school of New York tabloid journalism, where she had first come across Trump. The President would periodically heap abuse on her via Twitter; but he would also give her occasional access, and Maggie's sources and insight were peerless. And the new kid on the block was an Australian, Jonathan Swan, who started on the Hill, a Washington-based political website, but made his name on Axios, the instantly fashionable and successful news website launched in 2016 by a group of ex-Politico journalists.

Swan in particular gifted the world an understanding of how the President spent his day. There had long been stories about lack of structure and absence of access control. General Kelly, when chief of staff, had tried to change this, demanding as a condition of taking on the job the right to decide who could see the President and when. He also tried to bring some order and process to the task of briefing Trump: no more notes slipped to the President containing a single staffer's ideas or analysis. But it turned out that Trump didn't really want order, process and structure. He didn't want a diary full of formal meetings. He wanted to freewheel. He wanted to be able to decide, spontaneously, hour by hour, what he was going to do next. And there was no corralling the two family members who worked in the White House. I used to see a lot of John Kelly because, like me, he started early, so was always available for a 7 a.m. breakfast. I recall that he was hosting me once in the White House dining room, for an excellent cheese and ham omelette, when Jared Kushner walked in with guests. As he and Kelly gazed at one another, the temperature in the room dropped instantly by about ten degrees. And after about eighteen months in the job, a frustrated Kelly walked, his relationship with Trump wrecked.

The Swan story was based on an extraordinary leak. Someone inside the White House gave him three months of presidential daily schedules – from 7 November 2018 to 1 February 2019. These revealed that of the total of roughly 500 hours covered by the schedules, the President had spent 77 hours in meetings; 51 hours travelling; 38 hours in events; 39 hours having lunch; and no less than 297 hours doing something called 'Executive Time'. Though he rose early – often before 6 a.m. – he didn't usually arrive in the

The only photo I have of my mother and me, in Nairobi, Kenya, 1956.

The schoolhouse where my brother and I lived with our grandmother on our return from Kenya.

My father in front of his pride and joy, an MG Magnet, with me leaning out of the rear window.

My brother and I standing in front of a dormobile, on holiday in Cornwall, summer of 1964. Note the clothing appropriate to a Cornish summer.

Vanessa and I at Durham University. Photo taken in
the tiny garden of the miner's cottage on Mavin Street
where she was living.

Opposite: Receiving
the knighthood.

A group of university friends on a weekend away in London,
visiting Hampton Court. From the left, Lou Hazel, Mike
Wigglesworth, Lyn Clohosy, Vanessa, Nigel Graham and
me (wearing a scarf knitted by Vanessa!).

Opposite: With Tony Blair
at a European Council, 2007.
I was European Policy Adviser.

Signing a national security agreement with
the Singapore government in front of Prime
Ministers David Cameron and Lee Hsien Loong.

Attending talks between David Cameron
and Barack Obama during my National
Security Adviser days.

The imposing British Residence in Washington, seen from the garden. Designed by Edwin Lutyens, completed in 1928. It wasn't always extolled. In 1930, Sir Ronald Lindsay was the first to live there, before construction had been completed. His wife complained to Lutyens: 'We are dizzy with confusion, deafened by noise, poisoned by flies, exasperated by ineptitudes and overrun by rats.' If these problems existed, they have been solved.

The near-nightly ritual of remarks from the podium at the Residence.

The photo with Obama that went briefly viral. It's not that bad, is it?

My family with Obama. Rachel, our American daughter-in-law, second from the left, is looking suitably excited at meeting her hero.

A selfie at the Capitol on Inauguration Day.

So was the crowd bigger than Obama's? Definitely not!

The first meeting between Donald Trump and Theresa May, January 2017. Note the Churchill bust on the side table behind Trump. Within six months, most of the participants shown in the photo – Reince Priebus and Michael Flynn on the US side, and Fiona Hill and Nick Timothy on the UK side – were gone.

Talking to Senator for Texas Ted Cruz at our Inauguration Week Reception on 18 January 2017.

Greeting the President at the annual House Speaker's lunch to celebrate St Patrick's Day.

Talking to Madeleine Albright at a reception.

A conversation with Kellyanne Conway – always fun!

Accompanying Foreign Secretary Boris Johnson through the US Capitol building after calling on Senate Majority Leader Senator Mitch McConnell.

Shaking hands (again) with the President at the talks at Chequers during his 2018 visit to the UK.

Moments before the Blenheim Palace dinner for the President.

A surprise encounter with Carole King at a Residence reception. Carole, you've got a friend.

A black tie dinner at the Residence for Sir David Attenborough to mark the launch of his Netflix documentary series *Our Planet*.

Calling on Joe Biden in his Washington offices, early 2019.

President Trump inspecting the Guard of Honour at his official welcome ceremony for his state visit, Buckingham Palace, 3 June 2019.

State visit: The First Lady, Her Majesty The Queen and the President.

Kennedy and MacMillan, Reagan and Thatcher, Bush and Blair... Trump and Johnson? The Prime Minister and the President at the Biarritz G7 Summit, August 2019.

The President's characterful Twitter account.

The wacky Ambassador that the U.K. foisted upon the United States is not someone we are thrilled with, a very stupid guy. He should speak to his country, and Prime Minister May, about their failed Brexit negotiation, and not be upset with my criticism of how badly it was...

Donald J. Trump @realDonaldTrump
12:48am - 9 Jul 2019

...handled. I told @theresa_may how to do that deal, but she went her own foolish way-was unable to get it done. A disaster! I don't know the Ambassador but have been told he is a pompous fool. Tell him the USA now has the best Economy & Military anywhere in the World, by far...

Donald J. Trump @realDonaldTrump
12:48am - 9 Jul 2019

....and they are both only getting bigger, better and stronger.....Thank you, Mr. President!

Donald J. Trump @realDonaldTrump
12:48am - 9 Jul 2019

Peter Brookes' take on my resignation, from *The Times.*

. Downtime: sailing with some friends on the Chesapeake.

Monty and Pico enjoying Residence life.

At our son's wedding in 2016. Our daughter Georgina and her partner David O'Callaghan are on the left; on the right is our son Simon and his wife Rachel Racicot.

Oval Office until around 11 a.m. Instead, he spent those hours in his private quarters watching the news channels, scanning the newspapers, and making phone calls – to White House staffers, but also to members of Congress, to contacts in the media, and to his business, showbiz and golfing friends. As for Executive Time, it was used for 'concealed meetings' – there were apparently some encounters that were kept hidden from the majority of White House staff. But it was mostly more of the same: more phone calls; more talking to staffers; impromptu spur-of-the-moment meetings; and more watching of the news channels – the President insisted that there be TVs in every room he frequented. On one day – the day after the 2018 midterm elections – he had one thirty-minute meeting with his chief of staff and seven hours of Executive Time. The media turned to the presidential historians, who universally thought this was all pretty odd. The White House did the only thing it could, given that the story was impossible to deny: brazen it out. Sarah Huckabee Sanders issued a statement saying that 'President Trump has a different leadership style than his prede-cessors and the results speak for themselves.' She added that the schedules were designed to allow 'for a more creative environment that has helped make him the most productive President in modern history'.

This 'creative' environment didn't only serve the President. In one of the more extraordinary stories of Trump's first term, Michael Wolff, a freelance journalist and writer, was given months of access to the White House in the administration's first year so that he could write a book about the President. Wolff himself said that Trump had proposed the book because he had liked an article Wolff had written about him in the *Hollywood Reporter*; Trump has denied this and has said that he never spoke to Wolff about a book, let alone author-ised access. Other reports suggest it was Steve Bannon's idea. Whichever, Wolff seemingly hung out in the White House for most of 2017, conducting by his own account more than two hundred interviews and watching events unfold. The working title for his book was apparently 'The Great Transition: The First 100 Days of the Trump Administration'; the book was eventually published on

5 January 2018 under the rather more enticing title, *Fire and Fury: Inside the Trump White House*, and was an instant publishing sensation, topping the best-seller lists for weeks. It told a lurid tale of presidential tantrums, chaotic processes, and Steve Bannon's low regard for Jared Kushner. Trump tweeted: 'Michael Wolff is a total loser who made up stories in order to sell this really boring and untruthful book. He used Sloppy Steve Bannon, who cried when he got fired and begged for his job. Now Sloppy Steve has been dumped like a dog by almost everyone. Too bad!' (Trump clearly has a thing about dogs.) Wolff for his part claimed that '100% of the people around him' believed Trump unfit for office. Everyone in Washington read the book. And it felt authentic, even if not everything in it actually happened.

There was one further feature of the Trump presidency that broke the mould in a highly visible way. He shunned the fixtures of the Washington social calendar: the Alfalfa, Gridiron and White House Correspondents' dinners, and the autumn Kennedy Center Honors. In skipping these events, he broke precedent with his predecessors, especially in relation to the world-famous White House Correspondents': although Nixon and Carter had missed a couple each, and Reagan missed one (with the reasonable excuse that he was recovering from an attempted assassination), Trump was the first President almost since the event's creation to make a public point of never going. This was in part about his feud with the mainstream media; in announcing his non-attendance, he tweeted that the event was negative and boring. But it also reflected a long-term grudge against the event, dating back to his attendance at the 2011 edition, when he was lampooned mercilessly from the podium by both Obama and the comedian Seth Meyers. The cameras homed in on him looking stony-faced. As for the Kennedy Center awards, these were given annually to half a dozen artists – singers, dancers, musicians, composers, actors – in recognition of careers of exceptional distinction. The recipients were given lunch at the White House and a grand black-tie gala evening was held for them at the Kennedy Center, attended by the President. I knew a member of the organising committee, who told me of their efforts to persuade the President to attend. Trump said to them that the problem with the awards was that they always seemed to go to artists who had spoken publicly against him, never to those who supported him.

The fixture Trump did attend, presumably in recognition of the evangelical portion of his base, was the National Prayer Breakfast. But he took a little time to adjust to the pace of this particular wicket. On his first appearance, he arrived at the podium in front of an expectant crowd, congratulated the previous speakers, then said he had been looking at the audience figures for the *Celebrity Apprentice* TV show under his successor Arnold Schwarzenegger; and they were terrible: 'down the tubes, a total disaster'. So the audience should 'pray for Arnold, for his ratings'. The clip went viral. The media feigned outrage at the 'inappropriateness' of the comment. And Schwarzenegger responded within a couple of hours, commenting that since Trump was so good at gaining TV ratings, they should swap jobs: Trump should go back on *The Apprentice* and he would take over as President, so that the American people 'could sleep more easily'.

To complete the picture, I gained a couple of personal insights into the freewheeling nature of life in the Trump White House. On one occasion I took into the White House a British expert on a country of major strategic importance – a country, moreover, where we had particular access and insights that US experts couldn't match. We saw the relevant specialists in the National Security Council. And then, to our astonishment, my colleague was asked, 'Would you be prepared to brief the President? He would be interested.' Before he could even contemplate suggesting that he might not be sufficiently senior, I jumped in instantly to say, 'Yes of course'; and within about fifteen minutes we were ushered into the Oval Office. I thought we might be put at the back of the room or at the end of a table. Instead, we were shown to two chairs directly opposite the President, who was sitting behind the famous Resolute desk, a gift from Queen Victoria to President Rutherford B. Hayes in 1880, built from the timbers of HMS *Resolute*, the British Arctic exploration ship. Vice President Pence was off to the President's right-hand side, while everyone else – there must have been a dozen in the room – was seated around the edge of the room, like wallflowers at a programme dance.

The meeting lasted about half an hour. The President was friendly, informal, and seemed genuinely interested. He asked a series of questions about the political and economic situation in the country in question. And then he started asking me about Brexit, on which he seemed well informed. I had to give him the official position, which was that everything was going to plan (it wasn't – the Prime Minister was meeting serious resistance in Parliament). He listened politely, but was visibly sceptical. It prompted me to wonder who in the White House was briefing him on the subject.

The experience was repeated about nine months later; same British expert, same impromptu invitation to spend a few minutes with the President. But it panned out somewhat differently. We were taken to the anteroom to the Oval Office. But the door was shut, with the previous meeting still going on. I expected to be taken back to the waiting room. But we were allowed to stand there. Minutes passed. And I could hear the sound of loud, angry voices through the door – one voice in particular. I could only pick up the odd phrase, notably the words 'I have just had it with him'. It continued for perhaps eight or nine minutes, and it sounded lively. Eventually, the door opened and the White House press team emerged, together with Kellyanne Conway. Kellyanne looked unflustered – just a normal day. The others looked a bit shaken.

As we were shown in, I wondered in what mood we would find the President. The answer was . . . apparently completely normal. He was welcoming, and seemed relaxed. The only clue that he might be preoccupied was the speed with which we were in and out of the door. A few questions to my expert colleague, a few more questions to me about Brexit, and we were done, in about a quarter of an hour.

In my reporting to London, I tried to capture the flavour of this profoundly different White House: the *Apprentice*-style near-weekly firings, the medieval court atmospherics with internal feuding straight out of *Game of Thrones*, the war with the media, the permanent day-to-day unpredictability. In particular, I warned London that they shouldn't expect the traditional level of interaction and consultation before big decisions were made: we shouldn't take this personally, as it simply wasn't in Trump's makeup. Once he had taken a position, he wanted it out there immediately. This made, I argued, regular prime ministerial phone calls to the President all the more important, just to find out what was on his mind; to catch him before his mind was made up. And we counselled that phone calls with the President generally went better if they weren't just about business; he liked to shoot the breeze, especially on US domestic politics.

We in the embassy also put a lot of thought into how to influence the administration. Trump wasn't a man who easily, if ever, changed his mind. As he was fond of saying, he trusted his gut – and his (somewhat incomplete) world view. Our first thought was that the terms in which you made an argument were crucial. This was still at root an 'America First' President. We had a whole lot more traction with him if, rather than saying 'please help us with this', we could say 'do this and it's a win for you'. We also were hearing that, while once he'd decided, he was almost immovable, before that moment he tended to run things past a wide range of people: his staff, his cabinet secretaries (sometimes), certain senators and congressmen, his business and media friends. We reckoned that we needed to develop relationships with as many of these individuals as possible, in effect the President's kitchen cabinet, and ensure that wherever possible they, as well as our contacts in the White House, knew where the UK stood on the issues of the day.

Did these tactics work? Sometimes they did, sometimes not. But we were convinced, with some evidence, that they gave us a better chance. We had one notable success: after an intensive lobbying exercise at every level, we persuaded the President to expel sixty Russian diplomats in response to the Salisbury poisoning – by some way the most heavyweight response of any of our allies. Other results were invisible: using our network to persuade the White House not to comment about a lost Brexit vote or to convince the President that NATO partners were spending more on defence.

I also tried to bring out for London a particular feature of Trump that fascinates me to this day. He really didn't do strategy. White House insiders would confirm to us that the President started every day with a blank sheet of paper. Reportedly he would tell his staffers that they should see each twenty-four hours as a battle with those forces of darkness, in the media and in Congress, who were bent on bringing him down – and who equally saw each day as an opportunity to minimise or discredit his successes and amplify his setbacks. Each day was about fighting back, about getting the message out, and about delivering on his campaign promises. Decisions were about the immediate results and impact – roll the dice, see where they fall, deal with the unforeseen consequences tomorrow. Or perhaps I am missing the point here. This *was* the strategy: keep your eyes on the next twenty-four hours, treat each day as a new battle against a hostile media and deep state, never stop talking to your supporters, never surrender an inch to the critics, and the longer term will take care of itself.

I had spent a lot of years in a Whitehall that was obsessed with strategy. My old friend, David Richards, then chief of defence staff, would often say (to my intense irritation) at preparatory meetings for National Security Council sessions, 'You shouldn't put this to ministers until you have a strategy.' We always had a strategy: just not always one that David had approved. And secretly, I was something of a strategy sceptic, thinking that Mike Tyson had a point when he said, 'Everybody has a plan until they get punched in the mouth.' But I usually went along with the pro-strategy flow – which meant that the Whitehall foreign policy world was overflowing with papers setting out the beneficial consequences of recommended policies; how everything could work out perfectly in the best of desired outcomes. In my experience, foreign policy decisions were usually about choosing the least bad option, while understanding that there were countless known unknowns about how things would pan out. While it was important to think things through, the results should not be oversold: stuff would always happen.

But here was a President whose whole approach was 'my gut tells me – do this, let's see what happens'. It was the real-estate world writ large: buy this land, sell that building, roll the dice, see how it goes. And after three years he was still standing, not perhaps universally admired, but with a real prospect of re-election. Maybe he was on to something . . .

13

Foreign Policy and Trade

*

'Our allies are making billions screwing us'
— President Donald Trump, June 2018

*

IN THE mid-1990s, while I was head of the Foreign Office department handling the break-up of Yugoslavia, I had my first substantive encounter with some of the heavyweights of American foreign policy. I had, of course, met American diplomats before, many times, both socially and to swap information. But this was different. The war in Bosnia was still raging. The Srebrenica massacre had taken place a few months earlier, in July 1995. The transatlantic relationship was in poor shape. British and French soldiers were on the ground in Bosnia as part of the United Nations peacekeeping mission, UNPROFOR. An earlier joint peace initiative between the US and the UK, the Vance–Owen peace plan, had failed, as had a subsequent European Community effort. The Americans were staying out of the fray, had no troops on the ground, but were deeply critical, often publicly, of the performance of our troops. The most wounding accusation was that the British and French forces had become 'human shields for Bosnian Serb ethnic cleansing'. We were telling them that it was easy, and cheap, to criticise from the safety of 30,000 feet above the battlefield. It was, in short, becoming increasingly barbed and bitter, and infecting other parts of the relationship. Then we heard that a high-level US delegation was coming to Europe, starting with London, to discuss the crisis.

A meeting was duly set up in one of the grand rooms in the Foreign Office. The UK team would be led by the political director. As a medium-sized cog in the machine, I got the last seat on the UK side of the table, on the understanding that I would take the record of the meeting. We heard that the US team would be led by Tony Lake, President Clinton's national security adviser, and would include Dick Holbrooke, then the assistant secretary of state for Europe, and General Wesley Clark, a Vietnam veteran who would, a decade later, run unsuccessfully for President.

The meeting was one of the more dramatic of my career. Tony Lake spoke first. He said that the President, appalled at the civilian slaughter in Bosnia, had decided it was the moment for the US to take the lead. So he had authorised a peace initiative, which would involve bringing the parties to a location in the United States and forcing them to sit around a table for as long as it took to reach a deal. Hence the European tour, to inform allies and to seek their support, insights and ideas.

Dick Holbrooke then intervened, very obviously playing bad cop to Lake's inclusive, conciliatory good cop. He leant across the table, and in a tone that brooked no argument or interruption said that the President had been extremely clear in his mandate to them. 'We are going to do this. We hope you will be with us. But we will go ahead whether you are with us or not. This war has gone on too long and it has to be stopped.'

Watching discussions unfold, I was both intimidated by the show of power on the other side of the table, especially from Holbrooke, and dazzled by it. I knew instantly that while I was proud to serve as a British diplomat, there would never be a moment when I would be able to say, as Holbrooke had, 'we are going to sort this out, with or without you'. This was a superpower in action. It was an internationalist America looking outwards, showing leadership, addressing the world's wrongs, taking on the bad guys, making the world a better place. And it worked. Months later the Dayton Peace

Agreement was signed. Imperfect though it is, it has held to this day.

I tell this story only to make a basic point: Donald Trump's foreign policy was nothing like that.

So what was it? We in the embassy put a lot of effort into assessing how Trump in office might behave, for the obvious reason that decisions taken in the White House matter – in London, Paris, Berlin, Moscow, Tokyo and points beyond. London thought they knew what a Hillary Clinton presidency would look like. But Trump was an unknown quantity. So there was a market which we needed to satisfy. It wasn't easy. Trump made only one real foreign policy-focused speech, on 27 April 2016, at the Center for the National Interest, a Washington-based think tank founded by Richard Nixon: and I suspect he did it only because he was told he had to if he wanted his candidacy to be taken seriously. But a combination of this and some staples from his nightly campaign speeches gave us something to go on.

The story that these bits and pieces told was of someone who lacked any sort of global perspective; who seemed to have complete disdain for the largely American-designed international structures and organisations that make up the post-war international order; who criticised America's allies rather more than he condemned America's enemies; and who carried around with him a series of grievances about America's treatment by the rest of the world. The most prominent of his complaints was about trade. Trump would say in his campaign speeches, to a rapturous crowd, that America had done a bunch of terrible trade deals. He would target, in particular, the huge US trade deficit with China and the NAFTA trade agreement between the US and its neighbours, Mexico and Canada. And he would argue that these deals had opened American markets to unfair competition, destroyed American industry, encouraged huge trade deficits, and delivered virtually nothing for the US in return. He made something of the same argument about the Paris climate change agreement: that it was unfair and lopsided and would damage American business to the advantage of their competitors. The other campaign standby was

US entanglements in the Middle East and Afghanistan. Trump would claim that these foreign interventions had failed – 'Why don't we win any more?' – and that he would bring the troops home.

Then there was Iran. The Obama administration, together with the UK, France and Germany, had negotiated a deal with Iran which froze their programme to develop a nuclear weapon. Trump called it 'the worst deal ever', and said he would withdraw from it once he'd won the election and reimpose sanctions. He also promised to be the most pro-Israeli President in history – and to move the US Embassy in Israel from Tel Aviv to Jerusalem (in effect recognising Jerusalem as the capital of the Jewish state, a highly controversial step given the city's long history of division and conflict and its disputed status). He questioned NATO's relevance, and complained that the Europeans and Canadians were not spending what they had promised on defence. And he prompted much comment by steadfastly resisting criticism of Vladimir Putin, arguing instead that he could do deals with him to resolve some of the world's problems. Otherwise, the rest of the map of the world – Africa, most of Asia and South America – might as well have been a blank space.

I struggled to find a single phrase that encapsulated and made coherent these objectives. The best that I could invent was that it was a 'reset foreign policy'; that it was about turning the clock back and wiping out 'bad' deals, whether in trade, in the Middle East or on climate change. To the extent that it dealt with the future at all, it was by default: reverse the mistakes and America would be in a better place. Also, it was a unilateral reset: there seemed no place in the Trump vision of the world for allies. They were either ignored or abused in his campaign speeches. It was America Alone.

I also tried to understand, and explain to London, *why* Trump held these views, drawing on insights from those who knew him well. His contempt for America's trade negotiators seemed to be the most longstanding and deeply held position; it could be tracked back decades in his public pronouncements. It wasn't Republican

Party policy; they were the party of free trade, with the Democrats, the party of organised labour, likelier to tilt towards protectionism. But for Trump, it fitted perfectly with his campaign aim to target America's disaffected blue-collar workers. Here was a man promising to turn back the clock and reopen the factories and the coal mines.

Otherwise, Trump's targets looked like a combination of political expediency and personal antipathy to Barack Obama. On Iran, I doubt whether he had ever read anything more than the briefest summary of the deal. But the Republicans didn't support it; the Israelis hated it; and it had been Obama's achievement. On Israel, most would say that his unqualified support was a phenomenon that dated precisely from the beginning of his presidential campaign: but if Trump was late to the calling, he made up for it through the unquestioning and unconditional nature of his support.

On NATO and Putin, however, he was on his own. The Republican Party strongly supported NATO and believed fervently in a tough stance towards Russia. But from what I picked up from his entourage, his views on NATO were primarily about the bottom line: in a defence alliance of twenty-nine countries, the US was responsible for over 70 per cent of total defence spending.

As for the refusal to criticise Putin, this was a genuine mystery. His team declined even to try to explain or justify it. But there were several theories in circulation. The most colourful, linked to the Steele dossier, was that the Russians had something on him, dating back to Trump's visit to Moscow when he took his Miss Universe franchise there, or perhaps even to one of his flirtations with bankruptcy. But although plenty of investigative journalists tried, no one could ever stand the story up. The likelier explanation, in my view, was that Trump simply admired strong, dominant leaders, whatever their democratic credentials; and this went along with a belief that, if he could establish a strong relationship with Putin, together they could sort out the world's problems.

The Republicans didn't like these divergences from their basic beliefs. When I called on Republican politicians in their offices on the Hill, I heard quite a lot of private disquiet about Trump's campaign pronouncements. But I also heard a lot of complacent predictions about how things would change if Trump got into office; how as President, he would cleave to the Republican mainstream. They were wrong. This was a politician who believed emphatically in delivering on his campaign commitments; and moreover, someone without any sense of gratitude or obligation towards the Republican Party. It was his victory, not theirs; the gratitude should be flowing upstream not down. For Trump, 2017 was Year Zero: nothing was sacred, everything was up for grabs. It might be less a foreign policy, more a grievance policy. But he was going to follow his instincts. And so he did, leaving no campaign commitment untouched over the next three years.

Trade, the issue about which Trump had felt strongest for longest, was the first part of his agenda to surface post-inauguration. On 23 January, just three days into his term, President Trump announced US withdrawal from the Trans Pacific Partnership, or TPP, an ambitious trade agreement negotiated, but not ratified, during Obama's presidency. Trump claimed his decision would be a 'great thing for the American worker'. The deal would have involved a dozen countries around the Pacific Rim: apart from the US, it included Australia, Brunei, Canada, Chile, Japan, Malaysia, Mexico, New Zealand, Peru, Singapore and Vietnam. It would have created the third largest free-trade area in the world. The remaining eleven participants went ahead anyway with basically the same agreement, though renamed the CPTPP, or Comprehensive and Progressive Agreement for Trans-Pacific Partnership.

The new administration followed up on 1 March by publishing, through the office of the US trade representative, its trade policy agenda. This set four priorities: promoting US sovereignty, enforcing US trade laws, expanding exports, and protecting US intellectual property rights. Then on 18 May, with trade policy now led by newly appointed US trade representative and veteran negotiator Bob Lighthizer, Congress were notified of the White House's intention to renegotiate the North America Trade Agreement between the US, Canada and Mexico.

The trade dossier then went quiet – or at least was overshadowed by the relentless tide of bigger stories – for the rest of the year. Negotiations started with Canada and Mexico. We were picking up from sources within the administration that the President wanted to impose tariffs on China and perhaps on the EU. There was history here – and a classic Donald Trump story. Back in 1988, Trump had bid for, but lost at auction, the 'Play it again, Sam' piano used in the film *Casablanca*. He was beaten to it by a Japanese collector. A few months later, he called publicly for a 20 per cent tariff on imports from Japan. He said at the time, 'America is being ripped off. We have to tax, we have to tariff, we have to protect this country.' (He somehow resisted adding 'especially our pianos'.) Three decades on, tariffs remained his favourite trade instrument. Our White House contacts would tell us that whenever a trade issue landed on his desk, he would ask 'Where are my tariffs? Bring me my tariffs.'

Through 2017, it didn't happen: the President somehow got diverted down other tracks (as history would show, he certainly didn't change his mind). But, again thanks to an extraordinarily leaky White House, we were picking up that a ferocious war had broken out behind the scenes. On one side was the President's trade adviser, Peter Navarro. Previously an economics professor, he was a controversial and fringe figure in the American economic community thanks to his advocacy of an isolationist and protectionist American foreign policy; and because of his fervently anti-Chinese views, encapsulated in his subtly titled 2011 book, *Death by China*. But his views meshed well with the emerging Trump narrative, and he was invited to join the Trump campaign as an economic policy adviser. In that capacity, he and Wilbur Ross co-wrote an economic policy plan for Trump. I went to lunch with the two of them at around that time. Navarro didn't say much, but he did look as if he were permanently angry with, really, the rest of the world, for just not getting it. Perhaps he knew what was coming: shortly afterwards 370 US economists, including 19 Nobel Prize winners, signed a letter rubbishing the Navarro/Ross proposals. Navarro responded that the letter was 'an embarrassment to the corporate offshoring wing of the economist profession which continues to insist bad trade deals are good for America'.

And in the opposite corner, the President's senior economic adviser Gary Cohn. I got to know Gary quite well. He had risen to one job short of the top at Goldman Sachs. In a couple of meetings that I attended between the Prime Minister and the President, Trump introduced him by saying 'And this is Gary Cohn. He's made so much money.' He was a big, dominating personality and a real street fighter in the White House wars. He somehow inserted himself between Navarro and the President and would hint privately that he was stopping anything written by Navarro from reaching Trump's desk. This may have been the biggest single reason why 2017 was a tariff-free year. But the problem was that Trump basically agreed with Navarro, while Cohn was growing increasingly frustrated with life in the White House. On 22 December 2017, Trump signed into law the Tax Cuts and Jobs Act, the biggest tax reform package in more than thirty years, a measure on which Cohn had been the White House lead; on 6 March 2018, Cohn resigned, letting it be known that with tax reform done, he felt he'd contributed all he could.

It was no sort of coincidence that tariffs came straight back onto the agenda, starting with action under a hitherto obscure national security provision to protect the US steel and aluminium producers. We in the embassy had seen this coming, and I went to see Wilbur Ross to argue against the impending decision, in particular because action on national security grounds which impacted on America's strongest ally made no kind of sense. I gave him a list of UK producers who were potentially in the line of fire, highlighting in particular those that made specialist products for which there was no direct US competitor. Ross hinted that he had no prospect of changing the President's mind but would try to be helpful where he could. In early March, the administration announced it was imposing 25 per cent tariffs on imports of steel and 10 per cent tariffs on imports of aluminium. The tariffs applied to most of America's trading partners:

the EU, Canada, China, South Korea, Japan, Australia, Argentina, Brazil, Mexico, Norway, India, Switzerland. And there were some helpful exclusions for specialist steel products. The tariffs came into force on 31 May; on 22 June the EU retaliated with tariffs on $3.2 billion of US exports, in particular on iconic American products produced in Trump-supporting states: Harley-Davidsons, bourbon and orange juice. In April 2019, prompted by a World Trade Organisation ruling on illegal European government subsidies to Airbus, the US announced tariffs on a further $11 billion of European products.

Meanwhile, the trade war with China kicked off. The US trade deficit with China is huge. In 2018, it was $419 billion, by far their largest with any country. Moreover, nearly everyone in the West believes China breaks the rules: through government subsidies to China's emerging industries; through hidden barriers to imports; and through forced technology transfers, requiring companies who export to China to share their secrets. As I often said to contacts within the administration, we too were damaged daily by Chinese trade practices and would have been ready to discuss joint action. But the President wanted to act quickly. Over the course of 2018, he imposed three rounds of tariffs on China, amounting in total to tariffs on $250 billion of Chinese goods. Retaliation was inevitable and China imposed tariffs on more than $110 billion of US products. The counterpunching continued in 2019, with Trump raising one tranche of tariffs, on $200 billion of Chinese goods, from 10 per cent to 25 per cent in May; a few weeks later China responded with a hike on its tariffs on $60 billion of US products. The Chinese also targeted Trump-supporting states, especially the farm belt of Illinois, Indiana and Wisconsin, all of which were big exporters of agricultural produce to China. As evidence of the pain, farm bankruptcies reached their highest level for a decade.

I gained some personal insight into the impact of all this when I took a road trip around the Midwest in late summer 2018. Jaguar had just announced their first electric car, the Jaguar I-Pace, and they wanted some publicity for it. So the embassy's commercial and energy teams worked with them to construct a five-state road trip – to Michigan, Illinois, Indiana, Wisconsin and Minnesota – stopping off at Jaguar dealerships, at a world-leading research centre into battery technology, and at various governors' mansions on the way round, culminating with a visit to the Minnesota State Fair. I was intrigued to do this, provided I was allowed to drive the Jaguar. For social media purposes, it was christened The Great Green Road Trip.

The car was wonderful – a credit to British design, beautiful from the outside, spacious internally, and unbelievably fast. And for the record, I wasn't driving when we got the speeding ticket. In South Bend, Indiana, I met the Mayor, Pete Buttigieg – a Democrat in a state which Trump had won by 56 per cent to Clinton's 37 per cent in 2016. I had met Buttigieg briefly a year earlier at a residence reception and there was already a buzz around him as a rising politician. Our thirty-minute meeting stretched into an entire afternoon. I ended up chauffeuring him around South Bend in the Jaguar, while he showed me the projects which had been launched and the redevelopment that had taken place on his watch. We ended up drinking local craft beer in what looked like a film-maker's concept of the perfect neighbourhood bar. Buttigieg himself could not have been nicer or more welcoming, and I could sense even in that short time that he was an exceptionally impressive and gifted politician. He would go on to run for the Democratic nomination in the 2020 race, and despite being a mere town mayor in a field full of senators and governors, he was for a time the shock front-runner. No surprise to me.

Later in the trip we pitched up in Madison, Wisconsin, where we overnighted in an Airbnb on a bleak, windswept housing estate around which a pack of dogs seemed to be roaming. As a welcome offering, a head-high pile of old carpets was placed by the front door. But the house itself was fine. And we went to breakfast the following morning at a classic American diner with representatives of the Wisconsin farming community. They were as decent and nice a group as you could ever hope to meet, straight out of *The Waltons*. The conversation took place over a typical Midwestern breakfast, meaning that we gazed at each other across mountains of beige food: the foundations made from omelettes the size of frisbees, the slopes from hash browns and sausage links and bacon, the whole an impending heart attack. Vanessa would warn me daily about the perils of fried food and insisted on a healthy diet, but there was not a vegetable in sight. So here in the Midwest, I ate it all. It was delicious.

And the conversation was fascinating. The farmers said that they had been badly hit by the trade war with China, the soybean growers in particular. They confirmed that there was real hardship in their community. But all of them said that they trusted and still supported Donald Trump and that this was the wider view among Wisconsin farmers. They felt it was worth their taking the short-term hit for the potential long-term gain. And at a more emotional level, they felt that, unlike previous generations of politicians, Donald Trump really cared about them; he had their back. So they should repay his support. As it happens, there was some payback, shortly after my visit, when in September 2018 the US, Canada and Mexico agreed a new trade deal to replace NAFTA, called imaginatively the United States-Mexico-Canada Agreement. It was signed at the end of 2018; ratification is in hand but has yet to be completed. In truth, it doesn't involve radical change from NAFTA; but it does give American dairy farmers, of whom there are a lot in Wisconsin, increased access to the Canadian market.

The Paris climate change accord was next on the agenda. We also knew this was coming, and lobbied strenuously against US withdrawal. We had allies inside the system, notably energy secretary Rick Perry, Gary Cohn and Ivanka Trump. I heard from my French counterpart that President Macron had spoken several times to Trump himself, urging that the US stay on board. But it always felt like a losing battle. Trump was a climate change sceptic: he had tweeted, back in 2012, that the concept of global warming had been created by China to harm US competitiveness. And he had campaigned on a promise of US withdrawal. On 1 June, in a speech delivered in the Rose Garden in the White House, he announced that the US was pulling out. He said that the accord was 'simply the latest example of Washington entering into an agreement that disadvantages the United States to the exclusive benefits of other countries, leaving American workers – who I love – and taxpayers to absorb the cost in terms of lost jobs, lower wages, shuttered factories and vastly diminished economic production'.

Thereafter, climate change became a recurrent problem at international meetings, especially the G7: the US delegation would consistently resist communiqué language on the need to tackle climate change. And there was a huge outcry, both within America and internationally. In particular, thirteen US states and a number of city mayors recommitted to the Paris goals – including California, by itself one of the world's top ten economies. But leading Republicans like Senate majority leader Mitch McConnell supported the President. And Trump's polling figures barely shifted.

And so to the next 'bad' deal, Iran. The Iran nuclear agreement, the Joint Comprehensive Plan of Action – JCPOA for short – had been finalised in Vienna on 14 July 2015. The signatories comprised Iran (obviously), the US, the UK, France, Germany, Russia, China and the EU. All of the Western participants recognised the agreement's shortcomings. It didn't address Iran's development of medium-range ballistic missiles, nor the country's disruptive actions and policies in the Middle East, including its support for the Houthi rebels in Yemen, Hizbollah in Lebanon and Assad's murderous regime in Syria. But the Iranians had been developing nuclear technology, on and off, since the 1970s. They started to see it as a matter of national survival after the Iran–Iraq war of the 1980s, when the West supported Saddam Hussein and Iraq. And by 2015 Iran was judged to be about a year away from 'break out' – from having the capability to build and deliver a nuclear weapon. So constraining their programme was the priority.

And this the deal did, pretty effectively. It reduced the number of first-generation centrifuges (the means by which the useful stuff, uranium-235, is separated from lower grade uranium ores) held by the Iranians from 19,000 to 6,000; it reduced their holdings of advanced centrifuges from 1,000 to zero; and it reduced the stockpiles of low-enriched uranium from 7,000 to 300 kg, and of medium-enriched uranium from 200 kg to zero. It also required the Arak heavy water research reactor to be rebuilt so that it could not produce weapons-grade plutonium; and it required enrichment at the Fordow research facility to stop. Finally it provided for a comprehensive inspections regime, run by the International Atomic Energy Agency. All of these provisions were for ten years only, and were thereafter to be phased out over five years, so by 2030 the Iranian nuclear programme would in theory be unconstrained; but at least among the Western signatories, it was understood that there would have to be a follow-on agreement, or the reimposition of comprehensive sanctions.

The legislation under which US sanctions were suspended, the Iran Nuclear Agreement Review Act, required the President to certify in every quarter that Iran was complying with the limits set in the JCPOA. And the US, alongside other signatories, looked to the IAEA to confirm that Iran was complying with the deal. After taking office, Trump, though with a public show of reluctance, signed the April 2017 certificate and then the July version. But we in the embassy sensed that time was running out. In particular, the right-wing Washington think tanks were in full cry against the deal, as were many Republican politicians. At that stage, the Republicans had majorities in both Senate and House, while the President himself continued to call it 'the worst deal ever'. Our concerns proved well founded; when the October certification came round, and notwithstanding that the IAEA again declared the Iranians to be in compliance, Trump said he wouldn't sign.

The news triggered a flurry of activity in Washington. On the one hand, the opponents of the JCPOA, scenting victory, intensified their public campaign against it. On the other hand, the European ambassadors – myself and my French, German and EU colleagues – found ourselves in high demand, given that all of our governments had publicly recommitted themselves to the deal. Every week, there would be another debate, hosted by one or other think tank, where we would find ourselves lined up against the same hardened critics of the deal, some of whom might even have read it. We were also in demand on the Hill, where the entire Democratic caucus in the House asked us to address them. Of course we did so, to a sympathetic hearing (though not all Democrats supported the deal, any more than all Republicans opposed it). To my surprise, we started to pick up some grumbling from Republicans that this had been a 'partisan' act. As we pointed out to them, we would have done the same for the Republicans, had they asked us. But it illustrated how fractious the issue had become.

The issue, and the debate, dragged on. The State Department, at official level, largely supported the deal. And there were those inside the White House, notably National Security Adviser H. R. McMaster, who were trying to persuade the President not to withdraw. We heard that Defense Secretary Mattis also supported the deal. But we were also being told that the President was immovable in his determination to withdraw: another campaign commitment that had to be delivered.

As a last-gasp effort, State Department officials launched an exercise with us, the French and the Germans, about a text which they thought might just persuade the President to hold off. The idea was a collective statement by the four countries committing us to reimpose sanctions in a range of circumstances relating to Iran's broader behaviour as well as breaches of the JCPOA, together with a commitment never to let Iran complete development of a nuclear weapon. Officials made quite a lot of progress. By late April 2018, only a few sentences were still open. But the clock was ticking, with another recertification imminent and the President publicly reluctant. So Foreign Secretary Boris Johnson dropped everything and flew across the Atlantic to see if he and Rex Tillerson's successor as Secretary of State, Mike Pompeo, could find a solution for those last few sentences.

Johnson arrived with some drafting fixes in his briefcase. We went over to Foggy Bottom for the meeting with Pompeo, to discover that we were too late. Pompeo told us, in effect, that the decision had been taken – the US would be pulling out – and to forget about collective texts. At the end of the meeting, Johnson briefed the State Department press corps in strongly critical terms about the US decision. And in the wake of his abortive visit, I tried to find out what had happened behind the scenes in Washington. The picture was murky. There had been a private conversation between Pompeo and the President the day before Johnson's arrival, but no one would tell us exactly what had transpired; perhaps no one apart from the two principals actually knew. We wondered whether John Bolton, a noted Iran hardliner, who had replaced H. R. McMaster as national security adviser three weeks before, had made an impact, or whether Mike Pompeo had actually ever bought into it. In any case, on the next day, 8 May, Trump announced that the US was withdrawing from the JCPOA and reimposing sanctions.

The consequences of that decision included rising tensions in the Gulf, disagreement and disarray between the US and its European allies, and an Iranian economy suffering serious damage from US sanctions. The UK, France and Germany stuck with the JCPOA and didn't reimpose sanctions. But, as was inevitable, the big European companies with global networks, faced with a choice of trading with Iran or the US, chose the latter and disinvested from Iran. The sanctions also made it much harder for Iran to sell its oil, reducing a major stream of income. What didn't happen, however, was any concession by Iran, any move to meet American demands. As I had heard at those numerous think-tank events, the opponents of the nuclear deal had anticipated that renewed US sanctions would bring the Iranian economy to collapse within months and would force the Iranian regime back to the table to negotiate a greatly better deal than the JCPOA: in effect, to sign surrender terms. The European view was that the Iranians would eat grass before capitulating to the Great Satan. So far, the Europeans have been right.

What did happen was that the US and Iran came close to war. In May–June 2019, the Iranians started using mines against tankers in the busy shipping lanes in the Strait of Hormuz, the narrowest part of the Persian Gulf, and the route through which 20 per cent of the world's oil supply flows. This was an old Iranian play, one they had used in the late 1980s during the Iran–Iraq war as a reprisal for

Western support for Iraq. They also announced that they would no longer respect the JCPOA limit for their stockpile of enriched uranium. The attacks on tankers prompted increased Western surveillance of the Strait. And on 20 June, the Iranians shot down an unmanned US spy-in-the-sky drone which they claimed had breached their airspace. These drones may not have pilots, but they are, at $130 million each, somewhat pricier than the drones available for purchase on the high street; and at least among Republicans, there was pressure for a response. So the President, within a few hours, approved air strikes on the Iranian radar and missile batteries thought to have downed the drone. The planes took off; ships were in position; and we in the embassy had warned London that something was going on, not least because the Pentagon press corps had been told to expect some news late that evening. And then Trump changed his mind and called the strikes off. I believe this was his decision alone: I never heard, from either inside or outside the White House, any suggestion that someone got to him. Our Pentagon contacts were telling us that only twelve minutes had remained before missiles would have been released.

On the other side of the Persian Gulf, things went rather better. From the outset, Trump had prioritised good relationships with the ruling families of Saudi Arabia and the United Arab Emirates. This was presented as being about an alliance against Islamic terrorism – and against Iran. Washington cynics suggested it was more about a mutual preference for government as a family-run business – a theory bolstered by the relationship struck up between the 'three Crown Princes': Mohammed bin Salman (MbS) of Saudi Arabia, Mohammed bin Zayed (MbZ) of the United Arab Emirates, and Jared Kushner. The Kushner team in the White House presented this as a pair of genuine, close, personal friendships. I suspected that it was more about business than about socialising on WhatsApp. Whichever, there is no question that the lines between the three were busy – and that almost no one in the administration, especially not in the State Department, knew anything about the content of those conversations.

Confirmation of the Gulf's place in the global hierarchy came with the President's first big overseas trip, in late May 2017. Trump chose, not the neighbours, Canada or Mexico; nor Beijing, Paris, Berlin or London; but Riyadh, the Saudi capital. The visit seemed to go well. The administration claimed it had sealed a $350 billion arms deal, described in a typically Trump touch as 'the biggest arms deal in history'; in truth there was probably some double counting going on of deals concluded under the previous administration, or statements of intent that might never happen. Trump also met the Gulf Cooperation Council, and attended what was called the Arab Islamic American Summit – at which fifty-five Muslim and Arab leaders showed up.

But the visit was memorable above all for a video and a photograph. The video, preserved for the rest of time on YouTube, was of the traditional Saudi 'sword dance': a customary greeting for an honoured guest, in which squadrons of Saudi men chant and wave swords around. The President, newly arrived, was pressed to join in, which he did. He looked slightly awkward, though nothing like as static and uncomfortable as Commerce Secretary Wilbur Ross. Social media, of course, went wild. A year later, when Theresa May was mocked for an awkward dance during a visit to Africa, I wondered whether this might be a bonding issue between her and the President. Should she open their next phone conversation by commiserating over their joint embarrassment? But then, having pondered without inspiration on how to put this idea to the Prime Minister, I concluded, maybe not.

The photograph, however, was even better. At the end of the summit, Trump and his Saudi host, King Salman, starred at a brief event inaugurating a new Global Center for Combating Extremist Ideology. Somehow President Sisi of Egypt got himself in on the action. At the conclusion of the ceremony, the room went dark, and the three leaders laid their hands on a large glowing orb while staring mystically into the middle distance, in which position they stayed for around two minutes. The intention was to symbolise their joint commitment to lead the global fight against extremism and terrorism (the orb signifying the globe). Nice idea, but the reality looked beyond weird, and went globally viral in an instant.

Some likened it to the cosmic cube of the Marvel comics, which could 'turn any dream into reality'. Others saw the participants as the Three Soothsayers, waiting for the mists to clear in their crystal ball. The Church of Satan – a real body, currently headquartered in Poughkeepsie, New York – helpfully explained via Twitter, 'For clarification, this is not a Satanic ritual.' Personally, it took me straight to an early episode of the original *Star Trek* series in which Captain Kirk's body is controlled by telepathic aliens stored in globes.

In any case, blessed by this shared celestial experience, US–Saudi relations went from strength to strength. In March 2018, the real power in the land, Crown Prince Mohammed bin Salman, paid a return visit to the US which seemed to go on for months. He met American royalty, in the form of Oprah Winfrey. He saw a lot of Jared Kushner. And then everything was tested to its limits by the Khashoggi affair. Jamal Khashoggi was a Saudi dissident, in exile from his home country and resident in the US, and a journalist, contributing occasionally to the *Washington Post*. On 2 October 2018 he went into the Saudi Consulate in Istanbul to obtain some documents he needed to get married. He never came out. It emerged in the following days, mostly from Turkish intelligence (who had been bugging the consulate), that a Saudi hit team had travelled to Istanbul and had been inside the building. They had murdered Khashoggi, then had dismembered his body with a bone saw and taken it out of the building in suitcases.

The story made global headlines. The Saudis, never good at PR, changed their defence every day. The suspicion, inevitable given the power amassed by MbS, was that he had ordered the murder. He strenuously denied it, and eventually eighteen different Saudis were arrested for the crime. But a few weeks later, a highly classified CIA report into the affair leaked. The report noted that MbS had sent eleven electronic messages to the individual who had overseen the operation, and it concluded that the CIA had 'medium-to-high confidence' that MbS had 'personally targeted' Khashoggi and had 'probably ordered his death'.

The President, however, didn't accept his own agency's conclusion.

On the MbS issue, his conclusion was 'maybe he did, maybe he didn't . . . maybe we will never know all the facts'. And on broader relations with Saudi Arabia, he said, 'If we abandon Saudi Arabia, it would be a terrible mistake; we're staying with Saudi Arabia': a position he has held to this day, notwithstanding pressure from an angry Congress.

To be fair to the US administration, we and the French faced similar challenges. We both knew what had happened inside the consulate. But we both also had substantial stakes in Saudi Arabia, on which thousands of jobs depended. So we were really no more robust than the US in responding to the murder. A little less publicly defiant and dismissive than President Trump, perhaps, but no keener to impose sanctions.

For the Trump administration, the other central relationship in the Middle East was with Israel. There is no doubt that Jared Kushner had a big role in this, ensuring that Israel was the second country that Trump visited on that first trip, after Saudi Arabia. Trump also asked Kushner to lead in brokering a settlement between Israel and the Palestinians, and predicted that Kushner could do the deal that had eluded generations of politicians, diplomats and Middle East specialists. This was in itself a startling decision, diminishing for whoever sat in the Secretary of State's seat. But Kushner himself, to whom I and successive foreign secretaries talked regularly, was confident that he could bring a different, 'businessman's' approach to the challenge. I think he genuinely put hundreds of hours of work into it. But he waited a long time for the 'perfect' launch moment, when the stars would be in the ideal alignment. This being the Middle East, it never came. The proposals would eventually emerge in January 2020, at a far from propitious moment in the region. Meanwhile, relations between the administration and the Palestinians deteriorated dramatically.

The deterioration was the result not of random events, but of a series of deliberate US decisions. On 16 February, less than a month after taking office, the President met Israeli Prime Minister Netanyahu and implied afterwards that he was not committed to a two-state solution in the former mandate of Palestine, with a

Palestinian state side-by-side with Israel. Ten months later, on 6 December, he announced that he was fulfilling his campaign promise that the US Embassy in Israel would move from Tel Aviv to Jerusalem. Generations of previous presidential candidates had promised the same, then backed off once in office. Not Trump: the move proceeded quickly and the embassy was formally opened on 14 May 2018. Two of the cable news channels presented the event on a split screen: on one side, live coverage of the speeches marking the official opening; on the other, the riots in Gaza that accompanied the ceremony. Meanwhile, aid to the Palestinians was being cut. On 17 January 2018, the US halved, from $125 million to $65 million, the money it gave to UNWRA, the UN agency for Palestine refugees, and on 31 August cut funding to zero. Other aid programmes to the Palestinians were also cut. On 10 September, the PLO mission in Washington was forced to close, and on 17 September, the PLO representative had his visa revoked and was compelled to leave the country. All of this greatly pleased the Israeli government of the day; and it fulfilled Trump's campaign promise to be the strongest supporter of Israel ever to sit behind the Resolute desk. Whether it helped the prospects for Jared Kushner's peace plan or brought peace between Israelis and Palestinians closer is another question.

After Saudi Arabia and Israel on that first overseas trip came Brussels, for a NATO summit. But if the first two stops had been signals of a desire to build closer, stronger relationships, this was a different sort of message, something close to an ultimatum about the sharing of burdens. During his campaign, Trump had said that NATO was obsolete and had questioned why the US contribution was so disproportionate. He had a point: every NATO member had committed to spend 2 per cent of its gross domestic product on defence. Only four NATO members, among them the UK, actually did. Some of the richest countries, such as Germany and Canada, were among the worst offenders. Successive American Presidents had pushed for others to do more, but they had probably been too polite. Trump had no intention of striking a gentle tone. Instead he was brutal, even bullying, and in his speech to the assembled leaders, and apparently against the advice of most of his staffers, he deliberately omitted a personal endorsement of Article 5 of the NATO Treaty, the famous commitment to mutual defence, under which an attack on one was an attack on all. (There was a leak a few weeks later, confirmed to me by someone in the meeting, about a briefing session when Article 5 was explained to Trump. In response, he said, 'You mean, if Russia attacked Lithuania, we would go to war with Russia? That's crazy!' Ironically, the only time Article 5 has been invoked in NATO history was in support of the US after 9/11.)

Disdain for NATO would remain one of the core themes of the Trump presidency, and would cause serious friction between him and the Republican Party. When I talked to Republican senators, this was usually the issue where they would be most outspoken in their criticism of Trump. And it meant that NATO summits would become perilous exercises in managing the American President. The NATO secretary general, the Norwegian Jens Stoltenberg, became a master Trump-whisperer, always managing to keep the President just about on board. But Trump's basic views didn't really change. Friends in the White House would tell me about internal discussions where Trump said he would like to withdraw the US from NATO. He would say to his staffers that this treasured multi-lateral body – in its own words, the most successful military alliance in history – was in reality a giant scam designed to get America to pay for everyone's defence, while the rest of the membership spent their money on welfare. And when Trump met the Swedish Prime Minister, he told him openly that he would like the US to have the same posture as Sweden: outside NATO but cooperating when it chose.

The European Union was seen, if anything, even more negatively. There was his unjustified complaint to Theresa May at their first meeting that EU regulation was damaging his Irish golf course. He accused the EU of protectionism, and even said publicly, 'The EU is worse than China.' He focused in particular on the trade figures: the US tended to run a trade deficit with the EU of more than $150 billion, which was only partially balanced by a surplus in services of around $50 billion. And within these figures, the President fastened on the imbalance in tariffs on cars as a particular grievance. There was a 2.5 per cent tariff on EU vehicles sold in the US, but a 10 per cent tariff on US vehicles sold in the EU (not that US manufacturers put any effort into selling their products in Europe). Our friends inside the White House would tell us that the President was itching to raise the tariff on European vehicles to 25 per cent. So far, it hasn't happened, and the EU and US are trying to do a trade deal. But the threat remains.

But Trump's EU grievance always seemed to me to be primarily about Germany. Trump tended to be tough on female politicians: Hillary Clinton, Elizabeth Warren, Theresa May. So some critics saw it as being about Angela Merkel and labelled it straightforward misogyny. But it always felt like there was something deeper, rooted in Trump's family history. A German historian, Roland Paul, provided some insights. Though Trump himself had once publicly claimed Swedish ancestry, the Trumps actually came from Kallstadt, a small town of 1,200 people in the Palatinate region of southwestern Germany. Trump's grandfather, Friedrich, emigrated to America in 1885 at the age of sixteen, working as a hairdresser and a restaurant manager before moving west in the gold rush days, culminating in running downmarket hotels and boarding houses in the gold and silver mining town of Monte Cristo. But his homesick German wife wanted to go back to Germany. Having by then acquired US citizenship, Friedrich Trump had to apply for repatriation. The relevant authority at that time was the king of Bavaria, who rejected the Trump application, according to Roland Paul, because Friedrich as a young man had evaded the then compulsory military service (his grandson was similarly to dodge the draft decades later). Only the man himself can answer whether it was or is a factor in Trump's attitude to Germany. What isn't open to doubt is how aggressively and regularly he targeted Merkel and Germany. After one bilateral meeting with Merkel in July 2018, in the margins of a NATO summit, Trump told the media that 'Germany is totally controlled by Russia.'

By sharp contrast, the President initially got along famously with the new President of France, Emmanuel Macron. I think Trump saw in Macron's election victory in June 2017, coming from nowhere to defeat the established French politicians and parties, something akin to his own rise to the American presidency; notwithstanding the reality that as a centre-left politician, Macron came from a completely different part of the political spectrum to Trump. And Macron, sensing a 'Situation Vacant', moved rapidly to claim the position of Trump's 'new best friend'. The bromance flourished for a while. Macron invited Trump to attend the Bastille Day military parade (prompting Trump to propose a similar event on Pennsylvania Avenue). Trump in response gave Macron and his wife the first 'State Dinner' of his presidency (prompting much crowing in the French Embassy in Washington). And an expectant world was gifted some wonderful YouTube moments. The President had already had some awkwardly long handshakes with fellow leaders, but there was nothing to match the 29-second handshake with Macron after the Bastille Day parade: it looked to those of us watching on TV more like twenty-nine minutes. And then, when they met before the state dinner at the White House, the President, noticing a white speck on Macron's shoulder, leant across and picked it off while saying, 'Just removing some dandruff – there, now you're perfect.' A nation retreated behind their sofas.

We Washington cynics noticed, however, that, cosy as the relationship appeared, it wasn't actually delivering anything. Trump still imposed tariffs on EU steel and aluminium. He still withdrew from the Iran deal. Macron clearly felt the same way about these decisions as the rest of the Europeans. And within eighteen months, the bromance was turning into something close to a feud. In November 2018, Macron delivered a speech asserting that nationalism amounted to a betrayal of patriotism: 'By putting our own interests first, with no regard for others, we erase the very thing that a nation holds dearest, and the thing that keeps it alive: its moral values.' Trump responded by trolling Macron on Twitter. 'The problem is that Emmanuel suffers from a very low approval rating in France, 26%, and an unemployment rate of almost 10%.

He was just trying to get on to another subject.' There was more. On a visit to Paris to mark the one-hundredth anniversary of the Armistice which ended the First World War, and to honour the 20 million soldiers who died, Trump, to widespread media ridicule, ducked out of a visit to a military cemetery on the outskirts of Paris, supposedly because it was raining heavily. The French army put out on its official Twitter feed a photograph of a French soldier training in the rain, over the caption 'it is raining but it is not a big deal'.

Trump had one other rollercoaster relationship: with North Korean leader Kim Jong-Un. The North Koreans, like the Iranians, were developing nuclear weapons. Under Kim's leadership, they spent most of 2017 test-firing ballistic missiles into the Pacific Ocean and carrying out underground nuclear tests. To be fair to the President, the programme had been running for a while, without any of his predecessors doing much about it. Trump initially put public pressure on Kim, calling him 'little rocket man' and threatening him with 'fire and fury' – all the while trying to get China, which kept North Korea afloat economically, to use its leverage to force an abandonment of the nuclear programme. But then, against the advice of his staffers, Trump offered a summit without preconditions. It happened on 12 June 2018, in Singapore, in front of thousands of media and a global TV audience, and it produced a broad-brush agreement to work together towards 'complete denuclearisation'. The negotiations which followed haven't yet made any significant progress; there are plenty of experts around who say they never will and that Kim Jong-Un is just playing for time. Meanwhile, we have seen the narrative of the Kim correspondence: personal missives from the North Korean leader, dispatched in ridiculously oversized envelopes, contents private, but according to the President they are 'beautiful letters'. At one point, Trump said in a speech, 'and Kim and I fell in love', providing an instant meme for social media. I stole it for my Christmas party speech to embassy staff.

How does the profit and loss account look in relation to Trump's foreign policy? I think he can claim three successes. NATO is spending more on defence. Nine countries are now at or near the 2 per cent target. That might have happened anyway. But I reckon that Trump's pressure, crudely applied though it was, made a difference. I also think that the summit with Kim Jong-Un was a qualified success. Diplomatic groupthink is that he should have made the North Koreans pay a price for the prestige of a bilateral summit with the US President. That is actually a recipe for stalemate. Trump's unconventional personal diplomacy hasn't delivered a denuclearisation deal, but it has, for the moment, initiated a process and stopped the North Korean testing programme. That's worth having. And third, Trump's tactics did deliver a better trade deal with Canada and Mexico. It is only marginally better, but that's something.

Finally, how was all of this received in London? The short answer is that, across the Pond, preoccupied by Brexit, they found it difficult to grasp quite what a fundamental shift was taking place. This was an American President who didn't really believe in NATO and thought America was being ripped off by its allies. He disparaged the European Union and wanted it to fall apart, breaking with decades of US support for the European project. He unravelled international trade agreements, imposed tariffs on America's friends, and came close to wrecking the World Trade Organisation by blocking the appointment of judges to its court. He took the United States out of the most important international agreement of the new century, in the form of the Paris climate accord. He pulled out of the Iran nuclear deal, destabilising the Gulf region and endangering European security. And he arguably set back the prospects of a settlement between Israel and the Palestinians by moving the US Embassy to Jerusalem. These were not the actions of our most trusted ally or the leader of the free world: this was America First brought to life, a mixture of isolationism and unilateralism. Yet, judging by conversations with a succession of ministerial visitors, the Trump administration was being seen in London as a slightly coarser version of George W. Bush's administration of the early 2000s. Hence my enthusiasm for a National Security Council discussion on the transatlantic relationship, and my decision to write in stark terms to NSC participants about the challenges the Trump administration posed for us. I thought Whitehall needed a wake-up call. The consequences of that letter were to come later.

14

Domestic Policy: Obamacare, Tax Reform and Immigration

*

'Our economy is the best it has ever been'
                                    – President Donald Trump, July 2019

*

IN THE days when the British ruled India, the colonial government faced a particular public health challenge in the capital city of Delhi. The inhabitants were being endangered by a plague of poisonous cobras. The administrators accordingly put together an incentive scheme: they offered a bounty for every dead cobra produced before designated city officials. The scheme initially seemed to work well. Fewer cobras were seen around the streets. But instead of tapering off over time, the number of cobra corpses increased. Each month, more and more were presented for bounty payment.

What was happening, of course, was that cobra corpses had become valuable. So enterprising individuals had started breeding programmes. Those with a steady supply of dead cobras enjoyed a stable source of income: nowadays they might be called entrepreneurs. Moreover, it was much more convenient to kill the cobras being bred in captivity than to hunt down those living in the wild. So while more dead snakes were being produced for bounties, there was, after a while, also a rise in the number of cobras loose in the streets. Faced with this combination of rising costs and reduced effectiveness, the administrators understandably abandoned the bounty programme. The cobra breeders, stuck with nests of newly worthless cobras, simply released them into the city. The net result: more cobras on the streets than ever.

The French colonial administrators in Hanoi faced a similar problem: a plague of rats. They too introduced a bounty system. They didn't demand whole dead rats, just rats' tails. Before long, it became apparent that Hanoi was still engulfed with rats, but that a lot of them, though alive – indeed thriving – lacked tails. As in Delhi, enterprising residents were setting up rat-breeding programmes. The bounty scheme was accordingly stopped, and hordes of newly bred rats were released into Hanoi to join their mostly tailless comrades.

The point of these stories is that government is difficult. The problems administrators face are often complex. The simple solutions that sound good on the campaign trail often don't work. People sometimes behave counterintuitively rather than predictably. And someone will always try to scam the system. There are, in short, second-order effects, unforeseen consequences and feedback loops lying in wait.

In addition there is, in the case of the US, the balance of powers ordained by the authors of the American Constitution. Bill Vaughan, the American journalist and writer, wrote columns for the *Kansas City Star* from 1946 until his death in 1977. He was a world-class originator of folksy aphorisms. One of those attributed to him goes as follows: 'In foreign affairs, the President can do what he wants unless Congress says no. In domestic policy, the President can't do anything unless Congress says yes.' This isn't completely accurate: the President can do some stuff, by executive order, without Congress; but at the risk of his successor repealing it all at the stroke of a pen. And the story of the Trump administration's domestic policies, throughout my time in Washington, was one of endless, tortuous struggles with Congress and the courts.

(Incidentally, this isn't the best Bill Vaughan quote. That honour, in my view, goes to a rather quirkier example: 'We hope that, when the insects take over the world, they will remember with gratitude how we took them along on all our picnics.')

The Trump administration came into office with three big domestic policy objectives. They wanted to repeal the Affordable Care Act – ACA for short, and popularly known as Obamacare. They wanted to reform the US tax system. And they wanted drastically to reduce immigration into the US, by building a wall across the southern border to stop the flow of illegal immigrants from Latin America, and by cutting the programmes facilitating legal immigration. It amounted to the embodiment of Making America Great Again – for Americans – by giving them their money back while keeping foreigners out. They expected it to be straightforward; a senior White House official told me as much a few months after entering office. After all, there were Republican majorities in both houses of Congress. Instead, they faced legal challenges, political obstacles (from their own side) and shifting public opinion. What had seemed sure-fire vote winners in mid-2016 looked much less popular eighteen months later. And they faced an inevitable succession of unexpected challenges and distractions, from school shootings which reignited the gun control debate to the shocking toll on blue-collar America of the opioid epidemic. In short, though I doubt any of them had ever heard of it, they faced variations of the cobra effect.

Why should the British government have cared, and expected us in the embassy to track and report on these narratives? There are three reasons. First, in today's interconnected world, domestic can become international in an instant. When, for example, in January 2017, the newly installed Trump administration announced a ban on travellers from seven largely Muslim countries, there was chaos at London's airports within hours, accompanied by early hours telephone calls from the Foreign Office and No. 10 to, well, me. Second, some problems, notably immigration and healthcare, are common to all Western governments. If there were a perfect solution out there, everyone would have adopted it. So politicians are inevitably, and rightly, fascinated with what others are trying out, with the testbeds around the international scene. And third, the first question any leader wants to know about a counterpart is, how are they doing? Which can't be answered without an understanding of the domestic context.

Healthcare has been for decades one of the most combustible issues in American politics. There is nothing unique to America about this; it's the same in the UK. And every developed economy is struggling to cope with the simultaneous challenges of ever more sophisticated, and expensive, treatments and ageing populations. The particular challenge in the US has been the rising cost of private health insurance schemes, and its impact on poorer families. Healthcare costs are the number one cause of bankruptcy in the US. Moreover, the system produces some shocking population disparities: African Americans, for example, are twice as likely to die of diabetes as whites. And by 2013, more than 16 per cent of the American population, that is one in six Americans, had no health insurance. In other words, in the richest country on the planet, a country moreover where, according to the federally funded Centers for Disease Control and Prevention, 42 per cent of the population are obese, more than 50 million people cannot afford to visit the doctor.

Every US President, at least in recent times, has come into office with a legacy of promises to address healthcare. And there have been some reforms. In the mid-1960s, as part of Lyndon B. Johnson's Great Society revolution, both Medicaid and Medicare were introduced. Medicaid is, in essence, a means-tested government insurance programme for people of low income, which by 2017, according to the Kaiser Family Foundation, was providing free health coverage to some 74 million Americans. Medicare partially funds health insurance for people aged sixty-five and older, and now supports around 60 million Americans. And Barack Obama, at the start of his first term and exploiting the then Democratic majority in both houses of Congress, managed to get the ACA approved. It was signed into law on 23 March 2010.

Obamacare was designed to make health insurance more affordable and available. On the one hand, it required everyone to carry health insurance, or pay a tax penalty. On the other hand, it stopped the insurance companies excluding people with pre-existing conditions; it increased subsidies for the poorest through an expanded Medicaid programme; and it set minimum standards for the healthcare packages that the insurance companies put on the market. It was a landmark piece of legislation for Obama and the biggest reform of healthcare since the 1960s. And over time its provisions enabled 20 million Americans to acquire health insurance. But it was massively controversial, in particular the provision compelling everyone either to have insurance or pay extra tax. Critics presented this as the young and fit and healthy paying for the old, the chronically infirm, and most of all, the irresponsible – those who refused to live up to their personal responsibility to look after themselves and their families. The Republicans, in particular, were for the most part viscerally opposed. They vowed to repeal it when they got into power and made it the centrepiece of their 2010 midterm campaign – when they won big, with a swing in their favour of more than 6 per cent, and retook the House of Representatives. So it was understandable that they and Trump would try to make the same play in 2016, with repeal of Obamacare as one of their headline commitments.

Having won, healthcare therefore became the initial domestic priority for the new administration. With hindsight, it was a brave (or foolhardy) choice, for two reasons. First, President Trump had made it harder by insisting that he wouldn't just repeal the recent measure, leaving those who had been using the scheme without any protection at all; it had to be 'repeal and replace'. Despite having had six years to work out what the 'replace' bit of the picture should be, there was no agreed plan inside the Republican Party. And second, Obamacare had become more popular. In early 2014, opinion polls suggested that comfortably over 50 per cent of the US population had an 'unfavourable' opinion of the ACA, as against less than 40 per cent 'favourable'. By early 2017, however, 'favourable' was narrowly ahead. And the gap continued to grow; by early 2019, most polls had 'favourable' ahead by 50 per cent to 40 per cent. In effect, people had absorbed, and forgotten about, the extra costs, while a lot of Americans were experiencing the benefits.

Moreover, a lot of the 20 million Americans who had, often for the first time in their lives, acquired healthcare insurance because of the ACA were actually Trump voters. Republicans in marginal seats knew this. So as the party struggled to devise a scheme to replace the ACA, it split. The right were doctrinally against ideas to 'compensate' those who might lose out from repeal – for example, costly expansions of schemes like Medicare or Medicaid. But the moderate wing, and those standing for re-election in the 2018 midterms, wanted to be able to promise the voters that they wouldn't lose out. In the event, the two factions could never be reconciled. I talked to Republican politicians on both sides of the argument, and was struck by the pervasive mood of pessimism, even hopelessness: they just couldn't see a way through, and several resorted to arguing that they should never even have opened the dossier up. They struggled for months to find a formula, some bridging legislation around which they could unite. The field of battle became the Senate, where the Republicans had a wafer-thin majority. In the end, in late July 2017, there was a last-chance vote on a so-called 'skinny repeal' which ended the individual mandate but kept the expanded Medicaid programme. It failed by one vote, 51 to 50, notwithstanding that Vice President Pence voted in favour, when three Republicans voted against it: Lisa Murkowski of Alaska, Susan Collins of Maine, and John McCain of Arizona, who, though dying from brain cancer, flew into Washington to deliver the decisive (and literal) thumbs down.

That slender but decisive loss marked the end of the repeal and replace effort. Thereafter, the administration settled for wounding rather than killing: sharp reductions to the advertising and promotion budget, and what amounted to repeal of the individual mandate by reducing to zero dollars the penalty for not having health insurance. Despite all this, Obamacare limps on, bloodied but surviving, and still supported, the opinion polls say, by a majority of the American people. The 2020 election will determine its ultimate fate. Meanwhile, this was the first major legislative setback for the Trump administration. And it was the Republicans' own fault for wasting those six years out of the White House when they could have constructed and united around their alternative; six years of imagining that a soundbite about repealing Obamacare was the same thing as a plan or a policy.

With healthcare reform back on the shelf, tax reform took centre stage. It had long been a Republican Party objective. The last big tax reform had been under Reagan in the mid-1980s. And the failure on healthcare made it politically imperative. Within a few days of that John McCain-engineered defeat, Mitch McConnell, the majority (Republican) leader in the Senate, had summoned senior Republicans, especially members of the pivotal Budget Committee, and told them of the necessity of a tax reform package before the end of that year.

Again, they hadn't done their homework. During Obama's eight years in power, the Republicans had criticised him relentlessly for overspending, and for running up deficits and debt. But they had never agreed internally on how they would answer the question, 'If we were in power, what spending would we cut to pay for the tax reductions we want?' One idea, put forward by Kevin Brady, a senior congressman from Texas and chair of the House Ways and Means Committee, was a 'border adjustment' measure which amounted to a tax on imports. But the Republican right killed this. The solution they eventually, as a party, circled around was: don't pay for it at all; just add it to the debt mountain. The argument ran that the tax cuts would generate higher economic growth, a bigger economy and increased tax revenues, hence paying for itself. One does not need to be an economist to think this risky; history suggests that sometimes it works, sometimes it doesn't. But they were far from the first government to roll the dice in such a way. It also required eating a lot of the words they had spoken in the Obama era – but it meant that with one bound they were free. I would call on some of the avowed 'fiscal hawks' in Congress and ask them how they reconciled their political beliefs with the direction of travel. A lot just changed the subject. Some looked genuinely troubled. Others blamed their colleagues for failing to confront difficult decisions about cutting spending programmes. But none said to me that they would oppose.

Thereafter, progress was rapid. A $1.5 trillion tax bill was put together, with McConnell and House of Representatives majority leader Paul Ryan the major players. It represented an exceptionally sweeping reform package, delivering deep, permanent tax cuts to business, and smaller, temporary cuts to individuals. And shortly before Christmas 2017, it had passed both houses – 227 to 203 in the House and 51 to 48 in the Senate – and landed on the President's desk for signature. The big winners from the reforms were corporations: the corporate tax rate was cut from 35 per cent to 21 per cent. The bill also cut individual taxes across all income brackets for eight years. But it also tightened some tax breaks, notably capping the amount of state taxes which could be offset against the federal tax bill. This impacted most on those living in high-tax states, which tended to be Democratic. And it swelled the deficit. The budget shortfall rose by 17 per cent in 2018, to $799 billion; it is projected to exceed $1 trillion in 2020.

It can be argued that, thus far, in terms of delivering a boost in the polls, the tax package has been a disappointment. The November 2018 midterms didn't go well for the Republicans. The Democrats campaigned on the tax package being a giveaway to big business and the rich – and the results suggested their arguments struck home. Though the Republicans held on to the Senate, there was an 8.6 per cent swing to the Democrats, who retook the House on the back of winning 41 districts from the Republicans, and for good measure seven governorships. Exit polls taken on the day reported that 29 per cent of voters believed that the tax package had helped them, but 45 per cent said it had made no difference and 22 per cent claimed it had damaged them. And if anything, since the midterms, the polling figures have moved further against the package, despite non-partisan analysis suggesting that 65 per cent of American taxpayers are now paying less than they did. Moreover, although economic growth has been healthy, there has been little to substantiate the President's promise that tax reform 'will be rocket fuel for our economy'. Corporate tax revenue didn't rise. On the contrary, it fell 31 per cent in 2018. And the economy grew by 2.9 per cent in 2018, identical to the previous year.

All that said, there is no doubt about the popularity of the package in the business sector. In early 2019, Vanessa and I spent a week, part work, part holiday, down in Arkansas. This used to be Clinton country. He was born in Hope, Arkansas – 'The Man from Hope', as his campaign slogan would say – and was twice governor of the state, from 1979–1981 and from 1983–1992. But dating fairly precisely from the introduction of Obamacare, Democrats have been an endangered species there; Republicans control the Arkansas state legislature and the governor's mansion and Arkansas sends only Republicans to Washington. One of the Arkansas congressmen, French Hill, was a good friend and he hosted a reception at his house for us to meet the Little Rock business community. They were an interesting group. Every one of them seemed to own at least two businesses, one of which was always a rice farm; Arkansas, for a mixture of climatic and soil reasons, is a big rice producer. Every one of them had voted for Donald Trump in 2016. And every one intended to vote for him again in 2020. As one put it to me, 'He's made us so much money.'

Arkansas, incidentally, was also the place where we saw the best billboard ever. It sat on the roof of a jewellery store a few miles outside Little Rock and said 'Free Benelli Shotgun when you buy a Diamond!' Vanessa seemed quite keen on the diamond ring displayed on the billboard but was less sure about my acquiring the shotgun. I took a photo for posterity. When I showed it to American friends in DC they rolled their eyes and sighed in dismay. When I showed it to people in Arkansas they looked at me quizzically and said 'And your point is?' Well, America is a big country. A few months later, post-retirement, I did an (unpaid – not even a free sample) after-dinner talk to a group of senior executives from the South African diamonds group, De Beers. I told them that, notwithstanding my career as a diplomat, I was well placed to offer them some advice on how they should market their products; then I circulated the photo. They were kind enough not to call the police.

Next, 'the Wall'. On 16 June 2015, journalists and onlookers gathered in the basement of Donald Trump's New York hotel to witness his campaign launch. They were entertained while waiting by the mysterious choice of a looped soundtrack of 'The Music of the Night' from *Phantom of the Opera*. Eventually Donald Trump descended on the gold-painted escalator, announced his candidacy and raged about immigration, particularly from Mexico. And then he said, 'I will build a great, great wall on our southern border and I will have Mexico pay for that wall.'

A complete wall across the 2,000-mile length of the southern border of the United States is, in reality, conceptually flawed. There are a handful of heavily populated areas along the border where a physical barrier of some form would make sense. But the thousands of miles of border includes huge, desolate expanses hundreds of miles from human habitation – not to mention physical impediments to wall construction like rivers, canyons and mountains, and legal ones, like the private ownership of some of the land that would have to be acquired. So the idea was immediately, and widely, mocked in the media and on the late-night chat shows. Moreover, I couldn't find a single Republican congressman or senator from the border states who believed that the Wall, in its entirety, was a good idea. But away from the East and West Coast, it unquestionably resonated. It became the symbol of his campaign and the loudest applause line of his campaign speeches. I remember asking a Trump supporter at the Republican Convention whether he really believed that the wall would be built, with Mexico paying for it. 'Of course not,' he replied. 'It isn't a policy, it's an image which sends a message that we will be tough on immigration. It's worth a thousand words. People get it.'

The Trump supporter was wrong, however: President Trump did want to build his wall. The Mexican president, Enrique Peña Nieto, of course said Mexico wouldn't be paying, prompting an angry but fruitless phone call from Trump and the cancellation of a bilateral summit. Nevertheless, shortly after taking office, the President signed Executive Order 13767, a formal direction to the US government to start building the wall, using existing federal funding. Inevitably, this didn't work: every government department claimed every dollar was already committed. So the White House was forced to go to Congress for the money, prompting years of bitter, partisan argument and horse-trading. The Democrats to whom I talked were determined that not a brick of the wall would be laid without Trump paying dearly for it in terms of funding for their favourite programmes. And most Republicans, privately, would shake their heads sadly and question why this was a priority at all. The federal government even ran out of money and was partly shut down for thirty-five days, from 22 December 2018 to 25 January 2019 (the longest in US history), because Trump refused to sign any spending bill that didn't include $5 billion for border wall construction.

Eventually, in February 2019, the administration found a new way through: a declaration of national emergency around the situation at the US–Mexico border, requiring money to be reallocated to wall construction from other purposes. Congress tried to stop this through a joint resolution overturning the emergency order. Trump vetoed the resolution. The issue ended up in the Supreme Court, where the administration won. In July 2019, $2.5 billion was reallocated from a Defense Department anti-drug programme, and in September 2019, $3.6 billion from military construction projects.

Once funding was confirmed, the US media understandably became obsessed with the question of how much of the wall had actually been built, and at what cost. The official figure, announced at the end of 2019, was 93 miles, against a target of 500 miles by the time of the 2020 election (and a possible length of almost 2,000 miles if it were to stretch from 'sea to shining sea'). The media claimed that most of that 93 miles was replacement of existing barriers. The administration disputed this. As for cost, it was working out at about $20 million a mile – or, as the media gleefully declared, 'the most expensive wall in history'.

Meanwhile, the mockery continued. The election campaign pitch had been about a thirty-foot-high reinforced concrete wall. Once in office, and presumably on advice, the President started talking about 'beautiful vertical steel slats', on the grounds that the US border guards needed to be able 'to see what was happening on the other side of the wall'. In public, Trump would say 'You can call it a wall, or a slat fence, or a barrier, or whatever you want to call it' – once adding, mysteriously, 'name it Peaches, whatever you like.' As for its height, the joke during the campaign had been that a thirty-foot wall would lead to a classic cobra effect: a sudden sales opportunity for 31-foot ladders. The President dismissed this; when he visited the construction site in September 2019 he said that the wall had been tested by 'world class mountain climbers' who had found that 'this was the one that was hardest to climb'. So in December, social media went wild about the posting of a video showing a (presumably 31-foot) ladder being placed against a newly constructed length of 'wall', two men climbing it, and then each of them sliding effortlessly down on the other side on one of the steel slats; the whole escapade took about thirty seconds.

While the Wall was the headline, there were several more elements to the Trump immigration clampdown. The ban on travel to and from seven countries, announced hours after Theresa May's visit, was instantly blocked in the courts. But the third version of the legislation, Presidential Proclamation 9645, survived. The legal challenge against it went all the way to the Supreme Court, but on 26 June 2018, the court ruled 5–4 in its favour. The administration also cancelled 'temporary protective status' for tens of thousands of immigrants who had fled (they claimed for their own safety) from countries like Haiti, El Salvador, Nicaragua and Sudan. A bipartisan delegation from Congress went to see the President in January 2018, to suggest a deal restoring temporary protective status in exchange for toughening immigration legislation in other areas. They claim that Trump argued that 'these shithole countries send us people that they don't want' and that the US should instead take migrants from 'places like Norway'. The President subsequently denied that he had said this. And then there were the 'Dreamers': some 800,000 young adults brought illegally into the US as children by their parents. Obama had, in 2012, signed an executive order, 'Deferred Action for Childhood Arrivals' (DACA for short), allowing the Dreamers to work legally without fear of deportation. In September 2017, the Trump administration cancelled the order, though Trump did call for it to be replaced immediately with agreed legislation which would provide for continued protection. The cancellation was, however, put on hold by court order. It was then sent up to the Supreme Court for a final decision.

All of this was highly controversial and much criticised. But nothing came close to the explosion over family separations. April 2018, the administration announced zero tolerance of illegal immi-

gration across the southern border of the United States. This meant
that undocumented migrants caught crossing the border were
arrested, prosecuted and held in federal jails. If they had children
accompanying them, the children were not considered to have
committed a crime, so weren't jailed with their parents. Instead, they
were separated and placed under the supervision of the Department
of Health and Social Services. This meant, in effect, that children
were held in temporary facilities, some of which were wholly unsuit-
able, some located thousands of miles from the border. The hastily
arranged facilities included disused warehouses or hangars, the children being housed within them in 'wire mesh compartments' – hence
'children in cages', as the headline writers instantly dubbed the policy.
The administration's presentation of the decision was, moreover,
extraordinarily muddled, amid the usual stories of White House
splits. Sometimes the line was that they were simply implementing
policies introduced by the Obama administration, even though the
reality was that, while Obama had toughened some aspects of immigration policy, he had never enforced family separations. But other
representatives of the administration, notably Stephen Miller,
presented the policy as deliberately and specifically designed to
discourage would-be immigrant families from crossing the border.
And others, notably Homeland Security Secretary Kirstjen Nielsen
said, 'We do not have a policy of separating families at the border.
Period.'

Even a brilliant presentational strategy would, however, have
struggled to cope with the outcry that followed. The policy was
condemned across the mainstream media, and dominated the news
for weeks. Polls suggested a mere 25 per cent of Americans supported
it. Hundreds of thousands participated in protest demonstrations
against it across the country. Democrats in Congress united in
outrage, and demanded visits to the facilities where children were
being held. No fewer than seventeen states brought legal challenges
against family separations. More than a dozen religious groups
announced their opposition to the policy, including all four major
denominations of American Judaism and, from Rome, Pope Francis.
The UN High Commissioner for Refugees called for the policy to

be stopped. Governments around the world distanced themselves from the US action. Several US airlines refused to carry migrant children being transported away from their parents. And, most worryingly for the administration, a handful of moderate Republicans, notably Susan Collins, the senator for Maine, John McCain, Ben Sasse of Nebraska and even the usually loyal Orrin Hatch of Utah jumped ship and called for policy reversal. Many others in the Republican Party simply refused to talk about the issue, in the political equivalent of running for the hills.

We tracked proceedings closely from the embassy, stayed in close touch with opinion on the Hill and inside the administration, and kept London informed. I reached the view that the policy was unsustainable, such was the continuing volume of opposition. Indeed, the picture was growing darker by the day. At that stage something close to 2,000 children were being held. The media were uncovering stories that family separations had actually started in the summer of 2017, months before the policy was actually announced. Visits by politicians and journalists to children's holding centres revealed that some were grossly inadequate in terms of supervision, hygiene, nutrition, sleeping arrangements and communication facilities. And worst of all, it emerged that there may not have been proper arrangements and documentation for tracking and connecting separated families – raising the spectre that reunification might be difficult and even in some cases impossible. Theresa May was asked about it at Prime Minister's Questions: to her lasting credit, she didn't duck and weave. She said: 'The pictures of children being held in what appear to be cages are deeply disturbing. This is wrong.'

As I thought, it couldn't and didn't last. On 20 June 2018, after a torrid three months of assault from all quarters except a few Republican diehards, the President announced and signed an executive order reversing the policy, confirming that families would in future be detained together, and undertaking to reunite families which had been separated.

It wasn't, and isn't, over. There are ongoing Congressional investigations. And although the story has mostly moved to the inside pages, the media remain on the case. There have been painful interviews with mothers still separated from their children, notwithstanding the reunification commitment; and suspicions, which the administration denies, that faulty paperwork trails mean some families will never be reunited. There are eyewitness reports from Congressional visits of inadequate, overcrowded detention facilities. Meanwhile, the President said publicly, on 9 April 2019, that 'President Obama had child separation . . . we all know it . . . I'm the one that stopped it . . .'

The administration would claim, across the breadth of its immigration policies, that it was only doing what it had promised, and been elected, to do; to regain control of America's borders and to get immigration numbers down. There was, however, always an undercurrent to the President's rhetoric, a succession of coded signals to the base that were less about how many were coming in to the US than about who the immigrants were: or, some would say, classic dog-whistle politics.

The use of the dog whistle is as old as politics itself. It means using language or images that, on the surface, sound or look commonplace and unobjectionable, but which have a different or deeper meaning for some; to labour the metaphor, which are audible only to certain life forms. The term can be applied to all forms of political discourse, but it crops up most often in the context of immigration . . . or race. There are numerous examples. One of the most famous – or notorious – is the Willie Horton case from the 1988 US elections. This was the race between George H.W. Bush, nowadays seen somewhat as a father-of-the-nation figure, and as epitomising a 'kinder, gentler, America', and Michael Dukakis, then Governor of Massachusetts. Dukakis was a supporter of his state's 'weekend pass' programme, which allowed prisoners to leave prison for a day to work or visit family. The policy, incidentally, was introduced by a Republican governor. The Bush campaign launched a television advert – an 'attack ad' – featuring convicted murderer Willie Horton, who had escaped while using his weekend pass, and while on the run, had raped a woman and stabbed her fiancé. The centrepiece of the ad was a photograph of African-American Horton looking utterly terrifying; the dog-whistle message: vote for Dukakis and the country will be terrorised by rapists and murderers running amok.

Nor is the dog whistle confined to US politics. In the 2015 Canadian election, the incumbent Prime Minister, Stephen Harper, talked in a televised election debate about 'Old Stock Canadians' – meaning white Canadians. In the 2016 UK referendum campaign, UKIP produced a poster bearing the words 'Breaking Point', super-imposed on a photograph of hundreds of refugees fleeing the civil war in Syria (a poster from which fellow Leave campaigners like Michael Gove and Chris Grayling instantly disassociated themselves). And then there was the case of John Howard, multiple election winner, Australian Prime Minister from 1996 to 2007, and in the eyes of both the Australian media and his political opponents a master exponent of the dog-whistle art. He revived the term 'un-Australian' and used it to describe pretty much anyone who disagreed with him about any of his policies. But his 'finest hour', or his most controversial, perhaps offensive decision, depending on one's political viewpoint, was 'the Tampa Incident' in 2001. A Norwegian freighter, MV *Tampa*, en route to Australia, stopped in the Indian Ocean to rescue some 400 Afghan refugees from a sinking fishing vessel. Howard refused permission for the *Tampa* to enter Australian waters. The Afghans on board would certainly have qual-ified as refugees under international law. Some of them were seriously ill, so the ship would also have met the criteria for a maritime vessel in need. So Howard's position was, in the view of many, contrary to long-established international law. Howard justified his decision, however, by saying, 'I believe it is in Australia's national interest that we draw a line on what is increasingly becoming an uncontrollable number of illegal arrivals in this country.' Note the pejorative language: the refugees in question weren't illegal; and 400 were scarcely uncontrollable.

The ship eventually entered Australian waters anyway, without permission, but was immediately intercepted by the Australian navy and held offshore. The Australian government simultaneously intro-duced legislation, in the form of the Border Protection Bill, which applied retrospectively and forbade 'unauthorised arrivals' from landing on Australian territory. Eventually (thanks to financial inducements from the Australian government), detention centres were set up in some nearby Pacific islands. Some of the *Tampa* refugees ended up in New Zealand; others went back to Afghanistan. Hostile commentators highlighted the 'dehumanised' language that Howard had used, his disinclination to talk about the conditions on the vessel or the back stories of the refugees, as a way of concealing what they saw as the innate cruelty of the policy. But opinion polls suggested that some 90 per cent of voters supported the government's handling of the affair. And having been marginally behind in the opinion polls before the *Tampa* incident, Howard won a comfortable election victory a few months later.

Whether or not *Tampa* was any sort of deliberate template for the administration's approach to immigration, they made plentiful use of the dog whistle, though arguably much of Trump's language was so direct and unambiguous as not to qualify for the term. Mexicans, from the start, were a target: 'drug runners', 'criminals', 'rapists'. On the campaign trail, he claimed that a federal judge presiding over a case against Trump University was biased because of his Mexican heritage. In one of the campaign debates with Hillary Clinton he said that African Americans and Hispanics were 'living in hell' because their neighbourhoods were so dangerous; 'you walk down the street, you get shot'. He suggested four women of colour, Democrats newly elected to Congress, should 'go back and help fix the totally broken and crime-infested places from which they came'; three of the four were born in America. But the comment which hit the headlines, and which forever will be attached to him, was about the clashes in Charlottesville.

Charlottesville is an attractive city in Virginia, a couple of hours from Washington, on the edge of the Shenandoah National Park. Thomas Jefferson's plantation, Monticello, can be found on the outskirts, as can President Monroe's home, Highland. On 11 August 2017, however, just a few months into President Trump's term of office, Charlottesville was the venue for Unite the Right, a white supremacist rally that featured self-identified neo-Nazis, members of the Ku Klux Klan (the 'KKK') and white nationalists. The ostensible prompt for the rally was the proposed removal of a statue of Confederate General Robert E. Lee from Lee Park at the centre of the city. But the rally itself, judging by the TV coverage, involved a fair amount of marching around the city streets, carrying Tiki torches (more commonly seen outside Pacific island-themed restaurants), waving Confederate and Nazi flags, and chanting anti-Semitic slogans: 'Jews will not replace us' and the old Nazi favourite, 'Blood and Soil'. (Tiki Torches, incidentally, quickly condemned the event.) All of this was distasteful, if deeply ridiculous; but the episode turned into tragedy when a declared white supremacist, James Fields Jr, deliberately rammed his car into a group of counter-protesters, injuring nineteen and killing one, Heather Heyer. Fields was eventually convicted of first-degree murder, confessed to more than twenty other hate crimes, and was sentenced to life imprisonment.

The rally, the violence and Heather Heyer's death were a huge news story. Two hours after it happened, the President said that he condemned 'hatred, bigotry, and violence on many sides'. The media immediately asked what he had meant by 'many sides'. Over the next twenty-four hours, criticism mounted from quarters including a number of senior Republicans, who questioned whether the President should be equating racist thugs with peaceful demonstrators. In response, two days later, on 14 August, Trump issued a second statement, in which he said: 'Racism is evil and those who cause violence in its name are criminals and thugs, including the KKK, neo-Nazis, white supremacists and other hate groups that are repugnant to everything that we hold dear as Americans.' Both the media and some of the Republican critics, notably the African-American senator for South Carolina, Tim Scott, said the second statement had come too late.

All of which set the scene for a third Trump statement, on 15 August, this one delivered from Trump Tower in New York. The theoretical subject of the press conference was the state of US infrastructure (which was calamitous, at least around Washington). But as soon as the Q&A started, Charlottesville was the only subject. And the President went back to his original script, defending his first statement that there had been blame on both sides. He said:

'Not all of these people were white supremacists by any stretch . . . You had people that were very fine people on both sides . . . You had people in that group that were there to protest the taking down of a very very important statue and the renaming of a park from Robert E. Lee to another name.'

Charlottesville had been a big story. But until the Trump Tower outburst, it had been fading. This third statement didn't just revive it; it made it immense. I watched it live on one of the news channels: I was used to seeing wild Trump press conferences, but found it incomprehensible that he had chosen to reignite the controversy. I was also struck by how he appeared. Trump was always combative when talking to the media. But this time he looked enraged, steaming. Some of his team, notably chief of staff John Kelly, were in camera shot; they looked somewhere between stunned and stricken. And the more the journalists challenged the President on who the 'fine people' were among the neo-Nazis and white nationalists, the more that Trump doubled down on his assertion that some of the attendees had simply cared about the statues. Though he didn't articulate it in quite such terms, he was essentially arguing that some of the protests were justified, because removing these public celebrations of prominent Confederate figures amounted to a rewriting of American history in the cause of political correctness.

Within hours the condemnations started to flood in. Eventually more than sixty Republican and Democratic politicians condemned the President's remarks. One of the most senior Republicans, House Speaker Paul Ryan, said: 'We must be clear. White supremacy is repulsive. This bigotry is counter to all this country stands for. There can be no moral ambiguity.' An advisory group of senior American businessmen which the White House had put together unravelled, as some of the best known of them announced their resignations. It was now that Gary Cohn let the media know he was contemplating resignation (some eight months before his eventual departure). Public opinion also appeared to go against the President; opinion polls in the immediate aftermath reported that 56 per cent disapproved of Trump's response, while only 28 per cent approved. And 'fine people on both sides' remains one of the most remembered phrases of this soundbite-rich presidency. Leading Democratic candidate for 2020 Joe Biden cited it in his campaign launch, and it is bound to be quoted interminably as the race hots up. The President continues to say he was talking about statue enthusiasts.

What's the balance sheet, then, on the President's domestic policy successes and failures? Healthcare reform has been a comprehensive and decisive failure. The administration has succeeded only in making things worse: damaging Obamacare while failing completely to find a new approach. Tax reform has been a qualified success; qualified because cutting taxes without cutting spending is a cop-out, short-sighted, and piles up debt for the next generation. That said, the unstoppably dynamic US economy has continued to grow more strongly than anywhere in Europe. It is difficult to quantify how much of this has been down to the actions of the Trump administration; some economists claim that it has been largely a reflection of Obama's policies. On the other hand, nearly every American businessman I met attributed some of the economic growth to the tax cut boost.

And what of immigration? Trump is, of course, on to something when he talks about the importance of government gaining control of the flows over the borders. Some of my most liberal American friends admit it in private. Economic migration is one of the existential challenges of the age. Every European government is struggling with it too. It was unquestionably a factor in the Brexit debate, in Angela Merkel's decline in popularity, and in the rise of right-wing parties across Europe. But it can be argued that, in trying to turn campaign rhetoric into successful policy, there has been another comprehensive failure. The Wall may have been good campaign material but it is flawed as a policy idea: costly and ineffective. The initial attempts to restrict migrants from certain, mostly Muslim countries were bungled; some restrictions are now in place but their value is questionable. The family separation policy was a presentational disaster, doing huge damage to America's reputation and forcing an embarrassing policy reversal. And the dog-whistle politics accompanying all of this will have pleased the base but may have alienated voters whom the President will need in 2020, as well as reopening some deep divisions in the country.

In among the acres of newsprint, the immigration debate also generated some brilliant cartoons, especially after Charlottesville and the President's reference to 'very fine people on both sides'. Two in particular have stuck in my mind. The KKK costume, both ludicrous and menacing, features full-length white robes, with different markings according to rank, and tall conical hoods, covering (and therefore hiding) the whole head, apart from eyeholes. In the week after Charlottesville, the cover of *The Economist* featured a depiction of Trump shouting into a megaphone, depicted as a KKK hood. And the cover of the *New Yorker* the same week had the President sitting in a sailing boat, blowing into a sail which was also depicted as a KKK hood. From opposite sides of the Atlantic, the same imagery, the same repudiation of the President's words.

15

Uk–Us Relations: Brexit, Blenheim and the State Visit

*

'He told me I should sue the EU, not go into negotiations'
— Prime Minister Theresa May on Donald Trump's
advice about how to handle Brexit

*

'What a mess she and her representatives have created'
— President Donald Trump on Theresa May's
handling of Brexit

*

IT WAS 3 p.m. on Friday 24 May 2019. A group of us were gathered around the TV screen in the press section of the embassy, looking at an empty podium in Downing Street, set against the backdrop of that famous black door. The Prime Minister, Theresa May, emerged, strain etched on her face, and announced her resignation. She maintained her composure until the last sentence of her short statement, and then, voice breaking and tears starting to flow, turned and retreated to the sanctuary of No. 10. In Washington, silence hung over the gathering. Like everyone back in the UK, we had known this was coming. She had failed three times to get her Brexit deal through the House of Commons, and the cabinet were in open revolt. But this was a moment, not about politics, but about individual anguish, about broken dreams and about public acknowledgement of failure; and it moved all of us.

As I walked back to my office, I reflected that this was the second time in just forty months that I had seen a British Prime Minister stand in Downing Street, under the unsparing gaze of the media, and announce their resignation. It seemed as if there were no end to the damage Brexit was doing: to the British economy, to our international reputation, to national cohesion, to individual reputations and careers.

It hadn't always been like this. Back in June 2016, on the first Saturday after the Brexit vote, Vanessa and I were in the Georgetown Safeway, doing the weekly shop. It was normal, in the Georgetown village, to clash shopping trollies with someone you knew. That day was no exception. The lady behind us in the queue at the cash register was a well-known figure and hostess of classic Washington dinner parties. She greeted us and said, 'What wonderful news about the Brexit vote. I was so thrilled when it heard it. You are getting your independence back. Who do you think will leave next?'

I was to hear a lot of this sentiment over the next few months. Many Americans felt this way. And it was understandable; it would have been unimaginable for the US to share sovereignty in the style of EU members. But I was also to hear quite a lot of the opposite: alarm at our decision, concern about our future, and anxiety about what it would mean for the future of the EU as a whole. In a way, the US was as sharply divided as the UK on the issue, mostly on partisan lines, with Republicans applauding and Democrats worrying.

Personally, I wasn't a Brexit enthusiast: not because, in the clichéd trope of the Foreign Office, I was a lifelong disciple of a European superstate, but precisely because we had negotiated such an exceptional status for the UK – all of the good stuff and none of the bad – that we were already having our cake and eating it. But personal views have no place in the professional part of a diplomat's existence. So from the moment of the vote, for the next three years, I would find myself, in meetings with the administration and Congress, in public speeches, in TV and radio interviews, and several times in the supermarket queue, explaining and defending the decision the British people had taken, and expressing confidence about a golden future. All the while, the politics in my home country were becoming increasingly bitter, rancorous and partisan, and the Brexit process stumbled from crisis to crisis. I had never known a time like it, and it overshadowed every hour I spent in America.

In the immediate aftermath of the Brexit vote, two things about America became clear. First, no one outside a tiny handful of people in the federal government had heard of Theresa May. And second, apart from a few specialists in the State Department, Americans had only the haziest notion of what the European Union actually was: its history, its powers, its budget, its legislative sweep, its institutions. So in those first few months after the vote, the most common questions were: 'Why did Cameron resign?' 'Is Theresa May like Margaret Thatcher?' 'How is life now you've left?' On the last of these questions, I had to develop a mini-script which downloaded a summary of the post-vote reality in no more than about twenty seconds. This was the length of time I usually had before the eyes opposite me started to glaze over, the jaw fell to the chest, and some variety of unconsciousness kicked in.

Meanwhile, I was keeping a close track of political developments in London. It is often forgotten, in the light of how her premiership turned out, but Theresa May made a strong start. She looked and sounded the part. She was dominating the Opposition leader Jeremy Corbyn at the dispatch box. And she was exercising strong discipline over her cabinet and party from No. 10. We in Washington found the Iron Fist exceptionally useful. A new cabinet had been appointed – and a lot of the newcomers wanted to pay immediate visits to DC, usually at moments that made no sense whatsoever, such as when Congress was in recess. One minister even wanted to come over the Labor Day long weekend. We found that, with one quick phone call to one of the private secretaries in No. 10 – usually the excellent Jonny Hall – the notion of a visit would mysteriously disappear.

As 2016 progressed, however, there were some worrying signs. A new department, DEXEU, the Department for Exiting the EU, had been set up, with David Davis as its secretary of state. This had the effect of cutting the Foreign Office, and indeed the Treasury, completely out of the process. Olly Robbins, my former deputy national security adviser, was made its permanent secretary and would be the official-level lead in the exit negotiations. Olly was (and is) a friend and a brilliant official, and deserved the promotion. But there was something pointed, and odd, about this systematic rejection of departments and individuals with an EU background and negotiating experience. For example, had I been running the process, I would have tried to persuade Jon Cunliffe, my successor as UK ambassador to the EU, to lead the negotiations, simply because he was the best negotiator in the British system. It all looked like a pre-emptive concession to those backbenchers who instinctively distrusted any British official who had ever worked on the EU.

Then, during her party conference speech on 2 October, the Prime Minister stated that it was 'for the government alone to trigger Article 50'. She was referring to the provision of the EU treaties which a leaving member state invokes to launch negotiations about departure. A member of the public, Gina Miller, took the government to court over this refusal to hold a parliamentary vote. It ended up in the Supreme Court. At last there was something my American friends could recognise. And on 24 January 2017, the court decided against the government and for Gina Miller. This series of events – Parliament fighting with government, the courts getting involved and finding against the government – seemed at the time genuinely extraordinary. It was unprecedented, but it was a portent of the future.

There was another signal of the shape of things to come on 3 January 2017, when my friend Ivan Rogers suddenly resigned as UK ambassador to the EU. I had known Ivan for twenty years – initially as the Treasury man at the table in Whitehall EU policy debates, later as David Cameron's EU adviser while I filled the national security role. On EU policy, he was the ultimate expert; we all thought we knew stuff, but Ivan was encyclopedic. Sitting in Washington, I could imagine him taking ministers forensically through the implications of Brexit – the options realistically available to the UK and the likely positioning of the Brussels institutions and the other member states. The British media were reporting that some ministers and senior figures in No. 10 were finding his advice too gloomy and pessimistic, and that he was in consequence being cut out of key meetings. I didn't know if these stories were well-founded, but if they were, Ivan had no choice but to go. A big part of his job was to advise, as mine was from Washington. If you can't even get access to those you are meant to be advising, you might as well go and tend your garden.

If these decisions about structures and people looked like mistakes, they also looked manageable and recoverable; less so the Prime Minister's Lancaster House speech of 17 January 2017. This felt like an irrevocable and strategic error. The vote to leave the EU had been about a principle: membership or not. It had left undefined the nature of any future relationship between the UK and the EU. The strongest and most purist of the Leave campaigners wanted, and continued to advocate, a clean and complete break. They had every right to do so. But it was a reasonable assumption that the British public had an open mind on the form that Brexit should take. It was equally reasonable to assume that no one had voted to lose their jobs. May's Lancaster House speech, however, ruled out staying in the single market. It also rejected a customs union. Both of these would have been possible while the UK still left, but were dismissed as 'half in half out'. In ruling out these possibilities, she effectively aligned the government with the so-called 'hard Brexit' supporters, and declared war on those who supported softer options. She was taking the economically high-risk course. We did more than 40 per cent of our trade with the single market we were about to leave. She also said that she would not accept a 'punitive deal'; another declaration of war, this time aimed at the other member states and the Brussels institutions. It later became the soundbite 'no deal is better than a bad deal'.

The British media were suggesting that Nick Timothy, a Brexit enthusiast, had written much of the speech. From where I sat, across the Atlantic, I didn't think the Prime Minister needed to have been so emphatically categorical and sharp-edged about the shape of the future relationship. Why box yourself in so early in the process? But whatever my personal doubts about the speech, it became my personal script. I would from then on use it to explain our direction of travel, before pressing for a US contribution in the form of an ambitious UK/US Free Trade Deal, as partial compensation for the business we might lose in Europe.

The next big moment came in March. After the Supreme Court defeat, the government was required to get parliamentary approval to invoke Article 50. The Bill passed through its parliamentary procedures and received royal assent on 16 March. And on 29 March, Ivan Rogers' successor, Tim Barrow, delivered to Donald Tusk, the president of the European Council, the Article 50 letter, the formal notification of the UK's decision to leave the EU.

This also looked to me like a serious mistake. Article 50 set a two-year deadline for the completion of negotiations on the terms of departure. So from the moment it landed on Donald Tusk's desk, the clock was ticking and the pressure was on the UK. I thought the government should first have gained parliamentary approval for its approach to the negotiations: not just the terms of departure, but also a reasonably detailed proposition for the future relationship. There should have been a White Paper, an authoritative analysis of the tasks and options, followed by a sustained effort to find a cross-party consensus, and an affirmatory vote. Instead, the government looked set on bulldozing through its relatively 'hard' Brexit proposition, despite its narrow majority. It also knew that its own backbenchers were split, some wanting a much softer Brexit or a second, confirmatory referendum, others wanting an even harder Brexit. In short, it was asking for trouble, and trouble it got.

But not before the Prime Minister made her big decision. She played her ace, or perhaps her joker. On 18 April, out of the blue, and apparently on the back of a holiday walking in the Welsh hills (what was in the air?) she proposed a general election. Under the Fixed Terms Parliament Act, she needed a two-thirds majority of the total membership of the House of Commons to get this approved. But it is almost impossible for opposition parties to say that they don't want a general election and the opportunity to overthrow the government. So the proposition was passed on 19 April by a huge majority – 522 to 13. The election was set for 8 June. The logic behind the decision was obvious: the government enjoyed a big lead in the opinion polls – it was twenty-four points ahead in some polls – and winning a big majority would guarantee them straightforward passage of whatever deal they agreed with the EU. But elections are unpredictable creatures. As I heard the news, I couldn't help but think of some of the shock results of the past, such as John Major's win over Neil Kinnock in 1992, in defiance of all the polling predictions, or David Cameron's surprise overall majority in 2015. And the Prime Minister might have been thinking about Gordon Brown's 'election that never was'. In autumn 2007, his advisers pushed him to call an early general election on the back of a well-received first few months in office and a strong lead in the opinion polls. Racked by indecision, Brown dithered, then decided against, though not before the media had written that it was going to happen. He never really recovered his reputation. When the election eventually came round on its normal schedule, in 2010, he lost.

It's strange following an election campaign from overseas. Instead of the daily immersion, you get occasional vignettes, when you have time to tune into BBC World, or when something is newsworthy enough to make it onto the US news programmes. And that is genuinely rare, given the obsession with domestic news. But even on the basis of these brief, intermittent glimpses, it was clear that this was an odd campaign. In particular, whenever I caught a clip of the Prime Minister on the campaign trail, she looked deeply uncomfortable. She kept repeating that people should vote for her because she would provide 'strong and stable leadership'. It really wasn't her. I guessed that she was following the instructions of her election strategists. Why couldn't they see how pedestrian it looked and let her off the leash? Meanwhile, the Labour campaign had an old-fashioned, high-spending look, but with some obviously popular policies: super-taxing the rich and the corporations, free school meals, more police officers, the abolition of student tuition fees. And the polls were visibly tightening.

There is, in British embassies across the world, a tradition of 'election watch' parties. In Washington, there was little visible interest in the election campaign, but lots of interest in whether we would be holding a party. And of course we were, for about four hundred of Washington's finest. Given the five-hour time difference, however, the BBC exit poll, at 10 p.m. UK time, became public an hour before our party started. A group of us gathered in front of the TV in the Embassy political section, watching the BBC coverage. There was a suitably dramatic countdown, until on the stroke of 5 p.m. Eastern Time, the prediction came up: 314 seats for the Conservatives, a loss of 17, and 266 for Labour, a gain of 40. Taking the smaller parties into account, this meant a hung Parliament, with the government remaining the largest party but losing its overall majority. The presenters and pundits immediately provided the health warning: that it was only a poll, not a result. But my memory of exit polls was that they were usually strikingly accurate (as was this one: when the seat-by-seat counts were in, the final results were 317 Conservative, 262 Labour). Moreover, somehow, this also felt accurate, like the logical culmination of the campaign.

For the rest of the evening, with the party in full swing, I was asked repeatedly to explain how things had gone so badly. Why had the Prime Minister called an election she didn't need to hold, only to lose her majority? I talked about the inherent unpredictability of elections, about the setbacks and mistakes of the Conservative campaign, and about the poor record of pre-election polling in recent elections, including in the US. But I sensed a fundamental change in US views of the Prime Minister: no longer Thatcher's heir, but a politician who got big decisions wrong.

In the Brexit context, the next eighteen months were a slog. I continued to be asked about it several times a day. The questions had moved on a bit. 'Why did she risk the election?' 'Why is it taking so long?' And from the real experts, 'Who are the DUP?' and 'What's a confidence and supply agreement?' I continued to try to sound upbeat: the negotiations with the EU were going well, we were getting what we wanted, and we expected a deal and parliamentary approval before the exit date of 29 March 2019, exactly two years after the Article 50 letter. I remember in particular being invited to a dinner in a ritzy apartment in the fashionable Washington suburb of Rosslyn, hosted by a federal appeals court judge and his wife. Unusually for Washington, the guests were mostly Republicans, and the host asked me to 'entertain' them over the main course with a short speech about Brexit. I did my standard upbeat number. The guests seemed to like it and applauded politely. Vanessa said to me afterwards, 'That really reassured me! I thought Brexit was going badly but you lifted my spirits.' I explained, 'That was just my usual Brexit number . . .' But it was reassuring that it sounded so convincing.

Meanwhile, over in Brussels, the exit negotiations kicked off, and then dragged on, seemingly forever. 2017 turned into 2018. David Davis came through DC and briefed the administration, Congress, the think-tank community and the US media on the state of play. He did a good job, with a persuasive, if unjustified, tone of conviction and confidence. On 28 February 2018, the European Commission published the draft withdrawal agreement, as a work in progress. And there were endless positive 'lines to take' from DEXEU and the FCO, encouraging British embassies around the world to brief their host governments on how well it was all going. The parliamentary delegations coming through Washington were, however, telling us a different story, when they weren't fighting among themselves. They were increasingly sceptical, even while the negotiations were going on, that a deal could be done which would get through the House of Commons. The problem was, on the one hand, a solid bloc comprising opposition parties and rebel Conservatives who wanted a second referendum; and on the other hand, a group of hard Brexit supporters, the European Research Group (ERG), seemingly involving as many as seventy MPs, who didn't like the broad idea of a continuing close relationship between the UK and the EU. They specifically rejected the 'Irish backstop', an element of the emerging agreement which was designed to prevent a hard border between Northern Ireland and the Republic of Ireland. It provided for the United Kingdom of Great Britain and Northern Ireland as a whole to have a common customs area with the EU until arrangements could be agreed that guaranteed 'no hard border'. The ERG saw this as a trap which could keep the UK in a customs union with the EU forever. The Friends of Ireland Caucus in Congress were similarly suspicious, though for the different reason that we would somehow use the issue to do down the Irish or close off forever the prospect of a united Ireland. For my part, I had to talk regularly to the caucus in Washington to reassure them of the British government's intentions; I reckoned the Irish Embassy in DC, well though I got on with my Irish counterpart, were stirring things up. And the words I came to dread most were, 'Hey, can you explain this Irish backstop thing to us?' Add together these two entirely opposed factions, throw in the fact that there was no government majority, and there was the recipe for a government defeat.

And that's exactly what happened. On the way to the final deal, the Prime Minister lost a couple of Brexit secretaries: David Davis resigned on 9 July and his successor Dominic Raab on 15 November. But a deal was declared between the twenty-eight member states at a European Council on 25 November 2018. There were days of debate in Parliament. British embassies worldwide were briefed to speak positively about the prospects of parliamentary approval, although the British media assessed the chances as close to zero. A 'meaningful vote' on the deal was duly held on 15 January 2019. The government lost massively. Only 202 voted for the May deal; 432 voted against.

There was another 'meaningful vote' on 12 March, on the basis of a slightly revised deal. This one was lost too. Parliament was asked what it wanted, as opposed to what it didn't: all eight options failed to achieve a majority. Meaningful vote 3 was held on 29 March, and was also lost. And with the two-year deadline expiring, the government had to go back to its European partners and ask for a deadline extension – or, in fact, two, because the first one wasn't long enough.

While all of this was going on, our American contacts divided into three camps. The majority were simply bemused: 'What the hell is going on over there?' Inside the White House, the mood had darkened. I was hearing that the President was saying to anyone within earshot that the Prime Minister had 'made a mess of it', and that she should have followed his advice (which was, as the Prime

Minister later made public, to sue the EU; it wasn't clear for what). And third, I was increasingly hearing words of real concern from the American business community – both manufacturing and Wall Street. Some asked whether their investments were safe. Some warned that they had either frozen or decided definitively against future investment because of the uncertainty. And some just looked at me sadly and said: 'We expect this sort of chaos from others but never from you; what's happened to you?' I told them all that what they were seeing was democracy in action; that it was a difficult moment but we would get it sorted; and that the UK remained a great place to invest, with low corporation tax and strong economic fundamentals. Some looked reassured; some just shook their heads.

The government continued trying to find a version of the deal that Parliament would support. There were formal talks with the Opposition on finding a way forward which both sides of the chamber could support; they went nowhere and were abandoned after six weeks. On 21 May, the Prime Minister delivered a speech on a 'New Brexit Deal' which included a ten-point offer to MPs. But the reality was that time had run out on this negotiation and on this Prime Minister. The London newspapers were full of well-sourced stories of plots against her. Three days later, she resigned, effective from 7 June.

As I look back, I judge that, in terms of fronting up for the UK, this was as difficult an eighteen months as I had ever experienced. I was in Tokyo during the IRA hunger strikes, the death of Bobby Sands and those who followed; and that was difficult. There were many moments around the table during Brussels EU negotiations when I was required to make myself deeply unpopular, but if you don't revel in those moments you should be doing something else. But these were unpopular policies. There were reasons for them which you could explain and debate. Those months in the Brexit negotiations were different, because of the picture of total disarray: a government which was in office but not in power. This is not to criticise those in Parliament who were voting against the government; whichever side of the argument they chose, they did so because they had deeply held beliefs. But the cumulative damage to the British brand of those eighteen months of disarray was of Suez proportions, and may take a long time to repair.

In among the Brexit struggles we also had two visits by Donald Trump to the UK, both of them opportunities for resetting the 'special relationship' but fraught with risk. Wind the clock back to early 2018. Theresa May had been the first leader into the White House, a week after inauguration. But since then, the President had been to Saudi Arabia, China, Israel, Italy, Belgium, Poland, Germany, France, Japan, South Korea, Vietnam and the Philippines. French President Emmanuel Macron had positioned himself as President Trump's new best friend on earth. And there had been an angry exchange between Trump and the Prime Minister. The wildest Trump tweets tended to come in the early hours of the morning. On Wednesday 29 November 2017, he retweeted to his 50 million followers some Islamophobic video clips from a far-right extremist group called Britain First. None of these videos (example: 'Muslim migrants beating up a Dutch boy on crutches') were what they purported to be. May responded, as moderately as she could get away with, by saying that Trump had been wrong to promote the views of the group. Trump had responded waspishly that she should 'focus on the destructive radical Islamic terrorism taking place within the UK'. In short, putting all these elements together, I could sense that, absent a successful Trump visit, the British media would soon be writing a story that the 'special relationship' was special no longer. And to cap it all, I was hearing from friends in the White House that the President was missing his Scottish golf courses and wanted to visit them in 2018.

Whitehall didn't instantly embrace the idea of a Trump visit. Brexit was sucking up all the energy. There were understandable concerns about demonstrations, security and costs. In the wake of the Britain First bust-up, there were worries about what the President might say while in the UK. But No. 10 could also see the risks of Trump's continuing absence from the UK while he had been to France, Germany, Italy and Poland. So we were eventually given a flickering green light to begin planning.

On the detail of the programme, Whitehall essentially said to us:

tell us what will work best. In the White House, the chief of staff, John Kelly, and his team were in charge. It turned out to be an almost entirely painless process. The Kelly team were a pleasure to work with, provided I was happy to fit in with John Kelly's preferred meeting time of 7 a.m.; and Whitehall were in 'can do' mode. We rapidly decided to steer clear of London, simply because of the traffic disruption a US presidential visit on a working day would create, even if the predicted demonstrations didn't happen. In my time at No. 10, I had taken part in several summits at Chequers; it was a great venue, especially at the height of the English summer. As an army man, Kelly was keen for there to be an element in the programme showing how closely the British and American armed forces worked together. So we devised a visit to Sandhurst, not to inspect the students, but to see a mock attack on a 'terrorist compound' (some disused buildings on the Sandhurst estate) conducted jointly from helicopters by British and American special forces. Which left us to plan the meeting with Her Majesty the Queen, a traditional fixture in US presidential visits, and the welcome dinner on the first night.

The royal element of the programme was equally straightforward: a meeting with the Queen at Windsor Castle, a short helicopter ride from Chequers. But the first-night event needed some imagination. We guessed, and Kelly confirmed, that the President would want to do something 'different', something previous presidential visitors hadn't done. We kicked some ideas around. None really seemed quite different enough. And then we started hearing that the President was a big fan of the Churchill film that had recently been released, *Darkest Hour*. Its star, Gary Oldman, who played Churchill, won the Best Actor Oscar, a British success. We thought to ourselves – why not hold the welcome dinner at Blenheim Palace, Churchill's birthplace?

It was complicated. Blenheim would have to be closed to the public for almost a week, for security reasons. The police were not thrilled by the size of the secure perimeter they would have to establish. The Duke of Marlborough would have to be asked for his permission. But for history and grandeur, it couldn't be matched.

The White House loved the idea. And London, to their huge credit, overcame all the obstacles and made it happen.

The visit itself took place on 12–13 July. The Blenheim dinner was, on the surface, a great success. There was a military parade on the vast lawn. The President and First Lady had a private tour of the palace and were shown some Churchill memorabilia. There was a glittering guest list, including some American business friends of the President's. We had invited a selection of senior British businessmen, and encouraged them, in their brief pre-arranged audiences with the President, to highlight the breadth and depth of UK investment in the US. The Prime Minister and President sat next to one another at dinner and seemed, from where Vanessa and I were sitting on the opposite side of the table, to be getting along famously. But while the event unfolded, it seemed, exactly as planned, I was hearing that there was a big problem in the pipeline.

Trump had given an interview to the *Sun* newspaper on the eve of the visit; we heard from the White House press team that it had been a favour to his friend Rupert Murdoch. The journalist who interviewed Trump, Tom Newton Dunn, was someone I knew from my press spokesman days. I had a lot of respect for him as a talented, knowledgeable operator, with a brilliant nose for a story and a style of friendly interrogation that readily trapped the unwary into saying the unwise. And by the second course, I was hearing that Newton Dunn had delivered for his editor and that there would be some explosive stuff on the front page of the *Sun* the following day.

Back at the hotel after the dinner, I found the *Sun* story online. It was indeed really bad. The front-page headline was: 'TRUMP'S BREXIT BLAST. Donald Trump told Theresa May how to do Brexit but she wrecked it – and says the US trade deal is off.' In the body of the piece, Trump was recorded as saying that May had ignored his advice by opting for a soft Brexit strategy, and had added, 'If they do a deal like that we would be dealing with the European Union instead of dealing with the UK, so it will probably kill the trade deal.' He also suggested that European leaders had destroyed Europe's culture and identity by allowing in 'millions of migrants'. And he observed that Boris Johnson (who had just resigned as

Foreign Secretary) would make a great Prime Minister. What with proposing Farage for British ambassador and Johnson for Prime Minister, the President was a one-man headhunting agency.

The Sandhurst event was first on the agenda the following morning. Trump arrived by helicopter. I was a few steps behind the Prime Minister as she greeted him. He immediately launched into an apology for the *Sun* article. She told him not to worry: it was just the British press. He looked relieved. And they moved on to watch the special forces show together, still seemingly in the same convivial mood as at the previous night's dinner.

I admired at the time the Prime Minister's handling of the episode; it was genuinely gracious. But to this day I am genuinely puzzled by Trump's handling of the interview. For a few months afterwards, he would call the *Sun* 'fake news'. But there was no doubt that he had said those words: there was a recording. Did he think his remarks about the Prime Minister's handling of Brexit were not a story? Did he think his praise of Boris Johnson would be uncontroversial? As a man who had cut his media teeth in the brutal world of the New York tabloids, it's hard to believe that he would have been unaware of the impact of what he was saying. Perhaps he would say he was just answering the question truthfully; being authentic. Whatever, it reminded me of May's visit to the White House, when, as her plane was lifting off from the runway at Dulles, exhausts glowing in the night sky, the White House was initiating chaos at airports around the world by issuing the executive order banning citizens from seven Muslim countries from entering the US. It was really hard to arrange a wholly successful visit involving this President.

The Chequers session went fine. The sun shone. The President was in a mellow, conciliatory mood. He agreed with pretty much everything the Prime Minister proposed, and said lots of nice things about her at the press conference out on the lawn. Not something government officials, or even ministers, say often, but we had something for which to thank the *Sun*.

The state visit, a year later, was completely different, in two senses. First, it took place, of necessity, in London. And second, there was no real flexibility or need for creativity in the programme. Its main elements were unchanging, as though set down in the Magna Carta, or so it felt. As tends to be the case, the ceremonials would fall on the first day: the formal arrival at Buckingham Palace; the Guard of Honour; the 41-gun salute; the white-tie state banquet at Buckingham Palace. There were also more informal moments: a private lunch with the Queen and family; tea with the Prince of Wales and the Duchess of Cornwall. The second day was about work: a meeting with British and American businessmen; talks and lunch at No. 10; a press conference; all finishing with a return dinner at the American ambassador's residence. I set the visit up and finalised the programme with the new chief of staff in the White House, Mick Mulvaney, who proved an excellent collaborator. And it was exceptionally straightforward; they were happy with everything we suggested and didn't need any extra elements. The visit was to be one part of a four-leg European tour: after London, Trump would attend an event in Portsmouth to mark the seventy-fifth anniversary of the D-Day landings; he would visit another Trump golf course in Doonbeg on the west coast of Ireland and meet the Irish Taoiseach; and he would visit Normandy for further D-Day commemorations. And for the London leg at least, the President was bringing all but the youngest of his family with him: Donald Jr, Ivanka, Eric and Tiffany.

The visit took place on 3–4 June 2019. Vanessa and I were involved throughout. There was a degree of tension around the arrival ceremony: the previous year, at Windsor, the choreography at the Guard of Honour inspection had been awkward. This time it went flawlessly, and two sets of courtiers sighed unanimously in relief. And the private lunch afterwards, with early summer sunshine flooding in across the verdant Buckingham Palace lawns, was genuinely special. Later that afternoon, during tea at St James's Palace with the Prince of Wales and the Duchess of Cornwall, the Prince's strongly held views on climate change were on the menu. I would have been fascinated to listen in, but it was a private affair. And then the centrepiece, the state banquet. I have had the good fortune to be present at 'event' meals around the world: in the Elysée Palace, the White House, the Palazzo Chigi in Rome, Putin's private villa on the shores of the Black Sea, even one of President Xi's guest houses in Beijing. So I can say with some authority: we do it best.

The talks at No. 10 had an elegiac tone, the Prime Minister having already announced that she was resigning later that month. There was the sense, hanging in the atmosphere, that these were two people unlikely ever to talk again; and that, whatever their disagreements in the past, they wanted to part on a note of mutual respect, even warmth. At the press conference, Trump was inevitably invited to repeat his criticism of the Prime Minister's handling of Brexit. Instead, he did the opposite, saying she 'deserved a lot of credit for her work on Brexit . . . I think it will happen and I believe the Prime Minister has brought it to a very good point where something will take place in the not-too-distant future.' Trump was also prompted to repeat his comment of a year earlier that Boris Johnson would make a great Prime Minister. Spotting Jeremy Hunt, who was also running for the leadership, in the audience, Trump said, in an unusual display of textbook diplomacy, 'I know Boris. I like him. I think he would do a very good job. I know Jeremy. I think he would do a very good job.'

And then on to the final fixture, the American ambassador's return dinner at Winfield House. The pre-dinner drinks lasted forever as we awaited the arrival of the principals, the President and Melania, Prince Charles and Camilla: so much so that Trump's daughters joined Vanessa on the sofa, all escaping from the tyranny of vertiginous heels. The meal itself was done and dusted with striking speed. We have a friend in Yorkshire who is no fan of late nights or extended sessions over the cheese and red wine, and who is likely therefore to say to dinner guests, sometimes as early as about 10 p.m., 'Well, you'll be wanting to get home now, I imagine. Don't feel you have to stay longer to be polite.' It turned out that Ambassador Woody Johnson was cast from the same mould. No doubt prompted by a President eager to get to bed, he stood up to dismiss us all as the dessert plates were being cleared.

The third day was the Portsmouth D-Day commemoration. It was perfectly organised and movingly accomplished. Each of the leaders there took a turn on stage. Trump read out Franklin Roosevelt's famous prayer for the US troops involved in the landings, with that most resonant of lines: 'And let our hearts be stout, to wait out the long travail, to bear sorrows that may come, to impart our courage unto our sons wheresoever they may be.' Afterwards, he met the surviving D-Day veterans. One of them, 93-year-old Thomas Cuthbert, said to the President, motioning towards First Lady Melania, 'If only I was twenty years younger.' Trump replied: 'You could handle it, no question.'

Vanessa and I were part of a small delegation dispatched to Southampton Airport to see the President off. As we said goodbye, I congratulated him on his handling of the visit and suggested that the prospects for the relationship were bright. He agreed warmly: 'Relations are going to be better than they have ever been.' He may be right: he is clearly going to have a friendlier relationship with Prime Minister Boris Johnson than he ever enjoyed with Theresa May. I didn't know at the time, but I wouldn't be part of it. My reports, including the one on the state visit, would be leaked to the *Mail on Sunday* a few weeks later.

16

Resignation, Part Two

*

'*We will no longer deal with him*'
                         – President Donald Trump about me, 8 July 2019

*

'*I wish the British Ambassador well*'
                         – President Donald Trump, 12 July 2019

*

VANESSA WAS staying with her mother, up in East Anglia. I phoned her on the house landline at around 3 a.m. UK time, 10 p.m. in Washington. She picked up quickly, but the line was poor; it sounded at my end like she was on the deck of a sailing yacht in a gale rather than in a silent house in a quiet suburb. I apologised for waking her up and explained that I was calling because 'I think I'm resigning.' Unfortunately, the acoustics were equally bad at her end too; my words came across as 'I think I'm dying.' So I heard, 'Oh my God, what's the matter with you? What's happened?'

This took a couple of minutes to unravel. Having clarified that I was talking about career death rather than something more personal, I explained my reasoning. Vanessa instantly agreed, and said she had foreseen exactly this decision. Our daughter, Georgina, had come up from London that evening and Vanessa had suggested to her that, in the circumstances, I might feel that I had to resign. Vanessa added that I should have the announcement made quickly, to get myself off the front pages. I said I would get my resignation statement out the following day.

I reassembled the embassy team and broke the news to them. Some looked stunned, others like they had expected it. One or two suggested that I didn't need to decide then, I could wait twenty-four hours to see how the story developed. I said that if I was going, it was important that I looked to be ahead of the story: leaving at my chosen moment, not under pressure from any quarter. There was a short debate, but no one really pushed back. I asked them to help with my resignation statement, and set out what I wanted to say. They quickly produced a draft so near perfect that I barely changed a word.

Next I needed to talk to Simon McDonald, the FCO permanent secretary. But I felt I had to wait until 8 a.m. UK time. So I set my alarm for 3 a.m. Washington time and tried, unsuccessfully in the event, to get a couple of hours' sleep. Simon had already called me more than once in the preceding days, and had been hugely supportive throughout. This call was no exception. He tried briefly to persuade me to hold off, but I insisted that my decision was final, that I had a resignation statement ready and would forward it to him, and that I was keen for the announcement to be made that morning. He said that he would sort it out.

It was by then about 3.30 a.m. in DC. But I knew that there would be no end of phone calls from London about the timing of the announcement and the text of my statement. So it was a case of brewing a large pot of coffee and watching the dawn rise over the residence garden. The hours slipped by reasonably quickly, helped past by a succession of phone calls from my London colleagues, by then well into their working day. And Simon had clearly been as good as his word in impressing on everyone the need for urgency. Mark Sedwill called, as a friend rather than as cabinet secretary, to commiserate and to express his personal sadness that it had come to this. At about 6 a.m., I was told that the announcement would be made an hour from now, at midday UK time, and that the Prime

Minister wanted to speak briefly to me first. Her call came through at about 6.30. She was warm, sympathetic and gracious. The Foreign Secretary, Jeremy Hunt, also phoned to commiserate, living up to his reputation as one of the most decent men in politics. At the appropriate hour, I switched the TV on to BBC World, which always showed Prime Minister's Questions live. Theresa May referred to my resignation announcement as she stood up to speak. The leader of the Opposition, Jeremy Corbyn (whom I had never met) said some kind words about me when he stood up to speak. It was done.

I am sometimes asked how those hours felt, immediately after I had decided to resign. The answer is, a great deal less traumatic than might be imagined. I had in my career worked as chief of staff for three different Foreign Office ministers of state; I had been press spokesman for the Foreign Secretary; and I had worked twice in No. 10, as Europe adviser for Tony Blair and national security adviser for David Cameron. This succession of front row seats meant I had seen a lot of ministerial crises, some of which had ended in resignation, some not. And I reckoned that I had developed an instinct for which crises were survivable and which spelt doom. When these episodes happen, there is scarcely ever an instant resignation; everyone thinks they can ride it out until they realise that the rock-strewn path ahead of them is only getting steeper. The rule of thumb among those of us who have been press spokesmen is that, if the media storm is still raging after five days with no hint of abating, the individual concerned is almost certainly finished. The question is not if, but when.

Had I not resigned, I could see my story running on and on: more tweets from the White House, more commentary about me – whether for or against – in Parliament and the British and US media, and the certainty that more of our reports would appear in the *Mail on Sunday* the following weekend. I couldn't see how those in the administration, even if doors opened again, would speak to me with the same frankness and honesty as they had in the past, now that they had seen the tone of some of the embassy's confidential reporting. And without insights into what people were really thinking and doing, I would only be doing half the job. What was more, one of the two remaining candidates in the Conservative leadership race had said publicly that he would keep me in place, while the other had ducked the question, generating speculation that he wouldn't. I could see my name being weaponised in the final days of the race, as well potentially as months of unnamed sources briefing that I was about to be recalled and replaced. The more I turned it over in my mind, the more convinced I became that sooner or later I would have to go. At which point my media experience kicked in; if I was going to go, it was right to take the initiative, not wait until I looked as if I had tried to cling on, unwilling to accept the inevitable.

So having taken the decision, and knowing it was right, was cathartic: simultaneously liberating, energising and calming. I could spend the next few hours driving it through and dealing with the consequences, rather than thinking about what I was giving up. Immediately after the news became public, I took some telephone calls from friends and colleagues, replied to some emails, and declined all offers from the media to 'tell my side of the story'. The embassy media team were dealing with a blizzard of enquiries and requests for comment; they responded with my resignation statement and nothing more. I glanced briefly at Sky News on cable back in the apartment in the residence. My resignation was The Story, and by coincidence, two people I knew were being interviewed. The first was Robin Renwick, Lord Renwick, a former British ambassador to the United States, the architect of the Rhodesia settlement, and the most brilliant of his generation. He said I had been absolutely right to resign. And then, next on screen appeared David Mellor, long retired from Parliament, but one of the FCO ministers to whom I had been chief of staff. He was kind about his experience of working with me, but suggested I should probably have pulled the ripcord twenty-four hours earlier. Listening to his reasoning, I thought he was almost certainly right.

In among all this, there was a phone call I knew I had to make. By late morning Washington time, my phone screen showed a couple of missed calls from Boris Johnson, whose personal mobile number I'd had since his days as Foreign Secretary. I picked up the phone:

he answered immediately. He asked how I was and commiserated over the leak. He then said, 'But why did you resign? Wouldn't it all have blown over after a few weeks?' I said I couldn't be sure: this was a President who tended to hold grudges. Some people became permanent targets. Boris then said that the UK media were linking my resignation to his handling of a question about me in the hustings the previous evening. Had what he had said been the reason for my announcement? I said that there had been several factors behind my decision and his words had been one of them. The President's announcement that his administration would no longer deal with me had been another. Putting everything together, I had concluded that British interests would be best served by my swift departure. Boris said that he was sorry if what he had said had contributed to my decision; absolutely not his intention. He had been trying only to say that a televised debate was not the appropriate forum in which to discuss my future prospects. We left it at that. There was a certain tension in the atmosphere but our parting words were amicable.

I phoned Vanessa again and relayed the content of the phone calls from May, Hunt and Johnson. She said that she and Georgina had watched the leadership debate between Hunt and Johnson and had erupted in fury at the latter's failure to voice support for me. She likened it to 'siding with Trump' and thought it had been unforgivable. I was to hear a lot of that over the next few weeks. We also speculated about the silence from my son, Simon, and his wife Rachel, who hadn't been in touch since the story broke.

A few weeks later, we discovered the reason for their silence. The two of them had taken a group of Vanderbilt students on a fossil-hunting expedition in the Namibian desert. They had been completely off-grid at the time: no phone signal, no civilisation for hundreds of miles around. Simon told us the story of their journey, a couple of weeks later, to a fuel and supplies station a few hundred miles from the campsite. Having bought their supplies, they and the students had gone to the bar attached to the store for their first beers in a month. The students had all gone online; and within a few minutes, most of them were looking at Simon with a mixture of horror and fascination, waiting for him to come across the news.

Noticing this, Simon had asked, 'What are you looking at me for? What's happened?' One of them had silently pushed his iPad across the table for Simon to see the headline; and scrolling down, more headlines; and then still more . . .

Vanessa had also told me to look at the British newspapers, where I was as prominent as ever. I requisitioned a sheaf of cuttings and scanned through them. There was a lot of criticism of Johnson's 'refusal to back me' at the hustings. I thought (rightly as it turned out) that it wouldn't derail his march to victory. There was a partisan tinge to some of the commentary; merely because I had worked in Brussels twice, I was apparently a crazed Europhile, and therefore the wrong person to be representing modern Britain. But there was also some really funny stuff. The best came from Quentin Letts, a sketch writer who is occasionally cruel but also sometimes touched by brilliance. Commenting on the emergency Commons debate on my resignation, he wrote: 'All we needed was the tone of muffled bell, the crunch of guardsmen's boots to a funeral beat, the sorry clip-clop of Sir Kim's riderless horse with two empty boots reversed in the stirrups.' And then there were the cartoons. Trump is a gift to cartoonists, as is Boris Johnson. So there was a rich and varied collection, at least a couple of them portraying Johnson's tongue doing something unmentionable to a certain part of Trump's anatomy. Another one had Boris crushing me under a model London bus (he had bizarrely claimed a few days earlier that to relax, he liked to turn wine boxes into models of London buses). I've kept copies of them all, for eventual framing and display in the appropriate place, the smallest room in the house.

As the Washington day slithered on, the pressures started to ease. London closed down, and the embassy press team were holding the line with the US media. I was due to fly back to the UK on Friday evening. I brought it forward to Thursday, seeing no purpose in hanging around in Washington for another forty-eight hours. That still left me twenty-four hours in town, and with the phone ringing less and nothing operational to distract me, I had time to sift through the ashes of my Washington posting; to think about what had happened over the preceding five days; to apportion responsibility and blame.

So how did I feel during that slow walk through the remaining hours of my 42-year Foreign Office career? Time softens, conceals and heals; so as I trawl through my memory, those hours don't surge to the surface like some nightmarish monster from the deep. But I do recall anger, and remorse, and moments of existential bitterness.

My anger of course focused on the perpetrator of the leak. Having speculated endlessly about motive, I settled on three theories. Our reporting from Washington had been a great deal calmer than most of the content of the US media. But it had been seriously critical of the administration's performance. There had been good cause for this, and we had called it as we had seen it. I wondered whether someone, somewhere in the handful of Whitehall departments which saw our reports, had thought we were excessively, unfairly negative about the Trump presidency and had decided that this 'bias' needed to be exposed. Alternatively, since I was by then in my final six months, perhaps I had simply been collateral damage in some bigger battle about my successor – someone in the system wanting to ensure the appointment of a politician rather than a diplomat, the better to 'get' Trump. Or third, and most sinister, perhaps it had been a hack of the FCO communications system by some malign outside force.

Whichever, I wished I could meet the person responsible (in my mind, over a bare desk in a prison visiting room, following their prosecution under the Official Secrets Act for passing classified documents to journalists). I would ask them what they had thought would happen when the documents were published. Had they expected it to end my posting and my career? Or had they thought it would be a 24-hour story, a bit of a flurry, and then life would move on? In other words, had they intended to destroy, or were they just stupid?

As for remorse, I read and re-read the documents that had leaked and wondered if I should have written them differently. On this, however, it was easier to find peace of mind. First, the judgements and predictions in the reports stood up well; those from the first six months of the Trump presidency had proved strikingly accurate. Second, ministers hated dull, dry reports full of excessively long sentences, multiple sub-clauses and impenetrable jargon. They wanted brevity, clarity, insights, anecdotes and judgements. The previous year, Boris Johnson, in his role as Foreign Secretary, speaking to the annual gathering in London of British ambassadors worldwide, had singled out the output of the Washington embassy as 'the gold standard of diplomatic reporting'. He had also said that some of it deserved to be published for a wider audience: little did he know what was to come. And third, it was simply inconceivable that diplomats worldwide should start sanitising what we wrote because we anticipated that colleagues at home would give anything colourful or controversial to the newspapers. That way madness lay.

And then the existential bitterness. In essence, I'd had to resign for doing my job in the same way that I had done it throughout a career that had taken me to four permanent secretary posts, including advising two different Prime Ministers. And for the same crime, my life had been dissected across the pages of the British media. Journalists whom I had never met had claimed detailed knowledge of my personal politics, my conversations in Washington, my views on Europe, or Brexit, or Trump. A friend told me that there was even a ludicrous conspiracy theory circulating in the House of Commons that I had leaked the reports myself. While I was receiving a huge number of messages of solidarity and support, I was also conscious that some in London, for whom my having served as British ambassador to the EU was crime enough, were revelling in my departure. In short, it was hard not to feel a certain injustice in my circumstances. I consoled myself with the line beloved by TV football pundits when commenting on myopic refereeing decisions: 'Over the course of the season, your luck evens out.'

Also, especially through the long watches of that night, I couldn't help but think about the journey: the random chance that had led to my joining the Foreign Office, the long climb up the career ladder, the flashes of good fortune on the way, the decades of sixty- and seventy-hour weeks, the drab offices, the endless airports, the war zones and the gilded conference rooms. With in theory but six months left in Washington, I had been thinking about the final trips I would squeeze in: Alaska in October, North and South Dakota sometime, and Nebraska if possible (the latter motivated largely by the Bruce Springsteen album cover). I had been steeling myself for the long round of farewell parties for which Washington society was famous. I had been wondering who might succeed me. I had been counting my blessings that I would be leaving before the refurbishment of the residence started. And while part of me wanted to move on, another part wished I could do ten more months and see through the theatre, the spectacle and the drama of the 2020 election year. Instead, I would be getting on an aeroplane the next evening, probably never to carry out another official duty as British ambassador. Was this really how it was going to end?

The final day passed quickly enough. At lunchtime, I talked briefly to the embassy staff, assembled in the bright sunshine lighting up the residence lawn, to thank them for all the support they had given me. I sensed a mood of apprehension. Few other than the senior team had seen me for a couple of days; they were perhaps wondering whether I would be wheeled in on a stretcher. At the end of my remarks, I told them I was already considering writing a book about my Washington experience; I hoped they would all pre-order it in hardback. The mood lightened. I circulated for thirty minutes or so, said my individual farewells, then set off for Dulles Airport.

I generally flew to and from Washington on Virgin Atlantic: their schedule fitted best. As I boarded the plane, the first thing I saw was a selection of British newspapers laid out in the bar area next to the door. My face was on several front pages, above the story of my resignation. It was a sharp reminder: time to go, to retreat to our Cornish base, to put all the trauma behind us and think about what came next.

We flitted briefly back to Washington about six weeks later to say goodbye properly to the embassy and residence staff. Thanks to the passage of time, it was all less traumatic than it might have been. There was a proper farewell party in the residence for the entire embassy, and another speech to get through; I'd had long enough to dream up some more jokes about our time in Washington.

There was also the packing of our personal belongings to supervise. The bedrooms at the residence were arranged along each side of a long central corridor running the length of the building. And the staff had saved us a huge amount of time and work by emptying our apartment and displaying everything on trestle tables along that corridor, so that we could identify what was ours and what wasn't, what should go back to London, what should stay, and what should be thrown away. Even after a mere six weeks' absence, Vanessa and I felt like visiting anthropologists surveying the museum artefacts of a bygone age: Jay Gatsby's Long Island mansion after the music stopped. There were the reminders of some of the trips I had made as ambassador. Among them was a photograph of a small US Navy plane landing on the deck of the US aircraft carrier, the *George Washington*, somewhere off the coast of Virginia; I and the defence attaché had been on that plane, just about holding on to the contents of our stomachs as the arrester gear slowed the plane from 200 mph to a standstill within about 100 feet of carrier deck. There was a wooden plinth displaying a large rusty nail from the USS *Constitution*, given to me when I had visited the ship in Boston harbour: as the *Constitution* had defeated, in successive encounters, no fewer than five British warships during the war of 1812, it had been kind of the donors not to add the inscription 'To the losers'! And there were mementoes from a memorable meeting I'd had in Oklahoma with the leaders of no less than thirty-five Native American nations. Each had made a speech about their respective tribal histories, accompanied by a gift: so, correspondingly, there were thirty-five of them. Little would they have realised that I was returning to a modest house in the London suburbs. We wondered where on earth all of this stuff was going to go once we got home.

Then came the most emotional moment of the entire episode. Before we set off for the airport, the entire residence team, who had looked after us so brilliantly for the preceding three years, gathered at the doors to see us off. It felt exceptionally sad until, at the final moment, our cat, Monty, who was being adopted by the Residence Manager and his family, appeared from nowhere to join the throng, say goodbye and lift the mood. It was a quiet reflective drive out to the airport, the last moments of the job that had been the culmination of my career, and which had ended abruptly because someone, somewhere, had thought it was time to take me down. I kept trying to visualise the individual responsible: young or old? male or female? with what motive? And I felt saddest of all for the exceptional team I had left behind: talented, dedicated, loyal, as committed as I had been to a career of serving a country we were proud to represent.

At school, in English classes, I had studied a fair amount of Shakespeare, in particular an endless term dissecting *Macbeth*. As a result, while I am capable of forgetting things I did yesterday, I can retrieve lines from '*the Scottish play*' that I learnt fifty years ago. As the plane took off and soared into the twilight over Virginia, I remembered a quote from *Macbeth* which summed up the moment and the need to move on: 'Things without all remedy should be without regard; what's done is done'.

17

The Great Unravelling: Brexit, Trump and the Eclipse of Establishment Politics

*

'*You can take back control of a gun but it doesn't mean you use it to shoot your foot off*'
–William Hague, former Foreign Secretary

*

'*Tomorrow is going to be Brexit plus plus plus*'
– presidential candidate Donald Trump on the eve of the
2016 US election

*

'*I did say that I thought Brexit was the single stupidest thing any country has ever done, but then we Trumped it*'
– former New York mayor Michael Bloomberg

*

WHEN I arrived in Washington, in January 2016, Barack Obama was in the White House; David Cameron was in No. 10; and the UK was starting its forty-third year of membership of the European Union. As I write, just four years later, Donald Trump is in the White House; Boris Johnson is in No. 10; and the UK has just left the European Union. The UK remains split down the middle over Brexit, while America is bitterly divided over its President and whether he deserves re-election. The mood in both countries is angry, partisan and tribal. Populism is on the march in other Western democracies, not just in the Anglo-Saxon world. And the post-war multilateral structures which the US and UK constructed together, the anchorage points around which internationalist policies have been built for decades, are increasingly challenged, disparaged or ignored. The foundations of our post-war international order are trembling, perhaps even crumbling. And the existential question is: what has caused this great unravelling?

In trying to answer that question, my starting point is that there were striking and undeniable parallels between the forces, on each side of the Atlantic, that brought about these two political earthquakes: the vote for Brexit and the election of Donald Trump. And they revolve around the three I's: immigration, inequality and identity. But there were important differences too, starting with the nature of the two decisions. The American people were voting for a new President, for a four-year term, renewable once, and a position constrained by the balance of powers set out in the American Constitution. The British were voting to end forty-three years of involvement in the project of European integration and the sharing of sovereignty. One was, set against the long slow march of history, a short-term decision, a rolling of the dice: let's try something different. The other was the culmination of decades of mounting disillusionment with the European project, and a decision with the smack of finality about it; no reconsideration in four years' time.

Brexit first. This wasn't the first referendum on UK membership of the EU. On 5 June 1975, the British people voted by 17 million to 8 million – two to one – in favour of membership of what was then the European Economic Community. I subsequently spent twenty years of my career trying to deliver good outcomes for Britain from EU negotiations. So it's personal. And I have thought a lot about why the British people changed their minds so drastically. Historians will already be chronicling the hundreds of moments, events, decisions and mistakes that led to the outcome of the 2016 referendum. For me, however, it was in part about history; in part about the long-term impact and consequences of the 2008 financial crisis; in part about immigration pressures, in particular the surge of workers from central Europe into the UK after ten central European countries joined in 2004; and in part the result of mistakes by both London and Brussels in the run-up to the referendum itself. My version of the story starts with the European Council in Rome on 27–28 October 1990.

This was my first European Council; I would, later in my career, attend forty-five in succession. I was first secretary (EC and Economic) in the British Embassy in Rome, my first job focusing on European issues. In those days, European Councils were a travelling circus, taking place in the country which held the presidency: the Italians had the presidency, so it was Rome. Not for the first or last time, we disagreed radically with our EU partners on what this European Council should be about. Saddam Hussein's troops were occupying Kuwait. Negotiations on a new global trade round were at a crucial phase. Decisions were needed on support for Gorbachev's reforms in the Soviet Union. But the Italians were among the strongest supporters of further European integration, and they had designed this European Council around decisions on launching two 'intergovernmental conferences' – essentially high-level negotiations between the member states on amending the European treaties. One of these was to discuss political union, deeper integration between the member states, and the other economic and monetary union, the single European currency. Margaret Thatcher was Prime Minister. We were opposed to the single currency and had no intention of being part of it. And we saw no need for deeper political integration.

A few days before the European Council, a friend in the Bank of Italy tipped me off that the council's outcome had been more or less sewn up. A double-act comprising Umberto Vattani, the most senior official in the Italian foreign ministry, and Tommaso Padoa-Schioppa, vice director general in the Bank of Italy, had toured the other European capitals – though not the UK – and had secured agreement to the outcome they wanted. The two conferences were going to be launched, whatever the British thought. I breathlessly reported this insight to London; there was a deafening silence in response. Perhaps they already knew what was coming. Anyway, the European Council circus came to town, with my role, as a mere first secretary in the embassy, approximating to that of the workmen who erect the tents and feed the animals. But I could get into the building, if not the conference chamber, provided I hung around, out of eyeshot of the people who mattered, at the very back of the room.

I was too far from the action to have any idea what happened in the session that lasted through the first afternoon and evening. But on the second morning, a rumour swept through the conference centre that Mrs Thatcher was going to leave early – around mid-morning, three hours before the council was due to conclude. I joined the surge of journalists and hangers-on rushing to the British media room, where the Iron Lady was scheduled to speak to the press before heading to the airport. By the time I got there, it was standing room only and almost unbearably hot. When Mrs Thatcher came in, she apologised to the journalists for the crush, adding bitingly that the Italians had provided 'too small a room'. And she then set out, in a magisterial tone, her disappointment that the council had failed to address the truly important issues, like securing a world trade deal. The British press asked some combative questions about her one-vs-eleven isolation on the two intergovernmental conferences. Her response amounted to 'I don't mind being isolated when I'm right and they're wrong.' As she left, I spotted a friend of mine from the small cadre of British journalists based in Rome, and whispered to him 'That was okay, wasn't it?' He looked at me pityingly and said, 'But she lost . . . couldn't you see the wounds and hear the blood dripping onto the floor?'

Meanwhile, inside the conference room, the negotiations of the final text, the European Council 'Conclusions', went on, with Foreign Secretary Douglas Hurd substituting for the Prime Minister in the British chair. With casual brutality, and for the first time in the history of the European Community, the Italian Prime Minister, Giulio Andreotti, relegated British dissent to a handful of footnotes rather than including them in the main text. And within four weeks, Mrs Thatcher was gone. (We in the embassy would hear rumours of Andreotti's private exultation in his role in bringing her down. If he did celebrate, it was while the clock was ticking on his own career. Just three years later, as the post-war Italian political system collapsed amid multiplying corruption scandals, Andreotti himself would go on trial for, in effect, being in league with Cosa Nostra, the Sicilian Mafia. Though ultimately acquitted several years later, the courts concluded he had indeed colluded with Cosa Nostra, but much earlier in his career; he was saved by the statute of limitations.)

These Rome texts led, painfully but inexorably, to the Maastricht Treaty, signed on 7 February 1992. The Maastricht Treaty turned the European Economic Community into the European Union. It established the concept of European citizenship. It laid the foundations for economic and monetary union. It gave new powers to the European Parliament. It broadened substantially the use of qualified majority voting, meaning there were more policy areas where individual countries could be overridden. It created a common foreign and security policy. And it accelerated the realisation of the Schengen Agreement, 'Europe without Frontiers'. It was, in short, Europe's 'Great Leap Forward': perhaps the single biggest piece of integration in the EU's history.

The UK was to stay outside economic and monetary union. We cherry-picked participation in some elements of Schengen but kept our frontier controls. And parts of the Conservative Party would never be reconciled to greater powers for the European Parliament or increased use of qualified majority voting, let alone a 'common' foreign and security policy. By the time we came to ratify the treaty, I was the Deputy Head of the European Union Department in the Foreign Office. One of our main tasks was supporting government ministers trying to get the ratification bill through Parliament. It was a nightmare; endless rebellions, setbacks and nail-bitingly close votes. We got there, but at the cost of a profound split in the Conservative Party – which never healed.

The Maastricht episode also spoke to some deeper realities about Britain's tortured relationship with Europe. Maastricht was essentially about delivering the ambitions of Jean Monnet, Robert Schuman and the other founding fathers of the European project: the 'ever closer union among the peoples of Europe', to quote from the 1957 Treaty of Rome. They were motivated not by economics, or even politics, but by the objective, after centuries of war and destruction, of permanent peace in a Europe without national borders. When I was first in Brussels, the then German ambassador to the EU personified this. He would relate how his father had been killed on the Eastern Front in the Second World War, leaving him and his mother to flee, on foot, through the Prussian winter, steps ahead of the advancing Red Army: in his eyes, almost any sacrifice of national sovereignty was worthwhile to avoid future generations suffering as his family had done. And that spirit lived on in the other eleven leaders gathered around that table in Rome. They thought that further integration, making the project irreversible, was exactly what they should be doing, with political, economic and monetary union precisely the ultimate objective.

The majority of the British people never shared this vision. This reflected, I think, both our history and our character. We had suffered through two world wars. But we hadn't been invaded since 1066. We hadn't seen soldiers fighting building-to-building in our towns and villages, or had to flee our homes before an advancing army. We didn't have those memories passed on from generation to generation. And after centuries of Parliamentary democracy, we never entirely reconciled ourselves to the primary obligation of membership, the pooling of sovereignty and the consequent erosion of the powers of the British Parliament: it just didn't sit comfortably with the self-image of British exceptionalism. (Indeed, explicitly excluding the UK from the commitment to 'ever closer union' was one of David Cameron's lead objectives in his 2015 renegotiation.) Instead, generations of British politicians encouraged the misconception that the European project was primarily about markets and economics: British people of a certain generation to this day refer to the EU as the Common Market. We supported widening but never deepening.

And as a result, notwithstanding UK-inspired successes like the Single Market, and the successive expansions of the European Union, we were for most of the 47 years of our membership tugging on the handbrake while the other passengers pressed the accelerator. That said, the reality was that we had negotiated ourselves out of the Euro and Schengen, the two integration flagships, while still being able to exploit the Single Market: in effect, the EU which we had carved out for ourselves *was* mostly about economics.

Next, immigration. Fast forward to 2004: I was in No. 10 as EU adviser to Tony Blair. Eight central European countries – Poland, Hungary, the Czech Republic, Slovakia, Slovenia, Estonia, Lithuania and Latvia, together with Malta and Cyprus – had completed their accession negotiations and were to join the European Union on 1 May. This was the largest 'enlargement' in the history of the European Union, a triumph for British diplomacy, and something of a high point in our influence in Europe. But that success brought with it a big and far-reaching decision for all the established members of the EU: would we open our doors immediately to workers from central Europe, or would we invoke the seven years' delay allowed under the EU treaties?

As Blair's EU adviser, my responsibilities included canvassing views across Whitehall, notably in the Home Office, the Foreign Office and the Treasury; checking with my counterparts around Europe on what decisions they were taking; and then putting some consolidated advice to the Prime Minister. The picture around European capitals was clear: most would be imposing restrictions, though not necessarily for the full seven years; only Ireland and Finland seemed likely to open their doors. Views around Whitehall, however, were much harder to discern. The Home Secretary, David Blunkett, was, I was told, undecided. So, seemingly, was the Foreign Secretary, Jack Straw, though the Foreign Office institutionally was worried about the optics of championing enlargement but then pulling up the drawbridge to the citizens of the new member states. The Treasury, meanwhile, favoured the open door, for economic reasons. The British economy was growing strongly – and the biggest concern was wage inflation prompted by shortages of workers.

I duly put the question to the Prime Minister, noting the strong support from the Treasury, the history of British leadership on enlargement, the lack of strong objections from anyone else in Whitehall and the potential economic benefits – while also warning him that most of mainland Europe would be taking a different position, and that there was no authoritative analysis on the size of the likely inflow. I also told him that there was a safety net – in the sense that, should he decide on an open door policy but change his mind within a year or so, he could still impose restrictions. Blair reflected for a couple of days and concluded that we should, at least initially, open the door.

In the first two years after their countries joined the EU, close to two million central Europeans came to work in the UK. Thereafter, numbers stabilised somewhat but remained high: a decade later, arrivals were still running at more than 200,000 a year. It was the biggest mass immigration into the UK since the Huguenots, the French Protestants who fled the oppression of Louis XIV, the Sun King, in the late seventeenth and early eighteenth centuries. (By 1710, at least 5 per cent of the population of London were French Protestants.) It provided the boost to the economy that the Treasury had forecast; over the three years preceding the financial crash of 2008, the British economy was growing twice as fast as the Eurozone. And the phenomenon of the 'Polish plumber' was much discussed around London dinner tables. Suddenly it was possible to get builders, workmen, plumbers, cleaners, babysitters, without over-paying, or waiting months, or hiring cowboys.

But London is different: an international city and a wealthy, economically dynamic, full-employment enclave in a country with plenty of struggling post-industrial cities and pockets of rural poverty. Living in London in those boom years, I wasn't well placed to judge the impact of the central European influx on communities in the Midlands and the North. Ten years later, in the aftermath of the Leave victory, it became clear how much, outside London and the South-East, the newcomers had been resented. In the endless post-vote vox pops, the same themes kept emerging. It was taking two weeks, not two days, to get a doctor's appointment. You couldn't get your child into the local nursery, because it was 'full of Eastern Europeans'. You had to wait twice as long to get a council house. Your son or daughter couldn't get a job because they had all been snapped up by over-qualified immigrants. And as a multiplier for all of these resentments, 'no one asked my permission before letting them all in'. A lot of these complaints weren't well-founded. At least in the early years, the great majority of the incomers were young, single and healthy, coming just to work and contributing much more to the British economy than they took out of the social safety net. But perception and reality are different things, and foreigners an easy target.

To this day, and despite what has happened, I think that the migrants enriched the country, both economically and culturally. But I also think that, at a time when the Treasury coffers were full and the economy thriving, a strategic mistake was made which came back to haunt Remain supporters in 2016. Resources should have been pumped into these communities outside London once the size of the influx became clear: more doctors, more school places, more nursery places, more housing, more social infrastructure. And politicians should have been going to these parts of the country and saying, 'We know there is an issue, and we are addressing it.'

It wasn't just about the central Europeans. Two other factors amplified the immigration debate in the minds of British voters. The first was the European migrant crisis of 2015. The EU external border force, Frontex, estimated that more than 1.8 million migrants crossed into Europe that summer, in contrast to 280,000 in the whole of 2014. Most of them came by sea, particularly via the short sea route from Turkey to the nearest Greek islands but also by land through Turkey and the Balkans. The majority were refugees fleeing the Syrian war, but these huddled masses also included Afghans, Iraqis, Eritreans, Pakistanis, Nigerians and Iranians. The sea crossings were dangerous, with the migrants usually crammed into small, open, underpowered rubber dinghies: almost 4,000 drowned that summer, many of them children. And once on European soil, hundreds of thousands of them actually walked across Greece, central Europe and the western Balkans towards Western Europe. They walked across fields, along motorways and railway lines, tracked throughout by the cameras of the world's media, so that their approach was broadcast nightly on the TV screens of Europe. There was an obvious parallel with the periodic 'caravans' of central American migrants making their way to the southern border of the US, tracked with equal vigilance by the US media and much cited by President Trump. As a picture of sustained human misery, it was unmatched since the great population exoduses in the Bosnia and Kosovo conflicts of the 1990s. But it was also clear that the citizens of Western Europe would find these images unsettling, disturbing, even threatening.

In the end, most of the refugees went to Germany, thanks to the leadership, humanity and statesmanship of German Chancellor Angela Merkel – though she paid heavily for it in subsequent elections. German officials estimated that more than a million crossed the German border; by the end of 2015, more than 475,000 had claimed asylum there (though in terms of asylum applications as a proportion of population size, Hungary faced the biggest burden). But to communities across Britain, it must have felt as if the ultimate destination, the end of the road, for many of those walking westwards across Europe would be the UK: perhaps first by way of the Calais 'Jungle', the refugee and migrant encampment just across the English Channel, and then by small boat across to an English beach, or a hidden journey in the back of a lorry. People felt sorry for them, but didn't want them to turn up next door. The Cameron government said it would take 20,000 refugees over a five-year period, just 2 per cent of the numbers entering Germany. But, with the referendum less than a year away, while the EU tried to organise a mandatory sharing out of the refugee burden across the member states, resentment was still festering from the influx of central European migrants a decade earlier; and in the age of 24-hour news, social media and political polarisation, perceptions and fears readily override facts and reality.

Then, to complete the perfect storm, at the end of May 2016, in the midst of the referendum campaign, the Office of National

Statistics announced the second highest figure ever – 333,000 – for net migration into the UK. At that stage, the opinion polls showed Remain holding a small but significant lead. This announcement, however, was a gift of game-changing proportions to the Leave campaign; the British equivalent of the reopening of the Clinton email investigations. The Leave campaign spoke about almost nothing but immigration from that day on. And the poll figures closed to a virtual dead heat.

The irony here is that this public running total for net immigration amounted to a self-inflicted wound, a strategic mistake made by the Cameron government in 2010. The Conservative election manifesto had included a commitment to reduce net immigration, which was usually between 200,000 and 300,000 a year, to 'tens of thousands'. Even as election campaign promises go, this was stone cold crazy. We didn't know exactly how many people were leaving the country each year, having abolished comprehensive exit checks in the mid-1990s. (Since then, the Home Office has published 'estimates' for emigration, primarily based on small-scale surveys of passengers at airports and seaports. For example, in 2017, about three-quarters of a million survey interviews were conducted. Heathrow Airport alone saw 78 million travellers through its gates that year.)

Moreover, this net figure included foreign students. There were almost half a million of them, reflecting the inherent advantage of the English language and the qualities and competitiveness of the UK higher education sector. They contributed billions of pounds to the UK economy. And a 2016 study showed that only a few thousand overstayed their visas each year, as against an Office of National Statistics 'estimate' of 'close to 100,000 overstayers'. So in effect, we were counting them in but not counting them out.

All of this made UK net immigration statistics, as the Office of National Statistics eventually recognised, only a step up from guesswork. Indeed, they publicly admitted in August 2019 that their migration figures were inaccurate and re-categorised their data as 'experimental'. So the government in effect imposed on itself a target, against which it proceeded consistently to fail, judged against profoundly unreliable data. The policy amounted to a free hit for the media and the political opposition, a stick with which to beat the government around the head every time the figures came out. Nevertheless, bewilderingly, the commitment reappeared in the 2015 election manifesto.

Ironically, post-Brexit, policy on foreign students has now been relaxed. I'm not surprised. As mayor of London, Boris Johnson was an enthusiastic supporter of his city's international character. And as Prime Minister, he has taken what are, in my view, a series of admirable decisions on immigration. He has, in effect, abandoned the immigration target, saying in parliament that 'No one believes more strongly than me in the benefits of migration to our country' and talking about changing the profile of immigration rather than committing to a specific figure for total numbers. Realising that we are in international competition for the smartest students from overseas, he has reinstated the two-year post-study work visa for foreign postgraduates. And he has taken a principled stand on potentially opening Britain's doors to up to three million residents of Hong Kong.

But meanwhile, Brexit has happened. And the opinion poll evidence on the role of the immigration issue in the debate is compelling. One poll, published shortly before the referendum, showed that 55 per cent of respondents agreed that 'the Government should have total control over immigration even if this means coming out of the EU'. And in the same poll, 62 per cent of those surveyed wanted immigration levels reduced. Another poll, held on the day of the referendum itself, discovered that 33 per cent of those who had voted Leave had done so primarily because 'this offered the best chance for the UK to regain control of immigration and its own borders'. *The Economist* magazine reported that almost every area of the UK that saw increases of over 200 per cent in their foreign-born population between 2001 and 2014 saw a majority of voters back Leave. The town in the UK which voted most heavily for Leave, at 75 per cent in favour, was Boston in Lincolnshire. Between 2005 and 2015, the non-British population of Boston became sixteen times larger, from 1,000 to 16,000. In short, concerns about immigration were unquestionably a major factor in the Leave victory, and it is reasonable to conclude that these concerns were cemented in the minds of voters by a 'near-record' immigration figure that was at best 'experimental', at worst plain wrong. As Dominic Cummings, director of the Leave campaign, wrote in the *Spectator* in January 2017: 'Would we have won without immigration? No.'

Meanwhile, over in the United States, in a striking parallel, Donald Trump made immigration a central plank of his campaign platform. In doing so, he tapped into an issue which mattered as much to American voters as British – though greatly more to Republicans than Democrats. In 2015, there were more than 43 million immigrants residing in the United States, over 13 per cent of the total population. Almost one in seven US residents was foreign born. A Gallup poll in 2016 revealed that 62 per cent of Republicans wanted immigration reduced; even though only 23 per cent of Democrats agreed with them, that was a lot of people. Even impeccably liberal Washington acquaintances would express disquiet about the unending flow of economic migrants and the capacity even of America's vast spaces to accommodate them all.

Trump was far from the first American politician to try to tap into public anxiety about immigration. But there were three particular aspects to his campaign that amounted to political genius or distasteful populism, depending on your viewpoint. First, he focused heavily on undocumented migrants, the more than 11 million who had entered the United States illegally and could in theory be deported. Second, he characterised them in pejorative, even dehumanising terms. For the next eighteen months, he would repeat what he had said of Mexicans in his campaign launch speech in mid-2015: 'They're sending people that have lots of problems. They're bringing drugs. They're bringing crime. They're rapists. And some, I assume, are good people.'

And third, there was the Wall.

Whether Trump planned it or not, the point of the Wall was what it symbolised. Somehow the idea of constructing a physical barrier convinced voters that this candidate was serious about tackling illegal immigration while others were just mouthing platitudes. It captured his supporters' imaginations, even though, as I found out, many of them would tell you that they didn't expect it actually ever to be built. It became, not just an applause line at campaign rallies, but a moment for audience participation: 'Build the Wall!' they would chant, when they weren't chanting 'Lock her up'. And in an election decided by 70,000 votes, across three states, energising the base – getting every single supporter fired up and out voting – may have made the difference, at a moment when some of Obama's base from 2008 and 2012 weren't bothering to go out and vote for Hillary Clinton.

So immigration looks to have been as pivotal an issue in the 2016 US election as it was in the UK referendum the same year. Unlike Boris Johnson, however, once in office Donald Trump stayed on the offensive; he has continued to signal to his base and to outrage liberal America with attacks on illegal immigrants. Just before the 2018 midterm elections he complained publicly about 'an invasion' of violent criminals across the Mexican border. In terms of delivering his policy ideas, however, he has been less successful. Much of his agenda has been blocked in the courts. And only a small section of his wall (in the form of a metal fence) has been built. Even here there were problems: the US media gleefully reported that a section of it had been blown down in a violent storm on 29 January 2020.

If immigration is a big part of the narrative behind both Brexit and the rise of Trump in America, then inequality sits alongside it. The inequality story has deep roots. A recent study by the authoritative Pew Research Center noted that, in 1980, American households near the top of the income ladder had incomes about nine times higher than those of households near the bottom. By 2018, that gap had risen to 12.6 times higher. A recent analysis by the OECD concluded that the US had the highest level of income inequality of all the G7 nations, while a 2018 UN report noted that 40 million Americans lived in poverty. As to what lies behind this trend, globalisation – the integration of national economies through trade, investment, capital flow, labour migration and technology – has changed the face of the American workplace. Since the year 2000, the US has lost 20 per cent of its factory jobs. In 1960, one in four American workers was employed in manufacturing; today it is fewer than one in ten. And many of the jobs that have replaced those in manufacturing are poorly paid: one-quarter of American workers are earning less than $10 an hour, which means in most cases they have no health insurance or pension plan. Back in 1821, in his essay 'In Defence of Poetry', Percy Bysshe Shelley wrote: 'To him that hath, more shall be given; and from him that hath not, the little that he hath shall be taken away. The rich have become richer and the poor have become poorer; and the vessel of the State is driven between the Scylla and Charybdis of anarchy and despotism.' Who would have guessed that a nineteenth-century English poet would have described so accurately one of the leading causes of twenty-first-century populism?

The 2008 financial crisis exacerbated inequality, and must have raised the levels of anger and resentment among those already 'left behind' by several notches. It was the moment of the age: horrifying in the damage and destruction it caused; shocking for the greed and stupidity of those who caused and drove it, in New York, London and the other financial capitals; profound in its implications for politics across the developed world. This is not the place for a detailed analysis of what happened. But the Financial Crisis Inquiry Commission, otherwise known as the Angelides Commission, appointed by the US Congress to undertake a definitive investigation into the causes of the crisis, concluded that there had been 'widespread failures in financial regulation and supervision', 'dramatic failures of corporate governance and risk management at many systematically important financial institutions', 'a combination of excessive borrowing, risky investments, and a lack of transparency', 'a collapse in mortgage lending standards' and 'a failure of credit rating agencies to correctly price risk'. There is a blizzard of statistics on the costs of it all: a write-down of over $2 trillion dollars from financial institutions alone; and lost growth from the ensuing recession estimated at over $10 trillion.

But the political story here is the impact on individual Americans. This was the worst financial disaster since the Depression. The St

Louis Federal Reserve estimates that as many as 10 million Americans lost their homes. Statisticians like to group people in age ranges – Millennials, Generation X, and so on. The 'Silent Generation', those born between 1928 and 1945, and the 'Baby Boomers', those born between 1946 and 1964, are both significantly less wealthy now than they were in 2007. And annual income for the poorest households, the lowest 10 per cent, is actually lower now than in 2008. Added to this, it must have looked, to those living from wage packet to wage packet, profoundly unfair. Lehman Brothers went bankrupt and cast its employees out onto the streets. But none of the giants of the financial industry went to jail. Washington spent $700 billion bailing out US financial institutions. Within a few years, bonuses in the financial sector were returning to their eye-watering pre-crisis levels. And in the last few years, Republicans in Congress, urged on by the financial industry, have started weakening or even eliminating some of the financial regulations put in place after 2008. Since the 2008 financial crisis, those at the top of the income ladder have actually got richer, with a 13 per cent gain in median net worth, while those near the bottom are 39 per cent poorer in net wealth. It must have looked as if the conspiracy theorists were right: elites look after their own.

The UK was also hit devastatingly hard. British banks, some of which had played a major role in the worldwide selling of grotesquely overvalued and risky mortgage-backed securities, needed a massive government bailout. Indeed, Chancellor Alistair Darling led the way internationally with a £500 billion bailout fund and what amounted to a government takeover of Lloyds Bank and the Royal Bank of Scotland. The British economy went into a deep two-year recession, followed by the slowest and shallowest recovery since records began. Government spending was cut radically, with a 'decade of austerity'. Manufacturing slumped and government debt doubled. The housing market, one of the main motors of the British economy, has yet to recover, with prices in several parts of the country, ten years on, still lower than before the crisis. And real wages are still below pre-crisis levels. But as events unfolded, London was significantly insulated from the worst of the fallout. House prices started rising again. While a quarter of a million jobs were lost in the UK's manufacturing heartlands, employment in London stayed buoyant. With hindsight it is scarcely surprising that when, pre-referendum, the TV reporters, interviewing locals on the streets of Midlands and Northern towns, asked, 'Aren't you worried that leaving the EU will damage the economy?' they got the answer: 'That's your economy down there – up here it can't get any worse.'

After immigration and economic inequality, identity politics was, in my view, the third part of the trilogy. The term has been around since the 1970s. It lacks a generally agreed definition. Some argue that all politics is identity politics; but in current political discourse, it is often deployed as a form of disparagement, even abuse. A neutral definition might be that it is a description of political positions based on an aspect of identity – ethnicity, religion, sex, sexual orientation – shared by a group which feels that its concerns are not adequately recognised. And I believe that it was a significant factor in both Brexit and the Trump victory. These were, in both cases, narrow victories; Trump triumphed thanks to 70,000 votes cast across three states, while across in the UK, 700,000 votes the other way would have changed the outcome of the referendum. Donald Trump's biggest support came from white men without a college education; he beat Hillary Clinton by 72 per cent to 23 per cent in this demographic, a huge margin. His dominance of this demographic looks, moreover, to have been a key factor in his narrow victories in Wisconsin, Michigan and Pennsylvania. In the UK it was the English vote that clinched Brexit: while the majority of Scots and Northern Irish voted Remain, and the Welsh only narrowly favoured Leave, the English voted for Leave by broadly 15 million to 13 million, a margin of 53.4 per cent to 46.6 per cent.

This is delicate territory, but it merits some brief analysis. American political scientists have been studying the question, notably in a book, *Identity Crisis*, by John Sides, Michael Tesler and Lynn Vavreck. The central thesis here is that 'white identity', and a backlash against diversity politics, in the aftermath of Barack Obama's eight years in office, was a central factor in the outcome of the 2016 election, and that the further down the educational attainment ladder one looked, the greater was this 'white flight' from the Democrats to the Republicans. In 2007, before Obama's election, whites who did not attend college were just as likely to identify as Democrats as Republicans. By 2016, 54 per cent were calling themselves Republicans and 39 per cent Democrats. My own research in this area is rather more limited, perhaps a few dozen conversations. But in this context, I recall one in particular. In Little Rock, Arkansas, I was invited by the state's lieutenant governor to dinner with a group of local businessmen. As the wine flowed and the conversation opened out, the sense of resentment at Washington, and more broadly, at the East and West Coast elites, came out. One of those around the table said: 'They are trying to change our way of life, and with all this political correctness, they are trying to control what we think. It's not the country in which I grew up, and I don't like it.'

As for the disparity between English voting patterns in the referendum and those of the rest of the country, I struggle to explain what lies behind it. As poorer parts of the UK, Scotland, Wales and Northern Ireland received more money from the EU than most of England (Cornwall excepted). All three now have differing degrees of self-government, while there is a Scottish parliament and Welsh and Northern Irish assemblies but no English parliament. But this doesn't feel to me like the kind of issue to light the fire of English resentment. I suspect part of it was plain English contrariness. A few months after the Leave victory, I was seeing friends in Yorkshire (where cussedness is of course embedded in the DNA). These were successful businessmen at the end of their careers; manufacturers who made things, not financiers skimming off their 2 per cent. To my shock, every single one of them had voted Leave. And from what they said, it sounded less like a policy choice and more like an uprising against Westminster – two fingers to the Establishment. I was also struck by their indifference to the future of the Union. I expressed some concern about the implications of Brexit for Scotland's future as part of the UK. They looked surprised. One said: 'What's the problem? If they want to go, let them leave. What's it to us?'

I think that there has been one further factor in play in this shaking of the political kaleidoscope. Social media has changed the world, and has turned out to be a profoundly polarising force in modern politics. James Madison, statesman, diplomat, philosopher, Father of the Constitution and fourth President of the United States, co-founded the Federalist Papers with Alexander Hamilton and in 1787 wrote one of them himself, Federalist No. 10 (now regarded as one of the most influential documents in American history). His particular concern was factionalism – 'a number of citizens united and actuated by some common impulse of passion, adverse to the rights of other citizens or the permanent and aggregate interests of the community' – which he saw as a profound risk to the then nascent republic. But he concluded that 'the extent of the Union gives it a most palpable advantage . . . The influence of factious leaders may kindle a flame within their particular States, but will be unable to spread a general conflagration through the other States'. Communication was challenging in the late eighteenth century; I'm not sure that Madison could have reached such a reassuring conclusion in the age of Twitter and Facebook.

I vividly remember a lunch in the residence, towards the end of 2018, with a senior member of the Trump cabinet. The conversation turned to prospects for the 2020 election. I politely suggested that the President could have tried harder to reach out to independent voters, rather than only communicate with his base. My interlocutor looked at me with a touch of pity in his eyes, and said: 'That's not how you win elections nowadays. You have to realise that the political centre ground has become completely depopulated. The way you win elections now is getting your base riled up: making sure every single one of them gets out and votes.' If this is true, then social media is the tool for the age. It has also become a form of competition, and of grandstanding – numbers of Twitter followers, likes against dislikes, retweeting. Academic research suggests that social media posts exhibiting 'indignant disagreement' get twice the 'engagement' of calmer, more balanced contributions. And it is a modern truism that people find it much easier to be offensive or cruel when typing onto a blank screen than when talking to someone face-to-face. What's more, in 2019, 55 per cent of Americans of voting age got some or most of their news from social media, with Facebook as the market leader. So the politician who commands social media rules the world. And it is a world in which outrage is contagious. Users of social media platforms are actively encouraged to separate into tribes; superficiality, masquerading as brevity, is applauded, if not mandatory; brutality is acceptable; and the world is presented as a series of black or white images, when the reality is a myriad shades of grey.

Finally, the three I's aside, Brexit and Trump are not just down to the shifting of tectonic plates. In both cases the outcome was narrow, and could have gone differently. I admired and was proud to work for David Cameron. I thought that he was good at being Prime Minister. He took some brave decisions, notably with austerity policies that, in the wake of the financial crisis, were painful but essential. His instincts were good. Had he won the referendum, he would have delivered a series of socially liberal policies and initiatives that would have transformed the country. He was a true 'One Nation' Tory, in the honourable tradition of such figures. And he is, above all, a thoroughly decent human being; working for him, as for Tony Blair, was a pleasure. But with Brexit, and the benefit of hindsight, his Remain campaign was misjudged. It was essentially designed to frighten people, to tell them how much they would lose if they voted to leave. Something of the kind had worked with the Scottish independence referendum a couple of years earlier. But this time, it ran up against the argument that news reporters were hearing on the streets: 'We don't have anything to lose.'

David Cameron's second campaigning problem was this. If you have spent the previous five years publicly disparaging the EU, it is hard to sound authentic when persuading people that they should commit to continued membership. While campaigning for the Conservative Party leadership, he promised to take the party out of the European People's Party, the collective centre-right grouping in the European Parliament. This won him a few votes in the leadership ballot but did lasting damage to his relationship with Angela Merkel. She is a deeply tribal politician and I think he might have got more help from her on his pre-referendum renegotiation of Britain's relationship with the EU had he stayed with her group.

I also remember his first European Council, while I was still ambassador to the EU. He bonded effortlessly with his fellow leaders, won all his arguments in the session where the council conclusions were drafted and agreed, and provided at least one clever drafting fix to help one of his colleagues. But then, in his session with the British press, at the conclusion of the meeting, he was asked, mischievously, whether, since he appeared to have enjoyed himself, he was 'really a Eurosceptic'. I watched him closely. He paused, gathered his thoughts, and launched into a withering criticism of the EU, concluding that he indeed remained a Eurosceptic. Thereafter, on the journey out to each European Council, he would concoct with his press team a story to toss to the *Mail, Telegraph* and *Sun*, usually about a row with Martin Schultz, the German socialist president of the European Parliament, with the objective of swiftly burnishing his Eurosceptic credentials. All of which meant that, when campaigning, he struggled to offer a positive vision of continued EU membership; it was all about risk and downside. While against him, the Leave campaign was fuelled almost entirely on emotion, and a nostalgic, largely fantastical, Union-Jack bedecked vision of a 'Britain proud and free'.

But to complete the Brexit story, it wasn't only about a history of British exceptionalism and mistakes by the Remain campaign. My friends and former colleagues in Brussels would dispute this fiercely, but I think there was also a strategic mistake on the other side of the table. One of the founding principles of the single market is the 'four freedoms': free movement around the member states of goods, capital, services and labour (the last of these being the reason for the influx of central European workers into the UK from 2004). These are noble principles; but the reality is that they are only partially enforced within the EU. There is for example nothing like a completed single market in services. A 2019 IMF paper noted 'considerable implementation gaps' in the services directive and continuing 'administrative burdens and costs' for service providers when going cross-border. Germany, in particular, was always, in my negotiating days, a laggard on opening up the European services market. As for freedom of movement, it was conceived in a different age, when the EU was a smaller, richer, and exclusively Western European club. I do not believe that the principle was ever intended to facilitate huge population movements like the two million central Europeans who came to the UK after enlargement. Yet in the renegotiation of British terms of membership that preceded the referendum, the EU dug itself into a deep hole: they behaved as if the four freedoms were carved in marble and mounted on some celestial hillside, rather than the reality, which is a patchwork of partially delivered commitments.

In particular, Cameron badly needed a significant EU concession on immigration. One option was, in the EU jargon, an 'emergency brake': the right temporarily to suspend free movement of labour if the numbers entering in a single year were putting an unmanageable burden on a country's social services, health services, education system or housing supply. Another option was allowing the UK to limit welfare payments to EU migrants – a 'welfare brake'. (Though the scale of the problem was often exaggerated, the idea that EU citizens could turn up in the UK without a job and quickly take advantage of the UK's generous welfare payments, even to the extent of receiving child benefit for children who had never set foot in the UK, was understandably deeply unpopular.) In the end, an emergency brake was rejected on the grounds that it needs Treaty change (not that Treaty change was a problem when the Eurozone wanted it in the aftermath of the 2008 financial crisis). And Cameron could only get a watered down version of his welfare brake. As he outlines in his autobiography, he had wanted to be able to say 'no welfare for four years' and 'no sending child benefit home'. After the other member states, especially the central Europeans, had chipped away at the proposed deal, he could say only 'not much welfare' and 'not much child benefit'. In short, the EU could have done significantly more to help; instead they tended towards the rigidly inflexible and unimaginative, believing, in my judgement, that it was unimaginable that the UK would vote to leave. They misread British politics, as the UK, over the years, had often misread the politics in other member states. The result is an EU that is smaller, weaker, and substantially poorer. I have lost count of how many friends from EU governments have said to me since that UK departure is a disaster for the EU. I believe it could have been avoided had they shown a little more flexibility and creativity.

Meanwhile, across the Atlantic, Donald Trump was running one of the most unusual campaigns in US political history. Yes, his main themes, immigration and economic inequality, were resonating. Yes, he was exploiting a perfect storm, tapping into deep public anger. Yes, his campaign was essentially, in its central message, about recreating the past, the Golden Age of Fifties America, when the factories were full, when the coal mines were working, when the White House was the exclusive preserve of WASPs – White Anglo-Saxon Protestants. But that, by itself, would not have been enough, had he not been such an extraordinary campaigner. At the time, his messages were so harsh, controversial and divisive, the dog-whistle politics so glaring, that onlookers tended to overlook the enthusiasm he generated and the vast crowds he attracted. The Republicans thought they had assembled one of the strongest primary fields in their history, ranging from Ted Cruz and Marco Rubio on the right to Jeb Bush and John Kasich from the moderate centre. Trump, with a tiny campaign team behind him, blew them away. He had a killer's instinct for the weaknesses of his opponents, and a fairground barker's gift for pulling in the crowds.

There was more of the same when it came to the contest with Hillary Clinton. Trump campaigned tirelessly and endlessly, criss-crossing the country, shaking off setbacks, surfing on a wave of adulation while talking about criminals and rapists and walls and a corrupt establishment looking after its own. Hillary Clinton's carefully managed, data-driven, safety-first campaign seemed anaemic by comparison. And most of all, Trump understood grievances, because he was himself a tightly wound ball of deeply held grievances. His father had always been down on him. He was a boy from Queens, who had never been accepted among the Manhattan elite. No one gave him credit for his business successes. His TV show, *The Apprentice*, had never won the Emmy it deserved.

Barack Obama had ridiculed him at the nationally broadcast White House Correspondents' Dinner. The Republican Party didn't like him. The mainstream media had turned against him and his campaign, giving him no credit for destroying the rest of the primary field. In short, he was the outsider's outsider: the billionaire New York property developer who could connect with Hillary Clinton's 'basket of deplorables', or those small-town people described in Barack Obama's statement, on the 2008 campaign trail, as 'clinging to guns and religion and antipathy to people who weren't like them'.

Imagine how these campaigns, on each side of the Atlantic, would have looked to the voters. Trump supporters were by no means all blue-collar workers; he had much of the business community on his side. But envisage a 55-year-old white man living in Ohio, or Pennsylvania, or Michigan. He used to work on an assembly line in a factory down the road, pulling in nearly $25 an hour. Now he stacks shelves in the local Walmart at $10 an hour. During his factory days, he could support his family by himself. Now he can't; like so many others, he depends on his wife, who works as a nursing auxiliary in the healthcare sector, and whose hourly wage is a touch more than his. Overall, they are doing worse than twenty years ago, and there are so few jobs in their small town that their children have moved hundreds of miles away to find work. Meanwhile, his mobile phone keeps bombarding him with newsflashes describing a world he doesn't recognise: wars in countries he's never heard of, with American boys getting killed or wounded – why have they been sent to these hellholes, like Afghanistan and Iraq and Syria? What possible good are they doing? Closer to home, in the name of Islam, people with Middle Eastern names seem to be killing Americans on the streets of American cities. He hears on the news that white Americans will be a minority in the country by the mid-2040s. In the vacant lot down the road, they are building a mosque, or perhaps it is a Hindu temple. In what was once his local church, Andrew is getting married to William. And there is someone whose middle name is Hussein sitting in the Oval Office. So he is angry; he has grievances;

he feels he can't say what he thinks; he wonders what has happened to the America in which he grew up; and no one in charge, in that den of corruption called Washington, seems to care.

And then along comes someone new. He is a businessman, not a politician. He doesn't talk in code like politicians: he tells it like it is. He promises to bring the factories back, by getting rid of all these terrible trade deals which gave away American manufacturing to Asia and Mexico. He promises to reopen the coal mines and get rid of all that nonsense about wind energy and climate change. He understands that the immigrants have to be stopped – otherwise there will be no jobs left for Americans – and promises to build a great wall along the southern border. He says that America has to prevent the terrorists coming in, so he will stop flights from these terrible Middle Eastern countries. He says he's going to get American boys back from the sand and blood and death of the Middle East, because they aren't doing any good there and should never have been sent. And he hints, in some of the things he says, that he gets it: it has gone too far and real America has to be restored, with the right sort of people in charge. 'Make America Great Again'.

Envisage now a 35-year-old Englishman, in a small town in the West Midlands. He has a wife, two children of school age, and a mortgage on the edge of what he can afford. He works in sales for a small IT company; that too feels on the edge. His town has changed: now the people working in the shops, the restaurants and the pubs all seem to be from central Europe. When he goes to work on the bus, he hears foreign languages being spoken all around him. His wife complains that it is taking two weeks to get a doctor's appointment, while she can't get a place for their youngest at the local nursery, so she is stuck at home all day and can't take on a job. She puts this, too, down to the incomers, nice people though they are, with university degrees and perfect English. He watches the news every night and sees columns of refugees from Syria and Afghanistan and places he's never heard of marching across Europe, heading west; he wonders if they are coming to the UK.

He knows there is a big vote coming up on whether the UK should stay in the European Union. The Prime Minister is on TV, saying that it would 'damage economic growth' if we left the EU. The governor of the Bank of England appears, saying the same thing. He wonders where this economic growth actually is; his salary has been stagnant for years. On the other hand, there was an article in the newspapers saying that some people in the City of London are getting million-pound bonuses. This doesn't seem quite fair, to put it mildly. Other people in grey suits are saying that Leave would damage Britain's global role and international influence: on balance, he couldn't give a toss about either. And then that amusing likeable chap who used to be mayor of London, who was once trapped for hours on a zip wire, comes on and says that, on the contrary, leaving would be great. We would apparently save £350 million a week, which we could spend on doctors, do lots of trade deals with the rest of the world, and 'regain control of our borders' to stop the flood of foreigners coming in. On balance, this sounds better: when voting day comes, he goes with 'Let's Take Back Control'.

Put like this, it's a wonder that Trump and Leave didn't both win with landslides. The fact that they didn't is probably in part about credibility: it all sounds a little glib and short on detail and substance. But I also think that a lot of voters, though not enough, would have sensed that these aren't real visions of the future. They are actually pictures of an idealised, sepia-tinged past; before globalisation, before automation, before climate change, before the internet and inter-connectedness, before political correctness. It's a return to a golden age that never was. In my view it cannot work. As the Roman poet Ovid put it 2,000 years ago: 'Neither can the wave that has passed by be recalled, nor the hour which has passed return again'.

18

What Happened Next

'*There are decades where nothing happens; and there are weeks where decades happen*'

– Vladimir Ilyich Lenin

'*Never let the future disturb you. You will meet it, if you have to, with the same weapons of reason which today arm you against the present*'

– Marcus Aurelius

JEOPARDY! IS one of the longest running and most popular American television game shows. It debuted on NBC on 30 March 1975 and has been shown on one channel or another ever since, for more than 8,000 episodes. It features a quiz. On 28 February 2020, one of the questions was:

> Sir Kim Darroch resigned from this post in 2019 after the leak of some comments of his about the US administration. Which post was it?

The contestants found this too tough to handle: none of them could come up with the right answer, which was of course 'British Ambassador to the United States'. But within an hour or two, at least half a dozen friends and acquaintances had texted me to point out that I had featured: testimony, I guess, to the long-running popularity of the show, and, after months in the shadows, renewed fame of a sort, even if still more fleeting than Andy Warhol's fifteen minutes.

On returning to the UK, we couldn't immediately regain our house in the West London suburbs, since it was occupied by tenants on a lease running until Easter 2020. So we stayed initially with Vanessa's mother in her small house in a village on the Colne estuary on the east coast, an opportunity to walk daily along the windswept East Anglian salt marshes. And then, in late October, after the last holiday let, we went down to our cottage on the south coast of Cornwall. We had bought this for, by London standards, a pittance twenty years earlier as a crumbling and almost uninhabitable wreck; dating back to the seventeenth century, it had damp running down the walls, mould growing in the corners and a sizeable centipede and spider population living under the sodden carpets. It was made from Cornish cob, a folksy and reassuring name for a mixture of earth, clay, straw, rubble and possibly the odd dead cat to ward off the witches. We restored it step by step, year by year, despite setbacks aplenty, prompting us to conclude that we had purchased the most expensive mud hut in the country; and we knew we were near completion when our children considered it sufficiently cool to bring their friends down.

We stayed there through Christmas and the New Year until early February. The winter months on the Cornish coast are an experience: the storms line up in the Western Approaches, then hit land about once a fortnight, sending the waves crashing over the harbour walls, scattering seaweed, stones and seashells across the adjacent roads. But between the storms, there are days when the low winter sun emerges, lights up the landscape and transforms the sea, normally grey and threatening, into a shimmering, iridescent panorama that stretches to the horizon. It was the ideal refuge from which to follow the next chapter of the seemingly endless Brexit saga, as lengthy as *Game of Thrones* and with almost as much bloodshed; to watch from a safe distance the final year of Trump's first term; and to begin to write this book.

When we left Washington, Theresa May was still Prime Minister, though in a caretaker capacity. On 23 July, as every pundit had predicted, Boris Johnson won the votes of a comfortable majority of Conservative Party members and was elected party leader and

Prime Minister. And within three months, he had delivered a revised withdrawal agreement with Brussels. This was successfully presented to the British public as a brilliant negotiating coup, seeing off the EU apparatchiks. It wasn't really. Although both sides moved, it primarily entailed a substantial concession by the UK, agreeing to have its border with the EU in the Irish Sea rather than between Northern Ireland and the Republic. This was a solution the EU had actually proposed in February 2018. But as Churchill said, history is written by the victors.

The deal initially went less well in Parliament. Johnson imposed an arbitrary deadline of 31 October for its passage through the House of Commons, and memorably asserted that he would rather 'die in a ditch' than accept an extension. He then proceeded to lose a succession of Parliamentary votes, and, for a period, control of the House, forcing him to ask for an extension – though by that stage ditches had seemingly vanished from the landscape. But this was the last hurrah of the remainers. The votes were probably there for them to force through legislation mandating a second referendum, but they could never coalesce around a single proposition: what Freud called the narcissism of small differences, brilliantly lampooned by the Monty Python team in the film *Life of Brian* with the mortal enmity between the Judean People's Front and the People's Front of Judea. So the moment was lost: and at the end of October, in one of the more striking acts of self-destruction in British political history, Opposition leader Jeremy Corbyn, along with the leaders of the minor and regional parties, agreed to Johnson's demands for an early general election.

Down in Cornwall, we were in one of the Brexit heartlands. And it was clear from the talk in the pubs and the supermarket aisles that Brexit supporters were profoundly angry about Westminster's failure to deliver the outcome for which they had voted. Johnson's campaign was structured around the brilliantly simple though seriously misleading slogan 'Get Brexit done'; Corbyn's around Old Labour policies of splashing money around the public sector and taxing the better-off, allied to a position on Brexit so confusing and ambiguous it couldn't be described in less than half a dozen sentences. It was no surprise, at least to me, when Johnson won a landslide victory, guaranteeing a stable majority to deliver EU withdrawal, while Labour's result was their worst since 1935. In a tantalising glimpse of what might have been, the parties supporting either Remain or a second referendum got more than 50 per cent of the votes between them. But that counted for nothing with the Remain vote divided, the Conservatives gaining practically every pro-Brexit vote in the country, and the first-past-the-post constituency system.

The new government prioritised their promise to get Brexit done. The Withdrawal Agreement Bill gained royal assent on 23 January and at an hour before midnight on 31 January, the UK left the European Union. Down in our Cornish village, a few fireworks flared briefly, almost apologetically, in the night sky; otherwise most households seemed to have settled for an early night. In London, a campaign announced a few weeks earlier by the Prime Minister to crowdfund a temporary reopening of Big Ben, out of action during its restoration – 'bung a bob for a Big Ben bong for Brexit' – had thankfully collapsed within hours of its launch. So Johnson settled for delivering a brief address to the nation. He called it 'an astonishing moment of hope', asserted that his job was now 'to bring this country together and take us forward . . . it is potentially a moment of real national renewal', and sprayed around promises about 'defeating crime, transforming our NHS . . . the biggest revival of our infrastructure since the Victorians . . . and a Britain that is simultaneously a great European power and truly global in our range and ambitions'. Meanwhile, the media were starting to become interested in reports emerging from Wuhan in central China of the spread of an unknown pneumonia-type virus. The city of 11 million people had been closed off. The World Health Organisation had declared a global emergency. More than two hundred people had died and almost 10,000 infections reported worldwide in countries like Taiwan, Japan, South Korea and Thailand, as well as one in the United States. Alarming, but it all seemed a long way away.

And we were going back to America. I had been invited to do a three-month resident fellowship at the Institute of Politics, part of the Kennedy School at Harvard. Preparations for this included the unfamiliar task, after decades of hassle-free travel as a diplomat, of queuing outside the American embassy on a cold January morning to get a visa. I had expected to be there a couple of hours; such was the efficiency of the embassy's system, however, that it was all over in forty minutes, with the visa-replete passports arriving by post two days later. Who knew?

We wondered what we were going back to. While we had been away, the President had been impeached. This wasn't the Russia story that had transfixed Washington for two years, but something else entirely: an allegation that he had withheld both military aid to Ukraine and an invitation to the new Ukrainian President to visit the White House in order to pressure the country's government into investigating the activities there of Democrat Joe Biden and his son, Hunter (the latter had been appointed to the board of a Ukrainian natural gas company). As I had always thought would happen had the Russia affair ever led to impeachment, the process was going nowhere; the Republican majority in the Senate was solid in Trump's support, with the notable exception of Mitt Romney (the definitive acquittal would come through on 5 February). But it made Trump, after Presidents Andrew Johnson and Bill Clinton, only the third occupant of the Oval Office in history to be impeached.

We arrived in Boston on 3 February, a chilly Monday evening. On the flight, I watched *Midsommar*, a 'folk horror' film set in a pagan community in the Swedish countryside (though actually filmed in Hungary). It was clearly inspired by one of my favourite films of the Seventies, *The Wicker Man*, and it is unquestionably destined for the same cult status. I liked it so much that I have since insisted that friends sit through it, to the enduring trauma of some of them. Vanessa, meanwhile, ignored the new releases and chose *Contagion*, the 2011 film about a deadly virus sweeping the world; I am now considering how to market her precognitive abilities. And on landing at Boston, we found the airport mysteriously and spookily deserted, so we got through the entry formalities in what felt like seconds. The omens were piling up.

I was one of six resident fellows. The others comprised two political journalists, the former governor of Alaska, the chief of staff of a leading Democratic senator, and a former special assistant to President Trump. They were a great group. We saw a lot of each other, all being housed together in a cluster of apartments in Cambridge, near the Charles River and a few minutes' walk from both the Kennedy School and the main Harvard campus.

The teaching side required each of us to do individual two-hour sessions once a week. These were open not just to the students affiliated to the Institute of Politics, but also to the rest of the campus, and indeed to any residents of Cambridge who wanted to register and turn up. I had never 'taught' anyone anything in my entire career. So I turned to Vanessa for advice, she having taught in five different countries. She passed on the tricks of the trade, while confessing that her accumulated knowledge had been gleaned from a career teaching six- and seven-year-olds, and was therefore of questionable relevance to a class of the cleverest university students in America. Then, during the Fellows' induction week, we were treated to a talk from a resident expert on how to engage with students; and her advice exactly matched what Vanessa had told me. Who said that we are all children at heart?

The liberal invitation policy to these fellows' sessions made for an eclectic gathering each week; amongst my sixty-odd attendees there were a wide range of nationalities, reflecting the international nature of the Harvard intake, and an age range from the late teens to elderly retirees. I suspected that some of the locals were attending less to hear my thoughts on the world than to escape the frigid temperatures of the Boston winter. My theme was the rise of populism and the retreat of establishment politics across the West: broad enough to enable me to reminisce about my times in the Balkans during the Bosnia and Kosovo conflicts, Milosevic having been a classic user of the tools of populism, and to talk about the history of the UK's 'conscious uncoupling' (to quote one of the stars of *Contagion*) from the European Union. I think the sessions went okay, but how would I know? Everyone was far too polite to tell me otherwise.

Our time in Massachusetts coincided with a fascinating period in American politics: the Democratic primaries, the process through which the party would choose their candidate to go head-to-head with President Trump in November. The winnowing-out had already begun, with a preceding autumn of televised debates, campaigning, and most important of all in American politics, fundraising. And gradually the huge field, twenty or so at its peak, had narrowed down. By the time we arrived, though the field was theoretically still in double figures, the contest was really down to half a dozen: former Vice President Joe Biden, Senator Bernie Sanders, Senator Elizabeth Warren, Senator Amy Klobuchar and Mayor Pete Buttigieg, with Mike Bloomberg watching from New York, building his team and waiting in the wings. And the first primary, the Iowa caucus, was to be held the day after we arrived.

In my time as ambassador, I had met all of the leading candidates. One of them, Joe Biden, I had actually first spoken to when he was Vice President and I was national security adviser. He had attended and intervened at one of our National Security Council meetings. But when rumours sprang up that he was contemplating running for President, I went to see him. What should have been a thirty-minute encounter turned into ninety minutes, to the palpable discomfort of his staff: they eventually extracted him by telling him he had a plane to catch. He was warm, funny and wise, but also unstoppably talkative; anecdotes tumbled out of him. He was at that stage still declining to confirm that he was running; but when I asked him what sort of candidate could defeat Trump, his answer, tying together experience, empathy, a track record of working across the political divide, and the ability to connect with America's blue-collar classes, sounded uncannily like a description of himself. As I left his office, I concluded that I knew his intentions.

As for the others, I had kept in touch with Bloomberg whenever he had visited Washington. I had met Pete Buttigieg on his South Bend home turf. I first called on Bernie Sanders in the margins of the Democratic Convention in Philadelphia in 2016, and I subsequently went to see him a couple of times in his Senate office. He was always generous with his time, but generally spent most of the meetings quizzing me about Brexit, or European politics, or the Gulf; so much so that there was never time to get into his views on the state of America. Klobuchar and Warren I met in their Senate offices. Both were highly impressive: Klobuchar warm, sharp and witty, Warren the cerebral Harvard law professor.

The Iowa caucus, sometimes characterised as 'gatherings of neighbours', is a gloriously archaic construct. No paper ballots for the Iowans. Instead, they collect in school halls or indoor sports arenas, or even private houses; anywhere boasting a large covered space, out of the brutal Iowan winter. Once inside, they coalesce, discuss the candidates, and then indicate their support for one or other by dividing out to designated corners of the arena where eventually they are counted. Outdated or not, Iowa can be crucial in giving a candidate momentum. It memorably put Barack Obama on the road to the White House in 2008 when, in front of an astonished media, the almost exclusively white farmers of Iowa gathered in huge numbers in the Obama sectors of each arena, visibly spurning the hitherto front-running candidacy of Hillary Clinton.

This time, however, it was more like the caucus race in Lewis Carroll's *Alice's Adventures in Wonderland*, in which every contestant runs around haphazardly, in no particular direction, until the Dodo calls a halt and declares everyone a winner. A group of us gathered in front of the TV screens that early February evening to watch and wait for the drama to unfold. And waited. And waited. As the hours passed, and the sports arenas and community centres gradually emptied, it became clear that Something Had Gone Wrong. In a wonderful piece of solid gold irony, this most primitive of electoral processes had been sabotaged by malfunctioning technology, a newly designed mobile phone app intended to allow individual precincts to report their results more quickly and accurately. It didn't work. The results eventually emerged three days later. Buttigieg had won the most delegates, narrowly beating Sanders – a remarkable result for a mere mayor of the fourth largest city in Indiana, in competition with senators, governors and a former vice president. But the confusion and the delay robbed Buttigieg of much of the momentum he might have gained.

On to New Hampshire, a week later. This is the famous one: the first proper primary, with the voters casting ballots rather than meeting in the local school gymnasium. Like Iowa, it has sometimes changed political history: Dwight Eisenhower beating presumed front runner Robert Taft in 1954 on his way the White House; incumbent President Lyndon Johnson winning fewer delegates than the anti-war Senator Eugene McCarthy in 1968 and immediately withdrawing from the race; Ed Muskie, also presumed front runner, 'crying in the snow' over a defamatory press article while campaigning in 1972. The article, incidentally, was later alleged to have been the work of Richard Nixon's dirty tricks team, which included, to complete the circle to modern times, one Roger Stone.

There were no tears in the 2020 New Hampshire primary; not that much snow either. Bernie Sanders, for whom it was almost home territory, won. Buttigieg again exceeded expectations. The other mid-Westerner, Amy Klobuchar, also did well. But the big story was that Joe Biden came only fourth, with a mere 8 per cent of the vote. The first obituaries started to be written about this three-time failed candidate, the nearly man of American politics.

But as it turned out, neither Iowa nor New Hampshire was the defining moment in the campaign. Instead they were false trails on the road to the South Carolina primary on 29 February and the biggest comeback in recent political history. Buoyed by a massive turnout amongst African-American voters, Biden smashed the opposition, won every county in the state, and collected 48 per cent of the vote and thirty-nine delegates. Sanders came a distant second with 20 per cent and a mere fifteen delegates, while Buttigieg and Klobuchar were so far behind that, within twenty-four hours, they had dropped out and announced their support for Biden. Biden went on to dominate the 'Super Tuesday' voting across fourteen states three days later, winning ten states and a mass of delegates to Sanders' four. And a few days later, Elizabeth Warren also suspended her campaign, announcing her decision in an impromptu press doorstep outside her house in a suburban street in Cambridge, a few blocks from where we were staying during our time at Harvard. Though Sanders clung on for another month, it was in effect all over.

I found it interesting that among the Harvard students I canvassed, there wasn't a Biden supporter to be found: they were all enthusiasts for either Sanders or Warren, the two standard bearers for the 'progressive' wing of the party. The near universal view on Biden was a shrug and a 'meh'; 'like, what does he stand for?' I admired the idealism; but my travels in the Midwest had convinced me that Biden was the Democrat with the best chance of beating Donald Trump. I reckoned that Trump would be a formidable opponent for any of them, on the back of a strongly performing economy. But Biden could hope to recapture at least some of the blue-collar vote; in contrast to Hillary Clinton, African Americans would turn out for him; and after the roller-coaster ride of the Trump presidency, I thought Americans outside Trump's fervent base might yearn for a return to the calm and caution and rationality of the 'No Drama Obama' period, with an experienced and familiar figure from that era at the helm.

Biden, though no Obama, could also sometimes inspire; I remember in particular a brilliant speech he gave at the Gridiron dinner in Washington in February 2016, at the end of which Vanessa turned to me and said 'Why isn't he running for President? I'd vote for him.' But he had two unsuccessful runs behind him and a lot of Washington insider history to defend; and he had a history of gaffes (on which Biden himself once said, 'a gaffe in Washington is someone telling the truth'). And as he stumbled through the early debates, showing his age with now-archaic terms like 'record player' and allowing himself to be beaten up by California Senator Kamala Harris (who ran out of money and didn't even make it to the primaries), there were many moments when I doubted that he would come through. But on the back of South Carolina, he seemed transformed, his self-confidence renewed and his energy restored. For my part, I wished I'd had more confidence in my instincts and told London back in early 2019 that he'd be the Democratic candidate, when he hadn't even decided to run.

Biden's resurrection inevitably dominated the US media throughout early March. But in another part of the landscape, the world was about to stop. On 21 January, the US Center for Disease Control and Prevention, the CDC, had announced the first travel-related case of coronavirus, Covid-19 as we were all to learn to call it, in the US: a

35-year-old man living in Washington state who had just returned from Wuhan. The President said, 'It's one person coming in from China and we have it under control.' Ten days later, Trump announced a ban on non-US citizens travelling from China. It amounted to only a partial ban: Hong Kong, Macau and Taiwan were excluded and US citizens in China could still return to the US. According to the *New York Times*, more than 400,000 people flew directly from China to the US over that January-to-March period, including some 40,000 after the travel restrictions were imposed. The first publicly acknowledged Covid-related death, also in Washington state, 'Ground Zero' for the infection, was announced on 29 February. And on 6 March, three days after Biden had swept ten states on Super Tuesday, the President visited the CDC. At that stage the US had fifteen known cases, and the President said, 'Within a couple of days infections are going to be down close to zero . . . one day, it's like a miracle, it will disappear.'

These were words that will be quoted endlessly when the histories of the pandemic come to be written. The reality was the complete opposite: the virus was already spreading with terrifying speed. Just four days later, on 10 March, the number of confirmed cases in the US reached 1,000, with thirty deaths. And Harvard told all of its students to pack up and go home by the next weekend – when they would normally have been leaving for spring break – and not return until further notice. The campus was almost instantly swamped with piles of luggage, removal vans, and gatherings of disconsolate, sometimes tearful students saying goodbye to their friends and classmates; those in their final year never to return.

Late that evening, we went for a walk. The mood had changed. Almost every window was open in the unseasonable March warmth, and the night air was full of music and voices. Harvard was partying as if the end of the world was nigh and each drink might be the last: as if sensing that the tendrils of the virus were already twining around the pillars and staircases of the college buildings.

Our initial thought was to stick it out in Cambridge. The accommodation was available until the end of April. Harvard classes would be continuing online. But events were moving with unnerving speed.

On 11 March the President announced restrictions on travel from mainland Europe, extending the measure to the UK and Ireland a couple of days later. By 16 March there were over 4,000 reported cases across the US and more than forty deaths. The President announced a national emergency; some states started to close schools; and on 19 March, the first stay-at-home orders were announced by California and New York. As a sign that it was really serious, Broadway closed down and the college basketball finals were cancelled.

We had planned to spend spring break in Cape Cod, in a house borrowed from a Danish friend of ours, a lecturer at one of Boston's many universities. We went ahead; apart from the appeal of seeing the favourite landscape of the iconic and quintessentially American painter Edward Hopper, it was as isolated and safe a place as could be imagined. The house, an elegant expression of minimalist Scandinavian cool, nestled in a tree-filled hillside with the Atlantic Ocean glittering in the distance. The nearest village was Truro, an echo of Cornwall; and we were just a few miles from the relative metropolis of Provincetown at the tip of the peninsula.

We duly explored Provincetown, by its own account the gay capital of Massachusetts, and discovered a long and picturesque main street full of arty shops, though most were closed for the off season. With a state-wide lockdown coming into force from midnight that day, Vanessa got the last haircut in town, and we went for a final margarita before darkness descended. The barman commiserated, noting in particular that we would be missing one of the town's main attractions, a weekly drag revue that would have been held two days later: we would have gone. Instead, we spent the days walking for miles in sub-zero temperatures along deserted beaches beneath cobalt-blue skies, and in the evenings settled for Netflix. But every time I switched on the news channels, the crisis seemed to be accelerating. New York was emerging as the epicentre and its Democrat governor, Andrew Cuomo, as the most authoritative voice in American politics.

So we started to think we should head back to the UK, before Boston came to resemble New York, and before international travel closed down further. I telephoned Virgin Atlantic and discovered that they had already cancelled all their flights from Boston airport. But they rebooked us on a flight from New York's JFK on 25 March. The final, eerie few days in America were spent packing for departure, walking around a near-deserted Cambridge and tracking the ever-worsening impact of the virus. By our departure date, the death toll in the US had reached 1,000, though President Trump had declared two days earlier that he 'would love to have the country opened up' by Easter.

It should have been a five-hour drive from Boston to JFK, but the roads were so empty that we did it in barely more than three and arrived some four hours before our flight, to be greeted by a sight that will stay with me forever. JFK is the busiest international airport in the US, handling more than 60 million passengers a year. But the vast concourse was completely deserted: shuttered kiosks, rows upon rows of empty check-in counters and not a human being in view. I walked around searching for signs of life. Eventually I saw a couple of security guards wearing face masks, and then, in the far reaches of the check-in desks, a small huddled crowd of would-be passengers waiting to check in for a domestic flight. The airport was breathing, even if on life support.

So we waited, sitting on the concourse floor with our suitcases next to the Virgin check-in desks. Gradually we were joined by a handful of other evacuees, seemingly all fleeing the country at short notice; most of them were purchasing tickets before joining the check-in queue. To compound the dread-filled atmosphere, a clearly disturbed young woman was roaming the concourse, accosting passengers, under the indifferent gaze of the security guards. We passed the time by debating which post-apocalypse film we were now inhabiting. We settled on the (quite good) *I Am Legend* from 2007, starring Will Smith as the last human alive in New York after a virus had wiped out 90 per cent of humanity.

And then, mercifully, the check-in desk opened, we were through security and boarding our half-empty plane. The westerlies were so strong that the flight took barely six hours, so we arrived back at Heathrow at 6 a.m. It was busier than JFK – not a stretch – but still so empty that we were through in a few minutes. We got into a black cab for the short drive to our house in south-west London. Throughout my career I had interrogated London cabbies on my return from abroad, drawing on their insights to give me an instant snapshot of the mood of the country. So I explained to the cabbie that we had just returned from two months in America and asked how things were in locked-down London. He launched into an expressive tirade about how catastrophically his earnings had been hit by the lockdown, and how unfairly he and other self-employed were being treated by the government. (On 20 March the Chancellor had introduced a scheme under which the government would pay 80 per cent of the wages of employees of companies temporarily closed by the lockdown, but hadn't at that stage introduced anything similar for the self-employed, though he later did.) The diatribe reminded me how difficult it is to design a policy in which no one feels disadvantaged. And it made us feel truly back home.

My daughter, Georgie, and her partner, Dave, were already in residence at our house, while they climbed the mountain that is saving the deposit to buy somewhere of their own in London. Lockdown stretched timelessly through April, May and June, each day merging into the next. I shouldn't complain: it gave us time to unpack dozens of boxes in storage during our time in Washington; we joined the millions (or is it billions?) taking Adriene Mishler's online yoga classes; the sun shone, with the driest May for 150 years; the garden had never looked better. And Vanessa and Georgie cooked: sourdough, home-made pasta, selections from the pages of Yotam Ottolenghi and Nigel Slater, and perfect bagels; I may never again have to Google 'where to find New York-style bagels in London'. Most of all, it gave me time to read and to think about what was happening in the UK and America; about the consequences of the Covid-19 pandemic; about the future.

When we left Boston, the virus was raging through the north-eastern states, with New York the epicentre. As I write, in early July, with Europe tentatively reopening, it is surging across the Sun Belt, with numbers of new cases rising in thirty-five out of fifty states and reaching a one-day record of 62,000 on 8 July. Dr Anthony Fauci, the director of the National Institute of Allergies and Infectious Diseases, and a national figure from his appearances at the now-abandoned daily White House press briefings, has said that 'the US is going in the wrong direction' and has predicted that numbers of deaths, already at 128,000, are 'going to be very disturbing'.

This American carnage will reflect a multiplicity of causes and factors. But the contradictory messaging from the White House must have been a significant contributor. The President has repeatedly downplayed the threat from the virus: 'A lot of people will have this and it is very mild.' He has overstated the availability of testing: 'Anyone who wants a test can get one.' He has overpromised on the prospect of a vaccine: 'Now they have it, they have studied it, in fact we're very close to a vaccine.' He has made improbable claims about US readiness: 'The US is the most prepared country in the world.' He has promoted quack remedies like the antimalarial drug hydroxychloroquine, saying that he was taking it himself. He has repeatedly blamed China, calling Covid-19 'the Chinese virus' and 'Kung flu' and claiming that there is evidence it originated in a Chinese laboratory, the Wuhan Institute of Virology. He has invited ridicule by suggesting, from the White House podium, either that 'we hit the body with a tremendous ultra-violet light' or, since disinfectant 'knocks the virus out in a minute', scientists should look at the option of 'injection inside, almost a cleaning'. (The day after making that last pronouncement, he told reporters he was merely being sarcastic. Too late: social media had gone wild, one of the highlights being comedian and YouTube star Randy Rainbow's song 'A Spoonful of Clorox', to the tune of 'A Spoonful of Sugar', featuring the memorable line 'try some bleach in your beer and shove a flashlight up your ass'.)

Shortly after Disinfectant Day, the daily White House briefings were abandoned. This hasn't entirely stopped the stream of extraordinary proclamations. On 15 June Trump told reporters that 'if we stopped testing right now we'd have very few cases, if any'. And throughout, he has consistently struggled to convey empathy for the victims of the pandemic or their families, whilst unashamedly prioritising economic recovery, the buoyant economy having hitherto been his strongest claim to re-election. There is, moreover, little doubt that these messages have changed the behaviour of many Americans. In some states there have been public demonstrations against lockdowns. One or two state-level Republican politicians have argued that deaths from the virus overwhelmingly occur amongst the old, and are a cost worth paying for reopening the economy and saving jobs. And in chronically divided America, wearing a mask, or not, has become a political signal: Democrats wear them, Republicans, on the whole, do not. A friend of ours in Nashville told us that she was abused in the street for wearing one, and expelled from a garden centre on the grounds that her mask proved that she actually had the virus and was a danger to other customers.

Trump's problems haven't started and finished with the pandemic. He has also faced a wave of public disapproval over his reaction to the murder of George Floyd. On 25 May, Floyd, a 46-year-old African-American, was killed in Minneapolis while being arrested for allegedly using a counterfeit bill. A white police officer, Derek Chauvin, knelt on Floyd's neck for almost eight minutes while the dying Floyd said repeatedly 'I can't breathe.' The incident was filmed by a bystander on a mobile phone. The following day, Chauvin and his three colleagues were fired from the police force. Chauvin was charged with second-degree murder, the other three with abetting murder.

The mobile phone clip went viral, prompting protests, marches and demonstrations in over 60 countries worldwide under the Black Lives Matter banner: in the UK, tens of thousands participated in a series of almost entirely peaceful rallies across the country. In America, there were dozens of protests in cities from coast to coast. Some of them turned violent: on the one hand, rioting and looting, with over 500 businesses vandalised in Minneapolis alone; on the other, accusations of an aggressive and heavy-handed police response.

The President essentially scorned the protestors. He announced that he was 'the law and order President'. He ignored the George Floyd funeral, leaving the field clear to a Joe Biden video link to the mourners. He tweeted 'When the looting starts, the shooting starts', echoing (he later claimed unwittingly) a notorious phrase used in

1967 about African-American civil rights protesters by the then Miami police chief, Walter Headley. And on the afternoon of 1 June, he initiated a moment that came to symbolise his failure to respond as the nation expected: the Washington police used teargas and rubber bullets against peaceful protestors so that the President could walk from the White House to the adjacent St John's church, to be photographed brandishing a Bible. The photo-op won some praise from the evangelical community but backfired with the mainstream media and, judging by the instant slide in the opinion polls, with much of the public. The Bishop of Washington described herself as outraged: 'they cleared the way with teargas so that they could use one of our churches as a prop'.

But the most telling comment came from General James Mattis, once Trump's Defence Secretary. Mattis said on 4 June: 'The protests are defined by tens of thousands of people of conscience, who are insisting that we live up to our values . . . Donald Trump is the first president in my lifetime who does not try to unite the American people – does not even pretend to try. Instead he tries to divide us . . . Only by adopting a new path – which means in truth returning to the original path of our founding ideals – will we again be a country admired and respected at home and abroad.' Trump responded by tweeting that Mattis was 'the world's most overrated general'.

The pandemic is destined to live on in the images it has bequeathed us: the haunted look in the Prime Minister's eyes as he emerged publicly from his near-death experience after contracting the coronavirus; the two-metre distancing lines that have seemingly overnight appeared on pavements everywhere; the tented testing centres that have sprouted in empty car parks, with mysteriously short queues of supplicants waiting for their moments; the aerial video of coffins being loaded into a mass grave on New York City's Hart Island; and most of all, the unearthly sight of doctors and nurses in full protective equipment, masked, suited and gloved. They remind me of the plague doctors of the seventeenth century, who wore terrifying, nightmarish masks dominated by what appeared to be huge curved beaks but were – in fact, medieval respirators stuffed with herbs and spices and intended to filter away the 'miasma', the bad air thought erroneously to be the source of the plague.

Is Covid-19 going to change the world? Life before the pandemic already feels like a lost age; and absent either a cure or a vaccine, some things may never return to how they were. I suspect, however, that the impact will primarily be to accelerate existing trends: more working from home, more online shopping, a falling out of fashion of big prestige city centre company headquarters. And there is a risk that it will encourage one trend that is already of profoundly concerning: the fragmentation of international structures, of countries, and of societies. Multilateralism, as represented by the post-1945 international order, the United Nations , the IMF, the World Bank, the World Trade Organisation, even NATO and the European Union, has never been weaker or more disparaged. Independence movements are springing up everywhere. And as the culture wars across the West demonstrate, societies are increasingly and bitterly divided.

Viruses don't respect borders. On the face of it, one of the most obvious lessons of the pandemic is the need for international cooperation: to stop transmission from one country to another, to work jointly on vaccines and cures, to pool resources in producing and distributing drugs and medical equipment, to work together on economic recovery. The reality, however, is that countries have almost without exception pursued national responses, on issues ranging from when and whether to close borders to testing regimes, lockdown decisions, and quarantine rules. Efforts are being made to set up multilateral structures for consultation and coordination; but as of now, major countries like the US, Russia, and India are not participating. And there is hoarding, not sharing, of pharmaceutical supplies and medical equipment.

Alongside the public health challenge, the global economy has been wrecked. The IMF estimates that there is now an extra $6 trillion of government debt has been incurred across the developed economies. The immediate priority will be saving jobs and getting economies growing again, so there will be no early return to austerity. But free trade, already under attack with President Trump's dismantling of

American trade deals, his disdain for the World Trade Organisation, and his decision to launch a trade war with China, could be the most serious casualty. There is a risk of a comprehensive retreat from the globalisation of the last decade and a surge of economic nationalism, as companies look to shorten their long-distance supply chains and governments are tempted to pursue decoupling and self -sufficiency. This seems to me both likely and precisely the wrong answer to the challenges we collectively face, serving only to slow global recovery from the pandemic's ruinous impact. In short, it is a moment for visionary leadership of ambition and imagination, of the kind that rebuilt the world after the Second World War.

The pandemic may also have changed the political outlook in the US. Opinion polls are snapshots in time. They don't necessarily prefigure the future. I remember vividly that in the 2016 race, Hillary Clinton was ahead, often by substantial margins, in every opinion poll until the one that mattered: 8 November, election day. That said, there is no doubt that, as I write, the President is having a bad run. Biden enjoys significant leads in most of the battleground states, and a substantial leads nationally; one recent poll had him fourteen14 points ahead. And judging by the Trump's Twitter feed it bothers him, badly. My old friend Frank Luntz has recently said, on a CBS current affairs programme, that the election is now 'Biden's to lose'. Frank isn't alone: lots of commentators are saying the same and even Ladbrokes are making Biden the narrow favourite. But Trump is a formidable, inexhaustible campaigner. His base will turn out for him. By contrast, Biden has never excelled as a campaigner or a debater and seems to have spent his entire career either on the cusp of a gaffe or recovering from one.

So it's too early to call it. But I have started to wonder whether America has tired of the Great Disrupter and the daily strife and chaos. Perhaps Americans want some calm and quiet. Perhaps they don't want to hear about politics every day. Perhaps they have had enough of all the aggravation. The notorious British gangster Reggie Kray made a famous death bed confession about killing another gangster, Jack 'The Hat' McVitie, by stabbing him repeatedly in the face, chest and stomach. When asked why he'd done it, he said, 'I didn't like the man . . . . he was loud and aggressive . . . . he was a vexation to the spirit.'. Have the American people decided that Donald Trump is a vexation to the spirit?

What are the implications for the UK of the US election outcome? Whoever wins, I expect the foundations of the relationship – the defence, security and intelligence cooperation, the cultural inter-change – to remain as strong as ever. If Trump triumphs, I think we will get a quick free trade deal – provided we are prepared to make some substantial concessions, particularly in allowing hugely increased imports of low cost US agricultural produce. I don't see the US doing a deal on any other basis. As for a Biden victory, I see that the government are already briefing sympathetic journalists that this could be even better for the UK than the alternative; and in particular, that a bilateral trade deal wouldn't be needed, because both the UK and US would end up in the CPTPP, the Trans-Pacific Partnership. I think a Biden win would be better for the multilateral system and for NATO. Biden would want to repair relations with allies and rejoin the Paris Climate Change Agreement. But I question whether his winning would mean a new flowering of the bilateral relationship. The Democrats remember Boris Johnson's attacks on Obama. They are, in the main, not Brexit enthusiasts; Biden declared that if he'd had a vote, he would have cast it for Remain. They may not see a free trade deal with the UK as their first priority; remember, Obama said the UK would be 'at the back of the queue'. And Biden hasn't actually fully committed to joining the CPTPP; he has talked about renegotiating some aspects of it to make it a better deal for the US. That could take a while.

Meanwhile, in the UK, Boris Johnson is insulated from his own sliding poll ratings by an eighty-seat majority and another four and a half years before he has to face the voters. But he still has to deliver a post-Brexit deal with the European Union. His lead negotiator, David Frost, used to work for me in the Foreign Office on EU issues. He has a brilliant mind. But it looks as if he also has an impossible negotiating mandate, essentially around a comprehensive free trade deal with the EU without the obligations attached to membership of the single market.

I believe that the Prime Minister genuinely wants a deal. But I worry that he has locked himself into an unrealistic set of demands and parameters. I suspect that this in part reflects pressure from the faction in No. 10 and the Cabinet that would prefer no deal. They argue that the pandemic, by disrupting supply chains and encouraging a move towards economic nationalism, has greatly reduced the costs of falling back on WTO terms for future trade with the EU. And they think that the key to rebuilding the economy is the complete freedom to pursue a radical, liberalising, legislative and regulatory agenda; against this imperative, with whom you trade and under what terms is a secondary consideration. But it also in part reflects the widely held British view that, when dealing with the EU, economics will always override theology: as I was told often by ministers and MPs visiting Washington, 'they will still want to sell us their BMWs'.

Just as our EU partners consistently misread British politics, I believe this is a fundamental misunderstanding of the European project, which has never been about markets and trade. And while I hope I am wrong, I think this misconception makes no deal an all-too-possible outcome. In which eventuality, I wonder quite where we will then find our friends, partners and collaborators in this unquestionably interdependent world. The Brexit vision was based on a series of separate, beneficial free trade arrangements with the global big players: the US, the EU, China. A US deal will require some politically painful climbdowns. The EU deal is looking at risk. And relations with China are increasingly fraught, over Hong Kong, over Huawei, over China's trade practices. Who is going to line up with us if China retaliates? Or, to borrow a line from another of my lockdown reads, Max Brooks' *Devolution*: 'It's great to live free of the other sheep until you hear the wolves howl'.

An issue closer to my own world has been the spate of senior civil servants – friends and former colleagues of mine – leaving office. On 29 February, Philip Rutnam, the Permanent Secretary in the Home Office, resigned and announced he was suing the government for constructive dismissal over a 'vicious and orchestrated campaign' against him. Simon McDonald, Permanent Under Secretary at the Foreign Office, announced a few weeks ago that he was retiring earlier than expected. And Mark Sedwill, one of my closest friends in government, announced on 29 June his resignation as Cabinet Secretary and National Security Adviser. In each case, the departure was foreshadowed by a malicious briefing campaigns in the media.

There are a range of models for a country's senior civil service. It can be politicised, as it is in the US, where, when the administration changes from Republican to Democratic, or vice versa, some 4,000 jobs at senior official level also change hands. Or there is the British model: a politically impartial and independent civil service. But they cannot coexist simultaneously. The government appears to be wanting to create a political civil service by coercion, not legislation, and to be pushing senior figures out of the door for ideological rather than performance reasons. This fundamentally undercuts one of the roles of civil servants, which is to provide impartial and objective advice. A government which surrounds itself with courtiers and enablers and which banishes challenge is set on a troubling course.

On 7 October 1777, at the second battle of Saratoga, the British General John Burgoyne surrendered to the leader of the American forces, General Horatio Gates. It was a turning point in the American War of Independence, or as it is called in the US, the Revolutionary War. A painting of the surrender scene hangs in the United States Capitol's Rotunda; I would walk past it every time I visited Congress. Shortly after the defeat, a young British nobleman, Sir John Sinclair, wrote to the famous Scottish economist and philosopher, Adam Smith, and said, 'If we go on at this rate the nation must be ruined.' Smith replied: 'Be assured young friend, that there is a great deal of ruin in a nation.'

I, of course, hope that we aren't ruined. My misgivings about our circumstances are real, but I am a confirmed optimist. And I believe in a measure of British exceptionalism. We may not always channel efficiency, or discipline, or orderliness. But we have a genius for creativity and for improvisation. I hope that will see us through.

I write these closing words from our cottage on the south coast of Cornwall, as the lockdown lifts, the holidaymakers start to arrive and the village takes on its normal summertime appearance.

Down here in Cornwall, whatever the tumult elsewhere, it feels like time is standing still. As I stand in the cottage garden and look towards the sea, I can see one of the village fishing boats unloading its catch onto the harbour wall, as fishermen have done for generations. Beyond the harbour, in the summer calm, the waves are breaking lazily against the rocks. Featuring prominently in our living room is a framed photograph of our cottage in, I guess, the early 1900s: apart from the thatched roof, now slated, the quaint-looking clothes of the mother and children standing in front of the building and the large metal hoop embedded in the wall, presumably for tethering horses, the photograph could have been taken yesterday. This is about as far west as one can get from London without stepping into the Atlantic. And it feels it.

When the wind blows, which is often, it's the moment to head for the coastal paths; to experience the wild beauty of the Cornish coastline; and to discover that, unchanging though it may seem, history, in particular Anglo-American history, hasn't entirely passed the region by. A few miles up the coast is Plymouth, from where, on 6 September 1620, the pilgrims set sail for the New World. And scattered around this part of Cornwall are a series of beaches from which, on Tuesday 6 June 1944, American troops set out for Normandy on D-Day. Of these beaches, the one I know best is on the Helford river. Its part in history is marked by a simple metal sign, setting out brief details of who embarked, how many and where they were going. It reveals that the American troops were setting out for the slaughterhouses that were the Omaha and Utah landing beaches. Whenever I'm there, I'm prompted to wonder how those young men felt as they embarked; what sort of hell they found themselves in when they landed; and how many of them never returned. It reminds me of a moment when the UK-US relationship meant standing together, changing history, whatever the cost, against the greatest of evils. And it puts our present challenges into context.

Yesterday, I took another look at The Leak, the letter of June 2017 that led to my departure from Washington. I checked in particular the various predictions I had made about how the Trump administration would unfold, how it would look two or three years on. I concluded that it hadn't been a bad call; I was pretty much on the mark. As for the rest of my career – Tokyo, Rome, Brussels, Washington – every moment has been a privilege.

There is a splendid quote by the English actor, writer, theatre director, intellectual and Renaissance man, Peter Ustinov. He said: 'British education is probably the best in the world, if you can survive it. If you can't there is nothing left for you but the diplomatic corps.' It worked for me.

Acknowledgements

This book would never have happened without the encouragement, support and counsel of an extraordinary group of people: family, friends and guides to the hitherto mysterious world of publishing.

I have to start with my brilliant agent, Georgina Capel. I was given Georgina's address by a mutual friend. I contacted her with the email equivalent of cold calling. To my surprise and enduring gratitude, she offered a meeting in her agency offices, and responded positively to my half-formed ideas. She then led me through the whole process, from proposal to finished product. I feel extraordinarily lucky to have chanced upon her and her superb team: Rachel Conway, Simon Schaps and Irene Baldoni.

It was another stroke of exceptional good fortune to be published by Harper Collins; and to have as my editor the master of her craft and force of nature that is Arabella Pike. I would have been lost without her insight and reassurance and came to rely totally on her judgement. She too has an outstanding team: thank you to Jo Thompson, Katherine Patrick, Katy Archer and Jack Chalmers for all your help. And apologies for all the missed deadlines. Thanks also to Ellie Game for the wonderfully creative book jacket.

I must also thank Clive Priddle of Public Affairs over The Pond for his friendship and for handling the American side of business. Sorry, Clive, that COVID cancelled our lunch in Boston.

I would by now be only halfway through the book were it not for all the help I received from Patricia Boh; adviser, researcher, fact-checker and writer of the endnotes. Thanks Tricia: you and I know how hard you worked and how much you contributed.

I ran every word I wrote past a group of friends who are all much more talented writers than me: Charles Richards, friend for thirty years, author and former foreign correspondent of the *Independent*; Jacki Davis and Geoff Meade, doyenne and doyen respectively of the British journalists' community in Brussels; and Sir Anthony Seldon, educator and prolific contemporary political historian. I am eternally grateful for the time each of them devoted to wading through my prose and for the wisdom underlying their advice and comments. Thank you to Charles in particular for his unvarnished and unsparing judgements; I needed to hear it straight.

When Vanessa and I returned suddenly from America last year, our house was still rented out and we had nowhere to live. We stayed with friends: Julian and Susie Knott, Colin and Florence Matthews, Mariko Hasegawa, and for an extended period, Vanessa's mother, Penelope Jackson. Thanks to all for your generosity and hospitality.

I also benefitted throughout the writing process from the support and encouragement of friends: too many to name them all, but special mention of James Hooley, Paul and Denyse Adamson, David and Agnes O'Sullivan, Nigel and Lou Graham, Jon Sopel and Antony Phillipson.

Last but the opposite of least, I want to thank my family for their support and forbearance over the last eight months: Simon and his wife Rachel, and Georgina and her partner David O'Callaghan. The IT skills of Georgina and Dave saved me many times, notably in retrieving an entire chapter which had vanished into the iCloud. And the final word goes to Vanessa: love of my life, muse, adviser, purveyor of an unending stream of common sense and the reader of every word of this book, several times. It would not have been possible without her.

Kim Darroch
Cornwall, 6 August 2020

Notes

Chapter 1 Leaks and Tweets

more than twenty-five pages: Isabel Oakeshott, 'Britain's man in the US says Trump is "inept": leaked secret cables from ambassador say the President is "uniquely dysfunctional and his career could end in disgrace"', *Mail on Sunday*, 6 Jul 2019

invoked once in NATO history: NATO backgrounder on Article 5: https://www.nato.int/cps/en/natohq/topics_110496.htm

Trump campaign and agents of the Russian state: Michael Crowley, 'All of Trump's Russian ties in 7 Charts', POLITICO, Mar/Apr 2017, https://www.politico.com/magazine/story/2017/03/connections-trump-putin-russia-ties-chart-flynn-page-manafort-sessions-214868

less diplomatically clumsy and inept: Oakeshott, 'Britain's man in the US says Trump is "inept"'

Financial Times profile from a few months earlier: Edward Luce, 'Our man in the swamp: Sir Kim Darroch', *Financial Times,* 24 Oct 2018

'developments in their host countries': Naval Toosi, 'UK defends ambassador after disparaging Trump comments leak', POLITICO, 6 Jul 2019, https://www.politico.com/story/2019/07/06/uk-ambassador-trump-1399259

'We are not big fans of that man': 'Trump administration "uniquely dysfunctional", says UK ambassador to US', Reuters, 7 Jul 2019, https://www.reuters.com/article/us-usa-britain-idUSKCN1U2081

'soon have a new Prime Minister': Donald J. Trump, tweet, 8 Jul 2019, https://mobile.twitter.com/realDonaldTrump/status/1148298497189392384

statement saying that he supported me: 'Trump blasted the UK ambassador to the US, again. A British PM hopeful clapped back', Vox, 9 Jul 2019, https://www.vox.com/2019/7/9/20687710/jeremy-hunt-trump-uk-ambassador-leaked-cables

'more than well aware of my prejudices': Hansard Vol. 663, 'Urgent Question on UK Ambassador to USA: Leaked Emails', 8 Jul 2019, https://hansard. parliament.uk/Commons/2019-07-08/debates/A3571532-A0E0-4393-9B3E-459073220382/UKAmbassadorToUSALeakedEmails

was completely fine: Dominic Raab MP interview, BBC *Newsnight*, 9 Jul 2019, https://mobile.twitter.com/bbcnewsnight/status/1148714742703255552?lang=en

'continues to disgrace America, at home and abroad': Mia Farrow, tweet, 8 Jul 2019, https://mobile.twitter.com/miafarrow/status/1148416063027236864?lang=en

large crowd of angry protesters: NAACP Legal Defence and Education Fund, 'LDF Celebrates the 55th Anniversary of the Landmark Desegregation of the University of Georgia', 9 Jan 2016, https://www.naacpldf.org/press-release/ldf-celebrates-the-55th-anniversary-of-the-landmark-desegregation-of-the-university-of-georgia/

lead story out of the debate: ITV News, video clip from 03:17 to 03:45, 'Boris Johnson and Jeremy Hunt clash over Brexit', 9 Jul 2019, https://m.youtube.com/watch?v=GQLIpd5QjzM

Chapter 2 Off and Then On Again

'The son-in-law also rises': 'Callaghan's Son-in-law Named Ambassador to US', *New York Times*, 12 May 1977

huge loss to the country: Lord Heywood of Whitehall obituary, *Guardian*, 4 Nov 2018

Paris rather than Washington: 'David Cameron's former chief of staff made French Ambassador just weeks after receiving a peerage', *Daily Telegraph*, 23 Sep 2016

taking us to 3100, Massachusetts Avenue: 'Can This Man Keep the "Special Relationship" Special?', *Foreign Policy*, 29 Feb 2016, https://foreignpolicy.com/2016/02/29/can-this-man-keep-the-special-relationship-special/

'a quite unendurable winter': Dorian Lynskey, '"He typed in bed in his dressing gown": how Orwell wrote Nineteen Eighty-Four', *Guardian*, 19 May 2019

largest industrial conglomerate in the UK: 'ICI: from Perspex to paint', *Guardian*, 18 Jun 2007

died in office of a heart attack within months: 'Anthony Crosland Is Dead at 58; Foreign Secretary for Past Year', *New York Times*, 20 Feb 1977

bridge rather than a tunnel: Treaty of Canterbury, UNTS 25792 (signed 12 Feb 1986), https://treaties.un.org/doc/Publication/UNTS/Volume%201497/volume-1497-I-25792-English.pdf

the plaque commemorating the event: 'Canterbury celebration marks Channel Tunnel treaty', BBC News, 11 Feb 2011, https://www.bbc.com/news/uk-england-kent-12428702

Department, which was then dealing with the war in Bosnia: Julian Borger, *The Butcher's Trail: How the Search for Balkan War Criminals Became the World's Most Successful Manhunt* (Other Press, 2016)

Chapter 3 Discovering 'Real America'

transfixed by the Democrats' Blue Wall: Eugene Daniels and Beatrice Jin, 'Three reasons why the Democrats'B lue Wall crumbled', POLITICO, 16 Dec 2019, https://www.politico.com/interactives/2019/democrats-blue-wall-swing-states-pennsylvania-wisconsin-michigan/

owner of a small drapery business and lifelong Republican: Amy Chozick, 'Hillary Clinton Draws Scrappy Determination from a Tough, Combative Father', *New York Times*, 19 Jul 2015

to start his business career: Russ Buettner, Susanne Craig and David Barstow, '11 Takeaways from the Times Investigation into Trump's Wealth', *New York Times*, 2 Oct 2018

between the storm striking and the levees failing: Willie Drye, 'Hurricane Katrina: The Essential Timeline', *National Geographic*, 14 Sep 2005, https://www.nationalgeographic.com/news/2005/9/weather-hurricane-katrina-timeline/

had never really recovered: 'New Orleans East still rebuilding', WDSU News, 29 Aug 2016, https://www.wdsu.com/article/new-orleans-east-still-rebuilding/3393908

80 per cent of the city had flooded: Jamiles Lartey and agencies, 'New Orleans battles flash flooding as it faces possible hurricane', *Guardian*, 11 Jul 2019

had screwed up badly: Chris Edwards, 'Hurricane Katrina: Remembering the Federal Failures', 27 Aug 2015, https://www.cato.org/blog/hurricane-katrina-remembering-federal-failures

a sailor kissing a nurse: 'V-J Day in Times Square', *TIME* 100Photos series, 14 Aug 1945, http://100photos.time.com/photos/kiss-v-j-day-times-square-alfred-eisenstaedt#photograph

car driving into it in 2012: ‚Robert Eckhart „Unconditional Surrender» statue comes down after crash', *Sarasota Herald-Tribune*, 28 Apr 2012

died on 18 February 2019: Daniel E. Slotnik, 'George Mendonsa, 95, Most Likely the Sailor in a Famous Photo, Dies', *New York Times*, 18 Feb 2019

sprayed a #MeToo logo on the statue: Amy Held, '#MeToo graffiti scrubbed from Sarasota V-J Day kissing statue', NPR, 20 Feb 2019, https://www.npr. org/2019/02/20/696220627/-metoo-graffiti-scrubbed-from-sarasota-v-j-day-kissing-statue

broke into 'Amazing Grace' during his eulogy: 'Remarks by the President in Eulogy for the Honorable Reverend Clementa Pinckney, delivered at College of Charleston, 26 Jun 2015, https://obamawhitehouse.archives.gov/the-press-office/2015/06/26/remarks-president-eulogy-honorable-reverend-clementa-pinckney

Southern way of life: Mitch Landrieu, 'How I learned about the "cult of the Lost Cause"', *Smithsonian Magazine*, 12 Mar 2018, https://www.smithsonianmag.com/history/how-i-learned-about-cult-lost-cause-180968426/

Chapter 4 Snowzilla

'kind of a top-ten snowstorm': Sean Breslin, 'Winter Storm Jonas: At least 48 dead; roof collapses reported; D.C. remains shut down', Weather Channel, 26 Jan 2016, https://weather.com/storms/winter/news/winter-storm-jonas-impacts-news

dubbed it 'Snowzilla': Jason Samenow, 'How much snow fell from Snowzilla in the D.C. area, in detail', *Washington Post*, 24 Jan 2016

including three in Washington: '3 Local Deaths Attributed to Shoveling Snow', NBC Washington, 24 Jan 2016, https://www.nbcwashington.com/news/local/local-deaths-attributed-to-blizzard/101303/

1,000 mops for the governor: Nolan D. McCaskill, 'GoFundMe campaign offers mops for Christie', POLITICO, 27 Jan 2016, https://www.politico.com/story/2016/01/chris-christie-gofundme-mops-218278

Much accompanying ribaldry on social media: Adam Taylor, 'A very awkward photo of the British Ambassador and Obama: "It almost looks like a real human"', *Washington Post*, 1 Feb 2016

our largest bilateral market: Matthew Ward, 'Geographical pattern of UK trade', briefing paper no. 7593, 1 Nov 2019, London: House of Commons, http://researchbriefings.files.parliament.uk/documents/CBP-7593/CBP-7593.pdf

and women until 1994: Roxanne Roberts, 'The Alfalfa Club: still a place for the powerful to see and be seen', *Washington Post*, 24 Jan 2014

'202 years old. And very confused': 'President Obama cracks jokes at elite Alfalfa Club dinner', *Washington Post*, 29 Jan 2012, https://www.washingtonpost.com/blogs/reliable-source/post/president-obama-attends-elite-alfalfa-club-dinner/2012/01/28/gIQATk33YQ_blog.html

relationship with his daughters: Barack Obama, 'Remarks at the National

Prayer Breakfast', Washington, DC, 4 Feb 2016, https://obamawhitehouse. archives.gov/the-press-office/2016/02/04/remarks-president-national-prayer-breakfast-0

pre-programmed, robotic soundbites: Michael Barbaro, 'Once impervious, Marco Rubio is diminished by a caustic Chris Christie', *New York Times*, 7 Feb 2016, https://www.nytimes.com/2016/02/07/us/politics/chris-christie-marco-rubio-gop-debate.html.

second in South Carolina: 'South Carolina primary results', *New York Times*, 29 Sep 2016

money poured in (some $100 million): Metea Gold, 'Nearly $100 million in super PAC money couldn't save Jeb Bush', *Washington Post*, 20 Feb 2016

withdrew from the presidential race the next day: Ed O'Keefe, 'Jeb Bush drops out of 2016 presidential campaign', *Washington Post*, 20 Feb 2016

Chapter 5: The Brexit Vote

Bloomberg's London headquarters in January 2013: David Cameron, 'EU speech at Bloomberg', London, 23 Jan 2013, https://www.gov.uk/government/speeches/eu-speech-at-bloomberg

against President Assad's forces in Syria: Nicholas Watt, Rowena Mason and Nick Hopkins, 'Blow to Cameron's authority as MPs rule out British assault on Syria', *Guardian*, 29 Aug 2013

magnified British influence across the world: Barack Obama, 'As your friend, let me say that the EU makes Britain even greater', *Daily Telegraph*, 23 Apr 2016

'which is hugely inefficient': Anushka Asthana and Rowena Mason, 'Barack Obama: Brexit would put UK "back of the queue" for trade talks', *Guardian*, 22 Apr 2016

'doing an old British friend a political favour': 'Barack Obama says Brexit would leave UK at the "back of the queue' on trade', BBC News, https://www.bbc.com/news/uk-36115138

called Obama 'hypocritical': 'EU referendum: Boris Johnson accuses Barack Obama of "hypocrisy"', BBC News, 16 Apr 2016, https://www.bbc.com/news/uk-politics-eu-referendum-36057947.

'in a strong European Union': Toby Helm and Daniel Boffey, 'Hillary Clinton urges Britain to remain in the European Union,' *Guardian*, 23 Apr 2016

'make their own decision': Tara John, 'Donald Trump says UK "better off "out of European Union', *TIME*, 6 May 2016, https://time.com/4320675/donald-trump-uk-brexit-eu/

'anyone who makes it through the primary process deserves respect': David

Cameron, Prime Minister's Questions, BBC News, 16 Dec 2015, https://www.bbc.com/news/av/uk-politics-35114623/david-cameron-calls-trump-s-comments-divisive-stupid-and-wrong

Most of its output goes to Europe: Kimiko de Freytas-Tamura, 'Pro-"Brexit" City of Sunderland glad to poke establishment in the eye', *New York Times*, 27 Jun 2016

by a majority of about 6 per cent: Ben Riley-Smith, tweet, 23 June 2016, https://mobile.twitter.com/benrileysmith/status/746121163080929280

as against Remain at 39 per cent: 'EU Referendum results', BBC News, 2016: https://www.bbc.com/news/politics/eu_referendum/results

'angry about many, many things': 'Donald Trump in Scotland: "Brexit a great thing"', BBC News, 24 June 2016, https://www.bbc.com/news/uk-scotland-glasgow-west-36606184

'more people are coming to Turnberry, frankly': Chris Cillizza, 'Donald Trump's Brexit press conference was beyond bizarre', *Washington Post*, 24 Jun 2016

'just like we will take America back!': Donald Trump, tweet, 24 Jun 2016, https://twitter.com/realDonaldTrump/status/746272130992644096?s=20

Scotland voted by 62 per cent to 38 per cent to remain in the EU: 'EU Referendum: Scotland backs Remain as UK votes Leave', BBC News, 24 Jun 2016, https://www.bbc.com/news/uk-scotland-scotland-politics-36599102

Chapter 6 The Rise and Rise of Donald Trump

'which is why I alone can fix it': 'Full text: Donald Trump 2016 RNC draft speech transcript', POLITICO, 21 Jul 2016, https://www.politico.com/story/2016/07/full-transcript-donald-trump-nomination-acceptance-speech-at-rnc-225974

'I like people that weren't captured': Dion Rabouin, 'Donald Trump on John McCain: "He's a war hero because he got captured. I like people who weren't captured"; GOP candidate responds', International Business Times, 18 Jul 2015, https://www.ibtimes.com/donald-trump-john-mccain-hes-war-hero-because-he-got-captured-i-people-who-werent-2014674

securing his 1238th delegate: 'Donald Trump has delegates to clinch GOP nomination', CNN, 26 May 2016, https://www.cnn.com/2016/05/26/politics/donald-trump-has-delegates-to-clinch-gop-nomination/index.html

ninth grade level, 14-15 years old: Serina Sandhu, 'Donald Trump's use of grammar "typical of children aged 11 and under"', *Independent*, 17 Mar 2016, https://www.independent.co.uk/news/world/americas/us-elections/

donald-trump-uses-language-typical-of-children-under-11-a6936256.html

'best sex I've ever had': Jamie Ross, 'The story behind Trump's infamous "best sex I've ever had" headline', Daily Beast, 12 Apr 2018, https://www.thedailybeast.com/the-story-behind-trumps-infamous-1990-best-sex-i-ever-had-headline

industries such as steel, coal and textiles: Prasanth Perumal, 'Meet Wilbur Ross – Trump's pick for commerce secretary', Business Insider, 30 Nov 2016, https://www.businessinsider.com/wilbur-ross-profile-2016-11

present in the casinos as much as possible: Chris Megerian, 'Meet Wilbur Ross, who once bailed out Trump in Atlantic City and is now his pick for Commerce Secretary', Los Angeles Times, 8 Dec 2016

home for feral cats: Lori Hoffman, 'National Feral Cat Day, October 16', Atlantic City Weekly, 13 Oct 2014, https://www.atlanticcityweekly.com/archive/national-feral-cat-day-oct-16/article_faf16fbb-3fac-5b52-afcd-58b15df5f305.html

switched from Cruz to Trump: Patrick Svitek and Haley Samsel, 'Ted Cruz says Cambridge Analytica told his presidential campaign its data use was legal', Texas Tribune, 20 Mar 2018, https://www.texastribune.org/2018/03/20/ted-cruz-campaign-cambridge-analytica/

file for insolvency on 1 May 2018: Nicholas Confessore and Matthew Rosenberg, 'Cambridge Analytica to file for bankruptcy after misuse Facebook data', New York Times, 2 May 2018

would ultimately close down: Issie Lapowsky, 'Facebook exposed 87 million users to Cambridge Analytica', Wired, 4 Apr 2018, https://www.wired.com/story/facebook-exposed-87-million-users-to-cambridge-analytica/

credit for work done by others: Sue Halpern, 'Cambridge Analytica and the perils of psychographics', New Yorker, 30 Mar 2018

'Every claim about psychographics made by or about Cambridge Analytica is bullshit': Sam Dumitriu, retweet of Eitan Hersh's infamous tweet, 28 Aug 2019, https://mobile.twitter.com/Sam_Dumitriu/status/1166657949240102914

single-handed creation of the 'Euromyth': Jennifer Rankin and Jim Waterson, 'How Boris Johnson's Brussels-bashing stories shaped British politics', Guardian, 14 Jul 2019

'one of the greatest exponents of fake journalism': Martin Fletcher, 'The joke's over – how Boris Johnson is damaging Britain's global stature', New Statesman, 4 Nov 2017

'amazing explosive effect on the Tory party': Ellen Barry, 'Boris Johnson, political escape artist, lands in hot water. Again', New York Times, 26 Jun 2019

Johnson also delivered the Bentley: Steven Swinford, 'Britain's man in Washington swaps his Jaguar for a Bentley', Daily Telegraph, 23 Feb 2017

motoring correspondent for GQ magazine: John Pearley Huffman, 'Britain's new Prime Minister, Boris Johnson, wrote about cars. Not well', *Car and Driver*, 3 Nov 2019

Chapter 7 Fear and Loathing in Washington

Trump Organization bilking a succession of small-time contractors: Alexandra Berzon, 'Donald Trump's Business Plan Left a Trail of Unpaid Bills', *Wall Street Journal*, 9 June 2016

Trump's tax issues: David Barstow, Susanne Craig, Russ Buettner and Megan Twohey, 'Donald Trump Tax Records Show He Could Have Avoided Taxes for Nearly Two Decades', *The New York Times*, 1 October 2016

Trump Foundation's illegal activities: David A. Fahrenthold, 'New York files civil suit against President Trump, alleging his charity engaged in "illegal conduct"', *The Washington Post*, 14 June 2018

'gaining forty-two pounds': 'Donald Trump: Miss Universe Alicia Machado was "the absolute worst"', *Fox News*, 27 September 2016,

leaning Democrat in her election vote: 'Alicia Machado: Ex-Miss Universe claims Trump called her "Miss Piggy"', *BBC News*, 27 September 2016,

'grab them by the pussy . . . you can do anything': David A. Fahrenthold, 'Trump recorded having extremely lewd conversation about women in 2005', *The Washington Post*, 8 October 2016

rescinded their endorsements of his candidacy: 'John McCain withdraws support for Donald Trump over groping boasts', Guardian, 9 October 2016

he would not be voting Republican: Seth Kelley, 'Arnold Schwarzenegger: "I Will Not Vote for the Republican Candidate for President"', *Variety*, 8 October 2016

'who many expected to win it': J.A., 'Donald Trump boasts of groping women', *The Economist*, 8 October 2016, https://www.economist.com/democracy-in-america/2016/10/08/donald-trump-boasts-of-groping-women

Comey nevertheless went ahead: John Cassidy, 'James Comey's October Surprise', *New Yorker*, 29 October 2016

Chapter 8 Loose in Trump Tower

The District of Columbia had voted 92.8 per cent for Hillary Clinton: '2016 District of Columbia Presidential Election Results', POLITICO, updated 13 Dec 2016, https://www.politico.com/2016-election/results/map/president/district-of-columbia/

from the Egyptian and Turkish presidents: Reuters, 'Egypt's Sisi says spoke to Donald Trump by telephone, congratulated him on win', 9 Nov 2016, https://www.yahoo.com/news/egypts-sisi-says-spoke-donald-trump-telephone-congratulated-094905815.html

Chris Christie had been fired: Martin Pengelly, "You didn't get fired": Christie offers new evidence Trump avoids confrontation', *Guardian*, 16 Jan 2019

under serious pressure for the next few weeks: Peter Walker, 'Theresa May still awaiting call from Donald Trump', *Guardian*, 10 Nov 2016

suggestion from Trump that Farage speak at the rally: Adam Ganucheau, 'How Donald Trump and Nigel Farage met in Mississippi', *Mississippi Today*, 15 Nov 2015, https://mississippitoday.org/2016/11/15/how-donald-trump-and-nigel-farage-met-in-mississippi/,

upper reaches of Trump Tower: Jonathan Jones, 'The unholy power of that Farage-Trump buddy photo', *Guardian*, 23 Nov 2016

'O brave new world, that has such people in't': William Shakespeare, *The Tempest*, V.i.187–8

'He would do a great job!': Feliz Solomon, 'Donald Trump says "many people" want Nigel Farage to become Britain's Ambassador to the U.S.', *TIME*, 21 Nov 2016, https://time.com/4579571/donald-trump-nigel-farage-ukip-ambassador-theresa-may/

'most unpleasant conversations I've ever had': Joe Barnes, 'Farage clashes with TV host after being asked to pitch for Trump ambassador role', *Daily Express*, 25 Nov 2016

meeting with Trump in Trump Tower: 'Japan PM is first foreign leader to meet Trump', BBC News, 17 Nov 2016, https://www.bbc.com/news/world-asia-37946613

Obama White House had been furious: Joshua Hunt, 'Japan's pivot from Obama to Trump', *New Yorker*, 9 Dec 2016

two weeks before Christmas: Thomas Colson, 'Theresa May sent her two most senior aides to the US to defrost the UK's relationship with Donald Trump', Business Insider, 6 Jan 2017

most important piece of political real estate on the planet: Vivian Yee, 'Donald Trump's math takes his towers to greater height', *New Yorker*, 1 Nov 2016

descended in July 2015 to launch his campaign: 'Here's Donald Trump's presidential announcement speech', *TIME*, 16 Jun 2015, https://time.com/3923128/donald-trump-announcement-speech/

vetoing any UN resolution criticising Israel: Peter Beaumont, 'US abstention allows UN to demand end to Israeli settlements', *Guardian*, 23 Dec 2016

violating campaign finance laws: Mark Mazzetti, Benjamin Weiser, Ben Protess and Maggie Haberman, 'Cohen pleads guilty and details Trump's involvement in Moscow Tower project', *New York Times*, 29 Nov 2018

a few days after the inauguration: Victor Fiorillo, 'Here is the (apparently leaked) agenda for the Republican Retreat in Philly', *Philadelphia Magazine*, 25 Jan 2017, https://www.phillymag.com/news/2017/01/25/republican-retreat-agenda-philadelphia-donald-trump/

Congressional calls on the Monday: 'Boris Johnson meets Donald Trump's team in New York', BBC News, 9 Jan 2017: https://www.bbc.com/news/uk-politics-38549807.

Chapter 9 American Carnage

John F Kennedy's'Inauguration Speech, 20 January 1961: US National Archives, https://www.ourdocuments.gov/doc.php?flash=false&doc=91&page=transcript

President Donald Trump's Inauguration Speech, 20 January 2017: https://www.whitehouse.gov/briefings-statements/the-inaugural-address/

Article 2 of the Constitution: https://www.law.cornell.edu/constitution-conan/article-2/section-1/clause-8

introduced by the 2017 presidential inaugural committee: Michael C. Bender, 'Chairman's Global Dinner most exclusive event preceding Trump Inauguration'. *Wall Street Journal*, 16 Jan 2017

recurrent feature of presidential inaugurations: Federal Election Commission, background on inaugural committees, https://www.fec.gov/press/resources-journalists/inaugural-committees/

an unprecedented $107 million: Sarah Gray, 'How Trump's inaugural committee spent the record $107 million worth of donations to celebrate his election', Business Insider, 15 Jan 2019, https://www.businessinsider.com/how-trumps-inaugural-committee-spent-107-million-worth-of-donations-2019-1

shadowy Russian and Middle Eastern individuals: Maggie Haberman and Ben Protess, 'Trump Inaugural Committee ordered to hand over documents to federal investigators', *New York Times*, 4 Feb 2019

Investigations by federal prosecutors in Brooklyn and New York continue: Jonathan O'Connell, 'D.C. Attorney General sues Trump Inaugural Committee over $1 million booking at president's hotel', *Washington Post*, 22 Jan 2020; Rosalinda S. Helderman and Michael Kranish, 'Federal prosecutors issue sweeping subpoena for documents from Trump inaugural committee, a sign of a deepening criminal probe', *Washington Post*, 4 Feb 2019

when Gerald Ford was inaugurated in 1974: Krishnadev Calamur, 'A short history of awkward presidential transitions', *The Atlantic*, 10 Nov 2016, https://www.theatlantic.com/politics/archive/2016/11/presidential-transition-obama-trump/507257/

'That was some weird shit': Yashar Ali, 'What George W. Bush really thought of Donald Trump's Inauguration', *New York Magazine*, 29 Mar 2017, https://nymag.com/intelligencer/2017/03/what-george-w-bush-really-thought-of-trumps-inauguration.html

'more a primal scream aimed at Washington': Max Greenwood, 'Scarborough: Trump's inaugural speech a "primal scream"', *The Hill*, 20 Jan 2017, https://thehill.com/blogs/blog-briefing-room/news/315306-joe-scarborough-trumps-inaugural-speech-was-a-primal-scream

Chapter 10 Theresa May Meets Donald Trump

Theresa May press conference with President Trump, 27 Jan 2017: https://www.gov.uk/government/speeches/pm-press-conference-with-us-president-donald-trump-27-january-2017

'idealistic, daring, decent and fair': Andrew Glass, 'Reagan delivers his second inaugural address, Jan. 21 1985', POLITICO, 20 Jan 2017, https://www.politico.com/story/2017/01/reagan-delivers-his-second-inaugural-address-jan-21-1985-233668

'shameful and wrong': Sean Spicer, press statement, 21 Jan 2017, https://www.whitehouse.gov/briefings-statements/statement-press-secretary-sean-spicer/

Obama figure had been 513,000: Melanie Zanona, 'Metro ridership for Trump's inauguration far lower than Obama's', *The Hill*, 20 Jan 2017, https://thehill.com/policy/transportation/315277-dc-metro-ridership-for-trumps-inauguration-far-lower-than-obamas

about three times bigger than Trump's: Lori Robertson and Robert Farley, 'The facts on crowd size', FactCheck.org, 23 Jan 2017, https://www.factcheck.org/2017/01/the-facts-on-crowd-size/

' Sean Spicer gave alternative facts': Maxwell Tani, '"Alternative facts are not facts. They're falsehoods": Chuck Todd blasts Trump adviser over dubious briefing claims', Business Insider, 22 Jan 2017, https://www.businessinsider.in/alternative-facts-are-not-facts-theyre-falsehoods-chuck-todd-blasts-trump-advisor-over-dubious-briefing-claims/articleshow/56720308.cms

from her term at Oxford University: Molly Ball, 'Kellyanne's alternative universe', *The Atlantic*, Apr 2017, https://www.theatlantic.com/magazine/archive/2017/04/kellyannes-alternative-universe/517821/

became one of the phrases of the age: Chuck Todd, interview with Kellyanne

Conway, NBC, 22 Jan 2017, https://www.nbcnews.com/meet-the-press/video/conway-press-secretary-gave-alternative-facts-860142147643

pride of place in the library: Glenn Kessler, 'Here's the real story about the Churchill bust in the Oval Office', *Washington Post*, 23 Jan 2017

'ancestral dislike of the British Empire': Sewell Chan, 'Boris Johnson's essay on Obama and Churchill touches nerve online', *New York Times*, 22 Apr 2016

Martin Luther King had been removed: Nancy Gibbs, 'A note to our readers', *TIME*, 24 Jan 2017, https://time.com/4645541/donald-trump-white-house-oval-office/

departure from the EU had been completed: Adam Bienkov, 'FULL TEXT: Theresa May's speech to the Republican "Congress of Tomorrow" conference', Business Insider, 26 Jan 2017, https://www.businessinsider.com/full-text-theresa-mays-speech-to-the-republican-congress-of-tomorrow-conference-2017-1

prefer to be meeting the 'h-less' Teresa: Daily Telegraph Foreign Staff and Helena Horton, '"Teresa May": White House spells Theresa May's name wrong three times in memo ahead of visit', *Daily Telegraph*, 27 Jan 2017

Tomb of the Unknown Soldier: Anthony Lane, 'Theresa May's American adventure', *New Yorker*, 4 Feb 2017

Pakistani Prime Minister Nawaz Sharif: Drazen Jorgic, 'Trump offers to help Pakistan, calls PM Sharif a "terrific guy": Islamabad', Reuters, 30 Nov 2016, https://www.reuters.com/article/us-usa-trump-pakistan/trump-offers-to-help-pakistan-calls-pm-sharif-a-terrific-guy-islamabad-idUSKBN13Q398

$500 billion trade surplus with the US: Aimee Picchi, 'Fact check: Is Trump right that the U.S. loses $500 billion in trade to China?', CBS News, 6 May 2019, https://www.cbsnews.com/news/trump-china-trade-deal-causes-us-to-lose-500-billion-claim-review/

$700 million of aid to the Palestinians: Alex Lockie, 'Why Obama sent the Palestinians $221 million during his last hours in office', Business Insider, 24 January 2017, https://www.businessinsider.com/obama-queitly-sends-221-million-to-palestine-2017-1

prevented by EU regulations from building a sea wall: Danny Hankin and Sinead O'Shea, 'Tiny snail defeats Donald Trump in battle over Irish sea wall', *New York Times*, 7 Dec 2016

state visit to the UK: Eliza Mackintosh, 'Theresa May: Donald Trump to make state visit to UK', CNN, 27 Jan 2017 ,https://www.cnn.com/2017/01/27/politics/theresa-may-donald-trump-state-visit-uk/index.html

'confirmed that you're 100 per cent behind NATO': Rebecca Hershey, 'In meeting with Trump, U.K. Prime Minister pushes for future trade deal', NPR,

27 Jan 2017, https://www.npr.org/sections/thetwo-way/2017/01/27/512007797/in-meeting-with-trump-u-k-prime-minister-pushes-for-future-trade-deal

the chance of capturing moments such as this: 'Trump hand holding was "moment of assistance" – May', BBC News, 8 Sep 2017, https://www.bbc.com/news/uk-politics-41204204.

before advising The Queen to invite him': 'Trump state visit plan "very difficult" for Queen,' BBC News, 31 Jan 2017: https://www.bbc.com/news/uk-38805196.

signed Executive Order 13769: Executive Order protecting the nation from foreign terrorist entry into the United States (Executive Order 13769), 27 Jan 2017, https://www.whitehouse.gov/presidential-actions/executive-order-protecting-nation-foreign-terrorist-entry-united-states/

permanent legal US residents: Michael D. Shear and Helene Cooper, 'Trump bans refugees and citizens of 7 Muslim countries', *New York Times*, 27 Jan 2017

countries worldwide that are not affected: Brady Dennis and Jerry Markon, 'Amid protests and confusion, Trump defends executive order: "This is not a Muslim ban"', *Washington Post*, 29 Jan 2017

or about to be deported: Jonah Engel Bromwich, 'Lawyers mobilize at nation's airports after Trump's order', *New York Times*, 29 Jan 2017

attorney general of Washington state: Jim Brunner, Jessica Lee and David Guzman, 'Judge in Seattle halts Trump's immigration order nationwide; White House vows fight', *Seattle Times*, updated 4 Feb 2017

Court of Appeals in San Francisco: Matt Zapotosky, 'Federal appeals court rules 3 to 0 against Trump on travel ban', *Washington Post*, 9 Feb 2017

Executive Order 13780: Executive Order protecting the nation from foreign terrorist entry into the United States (Executive Order 13780), 6 Mar 2017, https://www.whitehouse.gov/presidential-actions/executive-order-protecting-nation-foreign-terrorist-entry-united-states-2/

This too would be challenged: David Cole, 'We'll see you in court, 2.0: Once a Muslim Ban, still a Muslim Ban', ACLU, 6 Mar 2017, https://www.aclu.org/blog/immigrants-rights/well-see-you-court-20-once-muslim-ban-still-muslim-ban?redirect=blog/speak-freely/well-see-you-court-20-once-muslim-ban-still-muslim-ban

temporarily suspended: State of Hawaii and Ishmael v. Donald J. Trump, et al – Order, filed 15 May 2017, https://www.aclu.org/legal-document/state-hawaii-and-ishmael-elshikh-vs-donald-j-trump-et-al-order

landmark judgment in June 2017: Michael D. Shear and Adam Liptak, 'Supreme Court takes up travel ban case, and allows parts to go ahead', *New York Times*, 26 Jun 2017

'Never glad confident morning again': Robert Browning, 'The Lost Leader', https://www.poetryfoundation.org/poems/43748/caliban-upon-setebos

Chapter 11 'No Collusion, No Obstruction'

'Trump fires FBI Director James Comey': Dave Lawler, 'Trump fires Comey as Russia probe intensifies', Axios, 10 May 2017, https://www.axios.com/trump-fires-comey-as-russia-probe-intensifies-1513302167-c391e308-a972-4090-ab86-3d061582cf07.html

FBI plane for personal journeys: Ronald J. Ostrow and Robert L. Jackson, 'Defiant FBI Chief is fired by President: Law enforcement: Alleged ethical abuses by Sessions are cited as reason for dismissal. He refused to resign', *Los Angeles Times*, 20 Jul 1993

opposition research on Trump: 'Christopher Steele, ex-MI6 officer, named as author of Trump dossier', *Guardian*, 12 Jan 2017

subject of gossip and rumour: Michael Rietmulder, 'The Seattle connection to the explosive Trump-Russia dossier', *Seattle Magazine*, updated 27 Nov 2018, https://www.seattlemag.com/news-and-features/seattle-connection-explosive-trump-russia-dossier

Bruce Ohr: Rosalind S. Helderman, Tom Hamburger, Kevin Uhrmacher and John Muyskens, 'The making of the Steele dossier', *Washington Post*, 6 Feb 2018

as early as March that year: 'Carter Page interviewed by FBI', The Moscow Project, https://themoscowproject.org/collusion/carter-page-interviewed-fbi/

'foreign policy adviser': Missy Ryan and Steven Mufson, 'One of Trump's foreign policy advisers is a 2009 college grad who lists Model UN as a credential', *Washington Post*, 22 Mar 2016

possibility of a meeting between Trump and Putin: Rosalind S. Helderman, Shane Harris and Ellen Nakashima, '"The engine of the entire Mueller probe": Focus on origins of Russian investigation puts spotlight on Maltese professor', *Washington Post*, 30 Jun 2019

deliberate political sabotage: Ellen Nakashima and Shane Harris, 'How the Russians hacked the DNC and passed its emails to WikiLeaks', *Washington Post*, 14 Jul 2018

Crossfire Hurricane investigation: Matt Apuzzo and Adam Goldman, 'Here's your unclassified briefing on secretary government code names', *New York Times*, 16 May 2018

which no one could ever stand up: Erik Wemple, '"The story stands": McClatchy won't back off its Michael Cohen-Prague reporting', *Washington Post*, 13 Dec 2019

trip to Moscow in July: Scott Shane, Mark Mazzetti and Adam Goldman, 'Trump Adviser's visit to Moscow got the FBI's attention', *New York Times*, 19 Apr 2017

share his findings with the Washington press: Jane Mayer, 'Christopher Steele, the man behind the Trump dossier', *New Yorker*, 5 Mar 2018

contents of the Steele dossier: Greg Miller, Rosalind S. Helderman, Tom Humburger and Steven Mufson, 'Intelligence chiefs briefed Trump and Obama on unconfirmed claims Russia has compromising information on president-elect', *Washington Post*, 10 Jan 2017

all thirty-five pages: Ken Bensinger, Miriam Elder and Mark Schoofs, 'These reports allege Trump has deep ties to Russia', Buzzfeed News, 10 Jan 2017, https://www.buzzfeednews.com/article/kenbensinger/these-reports-allege-trump-has-deep-ties-to-russia

excessively hostile to Islam: James Kitfield, 'How Mike Flynn became America's angriest general', POLITICO, 16 Oct 2016, https://www.politico.com/magazine/story/2016/10/how-mike-flynn-became-americas-angriest-general-214362

he sat next to Putin: Robert Windrem, 'Guess who came to dinner with Flynn and Putin', NBC News, 18 Apr 2017, https://www.nbcnews.com/news/world/guess-who-came-dinner-flynn-putin-n742696

Turkish Government wanted Gulen extradited: Carol E. Lee, 'Mueller gives new details on Flynn's secretive work for Turkey', NBC News, updated 5 Dec 2018, https://www.nbcnews.com/politics/national-security/mueller-gives-new-details-flynn-s-secretive-work-turkey-n943926

telephone conversation on 29 December: Sonam Sheth, 'Newly released transcripts show Michael Flynn asking the Russian ambassador not to "box us in" before Trump's inauguration', Business Insider, 29 May 2020, https://www.businessinsider.com/michael-flynn-sergey-kislyak-transcript-december-2016-phone-call-2020-5

Russian interference in the elections: Lauren Gambino, Sabrina Siddiqui and Shaun Walker, 'Obama expels 35 Russian diplomats in retaliation for US election hacking', *Guardian*, 30 Dec 2016

Mike Pence, the opposite: Jamie Ehrlich, 'Mike Pence: "I'd be happy" to see Michael Flynn back in the Trump administration', CNN, 10 May 2020, https://www.cnn.com/2020/05/10/politics/mike-pence-michael-flynn-interview/index.html

'impose censure against Russia': Josh Lederman and Carol E. Lee, 'Declassified calls show Flynn discussing sanctions with Russian envoy', NBC News, 29 May 2020, https://www.nbcnews.com/politics/politics-news/key-decision-awaits-new-intel-chief-over-release-flynn-call-n1218361

shortest tenure in history: Maggie Haberman, Matthew Rosenberg, Matt Apuzzo and Glenn Thrush, 'Michael Flynn resigns as National Security Adviser', *New York Times*, 13 Feb 2017

met Sergey Kislyak twice: Adam Entous, Ellen Nakashima and Greg Miller, 'Sessions discussed Trump campaign-related matters with Russian ambassador, U.S. intelligence intercepts show', *Washington Post*, 21 Jul 2017

Trump never forgave him: Mark Landler and Eric Lichtblau, 'Jeff Sessions recuses himself from Russia inquiry', *New York Times*, 2 Mar 2017

surveillance during the 2016 election campaign: Matthew Nussbaum, 'Justice Department: No evidence Obama wiretapped Trump Tower', POLITICO, 2 Sep 2017, https://www.politico.com/story/2017/09/02/obama-trump-tower-wiretap-no-evidence-242284

'before or after Election Day 2016': Senate Intelligence Committee, joint statement on wiretapping evidence at Trump Tower, 16 Mar 2017, https://www.intelligence.senate.gov/press/joint-statement-senate-intel-committee-leaders-wiretapping-evidence-trump-tower

'untrue and quite frankly absurd': Mark Hosenball, 'British security official denies UK spy agency eavesdropped on Trump', Reuters, 14 Mar 2017, https://www.reuters.com/article/us-usa-trump-wiretapping/british-security-official-denies-uk-spy-agency-eavesdropped-on-trump-idUSKBN16L2UV

which Comey had resisted: Matt Ford, 'James Comey finally tells his side of the story', *The Atlantic*, 7 Jun 2017, https://www.theatlantic.com/politics/archive/2017/06/james-comey-senate-testimony/529533/

'job security was on the menu': Mike Allen, 'Exclusive James Comey book excerpt: inside the "loyalty dinner"', Axios, 13 Apr 2018, https://www.axios.com/exclusive-james-comey-book-excerpt-inside-the-loyalty-dinner-d4db53c9-3560-44b7-80a4-57feb4fa7f92.html

rank and file of the FBI: Michael D. Shear and Matt Apuzzo, 'FBI Director James Comey is fired by Trump', *New York Times*, 9 May 2017

'a made-up story': Aaron Blake, 'Trump just decimated the White House's entire James Comey narrative', *Washington Post*, 11 May 2017

who had been investigating Watergate: Ron Elving, 'A brief history of Nixon's "Saturday Night Massacre"', NPR, 21 Oct 2018, https://www.npr.org/2018/10/21/659279158/a-brief-history-of-nixons-saturday-night-massacre

'investigation of him and his associates': 'Trump's firing of Comey is all about the Russia inquiry', *New York Times*, 9 May 2017

special congressional committee: David E. Sanger, Matthew Rosenberg and Michael S. Schmidt, 'Firing fuels calls for independent investigation, even from Republicans', *New York Times*, 9 May 2017

'phoney hypocrites': Donald J. Trump, tweet, 10 May 2017, https://mobile.
twitter.com/realDonaldTrump/status/862387734492663808

oversee the Russia investigation: Quinta Jurecic, 'DAG Rosenstein appoints
Robert Mueller as Special Counsel', Lawfare, 17 May 2017, https://www.
lawfareblog.com/dag-rosenstein-appoints-robert-mueller-special-counsel

'by-the-book' observation: Dareh Gregorian, 'Who is Robert Mueller, the
man behind the Trump report?', NBC News, 23 Mar 2019, https://www.
nbcnews.com/politics/justice-department/who-robert-mueller-man-behind-
report-trump-n974296

leading up to the meeting: Jo Becker, Matt Apuzzo and Adam Goldman,
'Trump's son met with Russian lawyer after being promised damaging
information on Clinton', New York Times, 9 Jul 2017

Azerbaijani pop star, Emin Agalarov: Daniella Diaz, 'Who is Rob Goldstone?
The man behind Trump Jr.'s meeting with Russian lawyer', CNN, 11 Jul 2017,
https://www.cnn.com/2017/07/11/politics/who-is-rob-goldstone-donald-
trump-jr/index.html

host – and presumably help finance – the event: Katie Rogers, 'How Trump's
"Miss Universe" in Russia became ensnared in a political inquiry', New York
Times, 11 Jul 2017

'especially later in the summer': Paul Owen, 'Full text of the emails between
Donald Trump Jr and Rob Goldstone', Guardian, 11 Jul 2017

former Russian intelligence officer, Rinat Akhmetshin: 'Donald Trump Jr
met Russian lawyer after promise of information on Hillary Clinton',
Guardian, 9 Jul 2017

'a wasted 20 minutes': Rolf Mowatt-Larssen, 'Trump Jr.'s Russia meeting
sure sounds like a Russian intelligence operation', Washington Post, 14 Jul
2017

'most ridiculous thing I've ever heard': Dave Lawler, 'Publicist at center of
Trump Jr.-Russia meeting breaks silence', Axios, 19 Nov 2017, https://www.
axios.com/publicist-at-center-of-trump-jr-russia-meeting-breaks-silence-
1513307045-5588d5ce-882d-46fe-a32f-964a93079d57.html

'hurt the campaign of Hillary Clinton': Pete Grieve, 'Warner: „Clear evidence"
that Trump officials met Russians to get info', CNN, 11 Jul 2017, https://
www.cnn.com/2017/07/10/politics/mark-warner-clear-evidence/index.html

to work with his investigation: Del Quentin Wilber and Byron Tau, 'Special
Counsel Robert Mueller impanels Washington Grand July in Russia Probe',
Wall Street Journal, 3 Aug 2017

one Dutch national – and three Russian organisations: Ryan Teague Beckwith,
'Here are all of the indictments, guilty pleas and conviction from Robert

Mueller's investigation', *TIME*, 15 Nov 2019, https://time.com/5556331/mueller-investigation-indictments-guilty-pleas/?amp=true

arrested in late July 2017: Paul Owen, 'George Papadopoulos timeline: Trump campaign adviser details Russia links', *Guardian*, 30 Oct 2017

his contacts with Russian agents: Michael D. Shear and Adam Goldman, 'Michael Flynn pleads guilty to lying to the FBI and will cooperate with Russia inquiry' *New York Times*, 1 Dec 2017

surrendered themselves to the FBI: Matt Apuzzo, Adam Goldman, Michael S. Schmid and Miatthew Rosenberg, 'Former Trump aides charged as prosecutors reveal new campaign ties with Russia', *New York Times*, 30 Oct 2017

'information warfare': Matt Apuzzo and Sharon LaFraniere, '13 Russians indicted as Mueller reveals effort to aid Trump Campaign', *New York Times*, 16 Feb 2018

releasing them online: Mark Mazzetti and Katie Benner, '12 Russian agents indicted in Mueller investigation', *New York Times*, 13 Jul 2018

reduced sentence himself: Dara Lind, 'Read: Rick Gates plea deal full text', Vox Media, 23 Feb 2018, https://www.vox.com/2018/2/23/17045484/gates-plea-deal-full-text-russia-investigation

hidden foreign bank account: Andrew Prokop, 'Paul Manafort was found guilty on 8 counts', Vox Media, 21 Aug 2018, https://www.vox.com/policy-and-politics/2018/8/21/17648760/manafort-trial-guilty-verdict-mueller-trump-russia

two counts of conspiracy: Dan Mangan, 'Former Trump campaign chief Paul Manafort agrees to cooperate with special counsel Robert Mueller, pleads guilty to conspiracy charges', CNBC, 14 Sep 2018, https://www.cnbc.com/2018/09/14/trump-campaign-chief-paul-manafort-pleads-guilty-to-conspiracy-charges.html

Loretto, Pennsylvania: David Voreacos and Greg Farrell, 'Paul Manafort released to home confinement over Virus Fears', Bloomberg, 13 May 2020, https://www.bloomberg.com/news/articles/2020-05-13/paul-manafort-released-to-home-confinement-over-virus-fears

with a white satin lining: Sharon LaFraniere and Emily Cochrane, 'Prosecution cites lavish spending by Paul Manafort in his fraud trial', *New York Times*, 1 Aug 2018

close to 300,000 electronic files: Matt Apuzzo, 'FBI raids office of Trump's longtime lawyer Michael Cohen; Trump calls it "disgraceful"', *New York Times*, 9 Apr 2018

surrendered himself to the FBI on 21 August: Brett Samuels, 'Cohen surrenders to FBI ahead of court appearance: report', *The Hill*, 21 Aug 2018, https://thehill.com/homenews/administration/402886-cohen-surrenders-to-fbi-ahead-of-court-appearance-report

sentenced to three years in prison: Laura Nahmais and Darren Samuelsohn, 'Michael Cohen sentenced to 3 years in prison', POLITICO, 12 Dec 2018, https://www.politico.com/story/2018/12/12/cohen-sentenced-to-3-years-in-prison-1060060

broken down in June 2016: Jeremy Herb, Gloria Borger and Manu Raju, 'Michael Cohen apologizes to Senate panel for lying to Congress', CNN, 26 Feb 2019, https://www.cnn.com/2019/02/26/politics/michael-cohen-senate-intelligence-committee/index.html

'The Torturers' Lobby': Matt Labash, 'Roger Stone, political animal', *Washington Examiner*, 5 Nov 2007: https://www.washingtonexaminer.com/weekly-standard/roger-stone-political-animal-15381

'launch counter-attack': Jeffrey Toovin, 'The Dirty Trickster', *New Yorker*, 2 Jun 2008

convicted on all seven accounts on 15 November 2019: Katelyn Polantz and Marshall Cohen, 'What Roger Stone's trial revealed about Trump and Mueller', CNN, 15 Nov 2019, https://www.cnn.com/2019/11/14/politics/roger-stone-trial-takeaways-mueller-report/index.html

his 'principal conclusions' from the report: 'Read the Attorney General's summary of the Mueller Report', 24 Mar 2019, https://www.nytimes.com/interactive/2019/03/24/us/politics/barr-letter-mueller-report.html

'election interference activities': Madeleine Carlisle and Olivia Paschal, 'Read Robert Mueller's written summaries of his Russia report', *The Atlantic*, 18 Apr 2019, https://www.theatlantic.com/politics/archive/2019/04/mueller-report-release-summaries-barr-trump/587182/

'related to Russian election interference': Carlisle and Paschal, 'Read Robert Mueller's written summaries of his Russia report'

'committed an obstruction of justice offence': 'Read the Attorney General's summary of the Mueller Report'

put the figure at 140: Karen Yourish and Larry Buchanan, 'Mueller report shows depth of connections between Trump campaigns and Russians', *New York Times*, 19 Apr 2019

Chapter 12: The Conduct of the Presidency

fired immediately after the election: Andrew Restuccia and Nancy Cook, 'Trump adviser steamroll Christie's transition', POLITICO, 15 Nov 2016, https://www.politico.com/story/2016/11/trump-christie-transition-231390

US Export-Import Bank: Zachary Warmbrodt, 'Trump fundraiser Scaramucci joins Export-Import Bank', POLITICO, 27 Jun 2017, https://www.politico.com/story/2017/06/27/anthony-scaramucci-export-import-bank-240019

White House communications director: Donald J. Trump, press release, 21 Jul 2017: https://www.whitehouse.gov/presidential-actions/president-donald-j-trump-appoints-anthony-scaramucci-white-house-communications-director/.

'strength of the President': Rebecca Harrington, 'Listen to the audio of Scaramucci's vulgar phone call with a New Yorker reporter that led to his firing', Business Insider, 3 Aug 2017, https://www.businessinsider.com/scaramucci-phone-call-audio-new-yorker-ryan-lizza-2017-8

resigned on 28 July: Peter Baker and Maggie Haberman, 'Reince Priebus is ousted amid stormy days for White House', *New York Times*, 28 Jul 2017

started until 25 July: Michael D. Shear, Glenn Thrush and Maggie Haberman, 'John Kelly, asserting authority, fired Anthony Scaramucci', *New York Times*, 31 Jul 2017

forty-plus states in 2020: Jesse Pound, 'Anthony Scaramucci: predicts "resounding" 40-state landslide for Trump in the 2020 election', CNBC, 3 Jul 2019, https://www.cnbc.com/2019/07/03/anthony-scaramucci-predicts-40-state-landslide-for-trump-in-2020.html

White House Office of Public Liaison: Lisa Marie Segarra, 'Omarosa says she resigned from White House in protest – and calls reports of being escorted out "ridiculous"', *TIME*, 14 Dec 2017, https://time.com/5064054/omarosa-not-fired-white-house-resigned-protest/

accusations of domestic abuse from two ex-wives: Andrew Restuccia and Eliana Johnson, 'White House aide Rob Porter resigns after allegations from ex-wives', POLITICO, 7 Feb 2018, https://www.politico.com/story/2018/02/07/white-house-aide-rob-porter-resigns-after-allegations-from-ex-wives-397407

But firing your Secretary of State is still something: Peter Baker, Gardiner Harris and Mark Landler, 'Trump fires Rex Tillerson and will replace him with CIA Chief Pompeo', *New York Times*, 13 Mar 2018

ultra-hawk John Bolton: Ashley Parker, Josh Dawsey, Philip Rucker and Carol D. Leonnig, 'Trump decides to remove national security adviser, and others may follow', *Washington Post*, 15 Mar 2018

accusations of ethics breaches: Leo Shane III, 'Shulkin out: Trump fires VA secretary after weeks of controversy', *Military Times*, 28 Mar 2018, https://www.militarytimes.com/veterans/2018/03/28/shulkin-out-trump-fires-va-secretary-after-weeks-of-controversy/

Wimbledon tennis tournament: Dave Philipps, 'Report faults V.A. Secretary Shulkin over travel to Europe', *New York Times*, 14 Feb 2018

series of ethics scandals: Coral Davenport, Lisa Friedman and Maggie Haberman, 'EPA Chief Scott Pruitt resigns under a cloud of ethics scandals', *New York Times*, 5 Jul 2018

Mira Ricardel: 'Melania calls for national security aide Mira Ricardel's firing', BBC News, 13 Nov 2018, https://www.bbc.com/news/world-us-canada-46202896

Patrick Shanahan: Michael D. Shear and Helene Cooper, 'Shanghai withdraws as Defence Secretary nominee, and Mark Esper is named Acting Pentagon Chief', *New York Times*, 18 Jun 2019

this volume of blood: Kathryn Dunn Tenpas, 'Why is Trump's staff turnover higher than the 5 most recent presidents?', Brookings Institution, 19 Jan 2018, https://www.brookings.edu/research/why-is-trumps-staff-turnover-higher-than-the-5-most-recent-presidents/

Jeff Bezos of Amazon: David Smith, 'Why does Trump hate Jeff Bezos: is it about power or money?', *Guardian*, 17 Jun 2018

the New York Times: Brian Stelter, 'Trump's love-hate relationship with the (not) "failing" New York Times', CNN, 2 Jan 2018, https://money.cnn.com/2018/01/02/media/new-york-times-president-trump/index.html

dwindled to almost nothing: Quint Forgey, 'White House press secretary says daily briefings aren't coming back any time soon', POLITICO, 23 Sep 2019, https://www.politico.com/story/2019/09/23/stephanie-grisham-white-house-press-briefings-1507288

surprised she lasted so long: Annie Karni, 'Her battles with the press corps behind her, Sanders plans a political future', *New York Times*, 24 Nov 2019

'a very stable genius at that': David Nakamura, 'Trump boasts that he's "like, really smart" and a "very stable genius" amid questions over his mental fitness', *Washington Post*, 6 Jan 2018

'my button works!': Peter Baker and Michael Tackett, 'Trump says his "nuclear button" is "much bigger" than North Korea's', *New York Times*, 2 Jan 2018

'#AlertTheDayCareStaff': Rebecca Savransky, 'Corker fires back at Trump: "Same untruths from an utterly untruthful president"', *The Hill*, 24 Oct 2017, https://thehill.com/homenews/senate/356831-corker-fires-back-at-trump-same-untruths-from-an-utterly-untruthful-president

have to go through training': Judy Kurtz, 'Animal control expert: Trump's use of "dogcatcher" as an insult is "degrading"', *The Hill*, 24 Oct 2017, https://thehill.com/blogs/in-the-know/in-the-know/356874-animal-control-expert-trumps-use-of-dogcatcher-as-an-insult-is

'seven hours of Executive Time: Alexi McCammond, Jonathan Swan, 'Read

Trump's "executive time"-filled leaked private schedules', Axios, 3 Feb 2019, https://www.axios.com/read-trumps-private-leaked-executive-time-schedules-00e9313a-3066-4988-a6dc-711a47de661e.html

'100% of the people around him': Brennan Weiss, 'The author of the explosive new Trump book says 100% of people around the president question his intelligence and fitness for office', Business Insider, 5 Jan 2018, https://www.businessinsider.com/michael-wolff-says-100-of-people-around-trump-question-his-fitness-2018-1

world-famous White House Correspondents: Lauren Egan, 'Trump to skip White House Correspondents Dinner for third year in a row', NBC, 5 Apr 2019, https://www.nbcnews.com/politics/donald-trump/trump-skip-white-house-correspondents-dinner-third-year-row-n991346

comedian Seth Meyers: 'Trump jokes from the 2011 White House correspondents' "dinner"', *Washington Post*, video, 27 Apr 2016, https://www.washingtonpost.com/video/entertainment/trump-jokes-from-the-2011-white-house-correspondents-dinner/2016/04/27/6a4384de-0bec-11e6-bc53-db-634ca94a2a_video.html

'pray for Arnold, for his ratings': Donald J. Trump, remarks at the 2017 National Prayer Breakfast, 2 Feb 2017: https://www.whitehouse.gov/briefings-statements/remarks-president-trump-national-prayer-breakfast/.

Chapter 13: Foreign Policy and Trade

founded by Richard Nixon: Ryan Teague Beckwith, 'Read Donald Trump's "America First" foreign policy speech', *TIME*, 27 Apr 2016, https://time.com/4309786/read-donald-trumps-america-first-foreign-policy-speech/

70 per cent of total defence spending: 'Trump: What does the US contribute to NATO in Europe?', BBC News, 3 Dec 2019, https://www.bbc.com/news/world-44717074

never ratified: Donald J. Trump, Presidential Memorandum, 23 Jan 2017, https://www.whitehouse.gov/presidential-actions/presidential-memorandum-regarding-withdrawal-united-states-trans-pacific-partnership-negotiations-agreement/

US withdrawal killed it: Kevin Granville, 'What is TPP? Behind the trade deal that died', *New York Times*, 23 Jan 2017

New Zealand and China: Willian Alan Reinsch, Jack Caporal and Lydia Murray, 'At last, an RCEP deal', Center for Strategic & International Studies, 3 Dec 2019, https://www.csis.org/analysis/last-rcep-deal

US intellectual property rights: President Trump's 2017 Trade Policy Agenda,

Office of the US Trade Representative, 1 Mar 2017, https://ustr.gov/about-us/policy-offices/press-office/press-releases/2017/march/annualreport17

the US, Canada and Mexico: Julie Hirschfeld Davis, 'Trump sends NAFTA renegotiation notice to Congress', *New York Times*, 18 May 2017

Japanese collector: '"Casablanca" piano eludes Donald Trump', *New York Times*, 17 Dec 1988

'good for America': Jim Zarroli, 'Economists warn: Trump "promotes magical thinking and conspiracy theories"', NPR, 1 Nov 2016, https://www.npr.org/2016/11/01/500264332/economists-warn-trump-promotes-magical-thinking-and-conspiracy-theories

Tax Cuts and Jobs Act: Donald J. Trump, remarks at the signing of the Tax Cuts and Jobs Bill Act, 22 Dec 2017, https://www.whitehouse.gov/briefings-statements/remarks-president-trump-signing-h-r-1-tax-cuts-jobs-bill-act-h-r-1370/

contributed all he could: Kate Kelly and Maggie Haberman, 'Gary Cohn says he will resign as Trump's top economic adviser', *New York Times*, 6 Mar 2018

Norway, India, Switzerland: Ana Swanson, 'Trump to impose sweeping steel and aluminium tariffs', *New York Times*, 1 Mar 2018

Harley Davidsons, bourbon and orange juice: 'EU tariffs on US goods come into force', BBC News, 22 Jun 2018, https://www.bbc.com/news/business-44567636

$11 billion of European products: Ana Swanson, 'US readies $11 billion in tariffs on EU', *New York Times*, 9 Apr 2019

largest with any country: 'US-China trade facts', Office of the US Trade Representative, https://ustr.gov/countries-regions/china-mongolia-taiwan/peoples-republic-china

$250 billion of Chinese goods: Gina Heeb and Bob Bryan, 'Here are all of the Chinese products that are set to face a 30% tariff this month', Business Insider, 2 Oct 2019, https://markets.businessinsider.com/news/stocks/trump-us-china-trade-war-products-to-face-30-tariff-2019-10-1028572345

$110 billion of US products: Eduardo Porter and Karl Russell, 'Firing back at Trump in the trade war with tariffs aimed at his base', *New York Times*, 3 Oct 2018

from 10 per cent to 25 per cent in May: Ana Swanson and Alan Rappeport, 'Trump increases China tariffs as trade deal hangs in the balance', *New York Times*, 9 May 2019

highest level for a decade: Se Young Lee and Lusha Zhang, 'China hikes tariffs on US goods after Trump warning', Reuters, 13 May 2019, https://www.

reuters.com/article/us-usa-trade-china-tariffs/china-to-impose-tariffs-on-60-billion-of-u-s-goods-idUSKCN1SJ1AM

56 per cent to Clinton's 37 per cent in 2016: 'Indiana results', *New York Times*, 1 Aug 2017

United States-Mexico-Canada Agreement: Alan Rappeport, 'US and Canada reach trade deal to salvage NAFTA', *New York Times*, 30 Sep 2018

signed at the end of 2018: Bill Chappell, 'USMCA: Trump signs new trade agreement with Mexico and Canada to replace NAFTA', NPR, 30 Nov 2018, https://www.nytimes.com/2018/09/30/us/politics/us-canada-nafta-deal-dead line.html

'vastly diminished economic production': Donald J. Trump, remarks on the Paris Climate Accord, 1 Jun 2017, https://www.whitehouse.gov/briefings-statements/statement-president-trump-paris-climate-accord/

then the July version: Nahal Toosi, 'Trump administration certifies Iran still complying with nuclear deal', POLITICO, 17 Jul 2017, https://www.politico.com/story/2017/07/17/trump-iran-nuclear-deal-240641

State Department press corps: Boris Johnson, 'Boris Johnson: Don't scuttle the Iran nuclear deal', *New York Times*, 6 May 2018

withdrawing from the JCPOA and reimposing sanctions: Mark Landler, 'Trump abandons Iran nuclear deal he long scorned', *New York Times*, 8 May 2018

world's oil supply flows: Mark Landler, Julian E. Barnes and Eric Schmitt, 'U.S. Puts Iran on Notice and Weighs Response to Attack on Oil Tankers', *New York Times*, 14 Jun 2019

$130 million each: Jamie McIntyre, 'US confirms $130M high-flying drone brought down by Iranian missile', *Washington Examiner*, 20 Jun 2019, https://www.washingtonexaminer.com/policy/defense-national-security/us-confirms-130m-high-flying-drone-brought-down-by-iranian-missile

called the strikes off: Michael D. Shear, Eric Schmitt, Michael Crowley and Maggie Haberman, 'Strikes on Iran Approved by Trump, Then Abruptly Pulled Back', *New York Times*, 20 Jun 2019

late May 2017: Mercy Benzaquen, Russell Goldman and Karen Yourish, 'President Trump's schedule for his first foreign trip', *New York Times*, 24 May 2017

$350 billion arms deal: Javier E. David, 'US-Saudi Arabia seal weapons deal worth nearly $110 billion immediately, $350 billion over 10 years', CNBC, 20 May 2017; updated 22 May 2017, https://www.cnbc.com/2017/05/20/us-saudi-arabia-seal-weapons-deal-worth-nearly-110-billion-as-trump-begins-visit.html

stayed for around two minutes: 'What was that glowing orb Trump touched in Saudi Arabia?', *New York Times*, 22 May 2017

seemed to go on for months: Mark Landler, 'Saudi prince's White House visit reinforces Trump's commitment to heir apparent', *New York Times*, 20 Mar 2018

out of the building in suitcases: 'Jamal Khashoggi: All you need to know about Saudi journalist's death', BBC News, 19 Jun 2019; updated 2 Jul 2020, https://www.bbc.com/news/world-europe-45812399

CIA report into the affair leaked: Warren P. Strobel, 'CIA intercepts underpin assessment Saudi Crown Prince targeted Khashoggi', *Wall Street Journal*, 1 Dec 2018

'probably ordered his death': Shane Harris, Greg Miller and Josh Dawsey, 'CIA concludes Saudi crown prince ordered Jamal Khashoggi's assassination', *Washington Post*, 16 Nov 2018

pressure from an angry Congress: Greg Myre, '"Maybe He Did, Maybe He Didn't": Trump Defends Saudis, Downplays U.S. Intel', NPR, 20 Nov 2018, https://www.npr.org/2018/11/20/669708254/maybe-he-did-maybe-he-didnt-trump-defends-saudis-downplays-u-s-intel

visited on that first trip: Peter Baker and Ian Fisher, 'Trump Comes to Israel Citing a Palestinian Deal as Crucial', *New York Times*, 22 May 2017

emerge in January 2020: Michael Crowley and David M. Halbfinger, 'Trump Releases Mideast Peace Plan That Strongly Favors Israel', *New York Times*, 28 Jan 2020; updated 4 Feb 2020, https://www.nytimes.com/2020/01/28/world/middleeast/peace-plan.html

side-by-side with Israel: Peter Baker and Mark Landler, 'Trump, Meeting With Netanyahu, Backs Away From Palestinian State', *New York Times*, 15 Feb 2017

move from Tel Aviv to Jerusalem: Donald J. Trump, Proclamation on Jerusalem as the Capital of the State of Israel, 6 Dec 2017, https://www.whitehouse.gov/briefings-statements/president-donald-j-trumps-proclamation-jerusalem-capital-state-israel/

formally opened on 14 May 2018: David M. Halbfinger, Isabel Kershner and Declan Walsh, 'Israel Kills Dozens at Gaza Border as U.S. Embassy Opens in Jerusalem', *New York Times*, 14 May 2018

UN agency for Palestine refugees: Gardiner Harris and Rick Gladstone, 'U.S. Withholds $65 Million From U.N. Relief Agency for Palestinians', *New York Times*, 16 Jan 2018

cut funding to zero: Karen DeYoung, Ruth Eglash and Hazem Balousha, 'U.S. ends aid to United Nations agency supporting Palestinian refugees', *Washington Post*, 31 Aug 2018

was forced to close: 'US to shut down Palestinian mission in Washington', BBC News, 10 Sep 2018, https://www.bbc.com/news/world-middle-east-45471420

compelled to leave the country: Yara Bayoumy, 'U.S. State Department revokes PLO ambassador family visas: envoy', Reuters, 16 Sep 2018, https://www.reuters.com/article/us-usa-palestinians/us-state-department-revokes-plo-ambassador-family-visas-envoy-idUSKCN1LW0RE

for a NATO Summit: Silvia Amaro, '5 takeaways from Trump's visit to Brussels', CNBC, 27 May 2017, https://www.cnbc.com/2017/05/27/trump-first-visit-to-brussels.html

an attack on all: 'Donald Trump tells Nato allies to pay up at Brussels talks', BBC News, 25 May 2017, https://www.bbc.com/news/world-europe-40037776

'The EU is worse than China': Jonathan Swan, 'Scoop: Trump tells Macron the EU is 'worse' than China', Axios, 10 Jun 2018, https://www.axios.com/donald-trump-emmanuel-macron-eu-worse-than-china-trade-tariffs-57f53e00-8b5c-4931-9d05-97ee0b510fd5.html

surplus in services of around \$50 billion: Linda Qiu, 'Trump Exaggerates Trade Deficit With European Union by \$50 Billion', *New York Times*, 7 Jun 2018

provided some insights: Kate Connolly, 'Historian finds German decree banishing Trump's grandfather', *Guardian*, 21 Nov 2016

'totally controlled by Russia': 'Trump: Germany is totally controlled by Russia', BBC News, 11 Jul 2018, https://www.bbc.com/news/av/world-europe-44793764/trump-germany-is-totally-controlled-by-russia

'there, now you're perfect': Julie Hirschfeld Davis and Katie Rogers, 'Le Bromance: Trump and Macron, Together Again', *New York Times*, 24 Apr 2018

In November 2018: James McAuley, 'The Broken Bromance? The Trump-Macron relationship is on the rocks', *Washington Post*, 10 Nov 2018

'its moral values': David Nakamura, Seung Min Kim and James McAuley, 'Macron denounces nationalism as a "betrayal of patriotism" in rebuke to Trump at WWI remembrance', *Washington Post*, 11 Nov 2018

'get on to another subject': Donald J. Trump, tweet, 13 Nov 2018, https://twitter.com/realDonaldTrump/status/1062333534214520832?s=20

'not a big deal': Ed Pilkington and Angelique Chrisafis, 'Trump ramps up Macron spat by mocking France in world wars', *Guardian*, 13 Nov 2018

'complete denuclearisation': Mark Landler, 'The Trump-Kim Summit Was Unprecedented, but the Statement Was Vague', *New York Times*, 12 Jun 2018

Chapter 14: Domestic Policy:
Obamacare, Tax Reform and Immigration

more cobras on the streets than ever: 'The Cobra Effect (Ep. 96): full transcript', Freakonomics, 11 Oct 2012, https://freakonomics.com/2012/10/11/the-cobra-effect-full-transcript/

join their mostly tailless comrades: Shay Maunz, 'The great Hanoi Rat Masscare of 1902 did not go as planned', Atlas Obscura, 6 Jun 2017, https://www.atlasobscura.com/articles/hanoi-rat-massacre-1902

'took them along on all our picnics': Bill Vaughan quotes, https://www.forbes.com/quotes/1236/

twice as likely to die of diabetes as whites: US Department of Health and Human Services, Office of Minority Healthy, Diabetes and African Americans, 19 Dec 2019, https://minorityhealth.hhs.gov/omh/browse.aspx?lvl=4&lvlid=18

had no health insurance: Rachel Garfield and Kendal Orgera, 'Primer – Key facts about health insurance and the uninsured amidst changes to the Affordable Care Act', Kaiser Family Foundation, 25 Jan 2019, https://www.kff.org/report-section/the-uninsured-and-the-aca-a-primer-key-facts-about-health-insurance-and-the-uninsured-amidst-changes-to-the-affordable-care-act-how-many-people-are-uninsured/

42 per cent of the population are obese: Craig M. Hales, Margaret D. Carroll, Cheryl D. Fryer and Cynthia L. Ogden, 'Prevalence of obesity and severe obesity among adults', Center for Disease Control and Prevention, 2017, https://www.cdc.gov/nchs/products/databriefs/db360.htm

cannot afford to visit the doctor: Center for Disease Control and Prevention, 'Access to Health Care: A record number of adults 18-64 years old are uninsured', https://www.cdc.gov/vitalsigns/healthcareaccess/index.html#Problem

supports around 60 million Americans: Kaiser Family Foundation, 'An overview of Medicare,' 13 Feb 2019, https://www.kff.org/medicare/issue-brief/an-overview-of-medicare/

signed into law on 23 March 2010: US Department of Health & Human Services, 'What is the Affordable Care Act?', updated 4 Aug 2017, https://www.hhs.gov/answers/affordable-care-act/what-is-the-affordable-care-act/index.html

most polls had 'favourable' ahead by 50 per cent: Mohamed Younis, 'Americans remain divided on "Obamacare"', Gallup, 4 Dec 2019, https://news.gallup.com/poll/268943/americans-remain-divided-obamacare.aspx

decisive (and literal) thumbs down: Russell Berman, 'John McCain's "no" vote sinks Republicans' "Skinny Repeal" plan', *The Atlantic*, 28 Jul 2017, https://www.theatlantic.com/politics/archive/2017/07/john-mccains-no-vote-sinks-republicans-skinny-repeal-plan/535209/

penalty for not having health insurance: Dan Mangan, 'Trump touts repeal of key part in "disastrous Obamacare" – the individual mandate', CNBC, 30 Jan 2018, https://www.cnbc.com/2018/01/30/trump-touts-repeal-of-obamacare-individual-mandate.html

before the end of that year: Elana Schor, 'McConnell plans to pass tax bill with just GOP votes', POLITICO, 1 Aug 2017, https://www.politico.com/story/2017/08/01/mitch-mcconnell-tax-bill-gop-votes-241212

amounted to a tax on imports: Richard Rubin, 'GOP lawmaker floats 50 year phase-in of border adjustment tax', *Wall Street Journal*, 13 Jun 2017

those living in high tax states: Heather Long, 'The final GOP tax bill is complete. Here's what is in it', *Washington Post*, 15 Dec 2017

rose by 17 per cent in 2018: Jim Tankersley, 'Budget deficit jumps nearly 17% in 2018', *New York Times*, 15 Oct 2018

exceed $1 trillion in 2020: Congressional Budget Office, *The Budget and Economic Outlook: 2020 to 2030*, Washington, DC: Government Print Office, 28 Jan 2020, https://www.cbo.gov/publication/56020#section0

8.6 per cent swing to the Democrats: Cook Political Report, 2018 House Popular Vote Tracker, 2 Jan 2019, https://cookpolitical.com/analysis/house/house-charts/2018-house-popular-vote-tracker/

for good measure seven governorships: Li Zhou and Emily Stewart, 'Here are the governor seats Democrats have flipped so far in the 2018 elections', Vox, 7 Nov 2018, https://www.vox.com/2018/11/6/18070682/democrat-governor-wins; Harry Enten, 'Latest House results confirm 2018 wasn't a blue wave. It was a blue tsunami', CNN, 6 Dec 2018, https://www.cnn.com/2018/12/06/politics/latest-house-vote-blue-wave/index.html

22 per cent claimed it had damaged them: CNN, 2018 exit poll question on 'Effect of new tax laws on your personal finances', https://www.cnn.com/election/2018/exit-polls

paying less than they did: Ben Casselman and Jim Tankersley, 'Face it: You (probably) got a tax cut', *New York Times*, 14 Apr 2019

fell 31 per cent in 2018: Peter G. Peterson Foundation, 'Corporate tax receipts took an unprecedented drop this year', 17 Oct 2018, https://www.pgpf.org/blog/2018/10/corporate-tax-receipts-were-down-by-nearly-one-third-in-fiscal-year-2018

grew by 2.9 per cent in 2018: Courtenay Brown, 'The U.S. economy grew 2.9%

in 2018', Axios, 28 Feb 2019, https://www.axios.com/united-states-2018-gdp-report-942280fa-1f51-4d31-97e1-dc557e2b46b2.html

witness his campaign launch: 'Here's Donald Trump's presidential announcement speech', *TIME*, 16 Jun 2015, https://time.com/3923128/donald-trump-announcement-speech/

Mexico wouldn't be paying: Cristiano Lima, 'Mexican President: "Of Course" Mexico won't pay for wall', POLITICO, 11 Jan 2017, https://www.politico.com/story/2017/01/mexico-trump-border-wall-233519

cancellation of a bilateral summit: Azam Ahmed, 'Mexico's President cancels meeting with Trump over Wall', *New York Times*, 26 Jan 2017

using existing federal funding: Donald J. Trump, Executive Order: Border Security And Immigration Enforcement Improvements', 25 Jan 2017, https://www.whitehouse.gov/presidential-actions/executive-order-border-security-immigration-enforcement-improvements/

$5 billion for border wall construction: Andrew Restuccia, Burgess Everett and Heather Caygle, 'Longest shutdown in history ends after Trump relents on wall', POLITICO, 25 Jan 2019, https://www.politico.com/story/2019/01/25/trump-shutdown-announcement-1125529

reallocated to wall construction from other purposes: Peter Baker, 'Trump Declares a National Emergency, and Provokes a Constitutional Clash', *New York Times*, 15 Feb 2019

Trump vetoed the resolution: Emily Cochrane, 'Senate Fails to Override Trump's Veto, Keeping Border Emergency in Place', *New York Times*, 17 Oct 2019

Defense Department anti-drug programme: Anya van Wagtendonk, 'In a victory for Trump, the Supreme Court frees up $2.5 billion for the border wall', Vox, 27 Jul 2019, https://www.vox.com/policy-and-politics/2019/7/27/8932874/border-wall-donald-trump-supreme-court-2-5-billion-us-mexico

$3.6 billion from military construction projects: Bobby Allyn, 'Appeals Court Allows Trump To Divert $3.6 Billion In Military Funds For Border Wall', NPR, 9 Jan 2020, https://www.npr.org/2020/01/09/794969121/appeals-court-allows-trump-to-divert-3-6-billion-in-military-funds-for-border-wa

replacement of existing barriers: Ted Hesson, 'Trump administration may not hit 2020 border wall goal, official says', Reuters, 17 Dec 2019, https://www.reuters.com/article/us-usa-immigration-border-idUSKBN1YL2FB

'name it Peaches, whatever you like': Meagan Vazquez, 'Trump says you can call his wall "peaches" for all he cares', CNN, 11 Jan 2019, https://www.cnn.com/2019/01/11/politics/donald-trump-national-emergency-peaches/index.html

sudden sales opportunity for 31-foot ladders: 'New business opportunities

for 31 foot ladders', https://31footladders.net/klymwuim7xp7n9yk5bsrofzk
mwisxs

'the one that was hardest to climb': Christina Zhao, 'Donald Trump Says
Border Wall Was Chosen After 20 "World-Class" Mountain Climbers Tested
It', *Newsweek*, 19 Sep 2019, https://www.newsweek.com/donald-trump-says-
border-wall-was-chosen-after-20-world-class-mountain-climbers-tested-it-
1460282

the whole escapade took about thirty seconds: Rosie Perper, 'A viral video
shows people climbing over the US-Mexico border fence with a ladder and
sliding down the other side', Business Insider, 5 Dec 2019, https://www.
businessinsider.com/video-people-easily-climb-us-mexico-border-
fence-2019-12

Presidential Proclamation 9645: Donald J. Trump, Presidential Proclamation
Enhancing Vetting Capabilities and Processes for Detecting Attempted
Entry Into the United States by Terrorists or Other Public-Safety Threats,
24 Sep 2017: https://www.whitehouse.gov/presidential-actions/presidential-
proclamation-enhancing-vetting-capabilities-processes-detecting-attempted-
entry-united-states-terrorists-public-safety-threats/.

Court ruled 5-4 in its favour: Ariane de Vogue and Veronica Stracqualursi,
'Supreme Court upholds travel ban', CNN, 27 Jun 2018, https://www.cnn.
com/2018/06/26/politics/travel-ban-supreme-court/index.html

Haiti, El Salvador, Nicaragua and Sudan: Richard Gonzales, 'Trump
Administration Ends Temporary Protected Status For Hondurans', NPR, 4
May 2018, https://www.npr.org/sections/thetwo-way/2018/05/04/608654408/
trump-administration-ends-temporary-protected-status-for-hondurans

'places like Norway': Josh Dawsey, 'Trump derides protections for immigrants
from "shithole" countries', *Washington Post*, 12 Jan 2018

provide for continued protection: Michael D. Shear and Julie Hirschfeld
Davis, 'Trump moves to end DACA and calls on Congress to act', *New York
Times*, 5 Sep 2017

southern border of the United States: US Department of Justice, Office of
Public Affairs, press release, 'Attorney General announces zero-tolerance
policy for criminal illegal entry', 6 Apr 2018, https://www.justice.gov/opa/pr/
attorney-general-announces-zero-tolerance-policy-criminal-illegal-entry

'separating families at the border. Period': Salvador Rizzo, 'The facts about
Trump's policy of separating families at the border', *Washington Post*, 19 Jun
2018

25 per cent of Americans supported it: William A. Gaston, 'As Trump's
zero-tolerance immigration policy backfires, Republicans are in jeopardy', Brookings Institution, 18 Jun 2018, https://www.brookings.edu/

blog/fixgov/2018/06/18/trumps-zero-tolerance-immigration-policy-puts-republicans-in-jeopardy/

legal challenges against family separations: Josh Gerstein, '17 states sue over Trump family separations', POLITICO, 26 Jun 2018, https://www.politico.com/story/2018/06/26/states-sue-donald-trump-family-separations-676377

from Rome, Pope Francis: Philip Pullella, 'Pope Francis slams Trump's family separation policy as "immoral"', Reuters, 20 Jun 2018, https://www.huffpost.com/entry/pope-francis-trump-family-separation_n_5b2a3458e4b0a4dc99 22a221

distanced themselves from the US action: Nick Cumming-Bruce, 'Taking Migrant Children From Parents Is Illegal, U.N. Tells U.S', *New York Times*, 5 Jun 2018

transported away from their parents: Richard Faussert, 'Airlines Ask Government Not to Use Their Flights to Carry Children Separated at the Border', *New York Times*, 20 Jun 2018

called for policy reversal: Amber Phillips, 'How Republicans are divided over Trump's immigration policy: For it, against it and keeping their mouths shut', *Washington Post*, 19 Jun 2018

before the policy was actually announced: Southern Poverty Law Center, 'Family separation under the Trump Administration – a timeline', 24 Sep 2019, https://www.splcenter.org/news/2019/09/24/family-separation-under-trump-administration-timeline

'This is wrong': Rob Merrick, 'Theresa May condemns Trump's family seperation policy and says she will challenge him on UK visit', *Independent*, 20 Jun 2018, https://www.independent.co.uk/news/uk/politics/theresa-may-donald-trump-migrant-children-us-mexico-border-family-separation-uk-visit-a8407846.html

families which had been separated: John Wagner, Nick Miroff and Mike DeBonis, 'Trump reverses course, signs order ending his policy of separating families at the border', *Washington Post*, 20 Jun 2018

'I'm the one that stopped it': Donald J. Trump, remarks before bilateral meeting with Egyptian president, 9 Apr 2019, https://www.whitehouse.gov/briefings-statements/remarks-president-trump-president-abdel-fattah-al-sisi-arab-republic-egypt-bilateral-meeting/

murderers running amok: Rachel Withers, 'George H.W. Bush's "Willie Horton» ad will always be the reference point for dog-whistle racism', Vox, 1 Dec 2018, https://www.vox.com/2018/12/1/18121221/george-hw-bush-willie-horton-dog-whistle-politics

instantly disassociated themselves: Heather Stewart and Rowena Mason, 'Nigel Farage's anti-migrant poster reported to police', *Guardian*, 16 Jun 2016

about any of his policies: 'Australia's un-doing', *Sydney Morning Herald*, 15 Mar 2005

'illegal arrivals in this country': National Museum of Australia, 'Defining Moments: "Tampa Affair»', https://www.nma.gov.au/defining-moments/resources/tampa-affair

supported the Government's handling: Patrick Barkham, 'Tampa is Howard's Belgrano', *Guardian*, 3 Sep 2001

'you get shot': Matthew Nussbaum, 'Trump at debate: Minorities in cities "are living in hell"', POLITICO, 26 Aug 2016, https://www.politico.com/story/2016/09/trump-minorities-living-in-hell-228726

born in America: Bianca Quilantan and David Cohen, 'Trump tells Dem congresswomen: Go back where you came from', POLITICO, 14 Jul 2019, https://www.politico.com/story/2019/07/14/trump-congress-go-back-where-they-came-from-1415692

killing one, Heather Heyer: Jason Hanna, Kaylee Hartung, Devon M. Sayers and Steve Almasy, 'Virginia governor to white nationalists: "Go home . . . shame on you"', CNN, 13 Aug 2017, https://www.cnn.com/2017/08/12/us/charlottesville-white-nationalists-rally/index.html

sentenced to life imprisonment: Sasha Ingber, 'Neo-Nazi James Fields Gets 2nd Life Sentence For Charlottesville Attack', NPR, 15 Jul 2019, https://www.npr.org/2019/07/15/741756615/virginia-court-sentences-neo-nazi-james-fields-jr-to-life-in-prison

equating racist thugs with peaceful demonstrators: Phil Helsel, Ariana Brockington and Marianna Sotomayor, 'Trump Takes Heat for Blaming Charlottesville Violence on "Many Sides"', NBC News, 12 Aug 2017, https://www.nbcnews.com/politics/white-house/trump-politicians-condemn-white-nationalist-rally-charlottesville-virginia-n792096

'everything that we hold dear as Americans': Donald J. Trump, official statement, 14 Aug 2017, https://www.whitehouse.gov/briefings-statements/statement-president-trump/

'from Robert E. Lee to another name': Libby Nelson and Kelly Swanson, 'Full transcript: Donald Trump's press conference defending the Charlottesville rally', Vox, 15 Aug 2017, https://www.vox.com/2017/8/15/16154028/trump-press-conference-transcript-charlottesville

'no moral ambiguity': Austin Wright, 'Ryan, House and Senate GOP outraged by Trump news conference', POLITICO, 16 Aug 2017, https://www.politico.com/story/2017/08/15/trump-charlottesville-ryan-republicans-241668

only 28 per cent approved: Scott Clement and David Nakamura, 'Poll shows clear disapproval of how Trump responded to Charlottesville violence', *Washington Post*, 21 Aug 2017

depicted as a KKK hood: Brittany Britto, 'MICA's David Plunkert wins ASME award for New Yorker's Trump Klan cover', *Baltimore Sun*, 9 Feb 2018

Chapter 15: UK-US Relations: Brexit, Blenheim and the State Visit

for Gina Miller: 'Gina Miller: Who is campaigner behind Brexit court cases?' BBC News, 25 Sep 2019, https://www.bbc.com/news/uk-politics-37861888

resigned as UK Ambassador to the EU: 'UK's ambassador to the EU Sir Ivan Rogers resigns', BBC News, 3 Jan 2017, https://www.bbc.com/news/uk-politics-38498839

speech of 17 January 2017: Theresa May, speech delivered at Lancaster House, 17 Jan 2017, https://www.gov.uk/government/speeches/the-governments-negotiating-objectives-for-exiting-the-eu-pm-speech

approval to invoke Article 50: 'Brexit: Supreme Court says Parliament must give Article 50 go-ahead', BBC News, 24 Jan 2017, https://www.bbc.com/news/uk-politics-38720320

decision to leave the EU: Daniel Boffey, 'Sir Tim Barrow to hand-deliver article 50 letter to Donald Tusk', *Guardian*, 27 Mar 2017

proposed a general election: Anushka Asthana and Peter Walker, 'Theresa May calls for general election to secure Brexit mandate', *Guardian*, 19 Apr 2017

317 Conservative, 262 Labour: Election 2017 results, BBC News, https://www.bbc.com/news/election/2017/results

a work in progress: Anand Menon, 'The EU and Britain are playing a high-stakes game of chicken', *Guardian*, 28 Feb 2018

Davis resigned on 9 July: 'Brexit Secretary David Davis resigns', BBC News, 9 Jul 2018, https://www.bbc.com/news/uk-politics-44761056

European Council on 25 November 2018: 'EU leaders agree UK's Brexit deal at Brussels summit', BBC News, 25 Nov 2018, https://www.bbc.com/news/uk-46334649

432 voted against: Heather Stewart, 'May suffers heaviest parliamentary defeat of a British PM in the democratic era', *Guardian*, 15 Jan 2019

This one was lost too: Heather Stewart, 'MPs ignore May's pleas and defeat her Brexit deal by 149 votes', *Guardian*, 12 Mar 2019

ten-point offer to MPs: Theresa May, speech on 'New Brexit Deal', 21 May 2019, https://www.gov.uk/government/speeches/pms-speech-on-new-brexit-deal-21-may-2019

effective from 7 June: Heather Stewart, 'Theresa May announces she will resign on 7 June', *Guardian*, 24 May 2019

group called Britain First: 'Donald Trump retweets far-right group's anti-Muslim videos', BBC News, 29 Nov 2017, https://www.bbc.com/news/world-us-canada-42166663

happened on 12 July: 'Donald Trump: US president meets Theresa May at Blenheim Palace', BBC News, 12 July 2018: https://www.bbc.com/news/uk-44802315.

The Sun the following day: Tom Newton Dunn, 'Donald Trump told Theresa May how to do Brexit "but she wrecked it –" and says the US trade deal is off', *Sun*, 13 Jul 2018

apology for the Sun article: Z. Byron Wolf, 'Donald Trump's kind-of, sort-of apology to Theresa May', CNN ,14 Jul 2018, https://www.cnn.com/2018/07/13/politics/theresa-may-trump-apology/index.html

American Ambassador's Residence: 'Donald Trump UK visit: All you need to know', BBC News, 4 Jun 2019 https://www.bbc.com/news/uk-38794886

3-4 June 2019: Peter Walker, 'Donald Trump's UK tour: the key things we learned', Guardian, 8 Jun 2019

a very good job: *Guardian*, video of US and UK joint press conference – highlights, 4 Jun 2019, https://www.theguardian.com/us-news/video/2019/jun/04/trump-and-may-hold-joint-press-conference-video-highlights

Chapter 16: Resignation, Part Two

when he stood up to speak: 'PMQs: May and Corbyn on Sir Kim Darroch's resignation', BBC News, 10 Jul 2019, https://www.bbc.com/news/av/uk-politics-48936501/pmqs-may-and-corbyn-on-sir-kim-darroch-s-resignation

most brilliant of his generation: Jack Hardy, 'British ambassador to US called Bill Clinton's White House "chaotic" and media-obsessed in confidential 1994 cable', *Daily Telegraph*, 18 Jul 2019

'reversed in the stirrups': Quentin Letts, 'A classic case of woe betides us', *The Times*, 12 Jul 2019

Chapter 17: The Great Unravelling: Brexit, Trump and the Eclipse of Establishment Politics

the then European Economic Community: Richard Nelsson, 'Archive: how the Guardian reported the 1975 EEC referendum', *Guardian*, 5 Jun 2015

'I'm right and they're wrong': UK House of Commons, debate on 'European Council (Rome)', Hansard HC vol. 178/cc869-92, 30 Oct 1990, https://api.

parliament.uk/historic-hansard/commons/1990/oct/30/european-council-rome

handful of footnotes: European Council, 'Conclusions of the Presidency', Rome, 27–8 Oct 1990, https://www.consilium.europa.eu/media/20554/1990_october_-_rome__eng_.pdf

statute of limitations: John Tagliabue, 'Giuliani Andretti, Premier of Italy 7 times, dies at 94', *New York Times*, 6 May 2013

challenge for the Major government: Owen Bowcott, 'John Major had a "full gloat" after defeating rebels on Maastricht', *Guardian*, 23 Jul 2018

the UK staying outside: UK Parliament, 'The ERM and the single currency', last updated Apr 2013: https://www.parliament.uk/about/living-heritage/evolutionofparliament/legislativescrutiny/parliament-and-europe/overview/britain-joins-erm-to-introduction-of-single-currency/

favoured the open door: Nicholas Watt and Patrick Wintour, 'How immigration came to haunt Labour: the inside story', *Guardian*, 24 Mar 2015

268,000 in 2014: Office of National Statistics, 'Migration statistics quarterly report: May 2015', 21 May 2015, https://www.ons.gov.uk/peoplepopulationandcommunity/populationandmigration/internationalmigration/bulletins/migrationstatisticsquarterlyreport/2015-05-21

5 per cent of the population of London were French Protestants: 'Legacies – Immigration and Emigration – The Huguenots', BBC News, http://www.bbc.co.uk/legacies/immig_emig/england/london/article_1.shtml

Pakistanis, Nigerians and Iranians: 'Migrant crisis: Migration to Europe explained in seven charts', BBC News, 4 Mar 2016, https://www.bbc.com/news/world-europe-34131911

many of them children: Jonathan Clayton and Herewood Holland, Tim Gaynor (ed.), 'Over one million sea arrivals reach Europe in 2015', UNHCR, 30 Dec 2015, https://www.unhcr.org/en-us/news/latest/2015/12/5683d0b56/million-sea-arrivals-reach-europe-2015.html

475,000 had claimed asylum there: 'Almost 1.1 million migrants registered in Germany last year', Deutsche Welle, 6 Jan 2016, https://www.dw.com/en/almost-11-million-migrants-registered-in-germany-last-year/a-18963088

2 per cent of the numbers entering Germany: 'UK to accept 20,000 refugees from Syria by 2020', BBC News, 7 Sep 2015, https://www.bbc.com/news/uk-34171148

only a step up from guesswork: 'EU migration to UK "underestimated" by ONS', BBC News, 21 Aug 2019, https://www.bbc.com/news/uk-49420730

'coming out of the EU': Ipsos MORI, 'Immigration one of the biggest issues for wavering EU referendum voters', 10 May 2016, https://www.ipsos.com/

ipsos-mori/en-uk/immigration-one-biggest-issues-wavering-eu-referendum-voters

'immigration and its own borders': Peter Roff, 'Brexit was about Britain', US News & World Report, 30 Jun 2016, https://www.usnews.com/opinion/articles/2016-06-30/poll-shows-brexit-vote-was-about-british-sovereignty-not-anti-immigration

majority of voters back Leave: 'Britain's immigration paradox', *The Economist*, 8 Jul 2016

Boston in Lincolnshire: 'Lincolnshire records UK's highest Brexit vote', BBC News, 24 Jun 2016, https://www.bbc.com/news/uk-politics-eu-referendum-36616740

from 1,000 to 16,000: 'Britain's immigration paradox', *The Economist*, 8 Jul 2016

'Would we have won without immigration? No': Dominic Cummings, 'How the Brexit referendum was won', *The Spectator*, 8 Jan 2017

13 per cent of the total population: Jie Zong and Jeanne Batalova, 'Frequently requested statistics on immigrants and immigration in the United States', Migration Policy Institute, 8 Mar 2017, https://www.migrationpolicy.org/article/frequently-requested-statistics-immigrants-and-immigration-united-states-6

23 per cent of Democrats agreed with them: Jeffrey M. Jones, 'New High in U.S. Say Immigration Most Important Problem', Gallup, 21 Jun 2016, https://news.gallup.com/poll/259103/new-high-say-immigration-impor-tant-problem.aspx

entered the United States illegally: Jeffrey S. Passel and D'Vera Cohn, 'U.S. Unauthorized Immigrant Total Dips to Lowest Level in a Decade', Pew Research Center, 27 Nov 2018, https://www.pewresearch.org/hispan-ic/2018/11/27/u-s-unauthorized-immigrant-total-dips-to-lowest-level-in-a-decade/

12.6 times higher: Katherine Schaeffer, '6 facts about economic inequality in the U.S.', Pew Research Center, 7 Feb 2020, https://www.pewresearch.org/fact-tank/2020/02/07/6-facts-about-economic-inequality-in-the-u-s/

40 million Americans lived in poverty: Jeff Stein, 'The U.N. says 18.5 million Americans are in "extreme poverty." Trump's team says just 250,000 are', *Washington Post*, 25 Jun 2018

20 per cent of its factory jobs: Heather Long, 'U.S. has lost 5 million manu-facturing jobs since 2000', CNN, 29 Mar 2016, https://money.cnn.com/2016/03/29/news/economy/us-manufacturing-jobs/index.html

10 million Americans lost their homes: William R. Emmons, 'The end is in sight for the U.S. foreclosures crisis', Federal Reserve Bank of St. Louis, 2

Dec 2016, https://www.stlouisfed.org/publications/housing-market-perspectives/2016/the-end-is-in-sight-for-the-us-foreclosure-crisis

lower now than in 2008: Matt O'Brien, 'The bottom 90 percent are still poorer than they were in 2007', *Washington Post*, 1 Oct 2018

bailing out US financial institutions: Jim Tankersley and Ben Casselman, 'Washington Weighs Big Bailouts to Help U.S. Economy Survive Coronavirus', *New York Times*, 18 Mar 2020

39 per cent poorer in net wealth: Juliana Menasce Horowitz, Ruth Igielnik and Rakesh Kochhar, 'Most Americans say there is too much economic inequality in the US, but fewer than half call it a top priority', Pew Research Center, 9 Jan 2020, https://www.pewsocialtrends.org/2020/01/09/trends-in-income-and-wealth-inequality/£500 billion bailout fund: Jon Swaine, 'Bank bailout: Alistair Darling unveils £500 billion rescue package', *Daily Telegraph*, 8 Oct 2008

changed the outcome of the referendum: Toby Helm, Michael Savage and Eleni Courea, 'Almost 700,000 march to demand "people's vote» on Brexit deal', *Guardian*, 20 Oct 2018

23 per cent in this demographic: Rob Griffin, Ruy Teixeira and John Halpin, 'Voter trends in 2016', Center for American Progress, 1 Nov 2017, https://www.americanprogress.org/issues/democracy/reports/2017/11/01/441926/voter-trends-in-2016/

53.4 per cent to 46.6 per cent: 'EU referendum results', BBC News, https://www.bbc.com/news/politics/eu_referendum/results

further down the educational attainment ladder one looked: John Sides, Michale Tesler and Lynn Vavreck, *Identity Crisis: the 2016 presidential campaign and the battle for the meaning of America* (Princeton University Press, 2018)

likely to identify as Democrats as Republicans: Clare Malone, 'The 2010s were a complicated decade for Democrats and white voters', FiveThirtyEight, 10 Dec 2019, https://fivethirtyeight.com/features/the-2010s-were-a-complicated-decade-for-democrats-and-white-voters/

39 per cent Democrats: 'Wide gender gap, growing educational divide in voters' party identification', Pew Research Center, 20 Mar 2018, https://www.people-press.org/2018/03/20/1-trends-in-party-affiliation-among-demographic-groups/

'general conflagration through the other States': James Madison, Federalist Paper No.10, 1787, available at: https://billofrightsinstitute.org/founding-documents/primary-source-documents/the-federalist-papers/federalist-papers-no-10/

Facebook as the market leader: John Gramlich, '10 Facts about Americans and Facebook', Pew Research Center, 16 May 2019, https://www.pewresearch. org/fact-tank/2019/05/16/facts-about-americans-and-facebook/

when going cross-border: Christian Ebeke, Jan-Martin Frie and Louise Rabier, 'Deepening the EU's Single Market for services', IMF working paper WP/19/269, Dec 2019, https://www.imf.org/~/media/Files/Publications/ WP/2019/wpiea2019269-print-pdf.ashx

List of Illustrations

Kim and his mother (personal collection)
Schoolhouse (personal collection)
Kim's father and car (personal collection)
Kim and his brother (personal collection)
Kim and Vanessa at university (personal collection)
Kim, Vanessa and university friends at Hampton Court Palace (personal collection)
Kim's knighthood (Anthony Devlin / PA Images)
Kim with Tony Blair at the European Council (Peter Macdiarmid / Getty Images)
Signing a memorandum with David Cameron and Singapore's Prime Minister Lee Hsien Loong (ROSLAN RAHMAN / AFP via Getty Images)
With David Cameron and Barack Obama (Official White House, Photo by Pete Souza))
The British Residence in Washington (personal collection)
Kim speaking at the British Residence (Riccardo Savi / Getty Images for Capitol File Magazine)
With Obama (personal collection)
With Obama and family (personal collection)
At Trump's inauguration (personal collection)
Trump's inauguration (personal collection)
Donald Trump and Theresa May in the Oval Office (Official White House, Photo by Shealah Craighead)
Kim and Ted Cruz (British Embassy Washington / Carrie Dorean)
Donald Trump shaking hands with Kim (personal collection)
Kim and Madeleine Albright (personal collection)

Kim and Kellyanne Conway (British Embassy Washington / Carrie Dorean)

Boris Johnson and Kim Darroch (dpa picture alliance / Alamy Stock Photo)Donald Trump and Theresa May greeted at Chequers (personal collection)

Kim and Vanessa at Blenheim Palace (personal collection)

Kim, Vanessa and Carole King (British Embassy Washington / Carrie Dorean)

Kim and David Attenborough (British Embassy Washington / Carrie Dorean)

Kim and Joe Biden (personal collection)

Donald Trump on a UK state visit (Official White House, Photo by Shealah Craighead)

Donald and Melania Trump with Queen Elizabeth II (Official White House, Photo by Andrea Hanks)

Boris Johnson and Donald Trump (Stefan Rousseau / Pool / Getty Images)

Donald Trump's Twitter thread (Twitter)

Cartoon of Boris Johnson (Peter Brookes / *The Times*)

Kim and Vanessa (personal collection)

The cats (personal collection)

Family wedding (personal collection)

Index

Kim Darroch, Baron Darroch of Kew, was appointed British Ambassador to the US in 2015. He resigned in 2019 after a series of cables containing unflattering descriptions of President Trump were leaked to a 19-year-old freelance journalist and Brexit Party employee and made public. Darroch received a life peerage in November 2019. Since Spring 2020, he has been a visiting fellow at the Institute of Politics at Harvard University.

PublicAffairs is a publishing house founded in 1997. It is a tribute to the standards, values, and flair of three persons who have served as mentors to countless reporters, writers, editors, and book people of all kinds, including me.

I. F. STONE, proprietor of *I. F. Stone's Weekly*, combined a commitment to the First Amendment with entrepreneurial zeal and reporting skill and became one of the great independent journalists in American history. At the age of eighty, Izzy published *The Trial of Socrates*, which was a national bestseller. He wrote the book after he taught himself ancient Greek.

BENJAMIN C. BRADLEE was for nearly thirty years the charismatic editorial leader of *The Washington Post*. It was Ben who gave the *Post* the range and courage to pursue such historic issues as Watergate. He supported his reporters with a tenacity that made them fearless and it is no accident that so many became authors of influential, best-selling books.

ROBERT L. BERNSTEIN, the chief executive of Random House for more than a quarter century, guided one of the nation's premier publishing houses. Bob was personally responsible for many books of political dissent and argument that challenged tyranny around the globe. He is also the founder and longtime chair of Human Rights Watch, one of the most respected human rights organizations in the world.

• • •

For fifty years, the banner of Public Affairs Press was carried by its owner Morris B. Schnapper, who published Gandhi, Nasser, Toynbee, Truman, and about 1,500 other authors. In 1983, Schnapper was described by *The Washington Post* as "a redoubtable gadfly." His legacy will endure in the books to come.

Peter Osnos, *Founder*